CONTINUITY

AND CHANGE

IN AFRICAN CULTURES

CONTINUITY

AND CHANGE

IN AFRICAN CULTURES

Edited by

William R. Bascom

and

Melville J. Herskovits

THE UNIVERSITY OF CHICAGO PRESS

CHICAGO & LONDON

SBN: 226-03879-3 (clothbound); 226-03880-7 (paperbound)
Library of Congress Catalog Card Number: 58-13135

THE UNIVERSITY OF CHICAGO PRESS, CHICAGO 60637
The University of Chicago Press, Ltd., London

This book grows indirectly out of an interdisciplinary conference on Africa, sponsored jointly by the National Research Council and the Social Science Research Council, which met at Princeton University in September, 1953. It was suggested that the papers delivered there by participants trained in the Department of Anthropology at Northwestern University be published, with articles by other Northwestern students, as a book which would give some of the results of their anthropological research in Africa.

Two grants, one from the Carnegie Corporation of New York and another from the Ford Foundation, made it possible to expand the department's interest in Africa, which dates from 1927, by establishing the present interdisciplinary Program of African Studies, which began in 1949. The program has provided fellowships and scholarships for the graduate study of many of the contributors to this volume and small supplemental grants toward their field projects. Various other foundations and agencies, through their fellowship programs, have provided the funds necessary to carry on the field research in Africa on which this book is based, as noted in the list of contributors. To all the institutions whose support has made this volume possible, we express our gratitude on behalf of those who have contributed to it.

WILLIAM R. BASCOM
MELVILLE J. HERSKOVITS

Preface

Since 1959, when this book was first published, most of Africa has become independent. A majority of Africans have emerged from a century of colonial status to become citizens of the new states which have taken their places among the nations of the world. Africa's emancipation was foreseeable, but the rapidity with which it has progressed could not have been predicted by even the most experienced experts in African affairs.

Yet these surprisingly rapid political changes have not destroyed the continuity of African cultures. Even in the violence which followed Belgium's sudden withdrawal from the Congo, the importance of ethnic bonds and traditional hostilities is clearly apparent; and they are still significant elements below the calm surface of Nigerian politics. "Tribalism" is no longer an obstacle to self-government in most of Africa, but it remains a problem for the leaders of Africa's new nations if national unity is to be maintained.

The continuity as well as continued change in the African institutions and customs which are discussed in this book have become even more apparent, so that little that is written here has been altered by the fact of independence. The problems faced by colonial officials, among the Mossi of the French territories of Upper Volta and Soudan, for example, are now being faced by African officials of the Voltaic Republic and Mali. The main difference that independence has brought is an even greater freedom of choice in selecting cultural innovations.

It is hoped that the discussions which follow will serve to interest more persons in Africa's rich resources for the scientific study of human behavior and will contribute to a more realistic understanding of a continent which is becoming increasingly important to all of us. For the United States and other countries which must now deal with Africa's new nations directly, and even for these new nations themselves, it is necessary to understand the strength of the diverse cultures of Africa and the role they are playing in shaping the changing African scene.

WILLIAM R. BASCOM
MELVILLE J. HERSKOVITS

Contents

In the pages that follow, the phonetic values of terms and names from African languages—except those place names where current usage is employed—conform, with a few modifications, to those given in the revised edition of the memorandum "Practical Orthography of African Languages" issued by the International African Institute, and in that of the American Anthropological Association, "Phonetic Transcription of Indian Languages."

Consonants: *d, c* (as in English "church"), *d, f, g, gb, gbw, h, x* (as *ch* in Scottish "loch"), *k, kp, kpw, l, m, n, η* (as *ng* in English "sing"), *ny, p, r, s, sh* (as in English "shut"), *t, θ* (*th*, as in English "path"), *v, w, y, z* (as in English "zebra")

Vowels: (the so-called "Italian" values are indicated unless otherwise stated), *a, α* (as English *a* in "hat"), *ε* (as English *e* in "met"), *e, i, ɔ* (as English *au* in "author"), *o, ⊖* ("half-close" between *u* and *o*), *u*

Clicks: ∥ lateral, ≠ palato-alveolar (cerebral)

Though many of the languages from which African words and names are taken are tonal, tone is not indicated.

1. The Problem of Stability
and Change in African Culture

This book may be thought of as one in a growing series of collaborative works on African anthropology. Together these volumes represent an international effort to further a sober and realistic understanding of the ways of life of the peoples who inhabit this vast area. As in the other works, all contributions in this book deal with Africa south of the Sahara and are written by trained anthropologists. However, the common orientation of the essays of this volume toward the concept of culture differentiates it from the others which, like most of the anthropological studies of African peoples of the past decade, have dealt principally with social institutions. We may therefore make explicit at the outset the theoretical formulations that give this book its unity of approach.

Rather than attempting, once again, a precise definition of culture, we can simply say that it refers to the way of life of a people, to their traditional behavior, in a broad sense, including their ideas, acts, and artifacts. Although many definitions of culture have been suggested, differing in wording and in emphasis, it is generally agreed that these ways of thinking and acting are patterned, so that behavior in any society is not haphazard or random. This does not mean that behavior thereby becomes fixed and inflexible; it varies from individual to individual and from time to time, within a range which is considered acceptable.

Culture, rather than social institutions, is what distinguishes man from the rest of the biological world. Other animals, and insects as well, have societies, but only man uses language, manufactures tools, and possesses art, religion, and other aspects of culture. The concern with culture rather than with society and social institutions thus emphasizes the specifically human elements of man's behavior.

Culture, being learned, is not instinctive, innate, or biologically determined, as behavior is among subhuman forms. Culture varies from group to group and from one period of time to another within any single group. From this follows a principle of fundamental scientific importance and, as regards the peoples of Africa, of equal practical significance: what has been learned can be modified through further learning; habits, customs, beliefs, social structures, and institutions can change.

From this also follows another factor which gives this book its underlying unity and again differentiates it from those collaborative studies of African anthropology with which it may be compared. Change and stability, in briefest summary, form its central theme and its theoretical rationale. If culture changes, if culture is dynamic, it must be studied in its historical dimension as well as in terms of the relationships among its components. Where new influences impinge on any society, a student of culture is at once confronted with the problem of how much of the preexisting body of custom and belief is discarded, how much is modified, and how much is retained. In the following essays the authors have attempted to give equal consideration to both these aspects of changing Africa.

CHANGE AND CONTINUITY

The suddenness with which Africa has emerged onto the world scene is one of the striking happenings of our day. Nowhere has the recognition of Africa's importance been more rapid than in the United States, where its repercussions are felt on the scientific level as well as the popular. Although this book is the fruit of a concern with Africa at Northwestern University that long antedates recent interest, its very existence reflects the growing recognition of the contribution that the study of African cultures can make to science. It indicates that the time has been reached when the acknowledgment of this contribution by American anthropologists, which though benevolent and permissive has long been formal and disinterested, is being replaced by a concern with Africa comparable to the active interest which for years has been directed toward other parts of the world.

The heightening of interest in Africa has been stimulated by a series of dramatic events since World War II. Seretse Khama in Bechuanaland and the Kabaka in Uganda were exiled, but they have returned to their home countries. There have been the violence of Mau Mau in Kenya, the disorders in the southern Sudan, the tensions arising out of the policy of *apartheid* in the Union of South Africa, and the manifestos of Africans in the Belgian Congo calling for a time schedule toward self-determination but suggesting that only moral force be used to achieve this goal. Still different in their consequences were the disturbances of a few years ago in Nigeria and the Gold Coast, following which these countries have made such rapid strides on the peaceful road to self-government. Independence has been achieved by the Gold Coast, now called Ghana, and is in sight for Nigeria and French Africa. These events are symptoms of the unmistakable ferment that has marked Africa's postwar years. They have been so dramatic, however, that they overshadow a fact of equal importance: the current African scene is marked not only by change but also by cultural continuity.

Both as individuals and as groups, Africans have reacted differently to the innovations with which they have been presented. The number of persons who can read and write, much less who have had higher education, is still small compared to those who follow the traditions of their ancestors with no more than surface modifications, or even compared to the growing number of those who, between the extremes of traditionalism and acceptance of the new, are interested in change and look for leaders among those who have been to school. Whether African or European, some are dismayed with the rapidity of change; others approve. But whatever their point of view or race, many of those charged with the direction of affairs are still faced with the problem of finding ways of inducing change in various aspects of African culture in order to implement policies they regard as desirable.

There is no African culture which has not been affected in some way by European contact, and there is none which has entirely given way before it. The cultures of Africa have been modified by contacts with Europe and the Near East which long antedate the events that have made headlines in recent years. Elements from outside, accepted generations ago, have been adapted to traditional African patterns. Tobacco, cassava, peanuts, and maize, which were probably introduced from the New World by the early Portuguese explorers, have been incorporated into many African cultures without weakening them. European legal principles and procedures, whatever their degree of acceptance, have not displaced the sanctions of traditional law—though in many cases both have been modified in the course of adaptation. Monogamy has been sanctioned in law without prohibiting polygyny when marriage is by "native law and custom."

Despite the intensity of Christian missionary effort and the thousand years of Moslem proselytizing which have marked the history of various parts of Africa, African religions continue to manifest vitality everywhere. This is to be seen in the worship of African deities, the homage to the ancestors, and the recourse to divination, magic, and other rituals. A growing number of Africans, to be sure, have been taught to regard the religion of their forefathers as superstition and to reject other beliefs and customs as outmoded. But there is no evidence which supports the assumption that so often underlies thinking about Africa's future, that African culture, whether in its religious or other aspects, will shortly and inevitably disappear.

If the studies of the New World Negro, in which we have also been engaged, contribute anything to the understanding of Africa, it is that African culture can and in fact has been able to accommodate itself to Euroamerican civilization. On the basis of our knowledge of Africans and their descendants in the New World, we have little reason to believe that African culture will have any difficulty in persisting with more than reinterpreted modifications. Despite the harsh conditions of acculturation under slavery in the New World, African religions, for example, have been able to flourish under conditions of industrialized, cosmopolitan, urban life.

The diversity of African cultures and of African reactions to European culture presents a major obstacle to understanding contemporary Africa, even for experienced observers. It makes the task of describing Africa to those who have never seen it the more difficult because of the temptation to draw generalizations that are valid only for specific African groups and particular African regions. Some of these cultural differences, which are far too numerous to detail, will become apparent in the following sections of this book.

It is not only Americans but Europeans as well who are having to reconcile the stereotype of the naked savage, perpetuated by Hollywood (with necessary modifications in clothing), with the impressions gained through personal acquaintance with the African students who in increasing numbers are attending European and American universities. Both images are partly true, but both are misleading. Mission accounts, through which many in Europe and America have become acquainted with African life, often emphasize and may even exaggerate the so-called savage features of African cultures, while the adventure books of the twentieth-century "explorers" tend to play up the exotic and the sensational. In the United States, the Pygmies and Bushmen, who are few in number and quite atypical, are more widely known than the Ashanti, Ibo, Hausa, Fulani, Kongo, Chaga, Swazi, or other important peoples. It is no wonder, then, that current developments, particularly in economics, politics, and education, have come as a surprise.

The degree of variation in African cultures is equaled by contrasts in the acceptance and rejection of Euroamerican innovations. Thus, in Kenya the Kikuyu were so eager to adopt European ways that, when frustrated in their desires, many resorted to the violence of Mau Mau. The Masai, Pakot, and other Nilotic peoples in the same country have followed the opposite course, remaining aloof and proudly indifferent to European influence; except for minor details, they have withstood the efforts to change their ways. Between these extremes, the Ganda of neighboring Uganda, with a cultural background which included a highly organized political system, have adapted to European culture with less resistance than the Nilotics but with less enthusiasm than the Kikuyu.

These differences in reaction to European contact cannot be explained solely, as is so often implied, in terms of variations in colonial policy or of duration and intensity of contact. Equally if not more important are the pre-established patterns of African culture. The tendency to neglect the factor of traditional modes of behavior and systems of belief has had far-reaching practical consequences where the framing of programs for economic or political development has been involved.

Nigeria affords a classic example of the effect of cultural backgrounds on the course of recent events. The policy of indirect rule was first applied among the Hausa in the north, where political authority was centered in the Emir and where taxation, courts, and other governmental institutions comparable to those of Europe were already in existence. It was extended with little difficulty to the Yoruba in the southwest, since their traditional political structure was sufficiently similar. But the attempt to apply it to the Ibo in the southeast failed because comparable political units on which to superimpose the new system were lacking. The development of Nigeria's federal form of government and of the different systems of representation which operate in its three regions cannot be explained without taking these cultural differences into account. Despite these differences and contrasts, of which any serious student of African culture soon becomes aware, there are underlying similarities between the cultures of neighboring African peoples and in the processes of culture change for sub-Saharan Africa as a whole; these should also become evident in the sections which follow.

Another complication that faces one who seeks to understand contemporary Africa arises from the fact that, even where it is least apparent on the surface, all groups take over innovations selectively. Some things are accepted, while others, not considered desirable, are rejected because they are incompatible with pre-existing custom or unsuitable to the natural environment, to name only two of the possible reasons. The Tutsi of Ruanda, for whom cattle are so important, have accepted modifications of earlier custom in political procedures, diet, and, to a degree, in agriculture, but they have stubbornly resisted and bitterly resented administrative efforts to destock their herds, although the population problem in their territory arises out of pressure not only of human beings on the land but of cattle as well. The Tutsi are by no means an exceptional case. Many other East African peoples have similarly resisted efforts to reduce their herds, have refused to put their cattle to the plow, or have been reluctant to sell cattle to purchase goods which they do not produce. Imponderables in African tradition may far outweigh the force of administrative measures which, from the point of view of an objective outsider, would improve the economic situation.

Even where selectivity in the acceptance of cultural elements from outside is recognized, analyses of the contemporary African scene too often fail to grasp the fact that selection is *additive* and not necessarily *substitutive*. European cloth adds to the range of fabrics and patterns; kerosene lamps are used together with traditional ones; and European-manufactured china and ironware expand the range of goods produced by African potters and blacksmiths. In time they may come to displace the African-made products, but despite the severe competition of European machine-made goods, African weavers, smiths, and potters are still active.

Literacy and schooling, which stand out among the many things of European origin because they are so widely desired by Africans, illustrate both the selective and the additive character of the acculturative process. The Africans' eagerness for a European type of education does does not mean that monogamy is equally acceptable, while the techniques of reading and writing do not compete with established traditions in non-literate societies. The desire for literacy is a response to a need which can be satisfied without inducing cultural conflict. Even when considered as modes of speech rather than techniques, the new European languages in which instruction is given are advantageous to learn but do not necessarily replace the African ones.

In religion, where substitution has clearly been the end of proselytizing, this principle clarifies an otherwise puzzling situation. For, whatever their verbalizations, Africans have by no means given over their allegiances to traditional supernatural forces when they have accepted the deity of another people. Rather, the new deity is added to the totality of supernatural resources on which they can call for aid. Comparable examples from other aspects of culture—economic, political, artistic, musical—will also become apparent in the pages of this book.

THE CULTURAL APPROACH AND THE HISTORICAL DIMENSION

Since the approach of this work differs from that of its predecessors in that it is cultural rather than sociological, its scope is broader. Precision in method and a sharper definition of problem are gained through concentration on a particular phase of social activity; yet this inescapably involves a narrower view of human behavior; a more restricted approach to the institutions, beliefs, customs, and traditions which man transmits through learning from one generation to another; and a disregard of the features which in essence differentiate human behavior from that of other animals.

Culture includes not only social institutions and their derivative forms of learned behavior but also those manifestations of man's creativity whereby the artist produces something new and distinctively individual within the range of forms and patterns which are a part of his tradition, the philosopher or priest reconciles apparent contradictions in religious belief, the narrator gives a new turn to the plot of a familiar tale, or the inventor introduces changes in technology derived from previous knowledge. The study of culture involves not only the institutions that frame man's reactions to the fellow members of his society but also the extra-institutional aspects of human behavior, including language, the relation between language and behavior, between personality and culture, and the system of values that gives meaning to the accepted modes of behavior of a people.

Studies in comparative sociology have often been concerned with the analysis of data lying on a single time plane. In the theoretical and conceptual scheme underlying cultural research, however, the historical dimension of culture is held to be equally indispensible for an adequate understanding of human behavior. That is, though intensive investigations of structure yield valuable insights into present relationships, other causalities are neglected if the factor of time is not taken into account.

The historical orientation that is basic to the theoretical structure of the essays that follow is most explicit in Fuller's discussion of the Gwambe. His projection of the results of ethnographic study against the available historical records is a striking demonstration of how fruitful this method can be in giving time depth, historically documented, for assessing the processes of cultural stability and change. It is gratifying to note that the value of this method, termed "ethnohistory," is beginning to receive the attention it deserves. Especially in West Africa studies are projected or under way which employ the resources of historical records, native tradition, and archeological findings in recovering the past of such peoples as the Bini and the Yoruba. The cumulative value of research of this kind is obvious, not only for the study of Africa, but in broader terms for testing hypotheses about the mechanisms of culture change, assumptions about paths of diffusion, or theories of myth which deny validity to oral history. It is worthy of note, however, that in Africa these studies have in the main been initiated and prosecuted by historians because sociologically oriented anthropologists have been so preoccupied with synchronic analyses of structure.

Ethnohistory, however, is only a recent addition to the historical methods that have figured in anthropological research. Anthropologists have often been confronted with historical problems when written records were not available. One of the approaches that has long been employed is indicated by Greenberg as a solution to the question of how Africa's linguistic complexity developed. The classification of languages into families, he explains, will "help us to decide—among other questions—whether the present diversity is of recent date, all of Africa having been settled by one linguistic stock at some not too remote period, or whether we must reckon with a more complex pattern of separate waves of settlement occurring at different periods." This quotation not only poses the problem of the historically oriented ethnolinguist but also illustrates a difference between the objectives and methods of the historical anthropologist and the historian. The anthropologist does not share the historian's concern with the particular event, its date, or even the exact sequence of events except in so far as they help us to understand either the form of present institutions, customs, and beliefs or the general processes of cultural dynamics—of change and stability in culture.

The historical component in culture, or in social institutions, cannot be rejected simply because written documentation is not available. The challenge of probing the past so as to understand the present remains. No problem disappears because we have imperfect or even inadequate means of solving it; if this were so, there would be little point to the study of either culture or social institutions, or to the whole of social science. But because the historical methods of anthropology have been specifically attacked by some social anthropologists, this point must be pursued further in a book whose central concern is change and stability through time.

Some of these criticisms have been directed against the methodology underlying sweeping reconstructions of the history of human culture on a world-wide basis, such as those of the cultural evolutionists and the diffusionists of the last century. With these criticisms we are in agreement, but there is a distinct difference between the reconstruction of the development of *culture*, and that of *a culture* or even of a group of related *cultures* within a restricted geographic area. Where the possibility of cultural influence can be demonstrated rather than postulated, and where due regard is given the complexity of the phenomena that are compared, historical reconstructions are on far more solid ground. Such reconstructions, based on the comparison of institutions and other elements of culture and translating their distribution in space into the dimension of time, can only be statements of probability rather than established historical fact. Yet even historical probability is an aid, not a barrier, in understanding the present forms and functioning of a given culture.

Certainly historical analyses which employ documentary or archeological evidence are preferable to those based on distributions, native traditions, or the recollections of old men and women, although, in terms of scientific validity, even these are not on a level with the results of intensive field research by a trained anthropologist working within the well-defined terms of reference of a carefully designed research program. But here we take another exception to objections raised against the consideration of the historical dimension.

We deny the reality of the dichotomy which is so often drawn between history and science. Historical analysis does not preclude scientific generalization. One can generalize from the development of a belief, a custom, or an institution as well as from its structural analysis, and by the same token, one can be as particularistic in the latter as in the former. The problems of anthropology do not end with detailed description, either of the form and function of a social system or of the development of a mode of religious belief, however essential both may be to the accumulation of data for developing and testing hypotheses in the search for an understanding of the regularities in human behavior and human institutions.

Granting that the cultural approach includes as an essential component the factor of dynamics and that some social anthropologists consider the historical dimension, much of what we have discussed comes down to the need to take into account both cultural stability and change in the study of African societies, as they are and as they were before European contact.

Certain conclusions derive from this position. It enhances the value of studies of African societies little affected by European contact by showing their relevance to the understanding of the contemporary scene. Such studies, and those of the traditional, the truly African elements in societies which have been considerably affected, are not ends in themselves but means of increasing the validity of scientific research by providing a base line from which change can be measured. Without a knowledge of earlier customs, institutions, and beliefs, the amount and kind of change involved can only be inferred from descriptions of the present. Moreover, by assessing responses to the varied cultural influences to which Africans have recently been exposed, we gain insights into the dynamics of African cultures which suggest their reactions at an even earlier period of time. There is much reason to believe that the present situation of cultural change in Africa is nothing new, except in terms of the multiplicity of innovations and the intensity of their manner of presentation; yet this point is rarely taken into account, either in scientific discussions or in administrative decisions.

This brings us to the difficult question of scientific law and prediction. The observed variety of customs, beliefs, and institutions that man has developed, not only in Africa but throughout the world, makes the problem of predicting the forms of even a given culture most difficult. Whether particularistic or general, predictions necessarily involve the dimension of time; cultural laws, and social laws as well, must involve both time and space if they are to be applicable to all cultures at all times. We believe that the answer lies not in predicting forms but in establishing laws of cultural processes. If this is accepted, the false dichotomy between history and science disappears, and both the historical dimension and the study of cultural stability and change become of utmost scientific importance.

Synchronic analyses of single societies provide data essential for formulating new hypotheses and for testing old hypotheses and previously accepted theories. On the planes of both social and cultural anthropology this testing of hypotheses and theories has constituted the classical anthropological contribution to the social sciences. It has been instrumental in emphasizing the importance of learning in understanding human behavior, and it has shifted interest and research away from instincts, from cataloguing traits of human nature, from racial determinism, and from biologically transmitted Oedipal complexes. What were formerly viewed as innate patterns are now largely accepted as learned behavior, to which each individual is enculturated as he grows to be a full-fledged member of his society as it is structured. However, the acceptance of this contribution of anthropology in the social sciences has not decreased concern with predictions and laws, which cannot be established by the study of any single society at any single point in time. Anthropological generalizations of this order, if they are to be valid, must be sought in the dimensions of both space and time, through the use of both historical and comparative methods.

SCOPE

The first five chapters of this book are intended to provide an overview of certain aspects of culture in Subsaharan Africa. All of the contributors have done field research in some part of Africa on the topic they treat, and here they generalize from their findings to develop broad surveys by drawing on the literature.

Each of the next three chapters examines a single culture as a whole. Fuller assesses the degree of change in the culture of a southeast African people, using historical records which cover a period of four centuries. Simon Ottenberg draws on the literature as well as on his own research among the Afikpo Ibo in trying to answer why the Ibo have been so receptive to European innovations. Schneider, on the other hand, seeks to explain resistance to change in a culture characterized by the cattle complex and to generalize again from his own field work among the Pakot to a larger group in East Africa.

The remaining chapters deal with more restricted aspects of specific cultures. In the order in which they are presented, they treat of social organization, economics, and religion, but the book is not subdivided into the usual sections dealing with these topics. To do this would be an injustice to the materials themselves and to the contributors' methodological approach, which recognizes the importance of the interrelationships among the various elements of a culture.

Wolfe is primarily concerned with the dynamics of lineage structure, which is clearly a feature of social organization, but his analysis takes relevant economic, political, and religious factors into account. Lystad focuses even more specifically on social organization because in his experimental design other cultural features, as well as natural habitat and demographic factors, can be considered as constants; in his study he relates kinship and marriage to the external factor of colonial policy. Phoebe Ottenberg's account of the economic position of women and Ames' discussion of co-operative work groups, viewed both as social and as economic units, overlap the fields of economics and social organization. Hammond, though primarily concerned with technology and economics, stresses the importance of religious beliefs and the ritual cycle in cultural adjustment under a program of planned resettlement and economic development. Christensen views priesthood both in terms of status and role and in terms of the theological constructs of the world view. Messenger concentrates on theological beliefs as affected by missionary activity but considers economic and political factors as well.

It will be evident that we have cast our net wide, both in geographical distribution and in the number of aspects customarily distinguished in the study of culture. While topics in the field of African social structure have a prominent place, with Dorjahn's study adding a wholly new dimension to them, the humanistic aspects of African culture are considered, both in the essays on specific peoples and in the general discussions of language, art, and music. There is no specific treatment of the verbal arts—narrative, proverb, and riddle—in which we both have long been interested,[1] though Fuller, Cordwell, and others draw on traditional lore. Despite their importance to the study of Africa we must also note with regret that neither archeology nor physical anthropology is covered, an omission explained by the fact that no studies in these fields have been made at Northwestern thus far.

RESEARCH DESIGN

Most of the papers in this volume are oriented toward the solution of specific scientific problems lying in the field of cultural dynamics.

[1] For general articles on this topic see M. J. Herskovits, "African Literature," in *Encyclopedia of Literature*, ed. J. Shipley (New York: Philosophical Library, 1946), I, 3–16 and R. A. Waterman and W. R. Bascom, "African and New World Negro Folklore," in *Funk and Wagnalls Standard Dictionary of Folklore, Mythology, and Legend*, ed. M. Leach (New York: Funk & Wagnalls, 1949), I, 18–24.

Each deals with variables in time and space in accordance with a research model, whether explicitly formulated or not, that has served to guide the study on which it is based.

As already mentioned, Fuller's contribution is the closest to conventional history because of his use of the ethnohistorical method, though the ethnographic component gives it a distinctive character. Greenberg's paper focuses on the problem of the development of African linguistic forms, while Cordwell examines both early historical accounts and the findings of archeology in seeking to understand the development and contemporary manifestations of African art. Though the historical dimension is relatively shallower in other essays, it is no less basic to their research designs.

Merriam considers acculturative factors in his discussion of African music, and his tentative classification of the music areas of Africa suggests a variety of historical problems. Dorjahn's comparative analysis of African demographic materials pioneers in attempting to answer, for the continent as a whole, a question that has profound implications for the understanding of many changes that are taking place in African life; it makes a dual contribution—to the understanding of the effects of demographic factors on polygyny and to the understanding of the effects of polygyny on the demographic composition of a people.

Wolfe's substantive contribution to the theory of segmentary systems which is being developed by social anthropologists derives largely from the historical perspective which is central to his research model; despite the lack of early historical documentation, his study of Ngombe lineages focuses clearly on dynamics rather than structure. Phoebe Ottenberg's account of the changing position of Afikpo Ibo women begins with an implied question: What factors changed Ibo women "almost overnight from an aggregate of peaceable, home-loving villagers into a mob of thousands who . . . attacked administration authorities while their men stood idly by"? The concern with change through time is also essential in Simon Ottenberg's consideration of the bases of Ibo willingness to accept European innovations, in contrast to the reluctance of the Pakot and other East African peoples shown by Schneider. It also underlies Christensen's discussion of the adaptations in Fanti religious belief and practice, and Messenger's analysis of how Anang Ibibio religion has responded to the pressures of Christian missions. To determine how the changes have taken place, Messenger compares the behavior of three age classes within the society, using a well-known research model to bring cultural change down from the level of abstraction to that of living, competing individuals.

The fact that continuity and change characterize African culture is apparent in all chapters but highlighted in the contrast between Ames's and Hammond's contributions. Ames, who suggests how Wolof co-operative work groups can contribute more effectively to the Gambia in the future and discusses what has happened to them in the past, emphasizes the principle that innovations must be related to traditional patterns if they are to be accepted and transmitted as a part of the cultural heritage to future generations. Hammond, on the other hand, shows how the attempt to re-create and perpetuate traditional African institutions has raised problems for French administrators, even when their policy was designed to ease the problem of cultural adjustment.

Though at first these two positions may seem contradictory, Ames is emphasizing the importance of cultural continuity, while Hammond is stressing the dynamic nature of culture. Both studies illustrate basic cultural principles which anthropologists have perhaps too often taken for granted or at least have not sufficiently stressed in communicating outside their own discipline. The problem of the French administrators seems to have been in underestimating the importance not of cultural continuity but of cultural change, despite the fact that they were trying to induce change by their program of economic development. Even more important, they seem not to have fully understood the intricate relationships between the various aspects of a culture and the principle that changes in one aspect may have unexpected and perhaps undesirable effects on its other aspects. For cultures, we now know, are never static, even in isolation, and it is impossible to alter one part of a culture without affecting its other parts.

The nature of the research design and the control of variables are most explicit in the studies by Hammond and Lystad. In the first, two parts of a single Mossi community are studied, one resettled under a large-scale, government-directed project of agricultural development, the other serving as a control group. Cultural changes are identified by comparing the life of those who migrated to their new setting in the Niger Office with the life of those who remained at home; Hammond also considers how those who return home after having participated in this project have impinged on traditional Mossi culture. In its design, it is apparent that this study makes a methodological contribution of considerable importance, quite aside from the theoretical implications of its findings or their relevance to the practical problems of economic development elsewhere in Africa.

Lystad compares two peoples who share a common historical and cultural background in terms of the effects of the independent variable of colonial policy. In his study the dependent variables are social institutions, but his research model is equally applicable to the analysis of other aspects of culture. This model could be developed because the Ashanti, who have lived under British control, and the Agni, under French control, share "a single precontact culture," which was one of the constants. Lystad's study takes on added significance as a design for research because of the many situations to which it can be applied: in all parts of Africa ethnic units have been split by political boundaries, each part having to adapt its mode of life to the exigencies of a different governmental policy. In addition to their significance for science, such studies have most important practical implications for resolving tensions arising in the course of the increasingly potent drive for nationhood in Africa— like those which have already assumed prominence in Togo and the Cameroons.

From the point of view of scientific method it should be obvious that an approach which takes into account the dimensions of space and time invites research designs in which variables can be controlled in a manner essential to the testing of specific hypotheses and the validation of generalizations. In the study of man, variables cannot be controlled by the observer as in a laboratory experiment in chemistry or physics. Because man, rather than atoms or elements, is his subject, the student of human behavior is faced at some point in his inquiries with social barriers to manipulation in his experiments. Like the astronomer and the geologist, who also study phenomena which they cannot manipulate, the anthropologist's answer lies in the analysis of data as they occur. He must seek out the situations which bear on the problem he wishes to study as they develop in various times and places, and he must design a research model that can test hypotheses or permit generalizations.

Here lies the importance of Africa for the scientific study of man, here where so many different situations have resulted from the variegated channels of the stream of history. It is essentially for this reason that all who have collaborated in this book have been attracted to the field of African studies, quite apart from the practical challenge that Africa presents for world adjustment, and all have sought by their works to expand the body of available data or the field of theory. For Africa affords a laboratory with untold resources for the scientific analysis of human behavior. We who have worked in this laboratory are confident that in it many important lessons can be learned—important lessons not only for Africa but for mankind as a whole.

2. Africa as a Linguistic Area

Africa is linguistically one of the most complex areas in the world, rivaled in this respect perhaps only by aboriginal South America and New Guinea; the usual figure of eight hundred languages for the continent is doubtless an underestimate. The first question we are likely to ask when confronted with this vast Babel of tongues is the historical one: How did such linguistic diversity come to exist? The accepted answer to such a question is a classification into families of languages, each independent and consisting of those forms of speech which are the differentiated descendants of a common original tongue. Such a result, if correct, will help us to decide—among other questions—whether the present diversity is of recent date, all of Africa having been settled by one linguistic stock at some not too remote period, or whether we must reckon with a more complex pattern of separate waves of settlement occurring at different periods. Indeed, in the absence of written records of any degree of antiquity for most of Africa outside of the northern littoral, and because of the paucity of the archeological data, there of necessity falls to linguistics a significant role in unraveling the history of the African continent over so many obscure millennia.

The language classifications which have successively held the field, from the early attempts of Lepsius and Mueller to the most recent one based chiefly on the efforts of Meinhof and Westermann, have all suffered from similar basic defects. They have been grand syntheses, reducing at all costs the number of distinct language families in Africa in accordance with some relatively simple theory of the peopling and racial composition of the continent. Only in small part have they presented concrete evidence for the classifications, which have thus rested largely on mere assertion. Most important, however, is the lack of attention to those specific types of resemblances which are probative of common origin.

For example, in the Meinhof-Westermann classification, linguistic phenomena indicative of true historical connections were inextricably mingled with considerations based on a supposed succession of language types reflecting an outmoded and oversimplified theory of language evolution. In this typological sequence, the languages of the "true Negro," those of the Sudanic type, were portrayed as having the most simple and primitive isolating structure, while the most advanced linguistic structures on the African scene involved a supposed Hamitic family blessed with inflection, grammatical gender, an abundance of cattle, and an appetite for conquest.

The question of what is relevant for determining common historical origin among languages is not difficult to grasp and needs no special training in linguistic science. Every meaningful form in a language, whether it is a lexical item like "house" or "run" or a grammatical item like the "-er" comparative of the English adjective, has a double aspect: it displays both a specific succession of sounds and a distinct meaning. If we compare languages, we find some resemblances in both sound and meaning—for example, the German forms which correspond to those cited above for English: *Haus, renn(en), -er*. Of course, there are different sounds with similar meanings (e.g., English "door" and Arabic *bāb* both mean "door") and similar sounds with different meanings, both in specific forms and in general systems (e.g., English "egg" and Hungarian *ég*, "sky," are pronounced in approximately the same way; English and classical Arabic both have a *th* sound).

The presence of resemblances in meaning only or in sound only would probably be rejected by ordinary good sense as having little or no bearing on the question of specific historical connection. The number of possible sounds is limited, and the occurrence of the same or similar sounds in different languages, if not used in forms with similar meanings, obviously proves nothing. Similarly, the converse may even seem pathological: "It is an evidence for the historical relationship of the English and Turkish languages that both have a word for 'water'; only in English it is 'water,' but in Turkish it is *su*." If the word designates some item for which, unlike "water," we do not expect every language to have a term, then the existence of a resemblance in meaning only, e.g., English "typewriter" and German *Schreibmaschine*, both meaning "typewriter," is the result of historical factors, the invention of the typewriter and its spread over a single cultural area—in this case, western Europe—but the terms here are obviously not the result of common origin if they only have the meaning in common. Resemblances in both sound and meaning in such items, English "telephone," German *Telefon*, are usually the result of borrowing, not common origin.

All this may seem so obvious and elementary as to be hardly worth stating. However, if instead of saying that languages are related because they both have a word for "water," we say they have grammatical gender, which merely means that they have forms meaning "masculine" and "feminine," and instead of resting our case on *th*, we say that they both have tonal systems, the argument sounds more impressive although in essence it remains the same as long as the resemblances refer to sound without meaning or meaning without sound. But such families as Sudanic and Hamitic of the older literature were defined almost entirely in terms of such irrelevant criteria and contained a hodgepodge of languages among which sound-meaning resemblances in basic vocabulary and grammatical elements could be shown; some were really related, and some had no real mutual connection.

THE LANGUAGE FAMILIES OF AFRICA

The classification outlined here is founded on a review of the total African evidence in which only the criteria relevant in the light of the foregoing discussion are considered.[1] According to this scheme, there are five distinct language families of major importance on the African continent; they occupy perhaps 98 per cent of the total precontact area and population. These are the Niger-Congo, Afro-Asiatic, Macrosudanic, Central Saharan, and Click families. In addition, there are seven groups of languages, or individual languages, which occupy relatively small areas—Songhai, Maban, Fur, Koman, Kordofanian, Temainian, and Nyangiya—making twelve families in all.

The Niger-Congo family is of vast extent and contains several hundred languages covering most of west central and southern Africa. It falls into seven subfamilies: West-Atlantic, Mandingo, Gur, Kwa, Ijo, Central, and Adamawa-Eastern.

The West-Atlantic subfamily includes the language of the Fulani, about which there has been much controversy. It is safe to say that Meinhof's assertion of the Hamitic affiliation of Fulani can no longer be seriously maintained. The closest linguistic relatives of the Fulani are the Serer-Sin, Wolof, Serer-Nono, and Konyagi, which together form a distinct group within the West-Atlantic subfamily.

The Mandingo and Gur languages are relatively obvious groupings about which there is little controversy. The Kwa is an important subfamily which stretches from Liberia, where the Kru languages are spoken, to the Edo (Bini) and Yala or Idoma group of southeastern Nigeria. The Ewe, Twi, and Yoruba groups all are affiliated with Kwa as well as with the Togo remnant languages, formerly classified in a separate branch. Ijo is a language of southeast Nigeria which forms a group by itself.

The Central group of the Niger-Congo family consists mainly of

[1] The detailed evidence for this classification has been presented in *Studies in African Linguistic Classification* (New Haven: Compass Publishing Co., 1955).

languages in Nigeria but contains the vast Bantu stock as a subgroup. Within this Central branch, Bantu has a particularly close relationship to Tiv, Batu, Ndoro, Bitare, Mambila, and Jarawa.

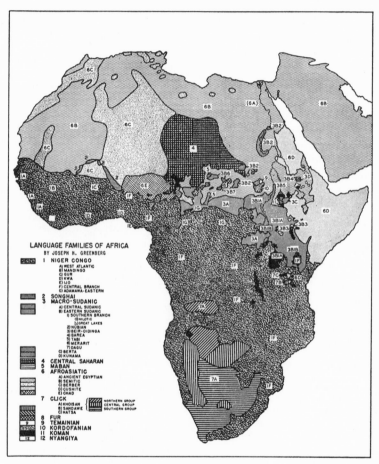

Fig. 1.

The Adamawa-Eastern group includes many little-known languages in eastern Nigeria and the Cameroons, along with such important languages farther east as Azande and Sango.

The Afro-Asiatic, like the Niger-Congo family, is of vast extent, covering all of northern Africa, adjoining portions of Asia, the Horn area of East Africa, and an extensive region in the vicinity of Lake

Chad. There are five branches: Berber, Cushitic, Semitic, Ancient Egyptian (extinct), and Chad.

The Chad subfamily contains perhaps as many as a hundred languages found for the most part in northern Nigeria and the northern Cameroons. The best-known language of this group is Hausa, probably the largest speech community in Africa outside of Arabic and widely employed as a lingua franca in West Africa.

The Afro-Asiatic languages correspond in general to those included under the traditional term "Hamito-Semitic." "Hamitic" has in the past been a cover term for all non-Semitic branches and represents no real linguistic entity. In view of the serious misunderstandings occasioned by the use of this term in physical anthropology and culture history, it is abandoned in the present classification.

The Macrosudanic languages are another major stock concentrated in the area of the Congo-Nile divide and extending eastward into the Upper Nile and northern Great Lakes region of East Africa. There are four branches: Eastern Sudanic, Central Sudanic, Kunama, and Berta. The Eastern Sudanic group includes Nuba, the Nilotic languages, and the so-called Nilo-Hamitic languages (Masai, Bari, etc.). Central Sudanic contains, among others, the Sara dialects near Lake Chad, Mangbetu, and the Moru-Madi subgroup. Kunama is a language of northwestern Ethiopia, and Berta is the designation of a small number of languages straddling the Ethiopian-Sudanese border.

Central Saharan covers a large but generally sparsely settled territory north and east of Lake Chad and near the lake itself. Included are Kanuri, Teda, and Zaghawa.

The Click family comprehends the languages of the Hottentots and the various Bushman populations of southwestern Africa as well as the Hatsa and Sandawe forms of speech farther north in East Africa. Here again, Meinhof's theory of the Hamitic affiliations of Hottentot is not seriously maintained at the present time. Hottentot is closely allied to the Bushman languages of the Naron and //Auen, within the much larger Khoisan branch of the entire Click family.

In addition to the twelve families enumerated earlier, there is Malagasy, a Malayo-Polynesian language spoken on the island of Madagascar. Meroitic, the extinct language of Meroe, an Egyptian-influenced culture of the Blue Nile–White Nile area which flourished in classical times and is only imperfectly known from inscriptional remains, appears to be independent.

THE ORIGIN OF BANTU

This review makes it clear that the present linguistic diversity of Africa cannot be reduced to a single source and that there has been a complex history of settlement over a very long period. This should not be surprising. Africa, on the evidence of paleontology, has been inhabited by hominids from very early times and rivals Asia as a possible home for earliest man. Some of the details of this long and varied historical development can, of course, be deduced from the language classification outlined here. One salient problem is that of the place of origin of the large Bantu group of closely related languages which occupies practically all of the southern third of the continent. The facts that Bantu is affiliated with the Central branch of the Niger-Congo family and that the other languages of this group are all spoken in Nigeria and the Cameroons point strongly to this general area as the original Bantu homeland. The special relationship of Bantu, within the Central group, to Tiv, Batu, Ndoro, Bitare, Mambila, and Jarawa serves to make this hypothesis more explicit. Since all these peoples live in a relatively restricted area near the central Benue Valley, this particular region is strongly indicated as the point of origin of the Bantu migration. The date at which such a proto-Bantu community still spoke a unified language may be estimated as approximately twenty-five hundred years ago.[2] The hypothesis that the Bantu spread first into the Congo rain forest and then into East and South Africa at this relatively recent date is in general accord with the archeological and paleontological evidence, which suggests that the earlier population of this area was of the Bushman and Pygmy types.

Hitherto the prevailing view (strongly championed, for example, by Sir Harry Johnston) has been that the Bantu originated in the Great Lakes area of East Africa.[3] The reason advanced has been that the Bantu languages of the East African lake area are more primitive in type than the other Bantu languages. What is presumably meant is that these languages have changed less from the parent Bantu language than others of the same stock. Scientific comparative linguistics rejects arguments of this kind. Closer examination of such assertions usually reveals that a few striking archaisms have been noticed that the innovations ignored. We expect that in a group of related languages all will have changed approximately to the same degree from the ancestral language. Even assuming that the Great Lakes languages are more archaic, the conclusion that this area is the Bantu homeland by no means follows. Similar reasoning applied to the Romance languages might lead to the conclusion that Latin originated in Sardinia, where

[2] The method employed is that of glottochronology, by which dates of separation of related languages are estimated on the basis of percentage of shared basic vocabulary. For a convenient exposition, see R. B. Lees, "The Basis of Glottochronology," *Language*, XXIX (1953), 113–27.

[3] In his monumental work, *A Comparative Study of the Bantu and Semi-Bantu Languages* (Oxford: Clarendon Press, 1919–22).

certain conspicuous archaisms are retained. It would certainly not lead to the conclusion that Latin originated in Rome.

On the other hand, the argument based on the geographical location of the genetically most closely related languages is a powerful one. It may be illustrated by the example of English. In the absence of written history, how could one choose among North America, South Africa, Australia, and the British Isles as the possible homeland of the English language? The language most closely related to English is Frisian, spoken by a small fishing population on the Dutch coast. The next most closely related languages are the Germanic group, found in northern Europe. Moreover, the remainder of the Indo-European family, of which Germanic is a branch, covers an adjacent area in Europe and western Asia. Each step, therefore, strengthens the case for the British Isles as against the other possible areas. In similar fashion, the relationships of Bantu point first to the central Benue, then to the Central group of Niger-Congo in Nigeria and the Cameroons, and finally to the Niger-Congo family, whose distribution centers in West Africa rather than East Africa.

The Great Lakes theory of Bantu origins has, at least in the minds of some of its adherents, been but one aspect of a general orientation which would, in its most extreme form, attribute virtually all the seminal events of African history to the stimulus of incoming, superior Caucasoids, both Semites and Hamites, as they exercised their influence on an indigenous, culturally passive Negroid population. Thus the Bantu languages, according to one view, arose in the area of the Great Lakes as the result of contact between a basic Sudanic-speaking Negro group and a Hamitic people.[4] In its racial aspect, this theory derives most of the population of sub-Saharan Africa, outside of a relatively small group of forest Negroes in West Africa, from varying Semitic and Hamitic admixture.

The linguistic counterpart of this theory has been the widespread extension of the use of "Hamitic" as a linguistic term. Indeed, the racial aspect of the Hamitic theory has been largely influenced by its employment in linguistic classification, the historical antecedent. The widest linguistic usage of the term "Hamitic" is found in Carl Meinhof's writings.[5] He considers as Hamitic Fulani, Hausa, and other languages in West Africa, Hottentot in South Africa, and Masai, Nandi, and other cattle peoples of the so-called Nilo-Hamitic subfamily in East Africa, in addition to the generally accepted groups of Berber,

---

[4] Cf. the statement of Carl Meinhof in his *Die Sprachen der Hamiten* (Hamburg: L. & R. Friederichsen, 1912): "Bantu is a mixed language, so to speak, descended of a Hamitic father and a Negro mother" (p. 2).

[5] Particularly in his *Die Sprachen der Hamiten.*

Ancient Egyptian, and the Cushitic of east Africa. Others besides the present writer have pointed to the weakness of the case presented by Meinhof for the Hamitic affiliations of Fulani and Hottentot. The Nilo-Hamitic group is still the subject of some controversy, but all writers agree that it is closely related to Nilotic, which would place it within the Macrosudanic family of the present writer. Some, however, maintain that it is a linguistic hybrid containing Hamitic elements.[6] On the other hand, Hausa and the many other languages related to Nilo-Hamitic in the Chad group are now generally admitted to be members of the Hamito-Semitic family. It is an ironic fact that these, the only non-cattle peoples contained in Meinhof's extension of traditional Hamitic, have also turned out to be the only valid addition to the family.

Finally, the view that Semitic and Hamitic are two branches of a Hamito-Semitic family can no longer be seriously maintained. The genetic picture that emerges from a careful review of the data is that of a linguistic family with five co-ordinate branches of which Semitic is but one. The term "Hamitic," therefore, lacks any linguistic foundation, since it is a term traditionally applied to four of the five branches of the entire family. It was for this reason that the present writer suggested the term Afro-Asiatic in place of the misleading Hamito-Semitic. In the light of these considerations, the racial and cultural-historical Hamitic theory lacks a linguistic foundation.

SPECIAL FEATURES OF AFRICAN LANGUAGES

Although we cannot prove an ultimate unity of all African languages, there are, just as in other aspects of African culture, features which set off Africa from other areas of the world. These result from later contacts among the languages of the continent, on a vast scale and over a long period. Practically none of the peculiarities listed below as typical are shared by all African languages, and almost every one is found somewhere outside of Africa, but the combination of these features gives a definite enough characterization that a language, not labeled as such for an observer, would probably be recognized as African.

Among sounds, the clicks of the Click family and certain South African Bantu languages are not found anywhere else in the world. The simultaneous labiovelar *kp* and *gb* sounds are distributed over a wide east-west belt of languages of diverse genetic affiliations from the Atlantic Ocean almost to the Nile Valley. Outside of Africa, these sounds are only known from a restricted area of Melanesia both in

[6] For a discussion of the recent controversial literature on this subject, see A. E. Meeussen "Hamitisch en Nilotisch," *Zaïre*, III (1957), 264–72.

Melanesian and in so-called Papuan languages. Implosive consonant sounds, in which the lowering of the glottis produces a rarefaction of the air followed by the ingress of outside air, are frequent in Africa but uncommon elsewhere. With few exceptions, African consonant systems are simple, without the variety of back velar sounds occurring in other parts of the world. Vowel systems are likewise simple, with the virtual absence of umlauted vowels or unrounded back vowels, the so-called abnormal vowels. Consonant combinations are usually few in number. They practically never involve more than two consonants medially or one initially. The syllable is characteristically open, that is, ending in a vowel. Initial *ng* sounds and initial combinations of nasal plus voiced stop, for example, *mb* and *nd*, are extremely common, and relatively rare elsewhere in the world.

Finally, tone is almost universal in Africa outside of the important Afro-Asiatic family. Even here, most—perhaps all—members of the Chad subgroup have tonal systems under the influence of neighboring languages.

In morphology, complex noun classifications like the well-known prefix classes of Bantu are widespread, though far from universal. The same feature is found in aboriginal Australia and in New Guinea, but without specific points of resemblance. The verb very often has a complicated set of derivatives to express such ideas as the causative, reflexive, passive, or motion towards the speaker. Characteristically, these ideas may be combined with each other. An example from Swahili will serve to illustrate such a system: *pata* (obtain), *patana* (make an agreement—reciprocal), *patanisha* (unite—reciprocal causative), *patia* (obtain for somebody—applicative), *patika* (be seized—passive), *patiliza* (make someone vexed—causative), *patilizana* (vex each other—causative-reciprocal), etc.

In the sphere of semantics, there are many idioms or metaphorical uses of terms with wide distributions found infrequently or not at all outside of Africa. Examples of such usages include the same term meaning "meat" and "wild animal"; the verb with the primary meaning "to eat" also meaning "to conquer," "capture a piece in a game," "have sexual intercourse"; the phrase "child of ———" to express the diminutive; the phrase "child of the tree" meaning "fruit"; widespread use of parts of the body to express position (cf. English "back of"), for example, "belly of" meaning "inside," "head of" meaning "upon," "buttock of" meaning "at the base of"; "he himself" often translates as "he with his head." A final example is the typical mode of expressing comparison in two variants—"x surpasses y in size" or "x is big, surpasses y" meaning "x is larger than y."

LINGUISTIC AREAS OF AFRICA

It is noticeable that various sections of the continent differ in the intensity with which they partake of such common characteristics. There is a large central area in which all of these characteristics are found in most of the languages. This core area consists mainly of the Niger-Congo languages, Songhai, the Central Sudanic subgroup of the Macrosudanic family, and, to a certain degree, the Chad subgroup of Afro-Asiatic.

Other areas which can now be roughly delimited are marginal in that they partake of some but not all of these features. In addition to their imperfect sharing of the most widespread African character-istics, each displays specialized phenomena which result from linguistic contacts within the area itself. One widespread area which can be described as marginal is the Khoisan-speaking part of southwestern Africa. Another well-marked linguistic area embraces approximately Ethiopia and the various Somalilands. The languages here are of heterogeneous origin—Cushitic, Ethiopian Semitic languages, Kunama, and Barea, the last two being members of different branches of Macro-sudanic. This area is marked by relatively complex consonantal systems, including glottalized sounds, absence of tone, word order of determined followed by determiner, closed syllables, and some characteristic idioms. Another rather less well-marked area can be discerned in the northern part of East Africa and in the Nile Valley, containing the Nilotic, Great Lakes, and Didinga-Murle groups, all belonging to Eastern Sudanic, and the Moru-Madi group of the Central Sudanic subfamily of Macrosudanic.

North of the Nile-Congo divide a whole series of languages which diverge sharply from languages to the south stretches across the eastern Sudan from Lake Chad in the west. Included are the Central Saharan languages, Maban, Fur, and the Dagu, Merarit, and Nubian languages of the Eastern Sudanic subgroup of Macrosudanic. Characteristics of this area include periodic sentence construction with the use of participles for subordination reminiscent in structure of classical Latin, a case system in the noun but without adjective agreement, and the absence of noun classificatory systems.

It should be emphasized that these language areas are tentative and in need of further investigation and documentation. A general re-semblance to Herskovits' standard culture-area classification is evident. The central or core area corresponds roughly to the Congo–Guinea Coast area, though it is somewhat more extensive, including especially the major part of the East Cattle area. The Khoisan area equates with the Bushman and Hottentot areas. The Ethiopian area outlined alone practically coincides with the East African Horn. The region which consists of the Nilotic, Great Lakes, Didinga, and Moru-Madi languages embraces the northern portion of the Eastern Cattle area. The group of languages stretching across Africa east of Lake Chad agrees well with the Eastern Sudanic area. Finally, the Berber- and Arabic-speaking areas that cover the northern stretch, though very similar, fall into two portions. In the western part of the area Arabic dialects, commencing approximately with the Egyptian-Libyan border, share many features derived from contact with Berber speakers, while Berber in turn contains large numbers of Arabic loan words and some sounds which have entered by way of Arabic influence. These two areas agree approximately with Herskovits' Egyptian area and the undesignated North African area.

EUROPEAN INFLUENCES ON AFRICAN LANGUAGES

The languages of Africa, in their sharing of fundamental features underlying a complexity of origin and in their areal differentiation, agree in general fashion with other aspects of African culture. So, too, the long-continued and persistent Moslem influences, which have to a high degree shaped the life patterns of Negro peoples in the entire Sudan and much of East Africa and even farther south, find their reflection in the numerous loan words of ultimate Arabic origin, even among non-Moslem peoples. What, then, of the European influences of the last several centuries which have transformed so many aspects of African life? The effects of these events on the linguistic life of Africa would probably have to be judged as relatively small, compared with that of Arabic. The essential continuity of African culture in spite of drastic changes is perhaps nowhere better illustrated than in language.

European contact has resulted in the importation of the large Afrikaans- and English-speaking populations of South Africa and much smaller or negligible European speech communities elsewhere. In the urban areas of Liberia and Sierra Leone, English in standard and Creolized form, respectively, has been established by repatriated Negro slaves. A few words, generally of Portuguese origin, have been borrowed for earlier items brought through the agency of Europeans, e.g., manioc from South America and the domestic pig in coastal areas (elsewhere it is older). In more recent times, borrowings have occurred chiefly from English and French for more modern items of contact, such as Hausa *kantini* (store), *kwano* (can), or *sati* (wages), from Saturday, the standard payday. Many borrowed terms of recent importation are not yet well established, and only the future will tell to what extent such words will continue or be replaced by indigenous expressions. The study of recent loan words of European origin is a field of great interest which has thus far hardly been investigated.

In addition, European languages have been used as lingua francas, particularly among educated Africans of differing tribal backgrounds, and as a vehicle of education, particularly on the higher levels. However, in all such cases except the Creolized forms already mentioned, European languages among Africans lack the basis provided by a large population speaking the language as its native tongue. Moreover, while serving in this fashion as a means of wider communication, such languages as English and French have to some extent been barriers to understanding: Africans with English and French education have, along with the language, acquired differing British and French cultural values.

In summary, the total direct linguistic influence of European contact has been the introduction of a few new speech communities of European origin, the use of European languages as lingua francas, and the introduction of loan words comprising but a very minor portion of the total vocabulary of any African language. The effect of European languages on the grammatical structure of African languages, as far as can be seen, is virtually nonexistent. In another direction, however, the indirect effects are of greater import. Language differentiation is the reflex of over-all communication conditions. Before intensive European contact, there were occasional instances of the spread of single languages over wide areas as the result of political expansion or in response to economic needs. One instance is the wide distribution of the Malinke language in its various dialectal forms in French West Africa, an event which must surely be connected with the existence of the vast Mandingo Empire in this region in the Middle Ages. So, likewise, much of the spread of Hausa as a second language beyond its original borders was a pre-European response to the growing indigenous trade needs of this segment of the western Sudan.

One of the chief effects of European colonizing activity has been the widening of communication through the abolition of slavery and intertribal warfare and the development of roads, railroads, and other forms of transportation. The more widespread traveling and commerce that result, as well as the modern administration and education and the cultural unity demanded by modern nationalism, all necessitate a higher degree of linguistic unity than existed prior to intensive European contact. The development of new lingua francas and the further spread of old ones, as well as the dying-out of the smaller speech communities, are the responses to these changing conditions. However, this readjustment is necessarily slow. A people does not abandon its language overnight. There are emotional attachments which people feel to their own language, and there must normally be at least one generation of bilinguals. Survival has been the rule rather than the exception thus far, even among relatively small speech communities. The impact of nationalism and the practical necessities of administration and education must in the long run considerably simplify the present complex linguistic situation, which is a heritage of other conditions, but such changes will take much time to accomplish. In the long run, such changes as well as the standardization in written form of many hitherto unwritten languages are of far greater significance than the superficial direct effects of European contact on the vigorous linguistic life of Africa.

3. African Art

For over fifty years artists, students, and collectors have been stirred by the aesthetic qualities of African art forms found in museums and private collections of Europe and America. Yet it is still difficult for the interested individual to find the information about their creators and cultural background that would give a richer understanding of these works of art. It is the purpose of this chapter to survey the material known to archeologists and ethnologists but not found in any one volume on African art, either general or iconographic in nature. African art forms of the prehistoric, precolonial, and modern periods are discussed in terms of their cultural setting and the dynamics of change expressed in the creativity of their makers.

THE PREHISTORIC PERIOD

Among the best-known forms of prehistoric African art are the vigorous rock drawings and paintings of South Africa and Rhodesia, and of North Africa as well. These portray men of different cultures and animals of the veldt and near desert. Done in ochre, red earth, charcoal, and white clay, whose colors are still fresh, they show a startling degree of movement and action in scenes depicting hunting and warfare. Relative dating is possible in some instances, as when drawings of Bantu and Europeans overlie those of animals.

Aside from the rock drawings and paintings, which have survived only on surfaces protected by overhangs where neither sand nor rain could obliterate them, prehistoric African art consists of work in stone, metal, and fired clay, which neither rain nor insects could destroy. The richest finds of ancient art in stone have been made in West Africa by French and British archeologists. Thus far, however, we have only the most fragmentary knowledge of the cultures which produced the small, roughly carved human heads in stone that are found from Dakar to Lake Chad and from the Sudan down to the Guinea Coast. It has been suggested that these heads are related to the hundreds of mysterious stone figures in a sacred grove near Esie, Ilorin Province, in southwest Nigeria;

one-third to one-half life size, they exhibit a combination of naturalism and stylized proportioning still common to contemporary, traditional forms of this area of West Africa. Nothing is known about their origins; they stand today as mute testimony of a people sophisticated in art forms and stone-working technique, a people who seem to have been of wholly African origin, for only Negroid features are depicted.

The most dramatic of the ancient terra cotta art forms are the naturalistic modeled heads and half-figures of Jos and Ife in Nigeria. The discovery in the Jos tin mines of small terra cotta heads, so similar to examples of more refined style found earlier in Ife, aroused speculation that they were actually part of the same tradition, though not contemporaneous with each other. The Jos finds, now identified with the Nok culture, have been dated by radiocarbon analysis as about three thousand years old (between 2000 B.C. and A.D. 200, most probably 900 B.C.); the Ife heads and half-figures are probably a thousand years younger.[1] Terra cotta forms extend to the Lake Chad area, where French archeologists have discovered what appears to be a similar ancient culture with walled cities and many objects of modeled clay.

The naturalism of these terra cotta art forms, more successful in some pieces than others, demonstrates what appears to be a gradual perfecting of style, perhaps by a specialized group of artists. The earlier heads are simple, with striated facial markings; but later ones, such as those of Ife, are more detailed and elaborate. A head from Nok shows a more stylized face, but with careful attention given to the decoration of the hair. Pottery that has survived the ravages of time includes containers once used for *Ifa* divination by more recent Yoruba. Modeled in high relief, the earlier pots depict various small animals and reptiles that serve as messengers of Yoruba deities. Frobenius' account of fired bricks with one face decorated in bas-relief on the palace at Ife, which had probably stood for centuries, suggests a relationship to the bas-relief designs in clay on the walls about inner doors in palaces and titled compounds in Benin and Dahomey. Stylized terra cotta heads of early workmanship still appear on the ancestral altars of titled members of the brass workers' quarter in Benin City. Their explanation is that while only the ancestors of the king could be depicted in large heads of brass or bronze, the titled members of the guild who married daughters of the king were allowed to have a life-sized head of terra cotta to represent them after death.

THE DEVELOPMENT OF METAL ART WORK

Iron appears to have replaced polished stone at a very early period in the adzes, hoes, knives, and spears of Africa. The use of stone tools is lost

[1] E. W. Barenson, E. F. Deevey, and L. J. Gralenski, "Yale Natural Radiocarbon Measurements III," *Science*, CXXVI (1957), 916.

in traditional history beyond the memory of the present inhabitants, though there are legends among the Khoisan peoples of the time before the coming of the Bantu that tell of their use. If iron art forms were made anywhere in ancient Africa, nothing remains, for iron does not long survive oxidation in the tropics without either deliberate preservation or repeated sacrifices of palm oil.

The people of Benin, however, have elaborate iron standards for the god of medicine, Osain, for some of which great antiquity is claimed. These standards, wrought in iron and standing the height of a man, have many branching arms at the top, each surmounted by a symbol of the needs and powers of man. The Bini also used lamp holders of wrought iron in basket shapes, some as large as sixteen inches in diameter, and made iron inserts in the eyes and foreheads of the carved wooden heads (*uhum elao*) of traditional chiefs used on family altars. The earliest known iron inserts are found on a great stone at Ife, whose origin is lost beyond traditional history; they form a pattern in a straight line, which has been interpreted as a record of some sort rather than as an artistic decoration. More recent are the Yoruba male figures of iron associated with Ogun, god of iron and war, some of which are mounted on horseback and carry a shallow circular dish on the head, thus serving as a lamp.

The Dahomean art forms in iron are still more modern, the earliest known being dated as not over two centuries old. They are discussed here because they are forerunners of an important art tradition in Dahomean culture. One technique was a wrought-iron plating attached to large, carved wooden forms of birds and animals that symbolized families of the royal clan. In one case, a wooden bird was covered with thin sheets of brass, and wings of wrought iron were attached. A more delicate technique in wrought iron produced the standard placed on the shrine of a high-ranking male member of the royal clan who had become governor of an area under the king or was perhaps the son of the king. This standard is a straight iron rod, four or five feet long; it has a pointed base to insert in the earth and is surmounted by a small round platform edged with pendants of brass or iron. Standing on the small platform are wrought-iron or brass symbols depicting forms such as animals or plants whose generic terms suggest tonal patterns similar to the names of the man and his family. Ceremonial gongs, common through West and Central Africa as musical instruments in percussion orchestras, were, and still are, made in unusually elaborate forms. Some of those in the old style have as many as three gongs connected by a stylized human figure.

Copper, silver, and gold, all fairly easy to abstract from ore at a low heat and readily worked in pure form, seem to have been in use from early times. Legends are vague about their origin and use. Copper ornaments in the form of bangles and bracelets are mentioned by Dapper as used by the commoners of Benin in the late seventeenth century, but they seem to have disappeared with the introduction of harder brass through European trade. The rest of Africa south of the Sahara appears to have had knowledge of copper through trade or actual smelting, but its path of diffusion and the extent of its use is clouded with speculation. Gold and silver were used for personal ornament and symbols of rank in West Africa. These metals seem to have been most used by the ancient kingdom of Ghana in the western Sudan for *repoussé* work on symbols of authority, and by the Ashanti, whose gold weights indicate the early weighing of gold dust. Travelers' accounts and the traditional histories of the Ashanti tell of thin sheets of gold used to cover the royal stool and of gold jewelry worn by members of the royal family. Small "masks" of gold, perhaps used as pendants and done in gold wire technique—as is most of the gold jewelry—are in the form of human faces and rams' heads. The Arabs discovered gold in use on the east coast in what is now Mozambique and forced the Africans to lead them to their small mines, which were then enlarged and worked for centuries, supplying a large portion of the Moslem world at that time with its wealth. Nothing is known of the forms into which this gold was worked by the Africans.

For a long time it was believed that bronze was used only for gold weights of the Ashanti and the art treasures of Benin, but discoveries since 1935 have given a fuller picture of the use of the medium in sub-Saharan Africa, though it does seem to have been concentrated in southern Nigeria. There are only scattered reports of its use to the west among the Ashanti and beyond. It should be made clear, however, that adequate metallurgical analyses have not been made on all the art forms which, from the patina usually associated with this medium, appear to be bronze. Actually, the alloys produced by African smelting in ancient times were of copper and zinc—that is, brass—and of copper and tin—bronze—though the percentage of zinc or tin seems to have varied greatly with the individual smeltings and in different areas.[2]

Cire-perdue casting reached as far west as what is now Liberia, where

[2] To avoid confusion in the discussion on *cire-perdue* casting, for which the following metals were used, we shall distinguish African brass and bronze from the European brass, which was introduced to the coast of west Africa by the Portuguese as early as the last quarter of the fifteenth century. Wherever casting was employed, the forms produced were for the use of the ruling class or for certain deities. European brass was eagerly accepted, but its use was still controlled by the ruling class, who in the case of the Yoruba and Bini allowed it to be used by nobles and members of certain religious cults, while the brass casters were allowed to sell a limited number of bracelets and bangles to the public. French archeologists have uncovered smelting works in the Sudan on ancient caravan routes which would seem to indicate that the African alloys of bronze or brass were cast into some rough form of ingot for shipment south to areas where skilled craftsmen worked in the *cire-perdue* process.

small figures, armlets, and containers were made. Among the Ashanti, African brass or bronze was most commonly used for the small, delicately modeled gold weights, small brass and copper masks, and brass *kuduos* or decorated jars which were probably intended to hold gold dust. The gold weights display less delicate modeling in genre human and animal subjects, geometric designs, and miniature artifacts, but this may be due to their small size and the simplicity of the casting process. A more complicated method of casting seems to have been used on larger pieces, such as one which represents the entire retinue of a chief who is being carried in a hammock, though this composition is itself not more than five inches in length at the base and two and a half inches high.

The African bronze or brass of Yoruba, Benin, and Nupe origin are more dramatic to Euroamerican tastes than the cast forms of the Ashanti to the west. The Yoruba are represented by the realistic, life-sized human Ife heads, the *Obalufon* mask, and a small torso in the costume of an *Oni* of Ife. There are a number of smaller pieces, such as figures and swords, but these are more stylized and do not have the perfect naturalism of the heads that brought them instant fame when they were discovered. In Nupe territory, to the north of Ife and Benin, are to be found a number of fine cast figures of what are known as the Tada and Jebba schools, probably influenced by Ife artists. The Tada figure is of a seated man done in a highly naturalistic style and has acquired a polished brown patina; the Jebba piece is much more stylized, suggesting the more rigid representations of Yoruba wood carvings.

The variety of bronze and brass forms extant in museums and private collections of Europe and America give a picture of Benin consistent with the descriptions given by travelers of the sixteenth and seventeenth centuries. Among the most dramatic and informative of these Benin pieces are the plaques which in the sixteenth century covered the wooden audience gallery of the king's inner courtyard. These depict the only landscapes in traditional African art, with scenes of hunters beneath trees, aiming bows and arrows at birds in the branches above. The plaques also record the deeds of nobles and the king (*oba*), with almost every type of rank indicated by the accouterments of the figures; these include many kinds of headdress, coral and jasper beads, tapestry cloth, leopard skins, tasseled skirts, and metal bells. Pendants on the dance costumes depict the face and headdress of members of the royal family, with heads of leopards to symbolize royalty and of rams, the beast sacrificed over the ancestral altars of royalty and nobles, also shown. Figures on plaques and pendants and free-standing forms accurately represent the Portuguese soldiers and explorers who visited Benin in the fifteenth and sixteenth centuries.

The balance of the Benin bronzes are intended for the shrines which each king had for his ancestors along the walls of a great inner courtyard of his compound. They include groupings of small figures of earlier rulers with their retinues, standing on a hollow base provided with an opening through which sacrifices to the spirit of the dead king could be poured. There are also a variety of bells, square at the top with flared sides, used to call the attention of the dead king to the sacrifices made for him; life-sized heads of royal princes having open tops into which were inserted great carved ivory tusks; and small oval heads with feet above and below symbolizing the messenger (Effoi) of the god of death (Ogiso). Large bronze leopards, which flanked the entrance to the audience chamber of the king, are the most prominent of the animal forms represented, though small leopard figures, which may have been sent with envoys as proof that they were from the king of Benin, have been found. To complete the list, swords, costume fasteners, and many other lesser accouterments of the royal household and favored nobles would have to be mentioned.

European brass, introduced to West Africa in the latter part of the fifteenth century, was traded to the interior, in some cases without the recipients ever having knowledge of its real source. Later, brass rods brought as gifts to the rulers along the coast became a standard of value, and in the nineteenth century they were as common as the earlier "manillas" of iron or brass used for currency. Wherever European brass was received, it was used for jewelry and art forms, in keeping with the tradition of other metals that had preceded it. Each society worked brass in its own way; some in *repoussé* technique, some in casting, and later, in East Africa and the Congo, by heating, hammering, and forming it into coiled arm and leg bands, earrings, and neck pieces. It was sometimes reserved for the use of rulers and deities, but some rulers allowed lesser nobles and commoners to have it. European brass was used by the Ashanti to cast gold weights, by the Yoruba and Bini for ceremonial forms, and by the Dahomeans for elaborate *repoussé* work on large wooden bases. The Bakota hammered it thin and nailed it to ancestral figures, as the Pongwe farther to the east did to religious figures, and the Ubangi made great coiled pieces of jewelry for their women, to cite but a few examples of its use.

Ife emerges as an early center of fine *cire-perdue* casting from the analysis of the early pieces and from the traditional history and early travelers' reports of Benin. It is said that small castings were sent by the king of Ife in the thirteenth century as gifts to the king of Benin, whose admiration for them caused him to request the king of Ife for a brass worker to teach the people of Benin. The Yoruba artist who was sent, so the account goes, remained in Benin, marrying a daughter of the king and founding the famous brass workers' quarter of Benin City. In Ife, casting of the quality of the famous heads does not seem to have survived much later than this period, though the casting of smaller pieces continued—wands linked by chains for the *Ogboni* society, small figures of Esu, the messenger god, and others whose dating is uncertain.

In Benin, on the other hand, the casting of African brass or bronze flourished. It is not possible to say that the simpler pieces were the earliest and that they grew more complex and artistically better as technical virtuosity progressed. According to the traditional brass workers today, talented artists and poor designers could have worked side by side or lived in different centuries. Since the figure of a dead king for his altar is always modeled by his first-born son, the ability of the heir to the throne also has to be taken into consideration.

Between the fourteenth and sixteenth centuries Benin expanded through southern Yoruba territory to the west and across the Niger to the east. The Bini arts expanded with the kingdom, and even today scattered evidence remains of their passing, as in the style of the Ijebu Yoruba brass castings and the few Benin castings which have turned up in Onitsha in Ibo country. By the eighteenth century more powerful Yoruba and Ibo groups were pushing the Bini back to their original territory; civil war and internal political strife drained the royal treasury, and for about two centuries apparently little art work was done. Traditional history reports the introduction of certain elements into the costumes of rulers and nobles which help the dating of later pieces. For example, wings of jasper beads were added to either side of the traditional crown of the king in approximately 1812, and the bronzes depicting these are thus no earlier than that time.

During the sack of Benin City in 1897, when the Bini fired their grass roofs and fled north into the forests and smaller villages, leaving everything behind them, the brass workers, wood carvers and ivory workers were among those who escaped. It was not until 1915, after the death of the exiled king and the ascent of his son to the throne of Benin City, that these artists were called back to their traditional home. Their work has received constant encouragement ever since from both the king and the British administration. The head of the brass workers' clan, who is also titular head of the quarter of casters and carvers, has been employed by the administration to teach not only the younger men of his family but outsiders as well. The work they produce, which is technically excellent but which strives for naturalism, is sold in a workshop with the work of the wood carvers. The rest of the extended family of brass workers, without encouragement from anyone in particular, continue in their ancient art in the back streets of the quarter, after working during the day as laborers or mechanics.

The Dahomean tradition of brass work is more recent than that of Ife,

Benin, or the Ashanti. African bronze or brass was not worked, and European brass did not come to the capital, Abomey, in any quantity until the middle of the last century. Earlier, the king had founded a quarter of wood carvers, weavers, and embroiderers near his palace, and with the introduction of European brass and cloth, brass workers and appliqué workers were added. At first large wood carvings of birds and animals were covered with thin sheets of the metal, while the iron standards for the ancestors were topped with brass. Large forms of this type, once stored in the king's small treasure house, are now housed in the museum in the restored palace at Abomey.

Some technique for casting must have existed as a basis for the present *cire-perdue* work, but it was probably restricted to the casting of earrings and arm bands in gold and brass. The Dahomean tradition of brass-casting is now well known in West Africa as well as in Europe and America, for the enthusiasm of French officials for the lively little human and animal figures has seen to their wide distribution. Casting is now being done by many members of the extended family which comprise the brass workers, and a great deal is produced for tourist trade; but the excellent quality of some of the early pieces is duplicated when special orders are given by discriminating customers, either African or European.

The traditional brass-casting of the Cameroons is centered chiefly in Bamum in the French Cameroons, though a small group of casters moved to Bamenda in British territory. The earlier work appears to have been made of European trade brass, which was cast into arm, neck, and leg coils, and into neck bands resembling the Portuguese "manillas" formerly made of iron. Though much of the later work is produced for commercial purposes, such as tiny genre figures, some is made for use in the indigenous culture—masks, both large and small, decorated with feathers for ceremonial dances, or elaborate pipes, based on those in modeled clay.

EARLIER WORK IN IVORY AND BONE

The extent of ivory- and bone-carving in prehistoric and precolonial times may never be completely known, for without particular care objects made of them—like those of wood—may perish in a tropical climate. Among the better-known centers of ivory tradition are the Warega in the eastern Congo, the Bapende and the Mangbetu in the northern Congo, Bamum in the Cameroons, and Benin City and the Ekiti or northeastern Yoruba in Nigeria. The Warega forms include highly stylized small figures and masks of half-life-size, though in some larger precolonial pieces a higher degree of naturalism was attempted. Though possessing charm and vigor, the Warega ivory carvings lack the competent handling of technique and design found in the small Bapende mask-faces used on ceremonial costumes or in the many small ivory carvings of the Mangbetu. The Mangbetu pieces are of small human subjects and, in more modern times, animal figures, carved pegs of a stringed instrument—each peg the head and shoulders of a woman—and carved pins for the elaborate coiffure for which Mangbetu women are famous.

The Benin ivories are not only the most elaborate but the best known. They were produced by a family in the quarter of specialists in Benin City and were made specifically for use by the king and nobles of Benin and for gifts to other rulers. Very large carved tusks were placed in the hollow top of life-sized bronze heads at either side of a royal ancestral altar; smaller ones were fastened to a projection set in a hole at the back of the wooden ancestral heads on the family altars of nobles. There were also large gauntlet-type bracelets, smaller bracelets, small figures of female worshipers of the messenger god (Esu), and wands for *Ifa* divination. From the earlier Portuguese period come fine small masks for ceremonial costumes, worn on the hip like those of bronze, and ivory gongs. More in European tradition were goblets with representations of Benin warriors and Portuguese soldiers surrounding the base.

In the designs found on the Benin ivories, the figure of the king (*oba*), dressed as the god of the sea (Olokun) appears most frequently, almost always supported by two figures, priests of the royal gods Ora and Uwen. The leopard represents the royal family, while the mudfish is a messenger of Olokun, as is the serpent.

The Yoruba of Owo were once under the influence of Benin, if not actually subjugated by it at the height of its conquests in the sixteenth and seventeenth centuries. Benin culture left its mark on the costumes and accouterments of the king (*Olowo*) and his nobles and war captains. Precolonial ivory carvings include small figurines of female worshipers of Eshu, as in Benin, wands for *Ifa* divination, decorations for ceremonial costumes, and Benin-type gauntlets and smaller bracelets. In 1952 there was still one ivory and bone carver in Owo, producing work in the old tradition, but his material was primarily elephant bone because of the present scarcity of ivory.

ART OF THE LATE PRECOLONIAL PERIOD: EASTERN AND SOUTHERN AFRICA

We turn next to a survey of the art forms of the various culture areas of Africa south of the Sahara before the beginning of the present century, starting with the Khoisan peoples of the south, the Bushmen and the Hottentot. At this time the Bushmen were already being pushed from their hunting grounds into the Kalahari Desert, while the Hottentots who had replaced them in the south and west were undergoing intensive contact with the white settlers of the Cape. The Hottentots, though they had a more stable economy based on herding and were able to support larger, more organized communities than the Bushmen hunters, never developed graphic and plastic art forms. Rock drawings and paintings depicting Bushmen and Bantu, as well as white settlers, have been attributed to the Bushmen, indicating that they continued this form of art to a relatively recent time, but by the early twentieth century it had apparently disappeared. The Bushmen and Hottentot

Fig. 2. Cultural areas and political divisions of Africa (revised, 1958)

made copper jewelry, iron points for arrowheads and spears, and pottery containers, but their art is simple, consisting of such decorative patterns as seriated incisions on Hottentot pottery and chevrons incised by the Northwest Bushmen on the ostrich egg shells used for storing water and on their stone and bone pipes. Skin bags were also ornamented with similar patterns, and occasionally wooden utensils and sticks were decorated with burned line designs.

In the East African Cattle area, stretching from the headwaters of the Nile to the Cape, the cultural focus is on cattle, and it is in terms of these beasts that the cultural values are expressed. Some peoples are nomadic pastoralists, but the majority practice subsistence farming as well as herding. So little graphic or plastic art is found, compared to the Congo or the Guinea Coast, that the area is often dismissed entirely. The Tutsi of Ruanda-Urundi—exposed to the Congo influences—and their sedentary neighbors like the Ganda did some wood-carving, but in most of this area plastic art consists of modeled clay figurines of cattle and humans, grass masks for puberty ceremonies, wooden masks for similar occasions made by the Makonde, and small wooden female figurines of the same people. Decorated pottery forms are found among the sedentary cattle peoples farther south and southwest, and the Lozi of the Zambesi River carve the great wooden bowls on whose lids are stylized elephants, rhinos, and other animals which serve as handles.

However, these forms are not the sole outlets for aesthetic expression and creative imagination. There is a profusion of beads, plaiting, brass rings, forms of hair dress, molded clay pipes, leather karosses, simply decorated shields, and beautifully proportioned and balanced spears of iron and wood. Costume, carefully designed for ceremonial occasions, becomes a means of aesthetic expression and is a distinct art form. Color photographs of the peoples of east and south Africa demonstrate that their expression is not limited to carving and casting, or by any of the restrictive definitions of graphic and plastic art of the Euroamerican world. Even the decoration of their houses with skins, mats, and pottery becomes by their arrangement a matter of creativity and aesthetic pleasure.

East Horn art need be touched upon only briefly here, for it is marginal to the rest of Subsaharan Africa. The art forms of the nomads resemble those of their neighbors in the East African Cattle area, but where Coptic sects flourished, as among a portion of the present Abyssinian nation, there are paintings in Byzantine style.

CONGO

The Congo area, which comprises central Africa west of the Great Lakes, has yielded so many of the art treasures in museums and private collections that it has the reputation of being the richest in the indigenous arts. Herding and subsistence farming are replaced by agriculture and trade, and the regions richest in art have craft specialists who produce articles used by other members of the society, including dyed and woven raffia cloth, ironwork, baskets, mats, pottery, and wood carvings. Interspersed in the deeper forest of the northern Congo area are the Pygmy groups. Farflung political structures are typical only of specific and scattered groups, such as the Bushongo (Bakuba) and Bakongo; nor does one find walled towns, great compounds, complex architecture in clay or terra cotta as on the Guinea Coast, since political organization generally was on a smaller scale.

During the precolonial period, masks and figurines may well have been the only major art forms of such peoples as the Bena Lulua among the Baluba and the Pongwe among the Fang. The art of many Fang groups, such as the Pongwe and Pahouin, has much in common with that of the Azande of the northeastern Congo, whence, according to tradition, they once came. The Bateke peoples are credited with the spread of small figure carvings of spirits or deities through the western Congo, to which they came from the south and the southeast, where these carvings are widespread.

The widespread Bushongo confederation was in contact with other areas whose art styles were mutually influenced thereby. Most of this is conjectural, but elements in their famous box and bowl work strongly suggest Bateke and Bayaka origin, while polychrome masks seem to have been adopted later from neighboring groups. According to their legendary history, Shamba Bolongongo, a Bushongo king in the seventeenth century, introduced both the famous commemorative statues of royalty and raffia-weaving, which reached its greatest complexity among these peoples. Although this is not verified by historical documents, it is just as possible for a single person to have introduced stylistic elements into the art of a society as it is for them to accumulate through the accretion of the work of many artists over a long period of time.

It is obvious that art forms must vary greatly in so large an area as the Congo. Most art forms produced in precolonial times were masks and figurines. As rich in plastic expression as they are by themselves, in their full ritual context they must have been startlingly effective. Almost universally the masks were polychrome and, though seldom so shown in books or museums, they were usually part of elaborate costumes and had great raffia manes, as in the lion masks of the Basonge. Some were worn with full grass skirts without attempt to conceal the dancer's body, which was decorated with clay, ash, or charcoal. Elsewhere, the entire body was covered with loosely falling cloth and raffia or with a crocheted costume of raffia. Though most of the masks coming from the Congo area are solely of painted wood, some combine cloth, metal, cowrie shells, and trade beads; others are entirely of crochet and knotting. The last two types are seldom mentioned in accounts of African art, but their artistic and dramatic quality in the context in which they were used is undeniable. In firelight or by daylight, in dance solos or in groups, the masks with full costume projected into the onlookers a sense of dignity and mystery of deities and spirits of the natural world, of ancestors, or simply a fear of the unknown.

Carved figurines also vary. They range from a few inches to several feet in height and from fairly crude workmanship to technical virtuosity. It would be impossible to generalize about the function of these carvings even if their cultural role were better known. In one area they are commemorative; in another they serve as temporary containers for the spirits of deities, while elsewhere they are used as charms. Commemorative portrait-statues and containers for the spirits of ancestors are more finished and artistic than figurines used in worship of the gods or for magical purposes.

Carved figurines are sometimes left half-finished, or their designs do not appear to have been considered as an artistic whole; but examples in use show that they may have been intended to be seen dressed in costumes of cloth, raffia, cowries, beads, or feathers and were never thought complete just as carvings. Combinations of materials were not limited to dressed figures; some Bakongo figurines have feather headdresses, glass eyes, and glass or porcelain inserted in the stomach. Unfortunately, lack of adequate ethnographic material makes it difficult to understand their religious symbolism and their indigenous appeal and restricts our observations to the level of description and speculation about their full meaning.

Except for the Bushongo, little is known of the actual context of the other art forms of the Congo basin. Torday wrote of the remnants of what must have been one of the most aesthetic settings of artistic work in the Congo. He described old villages in which he encountered decorated door frames, grass walls woven in patterns, beautiful thatch work, elaboration of simple furnishings such as boxes and pottery, and care in dress of the elders; all these bespeak a specialized society in which some members engaged in subsistence production and trade, while others were artists. Among the Mangbetu, also, the same careful workmanship that went into the effigy pots and ivory work went into costume, coiffure, painted murals on house walls, and the decorated utilitarian objects.

WESTERN AFRICA

The arts of the Guinea Coast and Western Sudan culture areas are more fully described in ethnological reports, accounts of early travelers and explorers, and the traditional histories of the many peoples within the area from Dakar to Lake Chad and from Timbuktu to the coast than is the case with any other part of Africa. The rise and fall of the great kingdoms of Melle, Ghana, Ife, Benin, and others are known, though the cultures of the first two are not fully documented. Ghana flourished until the tenth century; in the twelfth and thirteenth centuries Benin began to emulate Ife, which had developed earlier; Melle rose to its fullest development in the fourteenth century and the Ashanti and Dahomean states in the eighteenth and nineteenth centuries. Some of these kingdoms still exist on a reduced scale, including Ife within Yoruba territory, Benin (which includes only Benin City and its immediate surroundings), Dahomey, and Ashanti in the new state of Ghana.

However, simple farming societies living on a subsistence level, with art products limited to a few secret society masks or a few figures of spirits or deities, exist in the same area as the great West African kingdoms with their many specialists. The fact that even these societies, like the Baga and Mossi, whose artists were farmers, produced works of great sensitivity points to basic traditional factors that help to explain the profusion of forms in the more complex neighboring societies, where a man of talent could find economic support from political leaders and community alike, as among the Baoule, Dahomeans, and the Yoruba.

Conclusions as to past migrations and conquests in West Africa are reinforced by the analysis of stylistic distributions in the graphic and plastic arts. In examining masks, figures, and metal work of the precontact period, it is possible to see the evidence of borrowing of ideas, the reinterpretation and play with design elements that is part of the creative process. The influence of neighboring art styles is clearly apparent in such cases as that of Ife, Benin, Yoruba, and Dahomey; or of Baoule, Guro, and Senoufo; or of Sierra Leone and Liberia, where the Mende, Dan, Gola, and other peoples share the Poro society for men and the Bundu or Sande society for women.

The limitations of the literature make it difficult to give a generalized picture of the cultural context of graphic and plastic arts in West Africa in the precolonial period. Griaule has attempted this and has distinguished between the arts of the savanna and forest regions in terms of complex and simple cultures, respectively. But, the Ashanti, Baoule, Bini, and southern Yoruba, whose environment is almost totally or partially forest or forest-savanna, had complex political, social, and legal organizations and supported great numbers of specialists not only in the arts but in other fields as well.

Still, some generalizations can be made. The focus of these West African cultures may generally be said to be religion, though the forms of religion vary markedly from one group to another. One group emphasizes the power of nature deities, arranged in a hierarchical structure, in addition to ancestor worship; another stresses the worship of ancestors of the royal line, while nature deities are of secondary importance; still others recognize natural forces in specific deities but elevate minor local spirits over them. In representing religious concepts graphically or plastically in art forms, one group may concentrate on masks which are held to be the seat of power of nature deities, local spirits, or the dead; another may choose, as did the Bini, representations of the royal dead with their retinues or of gods with their familes and messengers in full figures in bronze or clay. In addition, traditional styles within a large ethnic grouping may vary greatly, as is the case with the Dogon and the Yoruba.

Masks have functioned religiously and aesthetically in West Africa from earliest times. Local tradition ascribes their origin variously to divine revelation, direction given by the dead in dreams, or, as among the Dogon, acquisition from earlier peoples. Though secret societies with varying degrees of religious sanction are found throughout the area, not all use carved masks. For example, members of some Yoruba societies wear only cloth costumes which completely cover the body, while one dancer representing the principal spirit may have a hard, flat platelet covered with cloth on top of his head to which the spirit may come during a ceremony, and another may wear an elaborate headdress of feathers symbolizing the powers of the spirit controlling the costume. As in the Congo, the total costume and its symbolism are of prime importance, and the carved mask, that portion which excites the artistic appreciation of Euroamericans, is but a detail in an elaborate complex of symbolism.

Some masks are used in puberty rites and to enforce social and re-ligious sanctions. Others enter into religious and semireligious ceremonies alike, representing such sophisticated concepts as the wedding of the sun and moon, as in the double masks of the Baoule. The power of the spirit of the tree from which a mask is made be known to the onlookers, as well as the power of the spirit which the mask itself represents—as among the Dogon. The power of a spirit may be so strong that three men wearing three identical masks are required to "carry" it, as among the Ijebu Yoruba, while another mask worn by one man may house the power of several spirits and their messengers, as among the Oyo Yoruba.

Masks in West Africa range from literal representations of deities or of human beings who manifested supernatural power while they lived to representations of the servants and messengers of the gods, which may be animals or human worshipers carrying symbols. Masked dancers appear singly or in groups just before the rainy season commences if their role is public and is not confined to the secret initiations that are part of puberty ceremonies. Their function is to drive away evil spirits and disease and to evoke the blessings and fortune of the gods or ancestors for whom sacrifices have been made. When not in use, masks are kept in shrines located in sacred groves near the village or in the house of the head of the society. Many masks are propitiated by sacrifices for special favors at other times of the year, as are such other repositories of supernatural power as the figures of deities.

Wooden figures seem to be of at least six types: representations of a deity or spirit; representations of a worshiper of the deity, holding symbols of the god; a symbol representing the god, such as something commonly associated with the deity, for example, a stone celt or a wooden copy of one, showing the possessor to be a worshiper of Shango in Yoruba society; representations of messengers or servants of a deity, perhaps in animal, insect, reptile, or fish form; representations of family ancestors, whether commoner, nobleman, or chief; and representations of persons or animals that hold religious connotation but serve purely decorative and aesthetic functions. Carved figures also may be the seats of the power of a deity or ancestor, or they may be employed as a medium through which the power of a sacrifice travels to touch a shrine and reach the spirit which is outside the figure.

The cultural function of these wooden figures varies. A carving that represents a deity may be kept in a shrine, attended by priests or priestesses who see to its decoration and renewal and assure that it receives the proper sacrifices, or a figure may belong to a family and be kept in a shrine in their compound or in the private room of the family head. Carved figures or symbols of a spirit or deity are sometimes carried by the attendants of masked dancers. Commemorative statues are generally in the possession of individual families. The families of one class of Benin chiefs keep carved wooden heads on the family altar, beneath which is buried the ancestor who founded the family; covered with blood and oil of many sacrifices, they serve to carry the sacrifice and messages of the living to his spirit. Carved wooden roosters serve the same purpose on the altars of female ancestors. Baoule commemorative figures are tended carefully, kept clean and polished, and on special occasions are brought forth for the family and neighbors to admire.

Pottery and weaving are considered as aesthetic forms by the Ashanti and Yoruba and undoubtedly by other peoples. Among both the Ashanti and Yoruba elaborate pots for religious purposes are decorated with figures of the messengers of the deities for which they were intended. Even water storage pots and cooking utensils are decorated for aesthetic reasons.

Weaving is practiced throughout West Africa, producing a variety of materials from simple raffia cloths for work clothes to elaborate gowns for kings and chiefs. Even before the introduction of European dyes there was an imaginative use of colors—red, yellow, orange, white, and an indigo blue which varies in shade from palest blue to almost black. The blue of indigo appears to have been the favorite of the Yoruba, and orange of the Ashanti, other peoples having their own favorite colors. The choices in modern fabrics often reflect these traditional preferences.

The early travelers to Benin describe tufted pile cloth, plain weaving combined with carried thread designs, and the attachment of tassels. Cloth was purchased by Europeans for sale in Brazil, where it was in demand among the freed slaves. However, by the late nineteenth century the weaving industry had died out in Benin, and the old techniques survive only in areas once subjugated by Benin, for example, among the Ijebu Yoruba and in one Ibo village on the coast. In the past, stricter social sanctions and political control probably saw to it that displays of wealth in rich costume remained in the hands of the privileged few; but wherever wealth and political power could command it, the art of the weaver and his designs were called into play. The work of the weaver has become available to all those who can afford to buy the more expensive hand-woven material, and as foreign political sanctions have loosened and a new pride in things African has appeared, the work of these weavers, particularly the men who weave strip cloth, is much in demand. The weavers themselves, it is apparent, enjoy the play with color and texture possible in imported European threads; they no longer have to search out dye plants or perform the laborious work of hand-dyeing thread.

Among all West African peoples care in the erection of wattle and mud walls and in thatching did not stop with the practical exigencies of construction. In the western Sudan, where Islam has taken hold, the influence of the architecture of the walled Moslem towns of North Africa is apparent. Walls of houses of important men are decorated in bas-relief, with geometric patterns. In the traditional kingdoms the compounds of chiefs and their relatives are also more elaborate than those of other members of the society. Among the Dogon, Baoule, Yoruba, and others, decoration was lavished on wooden doors which faced on the street. House posts are carved, or mud pillars are decorated in bas-relief, with designs that are either commemorative or religious in intent, depending on whether they are at the entrance of the house or in a family shrine. The most elaborate manifestations of this tradition are to be found in the carved, slender posts of the thatched palaces of the Cameroons kings, the bronze plaques which covered the wooden piers of the reception court in the palace at Benin, the painted mural designs on the compound walls of the Ibo, and the brightly colored figures in bas-relief on walls of the palaces of the kings of Dahomey which tell of the warlike deeds of the royal line. That we know little more than this of what was obviously one of the important arts of West Africa is due not only to the wars of the precolonial period and the African rains but also to a lack of interest in recording this aspect of African artistic expression.

THE CONTEMPORARY PERIOD

In all areas of Africa south of the Sahara, Africans have extended their very real aesthetic appreciation of form, color, and design by the employment of new media or of earlier media in new ways. Though the form is sometimes distasteful to those committed to the older forms of African art as the primary expression of African aesthetic drives, these newer productions have undoubted values in their own right.

The general impression gained from writings on African art is that the impact of the Euroamerican culture has destroyed that which it should have treasured and fostered, that the artists have been corrupted by Euroamerican tastes so that nothing is left of the classic arts in Africa. Yet this view distorts the picture. New ideas are utilized in old cultural patterns, and African societies that have been able to support specialists in the production of art forms now see new means of supporting more of them, though motivation may be directed away from old religious forms and concepts and from old prestige symbols to a new market and new terms of recognition for the artist. The seeds of destruction of classic art, to the extent that it has been destroyed, do not necessarily lie in European contact but in the indigenous cultural patterns, particularly the desire to accumulate wealth and prestige. It is neither strange nor blameworthy that the talented individual sees himself in the role of the specialist peculiarly blessed with a talent that has value in the world in which he lives.

To understand change in African art, it is necessary to understand first that with a few notable exceptions, such as the Bakuba, Baoule, Mangbetu, Dahomeans, and Yoruba, there are few African cultures where the concept of "art for art's sake" seems to have existed. There seem to be no specific systems of ideas concerning the aesthetic and no group of specialists who, as critics, have the function of interpreting art forms to others. Abstract terms for art, beauty, and design, so important in the vocabulary of those close to art in Euroamerican cultures, are restricted. Aesthetic factors are so intermingled with the religious, economic, political, and social aspects of a culture, to say nothing of its other aesthetic manifestations, that the vocabulary concerning what is beautiful or merely pretty or attractive may refer primarily to qualities such as wealth or prestige value, religious or political symbolism.

What is not ordinarily realized is that the work deplored by those who stress the exclusive values of classic African art is produced in the main not by traditional workers but by those who have taken up crafts which were alien to them, their families, or even to their society. They have usually been encouraged by missionaries, government officials, or educational institutions, or, as in the case of East Africa, even by businessmen who may supply wood, tools, and payment for a finished product.

In Brazzaville, Africans who never participated in the production of art forms in their own villages are reproducing on paper and canvas colorful designs and "abstracts" derived from motifs which in the indigenous culture were intended to be seen in a larger scale on the walls of houses and compounds. In Nigeria missionaries have encouraged Ibo girls to transfer the cicatrization patterns on their own bodies to cloth as embroidery motifs. Yoruba schoolboys are taught to carve thorns from the silk cotton tree, producing tiny human and animal figures. They are spurred on to perfect their work by the example of their African teachers, some of whom have become so well known that their carvings sell for very high prices.

Not all changes in African art have resulted from European contact. The dynamics of change are implicit in the creative process, even when change is less rapid or less apparent than in our own culture; playing with form, within the framework of culturally approved aesthetic symbols, is always present. Those whom we would term truly artistic individuals make small innovations, and because their work is admired within their own society, these are accepted.

Proportionately to the total population of the art-producing areas of Africa, there are few traditional carvers, even including the usual individuals of lesser talent whose primary motivation is economic rather than aesthetic. Of the total number of carvers, perhaps only 2 to 5 per cent are truly artists in the technical sense of the term, producing the great classical forms to be seen in museums and private collections. When the incentive is taken from this small percentage, or when it simply is not economically feasible for them to produce the art forms they love, less talented individuals produce what they believe the commercial trade will like, frequently on order from such traders as the Hausa, who are the greatest disseminators of the most carelessly made of the new art forms throughout West Africa and the northern Congo.

Those who do not believe that innovations in classic art were made by such a small percentage of the total number of carvers may profitably turn from the volumes that present only the best of African art to publications of colonial governments in the Congo and West Africa from about 1920 to 1940.[3] Here they will see photographs of literally hundreds of carvings, all in traditional style but poor in design, technically imperfect in workmanship, and generally lacking all the qualifications of the works that have been admired enough to be included in books on African art. One can only conclude that the same percentage of "hack" artists has continued to exist with only their subject matter changed as a result of the contact with Euroamerican norms they have experienced.

Yet encouragement by Europeans has been the stimulus that in many areas has kept art alive. The British were instrumental in bringing a member of the Benin brass workers' quarter to Kumasi in the Gold Coast, where he taught some Ashanti the art of *cire-perdue* casting, which had all but died out in that once important center of casting. Today, under government sponsorship, castings of old gold weight designs, rings, and bracelets using conventional motifs may be purchased in the bookshops and craft centers of Ghana.

It was British influence also that encouraged the Oba Eweke II of Benin not only to revive the traditional arts of Benin in 1915 but to include a type of carving heretofore unknown to the traditional carvers. This was the use of true ebony, the black heart wood of the type found in the immediate vicinity of Benin City. The king founded a school of carvers in his palace, using this medium as well as the more ancient one of coconut shells. The carvers were his sword-bearers, traditional attendants of the royal palace whom, since they must give a number of years in service and are thus not fitted for the world of skilled trades afterward, the king felt benefited from this training.

His son, Akenzua II, has carried on the tradition, and one of the latter's former sword-bearers, a man named Johnson, set up a workshop in Lagos where he took only Bini apprentices. When World War II brought thousands of British and American troops to West Africa, Johnson's carvings of heads of the king and his less elaborate busts of men and women sold well. His Bini apprentices branched off, founding their own workshops. Hausa traders bought up the practice pieces of the apprentices, selling them as curios along with their traditional hammered brass ash trays and leather goods from the Sudan. The Bini style emanating from the palace of the king himself thus spread across West Africa to Sierra Leone and as far south as the Congo. The fact that it was apprentices' work accounts for the poor quality of the originals, as well as that of the ethnic groups who copied them because

[3] Photographs of such carvings are to be found, for example, in nearly every issue of *Illustration Congolese* (Brussels) during the period mentioned.

they sold so well commercially. The fact that black heart ebony was not available was no deterrent, for in other localities white wood is simply blackened with European shoe polish.

At a time when forms of African art seem to be changing irrevocably to something bearing but faint resemblance to the traditional art and when the classic art itself appears to be dying out, a movement in the Congo and West Africa has quietly but surely been gaining momentum. This has been the work of men, most of whom are government officials or connected with governments in some capacity, who have seen to it that laws have been enacted prohibiting the export of old art forms in quantity. They have also been collecting the better old pieces to form the nucleus of national museums. Money and effort have also been spent quietly but persistently to recover fine pieces of classical African art from European and American museums, dealers, and collectors, as a conscious effort to foster pride in the rich heritage of the past and as an inspiration for the Africa of the future.

4. African Music

Much of African music remains to be described in other than subjective terms; yet there seem to be underlying unities which can be treated more precisely, and this discussion attempts to gather together materials which give an overview of the characteristics of this musical system. Available information primarily concerns structural factors; information on the integration of music with other aspects of culture is meager, so that here only some of the problems can be suggested. An attempt is also made, on a more general basis, to indicate the chief areas of agreement and disagreement among various writers, as well as the major problems which remain to be solved; finally, problems of change are discussed.[1]

FUNCTION

The stress placed upon musical activity as an integral and functioning part of the society is a feature that music shares with other aesthetic aspects of culture in Africa and one which is emphasized in almost all non-literate societies. In Euroamerican society, in contrast, there is a tendency to compartmentalize the arts and to divorce them from aspects of everyday life; thus we have "pure" art as opposed to "applied" art, as well as the "artist" and "commercial artist" or "craftsman," who are also differentiated both in role and in function. A further distinction is made in Western society in terms of "artist" and "audience," with the first group tending to be limited in number; relatively few persons in Western society participate in the arts, and even fewer are considered "accomplished" in music or the dance, for example. "It can safely be said that there are no nonliterate societies where distinctions of this order prevail. Art is a part of life, not separated from it."[2] This does not

[1] For bibliographies on African music see Douglas H. Varley, *African Native Music: An Annotated Bibliography* ("Royal Empire Society Bibliographies," No. 8; [London, 1936]); and Alan P. Merriam, "An Annotated Bibliography of African and African-derived Music since 1936," *Africa*, XXI (October, 1951), 319–29.

[2] Melville J. Herskovits, *Man and His Works* (New York: Alfred A. Knopf, 1948), p. 379.

mean, of course, that specialization is absent, but at the same time relatively large numbers of people within a non-literate society are competent in the arts, and aesthetic activities are closely related to the whole functioning culture. Thus, while the usual Western functions of music as entertainment, accompaniment for the dance, and in religious services are also present in non-literate societies, music is used in many other settings.

The Hutu in Ruanda, for example, recognize at least twenty-four general social song types, as distinguished from religious songs, including those played by professional musicians for entertainment, songs for beer-drinking, war, homage to a chief, hunting, harvesting, and general work; songs sung at the birth of a child or to admonish erring members of the society, to recount a successful elephant hunt, to deride Europeans; songs of death, vulgar songs, and others. Further, within each of these categories subtypes can be distinguished: certain songs are sung when taking a new canoe from the place it was constructed to the water, when paddling against a strong current, when paddling with a current, or to make the paddlers work better together.

Among the Tutsi of Ruanda there is a similar range of musical material: songs for boasting purposes, for war and greeting, songs sung when young married women meet together and reminisce about absent friends, children's songs, songs to flatter a girl, and many more. Of special importance to the Tutsi are songs dealing with cattle, and these subtypes include boasting songs called *ibiririmbo*, in which two men sing in competition with each other, alternating musical phrases; they may vie either in praising one cow or in singing of the merits of one cow against another. Special songs, not *ibiririmbo*, are sung in praise of cows, others to indicate the importance of having cows; there are songs for taking cattle home in the evening, for the herder when he is getting ready to take the cattle home, when he is drawing water for the cattle, when he is with other herders in the evening. Praises for the royal cattle, *inyambo*, are sung; children sing special cow songs, and other songs are sung when cattle are being shown to visitors. Special flute songs circumvent cattle thieves at night, and other songs recount historical events in which cattle have played a part.[3]

Music, then, plays a part in all aspects of culture. In political organization, for example, the functions of music are apparent in songs sung in praise of chiefs, but many other manifestations may also occur. Among the Tutsi the drum is the symbol of political power, and no individual other than the *Mwami* and the Queen Mother may possess

[3] Alan P. Merriam, "Field Notes," Belgian Congo and Ruanda Urundi, 1951–52.

sets of drums. "Le symbole de la royauté etait Kalinga, le tambour sacré. Posseder ce tambour signifiait être roi."[4] Or, again:

Il [Kalinga] est le tambour sacré par excellence, l'emblème de la souveraineté et le palladium du royaume. On ne le frappe pas habituellement. En principe, il doit suivre le roi dans ses déplacements. Il est porté dans un hamac et les autres tambours battent en son honneur. Il a droit aux mêmes égards que le roi et les gens frappent trois fois les mains l'une contre l'autre quand ils défilent devant lui. On l'oint de temps à autre, pour le conserver, de beurre et de sang de boeuf dont les entrailles ont 'blanchi', c'est-à-dire dont le sacrifice a été reconnu favorable par les devins-sacrificateurs.[5]

In the field of social organization functions of music for birth, *rites de passage*, marriage, and death are immediately apparent. One of the most widely known functions is that of social control; thus, in speaking of the Chopi, Tracey says:

They are often highly critical of those in authority over them, white or black, and . . . sly digs at the pompous, outspoken condemnation of those who neglect their duties, protests against the cruel and overbearing, outcries directed against social injustices as well as philosophy in the face of difficulties, are all to be found in their songs and shared through their music and dancing. . . . One can well imagine the forcefulness of the reprimand conveyed to a wrongdoer when he finds his misdeeds sung about by thirty or forty strapping young men before all the people of the village, or the blow to the pride of an overweening petty official who has to grin and bear it while the young men jeer to music at his pretentiousness. What better sanction could be brought to bear upon those who outrage the ethics of the community than to know that the poets will have you pilloried in their next composition.[6]

Herskovits speaks of the "song of allusion" in Dahomey,[7] and Waterman and Bascom note that a "type of song of great importance in . . . the Negro world is the topical song of current events used to spread news and gossip, and employed at times in a kind of blackmail."[8]

In economic life songs function as an aid to co-operative labor; canoe paddling songs, for example, have previously been mentioned. In speaking of the Dahomean *dokpwe*, Herskovits notes that the

---

[4] Jacques J. Maquet, *Le Système des Relations Sociales dans le Ruanda Ancien* ("Annales du Musée Royal du Congo Belge, Sciences de l'Homme, Ethnologie," Vol. I [Tervueren, 1954]), p. 147.

[5] Révérend Père Pages, *Un Royaume Hamite au Centre de l'Afrique* ("Institut Royal Colonial Belge, Section des Sciences Morales et Politiques, Memoires," Vol. I [Brussels, 1933]), pp. 371–72.

[6] Hugh Tracey, *Chopi Musicians: Their Music, Poetry, and Instruments* (London: Oxford University Press for the International African Institute, 1948), p. 3.

[7] Melville J. Herskovits, *Dahomey: An Ancient West African Kingdom* (New York: J. J. Augustin, 1938), II, 320.

[8] Richard A. Waterman and William R. Bascom, "African and New World Negro Folklore," in *Dictionary of Folklore, Mythology and Legend*, ed. Maria Leach (New York: Funk & Wagnalls, 1949), p. 21.

members of the co-operative work group are led to the field where they are to work "by a flutist whose shrill notes they can easily follow, for the distance is often great and perhaps not known to some of them. They have drums, gongs, and rattles, and use these to accompany the songs they sing."[9] The songs themselves are in turn used to emphasize a work rhythm.

In religion the function of music and musical instruments is too well known to repeat here; almost all ethnographies contain some account of the use of music in this aspect of culture. Perhaps not so well known, however, is the symbolic meaning which can be ascribed to a musical instrument itself. Thus among the Bambara:

L'anthropomorphisms de la harpe, ngoni, est très net dans la pensée des usagers.

La caisse rectangulaire de l'instrument représente le masque de Koumabana, l'ancêtre qui a reçu la parole; les deux éclisses latérales sont ses yeux, l'ouïe, son nez et sa respiration, le cordier, sa bouche et ses dents, les cordes au nombre de 8, ses paroles. Elle est aussi l'image de sa tombe et les deux baguettes qui la traversent représentent le deuxième et le troisième ancêtre qui l'accompagnèrent dans la mort. Le caisse représente aussi la face du devin et sa tombe, les deux baguettes étant les deux tiges de mil mises en terre avec le cadavre. A l'extrémité du manche, des sonnailles de cuivre ont le même rôle, à la fois technique et religieux, que celles fixées au tablier du tambour décrit plus haut.

Chaque son donné par chacune des 8 cordes est une prière. Les cordes sont pincées séparément par le devin, suivant leur rang et en fonction de la qualité du consultant et des questions qu'il pose....

[L'harpe] préside aux sacrifices, aux rites cathartiques ou de médication, aux purifications, aux rites apotropaïques, aux méditations solitaires. Ses notes hautes sont célestes et symboles de plénitude; les basses connotent les choses terrestres et l'incomplétude. Son jeu commande les arrivées et les départs, les proliférations et les amenuisements, les rappels à l'ordre; sa présence au bord d'une mare où elle a été déposée en silence, est gáge d'apaosement.

L'harpiste, avant de commencer son office, place sa bouche devant l'orifice de la caisse et murmure au mâitre du Verbe: "Maintenant c'est ton tour, organise le Monde."[10]

Some mention can also be made of the use of songs as a historical device. Waterman and Bascom note that "songs referring to battles of the 18th century are still current in Nigeria,"[11] and Herskovits, for Dahomey, says:

Songs were and are the prime carriers of history among this non-literate folk. In recounting the ritual associated with the giving of offerings to the souls of those who were transported into slavery, this function of song came out with great clarity. The informant at one point could not recall the sequence of

[9] Herskovits, *Dahomey*, I, 73.

[10] Viviana Paques, *Les Bambara* ("Monographies Ethnologiques Africaines," Institut International Africaine" [Paris: Presses Universitaires de France, 1954]), pp. 106–7.

[11] Waterman and Bascom, "Negro Folklore," p. 21.

important names in the series he was giving. Under his breath, to the accompaniment of clicking finger-nails, he began to sing, continuing his song for some moments. When he stopped he had the names clearly in mind once more, and in explanation of his song stated that this was the Dahomean method of remembering historic facts. The role of the singer as the 'keeper of records' has been remarked by those who visited the kingdom in the days of its autonomy.[12]

On a somewhat narrower basis, the Tutsi still sing their resentment of a government edict which forced them to sell cattle at a price they considered unfair; the order was intended to reduce the overpopulation of cattle in Ruanda, and although the event itself took place a good many years ago, it has been kept fresh in the consciousness of the people through the medium of song.[13]

Music itself, of course, falls within the aesthetic aspect of culture, and its relationship to other aesthetic aspects, such as folklore, dance, and drama, is too clear to require exploration here. The relationship of music and language, however, provides possibilities for the study of various forms of expression; thus among the Hima in Uganda and the eastern Congo truisms and proverbs form an important part of the text line—"A man who goes to market and listens to idle talk is liable to come home and fight with his wife; truth must be in the home"; "Don't cry for nothing." Of course, this also indicates the function of music in enculturation and education.[14] Finally, the use of poetic and dramatic expression further emphasizes the close music-language relationship in Africa.[15]

One of the most provocative problems arising in connection with music and language is that of the relationship between the speech curve, or melody, and the musical melodic line. Herzog has noted:

A slavish following of speech-melody by musical melody is not implied. Rather, the songs illustrate a constant conflict and accomodation between musical tendencies and the curves traced by the speech-tones of the song-text. Even when the speech-tones prevail, the musical impulse is not quelled but merely limited—urged, perhaps, to discovering devices it had not used before. The best proof of this is that often a turn which was evoked by speech melody immediately begins to lead its own melodic life, calling for repetition or balance, whether this agrees with the following speech-curve or not.

But accent (stress) is, with length, the important "musical" element of our languages, and it is this element that has figured in our musical development.[16]

The problem of the influence of language on musical melodic expression becomes even more complex when, as in many parts of Africa, one deals with the added factor of phonemic tone. Conflict between phonemic

[12] Herskovits, *Dahomey*, II, 321.

[13] Merriam, "Field Notes."

[14] *Ibid.*

[15] F. S. Herskovits, "Dahomean Songs," *Poetry*, XLV (1934), 75–77.

[16] George Herzog, "Speech Melody and Primitive Music," *Musical Quarterly*, XX (October, 1934), 466.

tone and interval direction is almost certain to occur in the course of a song, and Jones, who feels that the tone influence on melody is exceedingly strong, has considered this problem. "It explains why each verse of a song differs slightly in melody. The words of each verse . . . need separate melodic treatment to make the tune agree with the rise and fall of the syllables. . . . So powerful is its influence on African vocal music that there is one form of humorous song in which the humour is produced by making the melody for certain syllables run counter to the speech tones." And further:

> The result of all this is that African melody is in a strait-jacket. It is much more restricted in its scope by this very hide-bound system than was European music in the days of Bach and the strict rules of counterpoint. And the liberty of melody is still further restricted by the universal custom of singing *only one note to each syllable*. Anyone who tries to write a tune on these lines will find how very difficult it is to achieve interest and especially balance in melodic form. The African does succeed in doing this, but there is no question that the restrictions of the system have a conservative and limiting effect on the free development of African melody.[17]

Ward, in a less emphatic statement, reaches the conclusion that while it is possible "that accent may be . . . the guiding principle . . . at least we can no longer believe in the invariable agreement of tones and melody,"[18] and Hornbostel concludes:

> The pitches of the speaking voice, indeed, appear to determine the melodic nucleus; but they have no influence upon its inborn creative forces; these forces, and not any qualities of the speech, direct the further course of the melodic development. We need not be surprised at the fact that the hearer does not misunderstand the meaning of the words, even though the melodic movement is contrary to it. In the first place, the meaning in most cases is probably made unmistakable by the context, exactly as we understand what a foreigner says, although he may accentuate wrongly. Secondly, the melody of speech does not only depend on the passage of the voice through different pitches, but also on the clarity of the sounds of speech . . . and this remains unchanged—though not absolutely—in singing. Lastly, even in our languages chanted texts are always more difficult to understand than spoken ones; and it is quite possible that this difficulty is still greater in languages which have pitches as an essential element. But the difficulty only exists with regard to new songs; in a well-known one we imagine we hear the text distinctly and correctly, however distorted it may be.[19]

Brief mention may be made of the use of a musical instrument in communication; the phenomenon of "drum signaling" is made possible

[17] A. M. Jones, *African Music in Northern Rhodesia and Some Other Places* ("Rhodes-Livingstone Museum, Occasional Papers," No. 4 [Livingstone, 1949]), pp. 11–12.

[18] W. E. Ward, "Music in the Gold Coast," *Gold Coast Review*, III (July–December, 1927), 211.

[19] Erich M. von Hornbostel, "African Negro Music," *Africa*, I (January, 1928), 31–32. (In reprint.)

by phonemic tone present in many African languages. Since this method of communication has been widely studied and since, strictly speaking, it is a linguistic rather than a musical phenomenon, it will not be discussed here.[20]

In addition to the functions noted above, song texts as such play various roles; they frequently allow the expression of thoughts which might otherwise be repressed, and at the same time they may express underlying themes or configurations of the culture at hand. Thus, one could probably not expect to hear a Hutu express the following satiric thoughts directly; they were, however, composed and sung by a professional musical bow (*umunahi*) player in southern Ruanda:

An Englishman started to boast about his empire, and a Belgian started to boast about his empire. The Englishman said: "We have machines to make sugar. We have many cars, and they are driven by women. We have airplanes, trucks and shillings, and they are worth more than your francs. We have railways. We have traffic lights. Our people, the Baganda, who live in our empire, have cars, bicycles and motorcycles. Their houses have tin roofs. They are rich, you know." And the Belgian said: "We have the best country, Ruanda Urundi. We have *indarugaruga* (a group of people who helped drive out the Germans). We have *inyambo* (royal cattle); do you know how they are dressed? We have dancers; do you know how they dance? We have Abatutsi; do you know how tall they are?"[21]

A further example of the use of song to express what otherwise might remain hidden is found in a series of five songs sung by a group of Bashi girls on a coffee and quinine plantation in the Kivu area of the Belgian Congo. These songs were directed at the owner of the plantation, who was acting in the capacity of interpreter and thus could not fail to follow the texts. Because of a recent wage advance he had stopped giving the workers rations of salt and peanut or palm oil. The singers began by indicating the setting, the plantation; they continued with flattery which, by the third song, was in no sense subtle. In the fourth song the question of the cessation of salt and oil rations was introduced, and in the final song the singers threatened to take jobs elsewhere if the rations were not reinstituted. It is clear that the five songs represented a direct warning to the plantation owner of the discontent among his workers. This discontent was unknown to him; while the girls were unwilling to express their doubts directly, they seized this opportunity to inform him of the situation.[22]

[20] See John F. Carrington, *A Comparative Study of Some Central African Gong-Languages* ("Institut Royal Colonial Belge, Section des Sciences Morales et Politiques, Memoires," Vol. XVIII [Brussels, 1949]); and *Talking Drums of Africa* (London: Carey Kingsgate Press, 1949).

[21] Merriam, "Field Notes."

[22] See Alan P. Merriam, "Song Texts of the Bashi," *Zaïre*, VIII (January, 1954), 40–42.

In the same study of Bashi song texts, indications of a threatening social disintegration are pointed out; while not clear in ordinary relations among the Bashi or between Bashi and European, they are sharply manifested in the songs. The texts reveal deeds of violence, social rejection, and the indifference of the social group toward its individual members. Significantly, very rarely is comment made upon the injustices or distortions of perspective displayed by the individuals concerned; instead, the texts simply detail the occurrences without comment.

It should be noted that Europeans of long experience in the general area occupied by the Buniabungu are at present concerned with what they consider to be the disintegration of the Bahavu people, nearest neighbors of the Bashi to the north. Population figures seem to show that the birth rate of the Bahavu is dropping rapidly, according to these sources, and employers in the area regard the Bahavu men as physically weak and indifferent, preferring not to hire them if men of other tribes are available. If we are to accept these speculations, it seems clear that we may point to the song texts of the Bashi as indicative of what is quite possibly to come. Surely a society almost completely indifferent to itself shows signs of the beginning of disintegration. The impingement of a new culture and the attendant stresses and strains of readjustment to new patterns have clearly been of deep effect on the social awareness of the Bashi.[23]

It is possible to speak of function on at least two major levels: first, the way in which something is integrated into the workings of a society on a more or less conceptual basis and, second, the way in which people participate in a particular aspect of culture—in this case, we might speak of "functioning." We have paid most attention to the first, but it should be re-emphasized that in African societies large numbers of people participate in musical activities. The separation of the "artist" from the "audience" is not an African pattern—although specialists are always present, music is participative. Almost everyone can and does sing; many people play musical instruments; most people are competent in at least one type of musical expression. African music is functional on two levels—the music itself is integrated into daily life, and it is performed and enjoyed by large numbers of people within the society.

INSTRUMENTS

Description of musical instruments has occupied a large proportion of the literature dealing with African music, and it is neither necessary nor possible to review that literature here. A large number of articles have dealt with individual instruments in specific locales,[24] with the musical instruments of a particular group of people,[25] with instruments in mu-

[23] *Ibid.*, p. 43.
[24] Alice Werner, "On a Stringed Instrument Obtained at Ntumbi, Nyassaland, in 1894," *Bantu Studies*, V (September, 1931), 257–58.
[25] Alan P. Merriam, "Musical Instruments and Techniques of Performance among the Bashi," *Zaïre*, IX (February, 1955), 121–32.

seum collections,[26] with the origin and evolution of instruments,[27] with distribution and descriptions of instruments in political and geographic areas,[28] and from various other points of view. Under the classification proposed by Hornbostel and Sachs,[29] musical instruments have been divided into four major classes—idiophones, membranophones, aerophones, and chordophones—with at least ten major subdivisions and many still smaller divisions; it is safe to say that African musical instruments are represented in every division. This enormous variety is far too frequently overlooked in favor of the traditional view of African music which emphasizes drums to the exclusion of other instruments.

Two brief generalizations may be made here on the use of musical instruments in African culture. The first is simply that both instrumental soloists and groups of instrumentalists are found in Africa; the second is that accompanied song is perhaps more important in African music than solo instrumental performance. The second generalization is supported by the fact that almost all songs have words, whether or not those words are actually sung, so that when a song is played upon a musical instrument, words are automatically conceptualized, although they may not be verbalized.

RHYTHM

The importance of rhythm in the music of Africa has probably been more widely commented upon, by early as well as recent authors, than almost any other single aspect of African aesthetic expression. Early travelers' accounts emphasize the kinds, numbers, and varieties of drums and other percussion instruments, often to the exclusion of any further information. Wallaschek, in his very early attempt at a comprehensive description of the music of non-literate peoples, devoted his section on African music in great part to travelers' descriptions of drums and other percussion implements, and his section on drums themselves draws heavily upon African material.[30] Nor is the preoccupation of early trav-

[26] Olga Boone, *Les Xylophones du Congo Belge* ("Annales du Musée du Congo Belge, Ethnographie," Ser. 3, Vol. III, fasc. 2 [Tervueren, 1936]); and *Les Tambours du Congo Belge et du Ruanda-Urundi* ("Annales du Musée du Congo Belge, Sciences de l'Homme, Ethnographie," Vol. I [Tervueren, 1951]).

[27] Bernhard Ankermann, "Die afrikanischen Musikinstrumenten," *Ethnologisches Notizblatt*, III (1901), 1–134. Erich M. von Hornbostel, "The Ethnology of African Sound-Instruments." *Africa*, VI (April–July, 1933), 129–57, 277–311.

[28] Percival A. Kirby, *The Musical Instruments of the Native Races of South Africa* (Johannesburg: Witwatersrand University Press, 1953); K. P. Wachsmann, "The Sound Instruments," in Margaret Trowell and K. P. Wachsmann, *Tribal Crafts of Uganda* (London: Oxford University Press, 1953).

[29] Erich M. von Hornbostel and Curt Sachs, "Systematik der Musikinstrumente," *Zeitschrift für Ethnologie*, XLVI (1914), 553–90.

[30] Richard Wallaschek, *Primitive Music* (London: Longmans, Green, 1893), pp. 1–15, 108–16.

elers to Africa with rhythm and especially drums difficult to understand, for "in its use of percussion instruments and complex rhythms as a basis for a musical idiom, instead of harmony as in the Western world, West African music differs most markedly from the European musical concept although the basic idea of drumming is common to both cultures and thus provides some familiar ground for comparison. Again, the idea of the 'talking drum' complex is a fascinating one which appeals deeply to the imagination; and finally, the splendid drumming to be heard in parts of Africa must have stood out sharply for the early traveller as it does today."[31] No better description of the emotional impact of African rhythm is to be found in early travelers' accounts than the one given by Stanley in describing a dance of the "Bandussuma at Usiri" in northeastern Congo.

Half a score of drums, large and small, had been beaten by half a score of accomplished performers, keeping admirable time, and emitting a perfect volume of sound which must have been heard far away for miles, and in the meantime Katto, and his cousin Kalenge . . . were arranging thirty-three lines of thirty-three men each as nearly as possible in the form of a perfect and solid and close square. . . .

The phalanx stood still with spears grounded until, at a signal from the drums, Katto's deep voice was heard breaking out into a wild triumphant song or chant . . . and a mighty chorus of voices responded, and the phalanx was seen to move forward, and the earth around my chair, which was at a distance of fifty yards from the foremost line, shook as though there was an earthquake. I looked at the feet of the men and discovered that each man was forcefully stamping the ground, and taking forward steps not more than six inches long, and it was in this manner that the phalanx moved slowly but irresistibly. The voices rose and fell in sweeping waves of vocal sound, the forest of spears rose and subsided, with countless flashes of polished iron blades as they were tossed aloft and lowered again to the hoarse and exciting thunder of the drums. There was accuracy of cadence of voice and roar of drum, there was uniform uplift and subsidence of the constantly twirling spear blades, there was a simultaneous action of the bodies, and as they brought the tremendous weight of seventy tons of flesh with one regular stamp of the feet on the ground, the firm and hard earth echoed the sound round about tremulously. . . . It was certainly one of the best and most exciting exhibitions I had seen in Africa.[32]

Analysis of African rhythms, particularly those of drums, was attemped at an early date by Ward, who wrote, "Broadly speaking, the difference between African and European rhythms is that whereas any piece of European music has at any one moment one rhythm in command, a piece of African music has always two or three, sometimes as many as four." This principle is not to be confused with a simple elabor-

---

[31] Alan P. Merriam, "African Music Reexamined in the Light of New Materials from the Belgian Congo and Ruanda-Urundi," *Zaïre*, VII (March, 1953), 248.

[32] Henry M. Stanley, *In Darkest Africa* (New York: Charles Scribner's Sons, 1890), pp. 436–38.

ation of a single basic meter; different meters are used in combination so that while one drum is playing four beats, a second is playing three, a third, five, and so forth, over the same span of time. The organizing principle understood by Ward involves the fact that one drum, the biggest if more than one is used, plays regularly in duple meter with very little variation. The only change in this pattern is the subdivision of a single beat in each measure into two or the substitution of a rest of one beat in each bar; these variations do not change from measure to measure, although they may be applied to any beat in the bar. "This deep booming regular beat is the fundamental beat of the piece, and sets the time for all the other rhythms and instruments. The other rhythms may have no possible similarity to it and no connection whatever, but on the first beat of the big drum all must coincide." The following example illustrates both the diversity of rhythms (and meters) and the organizing beat of the "big drum":

A second characteristic of African rhythm is "that triple time is unknown. This is not to say that triple time-figures are excluded from African music. But even where a tune is in what sounds to European ears triple time, the underlying percussion rhythm makes it quite clear that the African feels it as duple time." Ward gives no explanation for this fact except to say that triple time "is foreign, if not actually repulsive, to the African musical experience."[33]

Ward's third point refers again to the simultaneous use of different meters; here he cites the independence of the separate instruments, which he says is "a characteristic of African music." At the same time, the rhythms coincide at regular intervals; thus there is, in effect, a set of bar lines representing a period of elapsed time. Finally, "the last characteristic of African rhythm is that the drummers are at complete liberty to extemporize variations, provided only that they keep to the length of time allowed for their figure—in other words they do not take more than one bar for their figure."[34]

[33] Ward, "Music in the Gold Coast," pp. 214, 217, 218, 219, 220.
[34] *Ibid.*, pp. 219, 220.

Ward summarizes four basic characteristics in African rhythm as "the absence of triple time, the importance of the fundamental regular beat, the independence of each instrument and its absorption with its own time-figure, and the freedom to vary the figure provided the time does not suffer."[35] It must be borne in mind that Ward wrote about music in the Gold Coast; although he drew his examples from this area, he seems clearly to have been attempting to generalize for all African music.

Hornbostel also accepted the concept of simultaneous use of more than one meter in African rhythm, but he added a new element in his interpretation of the actual act of drumming; in this act he saw a concept of syncopation fundamentally different from basic Western rhythmic assumptions.

African rhythm is ultimately founded on drumming. Drumming can be replaced by hand-clapping or by the xylophone; what really matters is the act of beating; and only from this point can African rhythms be understood. Each single beating movement is again two-fold: the muscles are strained and released, the hand is lifted and dropped. Only the second phase is stressed acoustically; but the first inaudible one has the motor accent, as it were, which consists in the straining of the muscles. This implies an essential contrast between our rhythmic conception and the Africans'; we proceed from hearing, they from motion; we separate the two phases by a bar-line, and commence the metrical unity, the bar, with the acoustically stressed time-unit; to them, the beginning of the movement, the arsis, is at the same time the beginning of the rhythmical figure; up-beats are unknown to them. To us, the simple succession of beats 𝄽 ♪ 𝄽 ♪ appears as syncopated, because we only attend to its acoustic aspect. In order to understand African rhythms as they really are, therefore, we must thoroughly change our attitude; and in order to write them down adequately we must place the bar-line before the rest or the up-beat.[36]

This concept, which Hornbostel found characteristic of ternary as well as binary time, is at the basis of his interpretation of African rhythms. Unfortunately, although numerous musical examples are given, no evidence is presented which indicates that the concept is really valid to the African. Such a rhythmic Gestalt is the result of a psychological process in which the succession of hand movements is organized in a specific way, and this must be related to the sound produced. The principle of "off-beating," which would result from such a concept, is undeniably present in African rhythm, but whether it is conceived as Hornbostel suggests, in terms of two-part motor behavior which is precisely the opposite of the Western concept, remains to be demonstrated.

Finally, Hornbostel points out that "rhythmical shapes . . . present themselves to the mind as unities; they are performed, and are received by the ear, without the smallest time-units being counted out. . . .

[35] *Ibid.*, p. 222.
[36] Hornbostel, "African Negro Music," pp. 25–26.

Rhythmic patterns do not arise until people join to sing in chorus and use drum rhythm along with it. But even then, melody and drum rhythm often go their own separate ways; and again, each of the drums may have a rhythmical *ostinato* of its own to balance the chanted part. This brings about a rhythmical heterophony which Europeans . . . find . . . difficult to disentangle."[37]

The concept of the simultaneous use of two or more meters is also central in Waterman's discussion of African rhythms; the phenomenon is designated "mixed" meter,[38] "multiple" meter, or "polymeter." In this case, however, two new factors are added in discussion. The first of these is what Waterman calls the "metronome sense," which involves "the development of a musical sense that, in the individual conditioned only to the norms of European music, usually lies somewhat dormant." Waterman explains this sense as follows: "From the point of view of the listener, it entails habits of conceiving any music as structured along a theoretical framework of beats regularly spaced in time and of co-operating in terms of overt or inhibited motor behavior with the pulses of this metric pattern whether or not the beats are expressed in actual melodic or percussion tones."[39]

This metronome sense is of considerable importance in African music, according to Waterman, so much so that "it is assumed without question or consideration to be part of the perceptual equipment of both musicians and listeners and is, in the most complete way, taken for granted. When the beat is actually sounded, it serves as a confirmation of this subjective beat." With the assumption of the operation of this subjective beat it becomes clear that the African musician is freed from actually emphasizing it, for he may assume that his listeners will automatically do so; he may elaborate the beat almost at will, whereas in European music it must be clearly stated at all times. Thus, "from the point of view of European music, African music introduces a new rhythmic dimension."[40]

If Waterman's theory of the metronome sense is to be questioned, it is on grounds similar to those involved with Hornbostel's theory. Again, a psychological process is involved which is not easily proved, and Waterman offers no empiric documentation save for the logic of the proposition itself. He implies that in view of the known complexity of African

[37] *Ibid.*, pp. 27–28.

[38] Richard A. Waterman, " 'Hot' Rhythm in Negro Music," *Journal of the American Musicological Society*, I (Spring, 1948), 4.

[39] Richard A. Waterman, "African Influence on the Music of the Americas," in *Acculturation in the Americas*, ed. Sol Tax ("Proceedings of the Twenty-ninth International Congress of Americanists," Vol. II [Chicago: University of Chicago Press, 1952]), pp. 212, 211.

[40] *Ibid.*, pp. 211, 212.

rhythms, some principle must be in operation which will allow the listener to orient himself in the music. The question involves the second fresh point made by Waterman, which deals simply with the fact that within the metrical framework set up by perhaps three drummers, shifts of emphasis occur, so that the European listener is puzzled by the fact that "rhythmic emphasis shifts back and forth from meter to meter."[41] To the lay listener, a song in 4/4 time may suddenly appear to have shifted to 3/4 or 6/8 time, for example, without noticeable changes in drumming patterns. The point here, according to Waterman, is that the African musician, as well as his African listener, is not upset by this apparent change because, in the first place, all three rhythmic components have been present throughout the particular song and, in the second place, the listener is comfortably oriented into a basic, over-all metric scheme through application (unconscious) of the metronome sense. It is here, then, that the logic of the proposition appears; without the metronome sense it would seem that the African listener could become fully as confused as the European, or, conversely, he is not confused because of the metronome sense. It should be pointed out here that Waterman does not conceive of the metronome sense as something innate or inherited by the African; rather, he sees it as learned behavior which is begun in childhood and which, through the processes of enculturation, becomes simply a normal part of musical behavior.

A. M. Jones's contributions to the study of African rhythm are of considerable importance both in re-emphasizing previous ideas and in expressing new concepts. In speaking of the importance of rhythm in African music, Jones says, "Rhythm is to the African what harmony is to Europeans and it is in the complex interweaving of contrasting rhythmic patterns that he finds his greatest aesthetic satisfaction"; and further, "whatever be the devices used to produce them, in African music there is practically always a *clash of rhythms*; this is a cardinal principle."[42]

Basing his conclusions on field research carried out in Northern Rhodesia but asserting that the same principles hold for "the Gold Coast in the West, Pemba Island in the East, and Kingwilliamstown in the South —that is, they are generally valid for Bantu Africa . . . and for the Ewe people in the Gold Coast who are generally held to be a non-Bantu people," Jones speaks of patterns of hand-clapping as well as drumming techniques. He reaches the conclusion that "an African song which has a clap is constructed so that either 2 pulses or 3 pulses go to one clap right through the songs, irrespective of word division, word accent, or melodic accent. The claps do not indicate any sort of stress; their

[41] *Ibid.*, p. 212.
[42] A. M. Jones, "African Rhythm," *Africa*, XXIV (January, 1954), 26, 27.

function is to act as an inexorable and mathematical background to the song." Thus hand-clapping acts as an organizing principle upon which songs are based; at the same time, it is of importance to note that in combined clapping, "all the various clap rhythms have a common beat on which to start."[43] Finally, in combined clapping patterns the principle of polymeter is employed.

In his study of drumming patterns Jones has introduced new concepts which are based upon using, in field study, an electrical apparatus so constructed as to mark rhythms upon paper as they are struck either in hand-clapping or drumming; thus Jones feels that his study of African drumming "has been tested by every objective means that [the author] could devise."[44]

Drumming is built up from combinations of rhythmic patterns, including both combinations of patterns within a single meter and combinations of patterns in more than one meter. Two absolutely fundamental differences exist, however, between the rhythms produced by hand-clapping and those produced by drums. The first is that "whereas in clapping, the various rhythm-patterns of the clappers have a simultaneous starting-point and so there is always one recurrent beat where they all coincide, in drumming . . . the main beats never coincide." Jones means that if two drummers are playing in a given meter, the pattern used by the second drummer never begins at the same place within a measure (to use a European concept) as does the pattern of the first. He gives two examples; two drummers are playing the following patterns:

To a European ear, the "natural" way of combining these would be:

To the African, however, two possibilities exist, says Jones, neither of which coincides with the European concept:

[43] *Ibid.*, pp. 26, 28, 39.

[44] *Ibid.*, p. 26. For description of the equipment used see Jones, *African Music,* pp. 65–78, Appendix I.

"We call this process 'crossing the beats': it is absolutely fundamental to African drumming technique. This crossing of the beat *must* be established."[45]

The second difference between clapping and drumming is that "the rhythm-patterns of the master drum are constantly changing. In clapping there is no variation: once the resultant has been established by the clapping parties, it continues unchanged over hundreds of repetitions. . . . [The master drummer] is forever changing the patterns, sometimes playing duple, sometimes triple time, sometimes using some rhythmic figure which fits into neither of these simple time divisions. As to the other drums, one sticks to a simple rhythm and never varies throughout; the other may have perhaps two rhythm patterns of a similar nature and he rings the changes on these."[46]

These, then, are the major concepts of African rhythm described by Jones. In view of his statement that the main beats never coincide in drumming, the rather vexing question of the use of bar lines in transcription is raised. In most transcriptions bar lines are applied to all instruments simultaneously; thus the pattern of drumming may appear highly syncopated and off-beated in the sense that the major drum pulses by no means necessarily coincide with the downbeats of the bar. This syncopation, or off-beating, is considered by most students to be axiomatic in African rhythm; that is, in any song the drumming can be organized into patterns which in turn lend themselves to being barred. Thus, from this point of view it makes no special difference whether a particular pattern falls within bar lines as $\frac{6}{4}$ ♩ ♩ ♩ ♪ ♩ ♩ ♪ or $\frac{6}{4}$ ♩ ♩ ♪ ♩ ♩ ♩ ♪ Jones's objection here is twofold. In the first place, he feels that his field research indicates clearly that each pattern, although meshed with all others, is independent in the sense that it has a definite beginning and ending as a pattern; thus, in the examples given immediately above, one would probably be correct and the other incorrect. His second point is that "looked at from the point of view of each player, African music is not syncopated nor is it complicated except for the master-drum rhythms," and he objects to the form of scoring which runs bar lines down the page on the specific basis that "it gives the impression that all but one of the contributors is highly syncopated and [that] the multitude of tied notes and off-beat accents makes the mind reel."[47]

The importance of rhythm in the music of Africa is an unquestioned

---

[45] Jones, "African Rhythm," pp. 39–40.
[46] *Ibid.*, p. 39.
[47] *Ibid.*, p. 44.

principle; in fact, it bulks so large that African music could perhaps be set off as a musical culture area dominated by this concept and opposed to other equally large musical culture areas. However, it is open to question whether the importance of drums and other instruments of percussion has not been exaggerated in most writing about African music, with the result that the wide range of musical instruments not idiophones or membranophones is too frequently neglected. We tend to think in terms of drums and drumming alone and to put aside that vast body of African music which in many cases does not use percussion instruments at all. For example, in speaking of the music of the Guinea Coast, Waterman has emphasized "drums, rattles, and gongs" and has said that "most African music includes, and depends upon, percussion instruments."[48] This excludes the large number of string and wind instruments as well as unaccompanied song. It would seem wiser to speak of African *music* as percussive, rather than to emphasize the use of percussion instruments exclusively. The trough zither, for example, found widely in East Africa, is used to produce music which is clearly percussive in effect, although as an instrument it can in no sense be called an idiophone or membranophone; similarly, trumpets of many kinds are played for percussive effect although the notes themselves are, of course, melodic. It is misleading to emphasize drums and idiophones alone as giving an accurate picture of African music; what is clearly important is that African music depends upon percussive effect, whether that music is sung, played upon wind or stringed instruments, or drummed.[49]

In summary, almost all students agree upon the fundamental importance of rhythm in African music as well as upon the fact that this rhythmic basis is frequently expressed by the simultaneous use of two or more meters. The organizing principles upon which multiple meter is based, however, are not agreed upon. Ward notes one drum playing a basically unvarying beat; Hornbostel sees the organization in terms of motor behavior which is the opposite of the Western concept; Waterman postulates the concept of the metronome sense; and Jones makes the point of lack of coincidence of the main beats. While these specific details remain to be worked out, the concensus about the use of multiple meter is so strong as to remain unquestioned as the basis for African rhythm. However, it must be emphasized that multiple meter is by no means necessarily present at all times or in all songs; though this would seem to be self-evident, some writers have made the assumption that a single song which lacks multiple meter provides the exception that destroys the rule.

[48] Waterman, "African Influence," p. 212.
[49] See Merriam, "African Music Reexamined," pp. 248–49.

MELODY AND FORM

The study of African melody is beset by the question of whether a generalization can be made which will serve to identify African melody as such. The most direct statement of the character of African melody has perhaps been made by Jones:

> Broadly speaking, the outline of an African tune is like a succession of the teeth of a rip-saw; a steep rise (not usually exceeding a 5th) followed by a gentle sloping down of the tune; then another sudden rise—then a gentle sloping down, and so on. The tendency is for the tune to start high and gradually to work downwards in this saw-like manner. There is no key change in the course of the tune. . . . There is however a distinct feeling in these tunes of hovering over and around a central note or notes, round which the melody seems to be built or towards which it works.[50]

Hornbostel indicates a structure felt to be typical of African melody: "a structure consisting of two halves, the first one resting on the upper fifth (dominant), and the second one built analogously on the tonic."[51] A third approach taken by Kolinski is mainly analytical rather than aimed toward an over-all impression of African melody.[52] In this case, melodic structure itself is broken down into smaller characteristic units: thus the triadic split fifth [musical notation], pendular thirds [musical notation], interlocked thirds [musical notation], and so forth.[53] This system of melodic analysis has been developed not so much to characterize African melody as to form the basis for melodic analysis in general, but it has been developed in connection with African studies.

In speaking of the nature of African melody, Waterman has introduced the concept of "off-beat phrasing of melodic accents," which functions in close association with the metronome sense.

> In transcriptions of African music this pattern appears in the form of notes tied together across bar lines or across other main beats. Melodic tones, and particularly accented ones, occur between the sounded or implied beats of the measure with great frequency. The beat is, so to speak, temporarily suspended, i.e., delayed or advanced in melodic execution, sometimes for single notes (syncopation), sometimes for a long series of notes. The displacement is by no means a random one, however, for the melodic notes not coinciding with the beat are invariably sounded, with great nicety, precisely on one of the points of either a duple or a triple division of the beat. Viewed a different way, this may

[50] Jones, *African Music*, p. 11.
[51] Hornbostel, "African Negro Music," p. 18.
[52] Mieczyslaw Kolinski, "Die Musik westafrikas" (unpublished MS).
[53] See Mieczyslaw Kolinski, "Suriname Music," in *Suriname Folklore*, Melville J. Herskovits and Frances S. Herskovits (New York: Columbia University Press, 1936), pp. 498–501.

be seen as a placement of tones on the beat of an implied meter at a tempo twice
or thrice that of the controlling rhythm.

The operation of the metronome sense creates in the listener an ex-
pectancy of a series of beats equally spaced in time, whether those beats
are actually sounded or not; if this beat

. . . is reinforced by an objective stimulus in the form of a percussive or
melodic tone, the metronome sense is reassured. . . . If the objective beat is
omitted, however, the co-operating auditor becomes very much aware of the
subjective beat, which thus attains for him greatly increased significance. If
the objective beat occurs ahead of time, the auditor, unprepared for it, perceives
it and assigns to it the additional importance always accorded the unexpected,
further reinforcing it with his subjective pulse which occurs at the "proper" time
in terms of his experience. If the objective beat is delayed, the period of suspense
between subjective and objective beats likewise increases the auditor's awareness of the rhythm. When the objective, audible beat occurs halfway between
two subjective pulsations, as is frequently the case, both mechanisms operate to
give the off-beat tone heightened significance.

If off-beat phrasing were constant throughout a song, however, so that
the melodic notes consistently occurred between the beats established by
the subjective metronome, the listener would readjust, and the total
effect would be lost; thus "the off-beat phrasing of accents . . . must
threaten, but never quite destroy, the orientation of the listener's subjective metronome."[54] The principle of off-beat phrasing, then, provides
a device whereby the listener, psychologically unprepared for the displacement of melodic beats, is thrown off balance, so to speak, and this
device tends to heighten musical excitement.

Some writers have denied that African music is characterized by
syncopation, which in one sense is the simple form of off-beating. Besides Jones, there is Ward, who says, "On the whole I think there is
surprisingly little syncopation in African melodies themselves. The
reason probably is that there is so much in the gong and small drum
parts that it is not necessary in the voice part, and in fact would be
wasted, if not actually worse than useless."[55] Probably the question of
bar lines once more enters the picture here; it is clear that in Ward's concept a change in bar lines could move the syncopation from percussion to
melodic line.

There seems to be fairly unanimous agreement about the formal
structure of African song; the major form is antiphony—alternate singing by soloist and chorus. It is also fairly well agreed that the melodic
line sung by the chorus identifies the song, while the leader's melody is
for the most part improvised, and that the chorus line remains basically
unchanged throughout a song while the solo line changes each time it is

[54] Waterman, "African Influence," pp. 213, 214.
[55] Ward, "Music in the Gold Coast," p. 221.

sung. It is finally agreed that the phrases of leader and chorus overlap, producing harmony of some sort.

According to Hornbostel, other forms develop from this antiphonal call-and-response pattern. The first of these is polyphony, derived from the overlapping between leader and chorus, which may lead to the singing of the two melodic lines simultaneously. Further, "when the refrain displays a greater variety of notes it develops into what is known as an *ostinato* . . . [which is] a free variation of the first solo phrase, but at variance with it by half a bar. . . . Again the chorus may simply repeat the phrase given out by the solo singer . . . at full length, and the two parts may overlap by exactly half the phrase. Thus a form is arrived at which we . . . are accustomed to think of as being highly artificial; namely, the *canon*."[56] Canon has also been noted in west African xylophone melodies by Herzog.[57]

Speaking of formal structure within the melodic line, Ward notes that "the germs of both binary and ternary forms are found though binary form is much commoner. Most of them are so short, consisting of only two or four phrases, that the form is only rudimentary. Generally speaking, the shorter melodies are in binary form, while the few instances of ternary are all among the longer examples. The binary form is often modified . . . by the ending of the second half with an imperfect cadence. Sometimes not only is this the case, but the second half of the tune is shorter than the first."[58] However, Ward often finds it difficult to distinguish clearly between binary and ternary form, although for the most part he feels the binary to be distinctly predominant in African music. This extends also to a wider view of African music—both melody and rhythm—and thus, as previously noted, Ward feels that triple time is virtually unknown in African music.

Jones also comments upon this predominance of duple forms: "But though the Bantu use in all their music both duple and triple rhythms, they seem to refuse to recognize the triple rhythm. If it is isolated and they are asked to sing or tap triple rhythm, they will naturally and quite unconsciously convert it into duple time."[59]

The preceding discussion applies especially to vocal music. In instrumental music form may vary considerably. Among the Chopi, for example, an analogy may almost be drawn between the integrated orchestral-dance-vocal forms and symphonic forms in Western culture; Tracey lists the following movements for an *Ngodo*, which he defines as an "orchestral dance in nine to eleven movements. Each movement is

[56] Hornbostel, "African Negro Music," pp. 17–18.

[57] George Herzog, "Canon in West African Xylophone Melodies," *Journal of the American Musicological Society*, II (Fall, 1949), 196–97.

[58] Ward, "Music in the Gold Coast," p. 206.

[59] Jones, *African Music*, p. 22.

distinctive and separate, and may last from a minute only, as in the case of some of the introductions, up to five or six minutes each. The whole performance takes as a rule about forty-five minutes, depending upon the intricacy of the dancers' routine and the mood of the moment." The movements, in order, are "First Orchestral Introduction, Second Orchestral Introduction, Third Orchestral Introduction, The Entry of the Dancers, The Call of the Dancers, The Dance, The Second Dance, The Song, The Councillors, The Dancers' Finale, The Orchestral Finale,"[60] although some movements, usually the orchestral introductions, may be omitted. While it may perhaps be said, then, that African singing is antiphonal in form, the dangers of generalization are apparent in the face of this exceedingly complex Chopi "symphonic" form.

In summary, the antiphonal form seems clearly to be characteristic of African vocal music; the song is identified by the chorus line, and the two parts of this particular form overlap. At present, it does not seem possible to generalize about the melody itself or about its structure.

SCALE

Types of scales or modes employed in African music have been relatively neglected as a subject for study. However, some controversy has been engendered over whether or not the African scale—if such a generalization can, indeed, be made at all—coincides with the diatonic scale used in Western musical expression.

As reported by Ward, Nicholas G. J. Ballanta Taylor maintained that the African scale is composed of sixteen intervals to the octave, which as Ward points out "would make it intermediate in type between the European 'pure scale' of nineteen intervals to the octave and the equally tempered diatonic scale." Such intervals would, of course, be difficult for the European-trained ear to distinguish, and Ward objects both upon this basis and upon others, saying in summary, "I am not prepared to accept the theory of a peculiarly African scale. I think that African music is perfectly intelligible on a diatonic basis." He further points out that if each tone in the scale represented one-sixteenth of an octave, it should be immediately noticeable in the melodic structure, since it would produce a "weird" affect or a feeling that the entire song was out of tune even though the individual intervals would probably not be distinguished by a European listener. What "weird" feeling there is, says Ward, is found at the beginning and end of songs; it can be accounted for by the fact that strong portamento existing at these points tends to give an unusual twist to the melodic line so far as Western listeners are concerned. Ward further points out that in his own experience African musicians accepted African music played on the piano save for the beginning and ending

[60] Tracey, *Chopi Musicians*, pp. 2, 10.

portamento. He concludes by saying, "In other words, I see no reason to suppose the existence of an 'African' scale, but rather I think that African melodies are essentially diatonic in structure, modified by a liberal, and unregulated, use of portamento. . . . If the African sixteen degree scale existed and were universally used for African music I should expect to find all the intervals forming a melody untrue by European standards. . . . I do not find it so."[61]

Apparently Hornbostel never subscribed to the concept of a peculiarly African scale. On the contrary, he observed that in regard to vocal melody, at least, the concept of scale as a succession of fixed degrees was inapplicable, although certain tones fit together aptly and thus any piece of music has tonality established by the "function and the mutual relations of the notes." He felt that modes could be established in African music but that scales could not. However, Hornbostel did not commit himself on the question of a "typical" African modal form.[62]

Pepper regards the African scale as a natural one, built up from the harmonics of a single tone.

Il existe en effet une échelle naturelle des sons, dont il n'est pas surprenant que le peuple noir, en contact étroit avec les phénomènes de la nature, ait adopté instinctivement la règle.

Cette règle, connue en physique sous le nom d'échelle harmonique, démontre qu'un son—émis par les vibrations d'une simple corde tendue, ou de la colonne d'air d'un tuyau—se compose en réalité d'un son fondamental et d'autres sons ou harmoniques qu'il engendre mathématiquement. Séparés, ils fournissent une échelle.[63]

With some modification, the natural scale is also the concept advanced by Jones, who further writes, "A more satisfactory theory is that the African scale is a series of conjunct 4ths. Here again we must be cautious for the subject is extremely difficult and the last word has probably not been said. . . . We can make selections from [these fourths] . . . and group them in several ways, e.g.

$$
\begin{bmatrix} s \\ f \\ m \\ r \end{bmatrix} \begin{bmatrix} f \\ m \\ r \\ d \end{bmatrix} \quad \text{or} \quad \begin{bmatrix} s \\ f \\ m \\ r \end{bmatrix} \begin{bmatrix} m \\ r \\ d \\ t_1 \end{bmatrix} \quad \text{or} \quad \begin{bmatrix} l \\ s \\ f \\ m \end{bmatrix} \begin{bmatrix} f \\ m \\ r \\ d \end{bmatrix} \begin{bmatrix} m \\ r \\ d \\ t_1 \end{bmatrix}
$$

[61] Ward, "Music in the Gold Coast," pp. 200–202.
[62] Hornbostel, "African Negro Music," pp. 7–10.
[63] Herbert Pepper, "Musique Centre-Africaine," in *Afrique Équatoriale Française* ("L'Encyclopédie Coloniale et Maritime" [Paris: Gouvernement Général de l'Afrique Equatoriale Française, n.d.]), pp. 3–4.

Each of these groups is a different scale; they are different because they each have different emphasis notes, i.e. those printed in heavier type. These emphasis notes are the chief notes of rest in the melody or the focal points round which the melody moves."[64] What Jones refers to as "scale" corresponds with Hornbostel's designation "mode," a word which, in fact, is probably more proper.

It is not irrelevant to point out here some of the difficulties which Tracey encountered in attempting to determine the scale of the Chopi *timbila*, or xylophone. While there was no difficulty in ascertaining that the musicians did not tune their instruments capriciously or by mere chance, some argument occurred among the musicians themselves as to the exact or desirable pitch of the *Hombe*, or tone center. The basis for various claims, however, was social rather than musical; thus, "Katini maintained that, as the Paramount Chief's musician, his was the one and only correct pitch, his was the 'king's note,' vouchsafed to him by his father, grandfather, and ancestors who had been hereditary leaders and composers of the king's music for generations. . . . The other musicians had equally good claims to hold the norm, but they were based upon the patronage of somewhat lesser chiefs." In any case, although there might be divergent opinion upon the exact starting pitch, "we can safely accept the assurances of the home musicians that, whatever the pitch of the Tonic, they are all in their own way attempting to achieve an even scale of equal intervals, a kind of tempered heptatonic scale."[65] Tracey, of course, does not attempt to indicate such a scale for African music as a whole, but although differences would occur in the size of interval steps, we are again dealing with a scale which does not differ from the diatonic nearly so widely as would a sixteen-tone scale, for example.

Among the Bapende, Maquet finds that the scale of the *madimba*, or xylophone, "présente donc une indéniable parenté avec la nôtre" and that the scale of the *gibinji*, or *sanza*, can be notated in European fashion without trouble.[66] Finally, Waterman dismisses the concept of a peculiarly African scale and speaks of the fact that "the western one-third of the Old World land mass is musically homogeneous . . . set off from the other major musical areas by the extent of its reliance on the diatonic scale" and other features.[67]

There has been some discussion of an African scale in which the third and seventh degrees are flatted or, more specifically, neutral between a major and minor interval. This concept has been advanced especially by those concerned with analysis of jazz music, since in jazz usage these two

[64] Jones, *African Music*, p. 10.

[65] Tracey, *Chopi Musicians*, pp. 124, 127–28.

[66] Jean-Noel Maquet, "La Musique chez les Bapende," *Problèmes d'Afrique Centrale*, No. 26 (Quatrième Trimestre, 1954), pp. 5, 10.

[67] Waterman, "African Influence," p. 207.

degrees of the scale—called "blue" notes—are commonly flatted and since the third degree, especially, is frequently given a variety of pitches in any single jazz performance.[68] Jones would clearly seem to support this proposition; he writes, "I have lived in Central Africa for over twenty years but to my knowledge *I have never heard an African sing the 3rd and 7th degrees of a major scale in tune,*" and "aural impressions do plainly verify the widespread use of the two 'blue' notes among Africans in Africa."[69] This is perhaps the only direct reference to this particular characteristic, and while Jones makes it more or less universally applicable to African music, he speaks primarily, of course, from an intimate knowledge of the music of East Africa. Since the concept is directly concerned with jazz, verification of its source must probably come from the music of the Guinea Coast and Congo regions; the present author found it only sporadically in the music of Congo.

A strong concept of an exclusively pentatonic African music has been popular with many writers; Phillips, for example, sees the pentatonic scale as the basis for almost all, if not all, Yoruba music.[70] In a recent study of Bashi flute music, however, all scales—or, rather, modes—were found to be heptatonic with one hexatonic exception,[71] and reference may again be made to the studies cited above. While the pentatonic is doubtless widely used, the characterization of all African music as pentatonic does not seem to be valid.

In view of the evidence above, it seems safe to say that the "scale" of African music, if such exists, is diatonic in its major aspects, although exceptions clearly occur and although there is certainly a considerable range of variation from area to area and even from tribe to tribe. The pentatonic is also widely used; the evidence for a sixteen-tone scale is scanty, indeed. Finally, the question of the flatted third and seventh of the diatonic scale must be referred to future investigation.

HARMONY

The usual assumption about African music is that harmony plays no part in it and that what harmony does appear is either accidental or due to Western influence on aboriginal musical patterns. This view, however, has been strongly contested by Waterman, among others; he feels that harmony along with the diatonic scale is a definite characteristic of

[68] Winthrop Sargeant, *Jazz Hot and Hybrid* (New York: E. P. Dutton, 1946), pp. 148ff.; Rudi Blesh, *Shining Trumpets: A History of Jazz* (New York: Alfred A. Knopf, 1946), pp. 45, 106, *passim*.

[69] A. M. Jones, "Blue Notes and Hot Rhythm," *African Music Society Newsletter*, I (June, 1951), 10.

[70] Ekundayo Phillips, *Yoruba Music* (Johannesburg: African Music Society, 1953).

[71] Alan P. Merriam, "The Bashi *Mulizi* and Its Music: An End-blown Flute from the Belgian Congo," *Journal of American Folklore*, LXX (April–June, 1957), 143–56.

African music. In this assertion three clarifying points are advanced. In the first place, he does not refer to the European school of literate music and musical theory which has elaborated harmonic ideas to an extent never used either in African music or in European folk music. In the second place, the existence of a broad, intrusive belt of Arabic influence divides the western third of the Old World into two parts; since this has existed over a long period of time, the fact that there is a continuous harmony-using area has been hidden. Finally, Waterman feels that the oft-repeated assertion that African music has no harmony stems "from certain preconceptions concerning the evolution of music which have proved inapplicable to the present case. The argument, in terms of these preconceptions, is simply that Africans had not developed enough culturally to be expected to have harmony. Given this bias, it is easy to see . . . how an ethnomusicologist of a decade or two ago could have listened to African music, and even have transcribed African music, without ever hearing harmony used, even though harmony may actually have been present." Waterman further points to the poor quality of early field recordings, the separation of the field worker and the laboratory scientist who analyzed the recordings, and the fact that within many African groups harmony does not appear as factors which have contributed to the lack of recognition of harmony in African music. As Waterman says, "not only in ethnomusicology does it occur that an authoritatively stated, although invalid, generalization comes to have considerable inertia of its own."[72]

Thus the concept of harmony in African music—indeed, as one of the major characteristics which allies it generally with European folk music traditions and structure—is strongly supported by Waterman. Most investigators do not share this point of view; they feel either that harmony is nonexistent or that it is rudimentary and plays but a minor role in African music.

Hornbostel, for example, sees African "harmony" as a form of polyphony. This arises from the antiphonal structure of African song; as Hornbostel explains it, singers sustain "the final note of a tune regardless of the metre or the uniformity of the bars, and accordingly the soloist is unable to know how long the sustained final note of the chorus will last." This leads to overlapping, and "the result is a dichord; but . . . it is accounted for by a melodic (and not by any harmonic) principle." This in turn may lead to splitting the final note of the song into a dichord without the necessary existence of overlapping, but the dichord may be an interval of any kind, since it is melodically formed. "The musical form arrived at in this way . . . is the *organum* in parallel motion which represents a primitive stage of polyphony." Thus, among the Wasu-

[72] Waterman, "African Influence," pp. 208, 209.

kuma, "only the three most consonant combinations of sound, octave, fifth, and fourth, are used. This kind of polyphony also is based on pure melody, and has nothing to do with harmony as we understand it." And finally, in elaborating his point of view, Hornbostel states that this "organum in parallel motion has no doubt prepared the way for harmony by making the ear familiar with the effect of simultaneous sounds."[73]

The same general viewpoint is held by Jones; in this case, however, while a "stage" of organum is postulated, it is merely intermediate between unison and harmony. "The idea is that part of the crowd sings the tune, and part of the crowd sings *the same tune* a 4th or a 5th lower. The Bemba for some extraordinary and unexplained reason always sing in organum in *thirds* and never in fourths or fifths."[74] Jones also points out the use of contrary motion among the Manyika. It is clear that he regards the phenomenon he explains as being harmonic in nature, while Hornbostel would not.

Ward cites instances of five-part harmony "of the broadest diatonic type. The general texture is of two, three, or four parts, and a fifth is often introduced to mark a cadence." However, Ward is not sure whether this represents an indigenous development or a borrowing from European patterns. Still, he says, "Genuine African harmony as far as I have heard it consists of thirds, fourths, fifths, and sixths, with of course the octave. The commonest harmonic structure is a string of consecutive thirds. . . . Fourths and fifths seem never to be consecutive, and fifths are rare altogether. Two-part harmony is far the commonest, and a third part is sometimes added; four and five-part harmony is much less common."[75] He gives the following example of three-part harmony:

The concept of harmony as such is Western and thus is difficult to apply to the music of non-Western peoples. By definition, harmony is "in general, any simultaneous combination of sounds, hence synonymous with chord. . . . Thus, harmony denotes the chordal (or vertical) structure of a musical composition, in contrast to counterpoint, i.e., its melodic (or horizontal) structure."[76] The problem involved, then, is whether African music can be said to be harmonic as opposed to contrapuntal or polyphonic; but, probably more important, it is also

[73] Hornbostel, "African Negro Music," pp. 13, 14, 15.

[74] Jones, *African Music*, p. 12.

[75] Ward, "Music in the Gold Coast," pp. 212, 213.

[76] Willi Apel, "Harmony," in *Harvard Dictionary of Music* (Cambridge: Harvard University Press, 1946), p. 322.

whether Africans themselves conceive of their music as vertical or horizontal, as the case may be.

Although a Western musician may feel that merely by looking at a piece of music he can ascertain whether it is harmonic or contrapuntal, this seems somewhat dangerous. Thus in the following example (which uses contrary motion), recorded among the Bashi in the eastern Belgian Congo, it is impossible to say whether the music is *conceived* horizontally or vertically:

It may be said that Ward's example is harmonic, while the Bashi example is polyphonic, but no matter what the conclusion, the examples are being viewed from the Western standpoint. It is impossible to say at present whether the Africans themselves would view the example in the same way, and it is doubtful that the African viewpoint would make a distinction between the concepts of vertical and horizontal music structure.

In any case, it is clear that the simultaneous sounding of more than one pitch by different singers or instrumentalists is common in much of African music. Whether it is to be viewed as harmonic or polyphonic, vertical or horizontal, cannot at present be ascertained.

VOCAL STYLE, TONE QUALITY, AND ORNAMENTATION

There are apparently no studies of African vocal style as such. In general, the singers seem to use an open, resonant voice quality of a type similar to that employed in western European folk music; the resonance possibilities of the various facial cavities are exploited rather fully. At the same time, a wide variety of tonal qualities is employed, although the open quality predominates. This variety in timbre sometimes leads to a rather persistent use of a "burred" tone, particularly in instrumental performance. Thus the *sanza*, for example—an instrument which sounds by means of plucked metal or bamboo strips—is inherently capable, by virtue of its construction, of clear, almost bell-like tones; as almost a general principle, however, various devices which result in a buzzing tone are added to the instrument. The same is widely true of xylophone tones; a material which will cause a buzz, often spider web, is placed over the holes in the gourd resonator.

Ornamental devices used by singers include various forms of the bend and dip, as well as the characteristic use of the glissando. Rising attack and particularly falling release also seem characteristic. Some songs are almost shouted rather than sung; the correlation, if any, of this style with factors such as emotional intensity or song type is unknown.

MUSIC AREAS

There have been three generalizations dealing with the music areas of Africa, no one of which seems to be totally adequate. Waterman lists five characteristics of African music intended to apply to Africa as a unit although based upon the study of the music of the Guinea Coast.[77] These characteristics have been contested on the basis that they do not always apply to the music of the Belgian Congo and Ruanda-Urundi,[78] and it therefore seems safer to regard them as typical of one particular area, although they certainly have application to other parts of Africa. The five points—metronome sense, dominance of percussion, polymeter, off-beat phrasing of melodic accents, and overlapping call-and-response pattern—probably serve to distinguish a Guinea Coast music area.

In a more general way, the music of the Belgian Congo has been said to be characterized by four major points: a lack of specific emphasis on percussion in the sense of the invariable use of idiophones and membranophones, although rhythm itself expressed in many ways remains characteristic; an enormous variety of musical instruments and musical styles; a heavy influence from the Islamic world in the northern parts; and a considerable amount of current change in process.[79] It is apparent that these generalizations are on a much broader plane than those made by Waterman and that so far as characterizing musical *style*, they are not particularly helpful.

A preliminary attempt at delimiting music areas has apparently been made by Schaeffner in a work not available to the present author. Hickmann notes:

Eine provisorische Aufteilung Afrikas in Musikzonen ist von A. Schaeffner versucht worden. Eine deutliche Grenzlinie ist zu ziehen zwischen den Musikarten arabisch-islamischer Kultur und der werklich afrikanischen Musik: der Chromatismus der ersten auf der einen Seite, der Diatonismus bzw. die fünfstufigen Leitern auf der anderen. Natürlich ist mit der fortschreitenden Islamisation seit dem MA, sowie dank des Sklavenhandels oder Einflüssen wie denen der Wander- und Handlervolker (Haussa) diese Grenzlinie immer häufiger überschritten worden.—Was nun die Gliederung der Musik des Inneren Afrikas anbelangt, so ist eine solche z.Z. noch unmöglich. . . . Hervorsuheben wäre endlich der deutliche Unterschied der Klangfarbe hamitisch oder semitisch durchdrungener Volkergruppen. So wohl im Gesang als auch in der Instr. Musik stehen sich leise, farblose und intime Klänge (hamitisch) und laut schrillende, scharfe und gepresste Klänge (semitisch) gegenüber. Unterschiede welche sich auch ander-

[77] Waterman, "African Influence."
[78] Merriam, "African Music Reexamined."
[79] *Ibid.*, p. 247.

weitig in der Negermusik festellen lassen: so gehort der ganze Süden mehr oder weniger den ersten Typus an.[80]

As far as can be ascertained, these three attempts at generalization for regions of Africa are the only ones in existence. Clearly, the lack of broad characterization represents a gap in our knowledge of the music of Africa which is manifestly difficult to fill. Most studies of African music have dealt either with characteristics of the music as a whole or, quite the opposite, with specific tribes or specific locales. Further, much of the literature dealing with African music is purely descriptive of musical instruments or is highly generalized to include affective descriptions of musical performances. With these reservations in mind, and with the realization that full documentation cannot be presented, a tentative approach to African music areas may be attempted with a view toward establishing at least a basic schema, subject to further revision.

It seems possible to distinguish the following music areas of Africa: (1) Bushman-Hottentot; (2) East Africa; (3) East Horn; (4) Central Africa; (5) West Coast; (6) Sudan-Desert, divided into (a) Sudan and (b) Desert; and (7) North Coast. These coincide in the main with the culture areas delimited by Herskovits.[81] To these must be added an eighth area which does not have geographic unity—this is the Pygmy area, found in rather widespread locations in central Africa; the music is characterized to some extent by yodeling, but particularly by the hocketing or *durchbrokene Arbeit* technique in which each individual in a group of singers contributes, with precision timing, one, two, or three notes to a longer melodic line.

The separation of a Bushman-Hottentot area is based upon description of musical instruments and styles presented chiefly by Kirby; unfortunately, very little recorded material is available for this area, and the separation must perforce remain tentative, although it seems apparent.[82]

The East Africa area can quite clearly be differentiated from areas to the west in terms of types of musical instruments used, the specific uses of drums and drumming, the Islamic influences, and some other characteristics, especially the absence of "hot" rhythm. The northern and southern parts of this area may have to be further divided into subareas

[80] Hans Hickmann, "Afrikanische Musik," in *Die Musik in Geschichte und Gegenwart*, ed. Freiderick Blume (Kassel and Basel: Barenreiter, Vol. I, 1949–51), cols. 125–26.

[81] Melville J. Herskovits, "A Preliminary Consideration of the Culture Areas of Africa," *American Anthropologist*, XXVI (1924), 50–63; cf. also *supra*, p. 37.

[82] See Percival A. Kirby, "The Musical Practices of the /?Auni and ≠Khomani Bushmen," *Bantu Studies*, X (December, 1936), 373–431; "A Study of Bushman Music," *Ibid.* (June, 1936), pp. 205–52; "Buschmann- und Hottentottenmusik," in *Die Musik in Geschichte und Gegenwart*, ed. Freiderick Blume (Kassel and Basel: Barenreiter, Vol. II, 1952), cols. 501–11.

because of the differences of musical instruments and an apparent difference in music style.

The music of the East Horn is clearly distinguishable from most of that of the East Africa area by the intensity of the Islamic influence. Although there is considerable variation here, and within any one of these

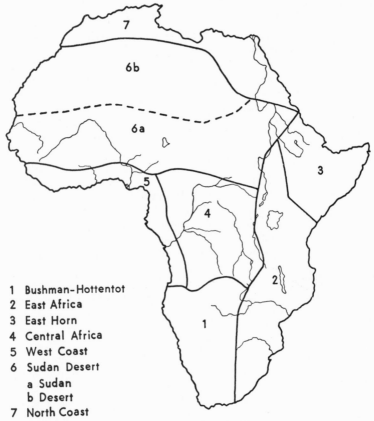

1 Bushman-Hottentot
2 East Africa
3 East Horn
4 Central Africa
5 West Coast
6 Sudan Desert
  a Sudan
  b Desert
7 North Coast

Fig. 3.   Music areas of Africa

areas, the Islamic influence is dominant. Where the East Horn area is to be distinguished from the eastern portion of the Sudan is also problematical.

The Central Africa and West Coast areas are differentiated from each other perhaps more in terms of degree than of kind. The West Coast area is distinguished by a strong emphasis on percussion instruments and especially by the use of "hot" rhythm.[83] This concept seems to be no-where in Africa so strong as it is along the Guinea Coast; while powerful rhythms and even group or solo drumming in other parts of the con-tinent are dynamic in affect, they seldom approach the "hot" concept of the Guinea Coast. The "hot" concept, as well as the traditional use of the three-drum choir and the consistent use of drums in a majority of types of music, extends southward in the coastal regions of French Equatorial Africa and the Belgian Congo; on the basis of recorded material from western Angola, this area must also be included. In moving inland from the coast, however, changes in musical concepts gradually occur. A clear belt of Arabic-African musical style exists to the north, while to the east, in interior French Equatorial Africa and the Belgian Congo, the musical concepts are similar to those of the West Coast area but, so to speak, a "dilution" of the characteristic concepts and patterns. In the interior Congo, for example, while drums and drumming are important, they do not seem to be so vital to musical expression; the three-drum choir or its variations are not so universally present, and, perhaps most important, the "hot" concept does not appear to be so strong. It is difficult, of course, to know where to draw the line separating two areas, but the existence of a coastal belt running roughly from Portuguese Guinea or perhaps even the Gambia on the north to Angola on the south, within which music style is reasonably uniform, can certainly be pos-tulated. The Central Africa area is clearly distinguishable on the east from the East Africa area, on the south from the Bushman-Hottentot area, on the north from the Sudan area, and, less clearly, from the coastal area to the west. The single reservation which may be entered here is that with more material it may conceivably be necessary to group the West Coast and Central Africa areas together.

The Sudan subarea represents an area of musical fusion between Islamic and Negro African styles, clearly differentiated from the West Coast. Again, it is difficult to draw a line for the boundaries of this spe-cific subarea, but as one moves northward into the Desert subarea, Islamic styles become increasingly influential. The peoples of the Desert subarea employ musical styles which are far more Arabic than Negro African, although Negro African influence can perhaps be detected. Finally, the North Coast area is clearly distinguishable in terms of its purely Arabic styles. Thus, areas 5, 6a, 6b, and 7 form a series of roughly horizontal belts across the map of Africa moving northward from Negro African to Islamic style, with the intermediate zones more or less transitional.

A further word of caution should be entered about the variety of musical styles which may be found within a particular area. For example,

[83] Waterman, " 'Hot' Rhythm."

in the vocal styles of the small area of Ruanda there have been isolated "trois variantes regionales Abatutsi, deux Batwa, et cinq Bahutu, chacune etant bien entendue representative de sa région,"[84] exclusive of instrumental diversities. However, the culture area concept, a taxonomic tool used by anthropologists, does not require that concepts within an area be identical; rather, they are more like each other within any given area than any of them is to those in other areas, and within Ruanda this requirement is basically met, although various substyles clearly exist. Variation is to be expected within any of the areas suggested here. Finally, the tentative nature of this exploratory delimitation of African music areas must again be stressed, although in view of the available data it seems justifiable.

CHANGE

In spite of differences from area to area there are some characteristics, especially the importance of rhythm and percussive-rhythmic techniques, which indicate a reasonably cohesive musical system in Africa. It is also clear that African music is a strongly functioning part of African society. From these two generalizations we may infer that music represents a stable aspect of African culture, but this does not mean that change is absent; on the contrary, African music has been subjected to considerable pressure from two major outside sources—the influence of Western and Islamic idioms.

In respect to Western influences, the probability of acculturation is enhanced by structural factors in the two musical systems themselves. It has been postulated that when the structures in two systems are similar, the potential for blending is much greater than when the structures are dissimilar, and that exchange of ideas thus will be frequent in the first instance, infrequent in the second.[85] Some similarities of African and Western music have previously been noted: both systems have an essential base of diatonic scale and harmony, the latter term at least employed here in the sense of the simultaneous use of two or more pitches, and both have the tradition of accompaniment of the voice not only with percussion instruments but with stringed instruments as well. The general structure of the melodic lines seems also to be fairly similar in the two systems, certainly more similar than either is to the music of other major music areas, and polyphony is strong in both systems. Concepts of voice production are not markedly dissimilar and, indeed, seem almost alike when either is compared, for example, with Plains Indian music. Other similarities are less specific, but it is clear that the two

[84] Alan P. Merriam, "Les Styles Vocaux dans la Musique du Ruanda-Urundi," *Jeune Afrique*, VII (Premier Trimestre, 1953), 16.

[85] Alan P. Merriam, "The Use of Music in the Study of a Problem of Acculturation," *American Anthropologist*, LVII (February, 1955), 28.

systems are compatible and that exchange between them therefore is almost inevitable if the opportunity for contact is established. This point of view is also taken by Kolinski, who, in speaking of the acculturative situation between African and European music in the Americas, says:

La música europa, con la que los negros entraron por vez primera en contacto después de su traslado al Nuevo Mundo, no fué de manera alguna una música artística exigente; por le contrario, se trataba de canciones sencillas del pueblos que al negro deberían aparecer más bien primitivas en vez de supercomplicadas, al compararlas con los cánticos de su tierra nativa, por lo menos cuando eran entonadas a una voz y sin accompañamiento. Pero la simplicidad relativa de la canción popular europea todavía no explica la sorprendente disposición con la que se aproprió el negro del resoro de la canción europea, y su notable capacidad de actuar muy pronto como creador de un estilo más o menos europeizante. Sólo cuando se tienen en cuenta las similitudes arriba indicadas en las estructure musical básica del cancionero africano y de la música popular europea, se comprenderá la adaptación, sin dificultad alguna, del estilo europeo por el negro.[86]

Among the instruments of change, the missionary has perhaps been most influential in the past; one of the major problems raised is the use of African music in Christian worship. Carrington has reviewed past endeavors in this field as well as some of the objections to them, including the attempted solution of "taking some tribal melody already in use and adapting Christian words to it." The major criticisms are two: "Some of the melodies . . . may be foreign importations and not real music of the tribe concerned," and "some melodies . . . are accompanied by such undesirable words that any attempt to introduce the tunes into church worship would be doomed to failure." "Because of the difficulty for African peoples of certain musical intervals and rhythms in European hymn-tunes," Carrington suggests "(a) teaching the correct European tune to African Christians; (b) allowing them to sing the tune as they wish, altering the different musical intervals and changing the rhythms to suit themselves; (c) recording the result on African lips after a suitable time has elapsed for the changes to become fixed. This will give the form of the tune to be introduced to newcomers and to be taught in schools." However, he admits that "many missionaries . . . will not be happy in using for worship what is essentially a hybrid form of music—neither truly African nor essentially European."[87]

Carrington also points out the relationships between phonemic tone and melody and thinks that singing African words to European melodies may be meaningless. He suggests that "instead of the hymn-writer first thinking of a favourite tune . . . and then fitting African words to the

[86] Mieczyslaw Kolinski, "La musica del oeste Africano," *Revista de estudios musicales*, I (December, 1949), 214–15.

[87] John F. Carrington, "African Music in Christian Worship," *International Review of Missions*, XXXVII (April, 1948), 198–99.

rhythm of the music, we begin with the words and then, from the tonal patterns of these words, the music emerges. The form of song having a solo lead . . . followed by a fixed chorus has been found to be most successful. . . . Perhaps the greatest value of hymns of the type described is that the words sung have meaning for the singer." Carrington lists four difficulties: that this type of African hymn-tune is only possible "where local music follows closely the tonal patterns of the spoken language," that four-part singing is not possible with this kind of hymn, that European musical instruments cannot be used to accompany the music, and that Africans trained in European ways often object to the use of African music, feeling that the assimilation of European music should accompany the assimilation of other European patterns of behavior.[88]

The use of African music in Christian worship has been discussed by a number of writers; Jones reaches conclusions similar to Carrington's, while Hornbostel disagrees rather strongly.[89] Another approach shows clearly that the acculturative processes taking place between Western and African music are not one way alone. In recent years at least five different Catholic masses have been scored by Europeans with the express intention of incorporating African melodies into the liturgical chants; in some cases drums have even been played as accompaniment during the services.[90] In summary, it may simply be said that Christian missionaries in Africa have exerted and continue to exert a considerable influence on African music.

A second factor has been the movement of Africans to urban centers where European musical patterns are accessible through the media of radio and phonograph. It is through these media that the guitar has emerged in recent years with ever-increasing popularity in the Belgian Congo and that the rumba and samba have quickly become highly popular musical forms. In Leopoldville there have been established at least three major recording firms whose libraries, reaching thousands of master recordings, are aimed directly at the African market. A considerable number of Congolese own mechanical phonographs, and recordings of this modern "jukebox" music are available in almost all African shops.[91]

This situation is not unique in the Congo. Through the radio and phonograph Africans across the continent are finding the opportunity to hear not only Western music but the music of other areas as well, and it is through these media that one of the most interesting acculturative

[88] *Ibid.*, pp. 201–5.

[89] A. M. Jones, "Hymns for the African," *African Music Society Newsletter*, Vol. I (July, 1950); Hornbostel, "African Negro Music."

[90] See Merriam, "The Use of Music," p. 32.

[91] See Merriam, "African Music Reexamined," p. 252.

processes is taking place. This concerns the so-called South American rhythms, the conga and samba, for example; while these forms are an established part of the European popular musical literature, they seem originally to have been rhythmically African. These "Latin American" songs—changed, of course, over a period of years—are returning to Africa by means of radio and phonograph and are being received enthusiastically as a new mode of expression for popular song.[92]

These two factors—the mission influence and the urban movement with its attendant results—seem to be the most important sources of change in African musical patterns so far as Western influences are concerned, and the spread of European idioms has brought some striking alterations in the musical face of Africa. Tin whistles have held sway along the Guinea Coast; in Zanzibar, and along the upper east coast in general, cowboy music from America as interpreted by Africans ranks high as a musical form. The former Gold Coast police band has made a celebrated recording of Duke Ellington's "Rockin' In Rhythm," and Zulu groups present a repertoire of songs ranging from ballads accompanied by concertina, through four-part songs strongly reminiscent of American Negro jubilee songs, to calypso-jazz combinations featuring trumpet, clarinet, and guitar.[93] Since the two systems are basically compatible, it may be expected that patterns of change will continue as long as Western and African cultures remain in contact.

The influence on African music from the Islamic world has been frequently recognized; yet relatively little direct study of this factor has been made. In Saharan Africa there is no question of the influences, and in the Guinea Coast region, the Eastern Sudan, and the Horn they are also clearly recognized. Farther south, the influences are neither clear nor so well known, although they are strong in the northern part of the East Africa area, along the east coast, and in the northern portions, at least, of the Central Africa area. In these areas the modified version of the Arabic *rebec*, or *ndingiti* as it is named in northeastern Congo, may be cited; in addition, the vocal style of the Tutsi in Ruanda and the Hima in Uganda shows clearly defined Islamic influences in "the use of a hummed introduction which sets the general modality for the music and text which follow, clearly akin to the Arabic *maqam*. The style of voice production, ornamentation of melodic line, general melodic characteristics, and the use of intervals smaller than half tones all suggest Arabic influence."[94] Thus Islamic characteristics in both musical styles and musical instruments are found farther south than is sometimes suspected. Although still unstudied as far as is known, it may be that Arabic

[92] See Merriam, "The Use of Music," p. 32.
[93] *Ibid.*
[94] Merriam, "African Music Reexamined," p. 251.

influences on the sociology of music have also influenced African patterns.

In the acculturative situation it is possible that the music of India may be another factor. Indian patterns, however, seem clearly to be less firmly established than the Islamic, although it may simply be that Indian influences are not distinguishable as such. The presence or extent of Indian influences is a problem which has received little, if any, attention; it seems probable that it is a factor in change which must be taken into account.

A fourth acculturative process may be noted here—the influence of African groups upon each other. The use of laborers drawn to specific South African locales and the general urban movements in Africa as a whole present many opportunities for exchanges of musical ideas and probably tend gradually to blur sharp tribal stylistic lines where they exist. As continent-wide systems of communication become more and more commonplace, as more and more African students studying both in Africa and in foreign countries come to learn traditional behavior patterns of other African students, the effects are certain to become continually more important.

Of the four forces affecting African music, Western patterns are probably the strongest and will continue to be so in the forseeable future; Arabic influences are fairly well fixed and at present cannot be expected to increase materially in intensity; Indian patterns cannot be assessed properly at this time; and African influences upon Africa will doubtless become steadily stronger. Nevertheless, the present author does not share the fear that African music as a style is rapidly disappearing and is destined to be overwhelmed within a relatively short period of time. This is not to overlook the changes that are taking place but to point to the large areas of Africa in which outside influences as yet have played little or no part and probably will not do so in the immediate future, as well as to those parts of the New World where African musical elements have persisted despite longer and more intense contact. If one is to postulate the disappearance of African music, he must be prepared to ignore the tenacity of well-established cultural patterns of behavior—of which music is certainly among the most tenacious—and to conclude that all parts of Africa must inevitably lose their identity under the impact of outside cultures. Both postulates are conceivable, but they do not seem inevitable.

PROBLEMS

It is clear from the foregoing discussion that our present knowledge of African music is far from extensive and that considerable research remains to be carried out even on the most elementary levels. It is useful to divide such research conceptually into the recording and analytical description of musical forms, on the one hand, and the relation of these forms to the cultural matrix in which they function, on the other.

The first of these does not present serious problems, for a number of students and interested laymen are currently recording or planning to record African music. The transcription and analysis of such recordings are somewhat more difficult, both because there are relatively few specialists equipped to carry out such analysis and because methods of analysis have never been standardized. More important, however, is the fact that so much of the writing about African music has been affective rather than analytical, providing only minimal aid to the serious student. Elementary problems, such as vocal quality in singing or the timbre of instrumental tone, have received little attention in these descriptions. Even the analysis of specific musical styles does not in itself contribute to generalizations about Africa or its music areas; preoccupied with the single village or district where his interest lies, the investigator often fails to realize that the music with which he is concerned represents but one phase of a larger pattern.

In a sense this bears upon the second aspect of research—the relating of music forms to the cultural matrix in which they function. Unfortunately, the chief concern of the investigator has frequently been solely to record the audible musical sound without reference to its ethnographic background and, too often, without any frame of reference whatsoever. We may distinguish the recording itself as primary in the sense that it preserves a record of music activity valuable as basic documentation. A second level of activity concerns the transcription and analysis of this material in the laboratory, resulting in technical description of music style; at present, far too few such descriptions exist. A third level includes both the preceding but adds the relationship of music to culture. While the first level alone has a certain utility, even when combined with the second it cannot give a total picture of the musical activity of a group of people. It is only by dealing with music as an aspect of culture that truly penetrating studies can be made; although the collector of music serves a purpose, the full rewards in the study of music lie in the depth analysis of musical patterns in culture.

Such studies have been rather consistently avoided in the past by non-specialists on the basis that they require highly technical knowledge. But it is no more difficult to study the role and status of the musician in a society than the role and status of a chief or of women, for example. It seems worthwhile here to speak briefly of some of the broader problems of African music which have received little attention but which are vital to the complete understanding of this creative aspect of culture.

In the study of musical instruments, for example, attention has been paid to the construction, processes of construction, instrumental techniques, ranges, notes, scales, and other similar aspects, but very few studies have been centered upon such problems as the ownership of musical instruments as part of the economic organization, special treatment of instruments, musical instruments used in specific types of musical or other activities, or the representation of particular moods or states of being by particular instruments. None of these things requires special knowledge of music as a technical structure.

Other problems of similar general nature, upon which virtually no information is available, include the role and status of the musician, the social levels from which musicians are drawn, the attitudes of the society toward the musician and his attitudes toward others, the training process of the musician, and the ownership of music. Music as a creative aspect of culture has hardly been acknowledged: where does music come from; what is the psychology of music; what are the processes of creation? Here, too, lies the fundamental problem of cultural variation. The allowable variation in individual rendition of songs gives immediate clues to the differences between ideal and real cultural behavior, which in turn lead to the total range of variation in individual behavior within a culture, thus comprising a basic attack on some of the mechanisms by which internal cultural change may be effected. The study of music can also yield information on problems of cultural patterning, diffusion, and acculturation, while, finally, the entire study of cultural values as expressed in connection with music remains obscure for Africa. Among the Navaho Indians this type of problem has been attacked by McAllester, who phrases his discussion partly in terms of existential values—"what music is conceived to be"—and normative values—"what is wanted or expected in a culture from its music,"[95] but this kind of study is completely lacking for African music.

The study of African music, then, must be attacked on all three levels, recording, musicological analysis, and the broader relationships to culture; unfortunately, the lack of a problem framework, so vital to any study, has been particularly noticeable in past studies. The simple recording of African songs as a collection of esoterica is not enough; the major contribution to be made through the study of African music lies in the broader view which recognizes the fact that this dynamic, creative aspect of culture can only be understood as it is related in time to itself and in culture to all other aspects. Thus far, our knowledge is largely restricted to structure, and even here there is much to be desired; our understanding of African music in relationship to African culture is almost nonexistent.

---

[95] David P. McAllester, *Enemy Way Music: A Study of Social and Esthetic Values As Seen in Navaho Music* ("Papers of the Peabody Museum of American Archaeology and Ethnology," Vol. XLI, No. 3; "Reports of the Rimrock Project," Value Ser. 3 [Cambridge, 1954]), pp. 4, 5.

5. The Factor of Polygyny
in African Demography

Demographers in the main have dealt with materials from the Euroamerican countries and to a lesser extent with those pertaining to the great civilizations of the Far East. They have largely neglected the possibility of using comparative data from Africa and other nonliterate areas, owing mainly to the paucity and over-all unsatisfactory nature of the quantitative material from these regions. Anyone concerned with sub-Saharan Africa and its problems in the changing world scene today, however, realizes that demographic data are basic to future planning in areas ranging from land policy to questions of labor and from medical and health problems to educational matters, as well as to the expansion of scientific knowledge. What data do exist often contain obvious errors and inaccuracies, as Kuczynski,[1] Taeuber,[2] and others have shown, and are thus a questionable foundation for planning or research.

These deficiencies are the result of a number of obstacles to the collection of demographic data which have long plagued investigators in sub-Saharan Africa. While they are gradually being eliminated, they are still important factors in most areas. Once these obstacles are recognized, the investigator can better judge the validity of the particular source materials which he wishes to apply to a given problem. Five important obstacles have been insufficient funds, shortages of trained personnel, illiteracy, the fact that many Africans do not know how old they are, and African opposition to demographic research.

Projects to set up and maintain effective census bureaus and compulsory birth and death registers are inadequately financed. Generally speaking, the African territories are poor and their annual budgets low. Many projects which can show more tangible and immediate benefits

[1] Robert R. Kuczynski, *The Cameroons and Togoland: A Demographic Study* (London: Oxford University Press, 1939); *A Demographic Survey of the British Colonial Empire*, Vol. I: *West Africa*, Vol. II: *East Africa* (London: Oxford University Press, 1948–49).

[2] Irene B. Taeuber, *The Population of Tanganyika* ("Reports on the Population of Trust Territories," No. 2 [Lake Success: United Nations, 1949]).

than population research, such as roads and harbor improvements, compete for the available funds. When funds are allocated for censuses, they are nearly always insufficient for the task at hand. Costs for the 1931 censuses in parts of British West Africa ranged from approximately 10¢ to $12.00 per thousand population enumerated in Nigeria—the latter figure referring to the intensive census of Katsina District—and were $3.00 and $1.50, respectively, per thousand population enumerated in the Gold Coast and the Gambia. For the High Commission Territories, comparable figures were $22.50 for Basutoland, $8.50 for Bechuanaland, and $7.60 for Swaziland. The 1950 census in the United States, on the other hand, cost roughly $400.00 per thousand population enumerated.[3] Once an enumeration has been completed, the data must be tabulated and a census report containing summaries of the raw data in one form or another must be prepared for publication. Funds for these purposes are generally set aside before the enumeration is undertaken; but, judging by the resultant publications, the amount reserved for making the data available is often deficient.

There is also a lack of adequate, trained personnel to administer the census and to compile and tabulate the collected data, owing partly to financial limitations. Trained demographers and statisticians command high salaries in terms of African rates of pay, and it is not surprising to find that only the most recent enumerations have been planned and administered by specialists. Past shortages of trained compilers to process the raw data into tabular form have introduced serious basic errors into census reports on numerous occasions. The administration of the French Cameroons, as Kuczynski[4] points out, reversed its opinion about the influence of polygyny on fertility at one point because of an arithmetical error.

Intensive demographic investigations have been extensively undertaken only by the government of the Belgian Congo, where a number of members of the medical service have been detailed to make such studies in areas of suspected depopulation. It is significant that the cost of such investigations, both in money and in the time of a high-salaried medical man, has been borne by governments only when they have been faced with serious population problems, and not as a general policy. One answer may be regional statistical offices, like those set up in British East and Central Africa, which supply expert services while the cost is shared by the member territories.

In many territories there has been a shortage of literate, trained

[3] Kuczynski, *Demographic Survey*. United States, *Appraisal of Census Programs* (Washington, D. C.: Government Printing Office, 1950), p. 1. The conversion rate used was $2.80 = £1.

[4] Kuczynski, *The Cameroons and Togoland*, p. 156.

Africans to serve even as enumerators and collectors of data in the field. Special efforts were made in connection with the most recent Nigerian census[5] to eliminate the errors of omission and commission introduced by untrained or partially trained enumerators who do not thoroughly understand question schedules and the system of marking them. Supervisors were nominated by the local groups in an effort to eliminate subsequent charges of imposition, while both supervisors and enumerators were given intensive training, including trial enumerations on prisoners.

The obstacle presented by widespread illiteracy in sub-Saharan Africa manifests itself other ways. Printed propaganda materials endeavoring to explain the true reasons for enumerations and to allay the fears of the populace are relatively ineffective. In areas of high illiteracy it is difficult to take even a count, for many of the village headmen and chiefs, upon whom the success or failure of such efforts depends, are incapable of handling and reporting results.

A very important obstacle is the fact that many Africans do not know how old they or their children are, having reckoned time by the European calendar only in recent years. Because a knowledge of the age composition of a population is prerequisite to many demographic analyses, recourse has been had to the visual assignment of age in accord with broad categories. Age breakdowns have been made in terms of "nonadult," "adult," and "aged," or in terms of "initiated" and "noninitiated" according to puberty ceremonies. However, visual signs of physical aging are far from reliable, while the dividing line in terms of initiation differs both from sex to sex and from society to society.

A. Ryckmans[6] suggests that more specific material can be gathered by means of an "age calendar," and J. C. Mitchell[7] has described his formulation and use of this device during the course of field work among the Yao of Nyasaland. An "age calendar" is essentially a chronology of remembered events which can be dated absolutely by historical records. Repeated interviewing permits rechecking and cross-checking against this chronology, enabling the investigator to classify the population into a number of age categories, with only the very old assigned ages by visual means. This device, however, is applicable only to relatively small groups among whom the field worker can spend an extended period of time in preparing and testing the age calendar and in lengthy repetitive interview sessions. Moreover, an age calendar constructed for one group is most unlikely to be workable for neighboring groups, and statistical problems of some magnitude would be involved in handling data sub-

[5] Melville J. Herskovits, unpublished field notes, 1953.

[6] André Ryckmans, "Étude sur les Statistiques Démographiques au Congo Belge," *Zaïre*, VII, No. 1 (1953), 3–33.

[7] J. Clyde Mitchell, "An Estimate of Fertility in Some Yao Hamlets in Liwonde District of Southern Nyasaland," *Africa*, XIX (October, 1949), 293–308.

divided according to different age groups as established by a series of such calendars in different societies, even if the expense involved in constructing them could be met. Thus, while this device might be used in simplified form in surveys, it has not been so employed to date to the writer's knowledge.

The final and most formidable obstacle to demographic research in sub-Saharan Africa is the opposition, both active and passive, of the African himself. Edge[8] lays stress upon this difficulty, underlining the equation of taxes and census in the minds of Africans. Whether or not this equation has a factual basis in administrative policy is of little import, for the obstacle is the same in either case. The African's opposition is manifested in various ways which can have different effects on the accuracy of the results. Entire villages have been deserted on the eve of an enumeration, with only the sick and incapacitated left behind. Headmen and chiefs may exaggerate the number of their subjects, or women may be concealed. Moreover, there may be strictures against any form of counting, as among the Pakot of Kenya,[9] which defeat attempts at accurate census-taking. N. J. Brooke, a district officer in northern Nigeria at the time of the 1931 census of this territory wrote:

> Such beliefs as that if their women-folk are accurately counted a number of them will run away, or that if the number of children is exactly given increased mortality amonst them will result, still linger among Pagan tribes. . . . One occasionally heard of an anxiety being expressed that during the year of the decennial census an abnormal number of deaths would occur among the population, but the more common reaction would be a suspicion that increased taxation is proposed.[10]

This same census report alludes to the difficulties entailed by the prohibition regarding personal names in determining the number of children in any given polygynous family.

Deliberate prevarication is encountered no less in Africa than in other areas of the world, and in fields other than demography. On an individual basis, it is difficult to find out, although it undoubtedly occurs and is variously motivated; but deliberate, prearranged conspiracies to misinform investigators may be more easily detected, as when inquiries into the number of children living or born per woman elicit identical responses. Passive resistance, apathy, and incomplete returns also doubtless occur, though references to them are rarely found in the literature. These reactions present greater difficulties in survey and formal census attempts than in intensive studies, where it is possible to recheck and cross-check information.

[8] P. Granville Edge, *Vital Statistics and Public Health Work in the Tropics* (London: Bailliére, Tindall & Cox, 1947), p. 22.

[9] Harold K. Schneider, unpublished field notes, 1952.

[10] Nigeria, *Census of Nigeria, 1931* (London, 1932–33), II, 12.

In one of the few accounts of how demographic inquiries appear to the Africans, Goldthorpe[11] has listed a number of difficulties in census work and vital registration in East Africa. Particular mention is made of the traditional belief throughout this area that it is impious or unlucky to count people, of suspicion of the government's motives in taking a census, and of the administrative decision to conduct the 1948 census during the rainy season, when travel was doubly difficult.

As literacy increases, it should be possible to lessen the Africans' opposition to census enumerations and vital registration by prior propaganda campaigns which endeavor to explain the purpose of the undertaking in terms of a preliminary step toward improvement in health, sanitation, and educational facilities. The enumeration in the recent Nigerian census[12] was preceded by a poster, press, and radio campaign stressing that the census was to be the basis for future planning and that each person who went uncounted meant fewer schools, hospitals, roads, and the like. Similarly, improvement in the accuracy of returns can be expected as increasing use is made of ethnographic reports in setting up the actual schedules and dates of enumeration. All in all, the active and passive resistance on the part of the African himself appears to be the major procedural obstacle to the collection of accurate demographic material on sub-Saharan Africa.

SOURCES OF DEMOGRAPHIC DATA

Our present knowledge of the demographic situation in sub-Saharan Africa is derived from various sources which can be considered under five general headings: formal census reports, sample census surveys, medical surveys, intensive demographic studies, and anthropological monographs containing data collected by either the census or the genealogical method.

The "censuses" of the various African territories are not censuses in the sense of enumerations made by entering the name and other particulars of each individual on the census form. In most cases, the population figures are no more than estimates by government officials or "counts" made either without any forms or with collective forms for villages or clans rather than for individuals. Kuczynski has demonstrated that in the 1931 census reports for British West Africa, censuses covered 4 per cent of the total population, compared to 12 per cent for counts and 84 per cent for estimates.[13] In British East and Central Africa for 1931,[14] "counts" covered roughly 40 per cent of the total population, while

[11] J. E. Goldthorpe, "Attitudes to the Census and Vital Registration in East Africa," *Population Studies*, VI (November, 1952), 163–72.

[12] Herskovits, unpublished field notes, 1953.

[13] Kuczynski, *Demographic Survey*, I, 2.

[14] *Ibid.*, II, 97.

"estimates" were made for the bulk of the remaining 60 per cent.

The basic purpose of formal administrative censuses is to collect, by means of territory-wide inquiries, reasonably accurate facts relating to the total number, distribution, and composition of the population. In a broad sense they are periodic tests of the socioeconomic condition of the population, while they serve a variety of other useful purposes. Essentially, they secure data on a limited range of topics for a broad population. Their greatest weakness is the limited range of topics which have been covered, while their strength lies chiefly in the large size of the population upon which it is based. A number of such formal censuses have been undertaken for the Union of South Africa and the many British African territories, excepting Somaliland, but few have been conducted by the Belgian, French, Spanish, and Portuguese administrations, though the Portuguese undertook enumerations for Angola and Mozambique in 1940 and for Portuguese Guinea in various recent years. No similar attempts have been made by the governments of Liberia and Ethiopia.

The sample census survey is a device only recently used in Africa to secure basic demographic statistics. The first rigorously scientific sample census on the African continent was conducted by J. R. H. Shaul[15] of the Central African Statistical Office on the African population of Southern Rhodesia in 1948, after a pilot study had been made in Hartley District in October, 1947. A discussion of the methodological and theoretical problems entailed in setting up sample inquiries is to be found in the various publications of Shaul and Myburgh[16] and in a volume by Yates.[17] Other sample censuses have been conducted by Neesen[18] in Ruanda-Urundi and by the Service de Statistique in French Guinea.[19] Some results of the sample census for the Sudan[20] have been published. Similar surveys have been proposed for the territories of British East Africa, to be conducted under the auspices of the East African Statistical Office.

It is difficult at the present time to evaluate the results obtained by

[15] J. R. H. Shaul, "Sampling Surveys in Central Africa," *Journal of the American Statistical Association*, XLVII (1952), 239–54.

[16] J. R. H. Shaul and C. A. L. Myburgh, "A Sample Survey of the African Population of Southern Rhodesia," *Population Studies*, II (1948), 339–53; "Provisional Results of the Sample Survey of the African Population of Southern Rhodesia," *ibid.*, VII (1949), 274–85.

[17] Frank Yates, *Sampling Methods for Censuses and Surveys* (London: C. Griffin, 1949).

[18] V. Neesen, "Quelques Données Démographiques sur la Population du Ruanda-Urundi," *Zaïre*, VII, No. 10 (1953), 1011–27; "Le Premier Recensement par Echantillonage au Ruanda-Urundi," *Zaïre*, VIII, No. 1 (1953), 469–89.

[19] French Guinea, *L'Enquête Démographique de Guinée* (Paris, 1956).

[20] Sudan, *The 1953 Pilot Population Census for the First Population Census in Sudan* (Khartoum, 1955); *First Population Census of Sudan 1955/56; First Interim Report* and *Supplement to Interim Reports* (Khartoum, 1956).

this method. Refinements in technique and the gradual assembly of a body of trained African enumerators will doubtless raise the standards. In general this method, though it may secure little beyond the most elementary demographic data on population composition and dynamics, is worthy of continued application if only because its relatively low cost makes frequently repeated enumeration possible.

Demographic statistics are often collected as an integral part of medical surveys.[21] These data provide the bulk of our information on mortality (especially of infants and young children), morbidity, and the incidence of disease. Owing to the intensive enumeration of relatively small populations, the validity of the data is undoubtedly higher than that collected by other methods. While some of the medical surveys, such as those conducted by FOREAMI[22] and other agencies in the Belgian Congo, cover total populations of several hundred thousand, the majority, such as those undertaken in British West Africa, deal with only a few villages containing at most a few thousand inhabitants. The primary aim of such surveys, however, is of necessity medical rather than demographic; hence they will not provide all of the basic data needed. At one time or other such investigations have been undertaken in most of the sub-Saharan African territories.

Special, intensive demographic investigations[23] of relatively small areas and populations have been undertaken in sub-Saharan Africa by missionaries, medical men, government administrators, interested lay colonists, and anthropologists. Judged by the published studies, the amount of knowledge of demographic theory, method, and results possessed by such persons varies widely, so that while some contain good data on most aspects of demographic interest, others are spotty and omit

[21] I. A. McGregor and D. A. Smith, "A Health, Nutrition, and Parasitological Survey in a Rural Village (Keneba) in West Kiang, Gambia," *Transactions of the Royal Society of Tropical Medicine and Hygiene*, XLVI (1952), 403–27. G. Muraz, "Résumé de l'Action, en A. E. F., pendant Huit Ans (1920–7), d'un Secteur de Prophylactic de la Maladie du Sommeil," *Bulletin de la Société de Pathologie Exotique*, XXI, No. 2 (1928), 141–58. M. J. Colbourne, G. M. Edington, and M. H. Hughes, "A Medical Survey in a Gold Coast Village," *Transactions of the Royal Society of Tropical Medicine and Hygiene*, XLIV, No. 3 (1950), 271–90.

[22] G. Trolli and Dupuy, *Contribution à l'Étude de la Démographie des Bakongo au Congo Belge* (Brussels, 1934).

[23] Enid Charles and C. Daryll Forde, "Notes on Some Population Data from a Southern Nigerian Village," *Sociological Review*, XXX (April, 1938), 145–60. Monique de Lestrange, "La Population de la Région de Youkounkoun, en Guinée Française," *Population*, V (October, 1950), 643–68. Meyer Fortes, "A Note on Fertility among the Tallensi of the Gold Coast," *Sociological Review*, XXXV (July–October, 1943), 99–113. L. Guerts, "Étude Démographique des Populations du Territoire de Lusambo," *Zaïre*, III, No. 9 (1949), 963–93; III, No. 10 (1949), 1068–89; IV, No. 1 (1950), 17–39. Annie Masson Detourbet, "Essai d'Étude Démographique des Kotoko (Région du Tchad)," *Population*, VI (July, 1951), 445–58. Mitchell, "Estimate of Fertility," pp. 293–308. Frank Lorimer, *Culture and Human Fertility* (Geneva: UNESCO, 1954).

crucial material. The size of the area studied in these intensive investigations varies from a few villages or a chiefdom to the population of an administrative district. Generally, the total population covered is from five hundred to twenty thousand. In most cases these studies, like the other types of investigations that have been discussed, have been based on a single interview, although it is safe to assume that these interviews are fuller than the brief sessions held by census enumerators. The one-interview method lacks opportunities for cross-checking and rechecking data, and these are the keystone of the intensive study which requires an extended period of time in a relatively small population. A lengthy period of ethnographic research is also prerequisite to constructing an age calendar and to overcoming African opposition to demographic inquiries.

The final major category of source material is that found in anthropological field reports.[24] As a general rule these are unsatisfactory, often consisting merely of data extracted from recent census reports pertaining to the area in question. In some cases, however, inquiries have been undertaken by the anthropologist himself, either by the local "census" or the "genealogical" method or both. The village or clan census method has long been recognized by anthropologists as a valuable field technique in the collection of various types of social data. Unfortunately, field workers using this technique have seldom been aware of the necessity for collecting subsidiary demographic data.

The genealogical method, according to Rivers, can yield useful data on the average size of the family, the proportion of the sexes at birth and as adults, class fertility, and intermarriage between various groups: "The genealogies will furnish a large mass of material on these subjects, and it may even be possible to obtain some idea of differences in these respects in different generations."[25] In spite of Rivers' claims, the genealogical method is no substitute for successive demographic studies of the census type. Theoretically, the genealogical method gives a picture of the situation at the time of the investigation, excluding immigrants not incorporated into the genealogies, but for past generations it gives a composite picture of many years rather than one picture at any specific point in time. Nevertheless, it may provide some indication of trend in popu-

[24] C. Daryll Forde, *Marriage and the Family among the Yakö* (London: Percy, Lund, Humphries, 1941). G. Hulstaert, *Le Mariage des Nkundo* (Brussels, 1936). Kenneth Little, *The Mende of Sierra Leone* (London: Routledge & Kegan Paul, 1951). Northcote W. Thomas, *Anthropological Report on the Edo-speaking Peoples of Nigeria* (London: Harrison & Sons, 1910); *Anthropological Report on the Ibo-speaking Peoples of Nigeria* (London: Harrison & Sons: 1913); *Anthropological Report on the Timne-speaking Peoples of Sierra Leone* (London: Harrison & Sons, 1916).

[25] William H. R. Rivers, "A Genealogical Method of Collecting Social and Vital Statistics," *Journal of the Royal Anthropological Institute*, XXX (January, 1900), 74–78.

lation change. Under ideal conditions the genealogical method and the census method would give identical results for the living population. In practice, where memory failure and prevarication bring about discrepancies, these point the way to further questioning. Since the census and genealogical methods should validate one another, both should be used in intensive studies of small populations.

While demographers have developed and employed highly refined methods for the statistical analysis of particular types of quantitative population data, it is only recently that they have begun to devise comparable methods of analysis where these data are incomplete, which is the case for most if not all of the area in question. A number of demographers have made significant advances in the treatment of fertility.[26]

DEMOGRAPHIC CHARACTERISTICS OF AFRICA

No accurate answer can be given to the question of how many people there are today in sub-Saharan Africa. The United Nation's compilation[27] of estimates for mid-year 1954 indicates roughly one hundred and sixty million as compared with two hundred and ten million for the continent as a whole; the possible error being about 5 per cent. In view of the tentative nature of most of the component data, this is as accurate an approximation as can reasonably be expected.

Sub-Saharan Africa is marked by a relatively low population density in comparison with other areas of the world.[28] Excepting the urban areas, the Niger delta, Ruanda-Urundi, and small sections of Nyasaland, Uganda, and the Union of South Africa, the over-all density rarely exceeds a figure of twenty-five per square mile. Furthermore, large sections of French West Africa, Kenya, Tanganyika, Angola, Bechuanaland, South-West Africa, and the Union of South Africa are all but uninhabited largely because of a shortage of water during much of each year. Large tracts of the tropical rain forest area in French Equatorial Africa and the Belgian Congo are also thinly populated.

The official census data, summarized below in Table 5, indicate that there are probably more females than males in sub-Saharan Africa as a

[26] W. Brass, "The Derivation of Fertility and Reproduction Rates from Restricted Data on Reproductive Histories," *Population Studies*, VII (November, 1953), 137–66; "The Estimation of Fertility Rates from Ratios of Total to First Births," *ibid.*, VIII (July, 1954), 74–91. C. J. Martin, "Note on the Use of Statistics of Total Fertility To Provide Estimates of Crude Birth Rates," *Population Studies*, VIII (July, 1954), 88–91. C. A. L. Myburgh, "Estimating the Fertility and Mortality of African Populations from the Total Number of Children Ever Born and the Number of These Still Living," *Population Studies*, X (November, 1956), 193–206.

[27] United Nations, *Demographic Yearbook* (New York: Statistical Office of the United Nations, 1955), Table I, pp. 99–103.

[28] Walter Fitzgerald, *Africa* (London: Methuen & Co., 1950), p. 108.

whole today. Striking local imbalances of the sex ratio occur in "labor-reservoir" areas, such as Nyasaland and the Rhodesias, where large numbers of adult males are absent for extended periods of time, in the urban and industrial areas,[29] where there are shortages of women, and wherever else sex-selective factors are in operation. The fluctuations of the sex ratio through the different age groups in response to differential mortality factors are imperfectly known, though it appears likely that male mortality is relatively higher at all ages except some of the childbearing years.

The fact that many Africans do not know how old they are is largely responsible for the rudimentary, and to formal demographers totally unsatisfactory, nature of the data on age structure. In view of the over-all low level of general health and nutrition by Euroamerican standards in much of sub-Saharan Africa, it is not surprising that the populations have relatively fewer old people and relatively more young people. In general, the African populations are "young" and possess the strengths, weaknesses, and potentialities of any "young" populations.

The reliable material dealing with fertility is limited to a relatively small number of intensive demographic studies which have been undertaken in various local areas. Many investigators have collected data relating the number of children fifteen years and younger to those more than fifteen years old in sample populations, which is essentially a fertility ratio, and some have tried to approximate gross and net reproduction rates.[30] Charles and Forde,[31] in their study of the Yakö of southern Nigeria, concentrated on a male net reproduction rate, while the Culwicks[32] tried to determine a female net reproduction rate in their study of the Ulanga Valley, Tanganyika. Fortes,[33] studying the Tallensi of the Gold Coast, considered both. Mitchell,[34] using an age calendar to determine ages, calculated gross reproduction rates for Yao women in five-year age groups, then combined these data in ten-year age groups, thus giving some idea of the past trend of fertility, and he ultimately derived a net reproduction rate. Though the methods used by these and other investigators do not produce true reproduction rates as derived

[29] V. Charles, "Le Mal Démographique de Léopoldville," *Zaïre*, II (1948), 897–901; "L'Équilibre des Sexes parmi les Adultes dans les Milieux Extra-Coutumiers," *ibid.*, III (1949), 47–53. R. Grévisse, "Le Centre Extra-Coutumier d'Élisabethville," *Bulletin du Centre d'Études des Problèmes Sociaux Indigènes*, XV (1951), 287–304.

[30] A comparative analysis of the many measures of reproduction is beyond the scope of this contribution.

[31] Charles and Forde, "Notes on Some Population Data," pp. 145–60.

[32] A. T. Culwick and G. M. Culwick, "A Study of Population in Ulanga, Tanganyika Territory," *Sociological Review*, XXX (October, 1938), 365–79; XXXI (January, 1939), 25–43.

[33] Fortes, "A Note on Fertility," pp. 99–113.

[34] Mitchell, "Estimate of Fertility," pp. 293–308.

from reliable census statistics, they nevertheless are the best means of studying population replacement where census records are unavailable. The difference in results arises because the treatment of mortality is approximate and the survival tables used in calculating the reproduction rates are makeshift. Any assumption of a constant mortality for several decades, implicit in some studies, is doubtless an oversimplification which can introduce sizable errors.

Specific studies of mortality are rare in the literature, though Gamble,[35] to cite one out of many, has dealt with infant mortality in the Gambia. The results of these studies show that infant and child mortality vary greatly in response to local conditions. The intimate relationship between child deaths, general nutrition, and seasonal shortages deserves further study in connection with the collection of mortality data.

Given the shortages of fertility and mortality data and the fact that even where both are available for a given population they reveal only the past and present, it is clear that the prognostication of future population trends is most precarious. It is definitely established, however, that while some populations, such as the Yao,[36] are increasing, others are decreasing. The Culwicks' data on Ulanga Valley[37] and the numerous studies on the Nkundo-Mongo population of the Belgian Congo summarized by Boelaert[38] show that these groups are not at present replacing themselves. Whether these local increases and decreases average out into an over-all population growth for sub-Saharan Africa is not incontrovertibly proven, but it seems likely that an over-all slow growth is occurring. It should be stressed, however, that with relatively high fertility and mortality rates, much of sub-Saharan Africa is an area of potential rapid growth. Any factor that decreases mortality, such as improved sanitation, medical services, or a higher level of general nutrition, could trigger a sudden population increase, but a number of other factors arising out of the contact situations tend to decrease the population through lowered fertility. In areas of migrant labor-recruiting husband and wife (or wives) are separated for long periods of time, while both there and in urban or industrial areas the loosening of the tribal family structure and increased rates of venereal infections also tend to lower birth rates. These and other factors, however, operate against a background of traditional African demographic patterns, some of which increase, while others decrease, total populations through their effects upon mortality and fertility. Mention need only be made of the African's desire for children, a

[35] David P. Gamble, "Infant Mortality Rates in Rural Areas in the Gambia Protectorate," *Journal of Tropical Medicine and Hygiene*, LV, No. 7 (1952), 145–49.
[36] Mitchell, "Estimate of Fertility," pp. 293–308.
[37] Culwick and Culwick, "Study of Population," pp. 25–43.
[38] E. Boelaert, *La Situation Démographique des Nkundo-Mongo* (Élisabethville: Centre d'Études des Problèmes Sociaux Indigènes, 1947).

crucial factor documented beyond question in the ethnographic literature.

Despite the marked limitations of the African demographic data, with care they can be used critically for the analysis of a variety of anthropological and demographic problems. They have been found sufficient as a basis for a study of the demographic aspects of polygyny,[39] a subject which, although of considerable importance to both anthropology and demography, has been largely neglected by scholars in these fields. The mechanisms by which it is possible for one hundred married men to have as many as one hundred and fifty to two hundred wives when the sex ratio appears to be about equal and the effect of polygyny on fertility were among the problems which were phrased as hypotheses and tested in terms of the available data.

THE INCIDENCE AND INTENSITY OF POLYGYNY

Basic to the clarification and testing of hypotheses dealing with these and other demographic aspects of polygyny, however, is a consideration of the *incidence* of polygynous households in various populations and of the *intensity* of polygyny or the size of these polygynous households. Many writers have had and still have misconceptions about the frequency or incidence of polygyny in sub-Saharan Africa. In regard to French Togoland, for example, Kuczynski notes that "the administration had assumed so far that polygamy was the 'general rule' and that one husband had on the average, 'slightly over two wives.' This, of course, was a delusion."[40] Prior to the first numerical inquiry into this question, which was not made until some years later, French official opinion held that the incidence of polygyny in Togoland was extremely high, much higher, in fact, than the subsequent quantitative data showed it to be.

The incidence of polygyny was also much overstated by early unofficial writers. Martin,[41] for example, wrote about the Basutos that "almost all the heathen males possess at least two or three wives." Lindblom, however, was more circumspect in speaking of the Akamba of Kenya:

The most usual number of wives is 1 to 3, and, if statistical investigations were made, the percentage of those who had more than 3 would be found to be very low. We should find the same state of things among most of the Bantu peoples, so that the popular conception of polygamy, that every man has a large number of wives, is far from being correct.[42]

[39] Vernon R. Dorjahn, *The Demographic Aspects of African Polygyny* (Ann Arbor: University Microfilms, 1954), chap. i.

[40] Kuczynski, *The Cameroons and Togoland*, p. 452.

[41] Minnie Martin, *Basutoland: Its Legends and Customs* (London, 1903), p. 41.

[42] Gerhard Lindblom, *The Akamba* (Upsala, 1920), p. 81.

The popular conception, however, is by no means entirely outmoded. Huntingford writes of the Barabaig of Tanganyika that "polygyny is common, and the average Barabanda man has at least two wives: many have 3 or 4, and some, the very rich, as many as 18."[43] This type of statement is usually marked by an absence of supporting quantitative material, and it is impossible to tell in most cases whether the phrase "average man" refers to the arithmetic mean, median, or mode, or indeed to any of these. However, if we can define the "average man" in terms of these statistical measures, we can rephrase the opinions quoted above as an estimate, *that the "average" number of wives per man in polygynous societies is two or more,* the word "average" being equated in turn with each of these three statistical measures of central tendency.

The estimate as stated does not specify the delimitations of the male group under consideration, since these are rarely stated in the ethnographic literature. Even if we assume that "man" refers to "adult male" and that an adult is anyone fifteen years of age and over, an additional difficulty arises in that writers such as Huntingford fail to state whether they mean all adult males or all adult married males. It is thus necessary, in testing the hypothesis, to consider for each sample both of these male groups in regard to each of the three measures of central tendency. The estimate thus must be considered separately in six distinct forms of statement.

The accessible quantitative material dealing with the incidence and intensity of African polygyny are characterized by their extreme variability.[44] It should be stressed that the size and hence the reliability of the sample populations differ considerably, while in some cases the size of the sample is unknown, or at least unstated. For only a few studies could any claim to a random sample be made.

The great majority of the studies upon which the present investigation is based present the incidence of polygyny as it appeared in the living population at the time the investigator was conducting his inquiries. It is impossible to designate the situation as that which was found on October 21, 1948, for example, which is the demographic procedure for census enumerations, but in most cases the year in which the stated distribution was observed can be designated.

In some studies, on the other hand, data are presented in the form of the number of men and women "ever polygynously married." Calculations based on such data are obviously overestimates for any given

[43] G. W. B. Huntingford, *The Southern Nilo-Hamites* ("Ethnographic Survey of Africa, East Central Africa," Part VIII [London: International African Institute, 1953]), p. 98.

[44] Dorjahn, *African Polygyny*, pp. 33–147. Lack of space has made it impossible to include here the critical analysis of each set of data, the summary tables, or a bibliography of the original sources, all of which may be found in the cited source.

time, and it has been necessary to eliminate this type of data from the following analysis, for it deals, essentially, with another phenomenon—the marital history of a population over an extended period of time. We are concerned here with the picture as it existed at a given point in time, or at least over such a short period of time that the situation remained sufficiently static for the investigator to comprehend and make allowances for the few changes that occurred through divorce, marriage, or death. The difference is analogous to that made by formal demographers in presenting the marital composition of a given population at a given date as opposed to the marital history of a generation of men or women through the number and per cent of each "ever married." This distinction is particularly important where, as is the case in much of sub-Saharan Africa, men acquire additional wives late in life.

Based upon the acceptable available data, the summary statements in Table 1 can be made regarding the estimate of incidence.

TABLE 1

PERCENTAGES OF CASES IN WHICH THE NUMBER OF WIVES
IS TWO OR MORE IN SUB-SAHARAN AFRICA*

Mean number of wives per adult man........ 3 per cent (2 out of 59 cases)
Mean number of wives per married man.....10 per cent (13 out of 136 cases)
Median number of wives per adult man...... 6 per cent (5 out of 76 cases)
Median number of wives per married man....13 per cent (20 out of 155 cases)
Modal number of wives per adult man....... 4 per cent (3 out of 76 cases)
Modal number of wives per married man..... 6 per cent (9 out of 155 cases)

* Dorjahn, *African Polygyny*, Table 96, p. 137.

The estimate that the average number of wives per man in polygynous societies is two or more does not hold for any of these measures of central tendency based upon either all adult men or all married men, though this estimate does hold for *some* polygynous societies.

Before a new estimate of the incidence of polygyny is computed, the impossibility of making valid statements based on quantitative data about the increase or decrease of polygyny should be emphasized. The data are largely synchronic, and with few exceptions there are no re-studies of the same population.[45] Data collected at any one point in time for different generations are difficult to utilize, since the younger age groups taken alone may not show the same incidence as the total adult male population when many men marry only late in life. The potential errors in such a procedure can obscure the smaller diachronic differences which are of crucial importance. Lacking the necessary quantitative

[45] Such restudies have been made in Basutoland and Swaziland, where the incidence of polygyny seems to be decreasing, in French Togoland, where there was little change during the period for which statistics are available, and in some areas of the Belgian Congo, where the incidence appears to be increasing.

data, one can only say that no certain over-all tendency toward increase or decrease is discernible for sub-Saharan Africa during the last forty years. The unquantified statements on the increase or decrease of polygyny found in the ethnographic literature indicate that examples of trends in both directions can be found for different populations. Generally speaking, the data are insufficient to consider the dynamic aspects of the problem, and it is assumed in the following discussion that the situation has remained relatively unchanged.

Since the incidence and intensity of polygyny are facets of cultural behavior, it is necessary to consider their areal variability. For this purpose

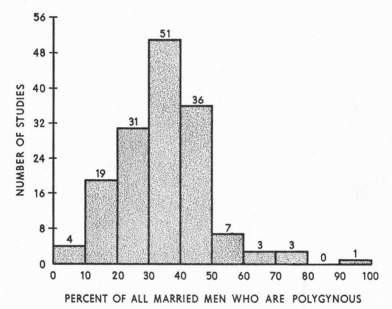

Fig. 4. Frequency histogram of data of Table 2, Sub-Saharan Africa

the culture areas of Africa according to Herskovits[46] have been used, but, owing to the paucity of data, the East Horn and Eastern Sudanic areas have been omitted, while only the arithmetic mean has been computed for the Khoisan area. Sample size has been disregarded in the following discussion, since if weightings were employed in accordance with sample size, undue importance would be placed upon the few general censuses that have dealt with polygyny to the detriment of the intensive studies based upon much smaller samples which, in all probability, more accu-

[46] Melville J. Herskovits, *Cultural Anthropology* (New York: Alfred A. Knopf, 1955), p. 402.

rately represent the actual situation. The dates of collection of the various samples are ignored on the assumption that, as the evidence itself suggests, the incidence of polygyny has been roughly constant in most parts of Africa during the period under consideration.

TABLE 2

PERCENTAGES OF ALL MARRIED MEN WHO ARE POLYGYNOUS, SUB-SAHARAN AFRICA BY CULTURE AREAS*

Area	N	Mean	Median	Mode	Range
Khoisan...............	4	24.5	....	....	4–40
East African Cattle......	24	24.7	21.6	15.6	5–75
Congo.................	38	32.6	32.1	31.1	12–48
Guinea Coast...........	46	43.0	41.4	38.0	24–91
Western Sudan.........	31	33.8	33.0	31.4	20–80
Sub-Saharan Africa†.....	155	35.0	34.1	32.2	4–91

* Dorjahn, *African Polygyny*, Table 97, p. 140.
† Includes some studies not incorporated in the computations for the individual culture areas.

The data in Table 2 again show that the estimate under consideration does not hold for all married men, either for Africa as a whole or for any of its areas; and since the percentages are bound to be lower for all adult males, it is not necessary to include these computations. The percentage of all married men who are polygynous is a measure of the incidence, as distinguished from the intensity, of polygyny throughout the male population, and the data in Table 2 show that the incidence of polygyny is lower in southern and eastern Africa than in the Congo and Western Sudan areas and highest in the Guinea Coast. It may be concluded that "West and central Africa" contain the areas of highest incidence. The data in Table 2, however, are at best only rather crude approximations because the samples are not randomly selected and are not comparable in size or date, thus necessitating assumptions about their accuracy and about the dynamics of the situation. The non-randomness of the samples precludes the use of statistical tests of significance.

The incidence of polygyny as measured by the number of wives to one hundred married men is also lower in southern and eastern Africa than in the Congo–Guinea Coast–West Sudan areas, as is shown by the data in Table 3. These averages are minimums, since they are based, in many cases, upon "open-ended" samples in the primary sources. For example, when five men are listed as having "six or more wives" or ten men as having "four or more wives," there are at least thirty and forty wives, respectively, but the actual numbers are unknown and are probably somewhat larger. The averages in Table 3 thus are underestimates of the actual situation, but not to such an extent that we can assume the correctness of the original estimate.

The data in Table 4 are also based upon a number of "open-ended" samples and are therefore also underestimates. The number of wives to one hundred *polygynously* married men is a direct measure of the intensity of polygyny, and the data in Table 4 suggest that southern and

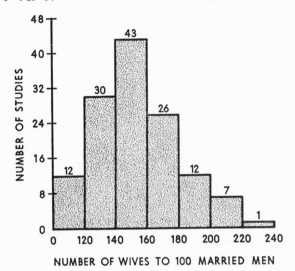

FIG. 5. Frequency histogram of data of Table 3, sub-Saharan Africa

eastern Africa do not have as high an intensity as is found in the Congo–Guinea Coast–West Sudan areas. East Africa appears to lack the very large households found in the remainder of the continent.

TABLE 3

NUMBER OF WIVES TO ONE HUNDRED MARRIED MEN,
SUB-SAHARAN AFRICA BY CULTURE AREAS*

Area	N	Mean	Median	Mode	Range
Khoisan..................	4	*ca.* 130.0	....	....	104–154
East African Cattle........	19	124.5	129.0	138.0	107–168
Congo...................	29	159.9	154.0	142.2	129–211
Guinea Coast.............	37	153.7	158.0	166.6	131–234
Western Sudan...........	32	151.8	150.0	146.4	127–190
Sub-Saharan Africa†	131	153.7	151.5	147.1	107–234

* Dorjahn, *African Polygyny*, Table 98, p. 141.
† Includes some studies not incorporated in the computations for the individual culture areas.

The following conclusions may be drawn from this analysis of the quantitative data: (1) The mean incidence of polygyny varies, as measured by the percentage of all married men who are polygynous, from a low of about 25 per cent in the Khoisan and East African Cattle areas to a high of 43 per cent in the Guinea Coast area, with a sub-Saharan

African average of about 35 per cent. (2) Measured by the number of wives to 100 married men, the mean incidence of polygyny varies from a low of about 124 in the East African Cattle area to a high of about 160 in the Congo area, with a sub-Saharan African average of about 154. (3) The number of wives to 100 polygynously married men, the measure

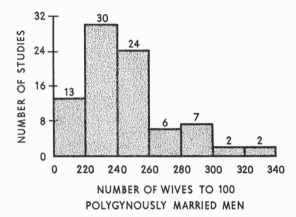

FIG. 6.   Frequency histogram of data of Table 4, sub-Saharan Africa

of the intensity of polygyny, varies from a low of about 215 in the Khoisan area to a high of about 257 in the Guinea Coast area, with an average of about 246 for sub-Saharan Africa. (4) Both the mean incidence and mean intensity of polygyny are higher in the Congo, Guinea

TABLE 4

NUMBER OF WIVES TO ONE HUNDRED POLYGYNOUSLY MARRIED MEN,
SUB-SAHARAN AFRICA BY CULTURE AREAS*

Area	N	Mean	Median	Mode	Range
Khoisan	4	214.0	. . . .	. . . .	201–232
East African Cattle	20	232.5	225.0	210.0	207–307
Congo	15	251.2	240.0	217.6	224–322
Guinea Coast	24	257.0	250.0	236.0	217–325
West Sudan	21	244.5	243.3	240.9	211–293
Sub-Saharan Africa	84	246.5	245.3	242.9	201–325

* Dorjahn, *African Polygny*, Table 100, p. 145.

Coast, and Western Sudan areas than in southern and eastern Africa. (5) In general, the data show that about 35 per cent of all married African males are polygynous, that this 35 per cent averages about 245 wives per 100 polygynously married men (or households), while the number of wives to 100 husbands, monogamously and polygynously married, is about 150.

The quantitative data thus indicate that for all sub-Saharan Africa *the mean number of wives per married man is 1.5 and that the ratio of married women to married men is 3 to 2*. This estimate will have to be re-evaluated in the future as definitive trends for increase or decrease in the incidence of polygyny emerge in the various subareas.

THE SOURCE OF SURPLUS WIVES

Given a polygynous system of marriage, it is evident that at any time there will be more married women than men, and wherever the practice is at all extensive, the problem of the origin of the surplus wives arises. To many writers the obvious explanation is a biologically determined female predominance in the sex ratio at birth, or at least among adults. Sonnabend outlines this position as follows:

The relationship between sex distribution and the extent of polygamy is of some importance. It is not an uncommon belief that an excess of female births is a *sine qua non* condition for this form of marriage. This idea is based on the fact that in certain polygamous communities, like that of the Bantu, a number of men have two or more wives, while there are very few men who remain unmarried.[47]

The following quotation from Monteil's monograph on the Khassonké is indicative of the point of view to which Sonnabend referred: "Il n'est pas sans intérêt de remarquer que, dans une société où le célibat les mâles est inexistant ... comme c'est la cas pour les Khassonké ... la poligamie ne saurait être et se maintenir que par la prédominance du nombre des femmes sur le nombre des hommes."[48] Therefore it is necessary to investigate the hypothesis that *polygyny is possible because there are more women than men in the various African territories*.[49] While it is desirable to study the purely genetically determined trend of the sex ratio, it is impossible to eliminate the influence of environmental factors, both natural and cultural. Fertility and mortality rates, both of vital importance, will vary considerably in response to local conditions. Furthermore, sex-selective migration can skew the sex ratio for local populations, as illustrated by the predominance of females in the "labor reservoir" areas compared to the male predominance in the urban areas of central and southern Africa. For sub-Saharan Africa as a whole, however, these irregularities in the resident populations cancel out, and sex-selective migration can be dismissed as a factor providing the surplus females required by a polygynous system. The same can be said for obtaining wives by raiding, enslaving, or buying children, all of which have been em-

[47] Enrico H. Sonnabend, "Demographic Samples in the Study of Backward and Primitive Populations," *South African Journal of Economics*, II (1934), 319.

[48] C. Monteil, *Les Khassonké* (Paris, 1915), p. 195.

[49] Dorjahn, *African Polygyny*, pp. 148–264.

ployed in various parts of Africa. The females gained by one group are, of course, lost to the other.

The data in Table 5, largely computed from official statistics, indicate a female predominance in most African territories and hence for sub-Saharan Africa as a whole. It should be stressed that any lengthening of the expectation of life through lowered mortality rates would increase this female predominance. What material exists on the sex ratio at birth

TABLE 5

Sex Ratios, the Number of Females per Hundred Males, of Total Populations of African Territories, by Regions, and for Various Years*

UNION OF SOUTH AFRICA, SOUTH-WEST AFRICA, AND THE HIGH COMMISSION TERRITORIES

Territory	1891	1904	1911	1921	1936	1946
Union[a]	....	101.0	98.7	97.2	98.0	95.9
South-West Africa[a]	....	....	....	....	105.4	104.9
Basutoland	107.6	113.0	120.1	123.1	134.3	127.8[a]
Bechuanaland	....	103.4	100.6	92.9	101.2	100.9[a]
Swaziland[b]	....	130	109	108	107	107

BRITISH CENTRAL AND EAST AFRICA

Territory	1911	1921	1926	1931	1945	1948
Southern Rhodesia[c]	....	....	....	....	....	101
Northern Rhodesia	....	118.8	....	123.1	....	....
Nyasaland	....	115.0	114.8	112.7	103.3	....
Tanganyika	....	103.9	....	106.8	....	106.4[d]
Kenya	....	....	....	105	....	102.6[e]
Uganda	121.2	116.8	....	108.1	....	100.0[f]

BELGIAN AND PORTUGUESE AFRICA

Territory	Year	Sex Ratio
Belgian Congo	1917 / 1929	100.2[g] / 103.6[h]
Congo Kasai	1929	108.0[h]
Equateur	....	108.4[h]
Orientale	....	95.8[h]
Katanga	....	109.8[h]
Bas-Congo	1933	107[i]
Ruanda-Urundi	1951	114.4[j]
Angola	1940	111.5[k]
Mozambique	1940	110.8[l]
Portuguese Guinea	1950	103[m]

FRENCH AFRICA

Territory	Year	Sex Ratio
French Equatorial Africa	1948	104[n]
French Cameroons	1926 / 1933	105.2[o] / 115[p]
French Togoland	1933 / 1934	99.7[q] / 101.3[q]

TABLE 5 (Continued)

BRITISH WEST AFRICA

Territory	1891	1901	1911	1921	1931	1948
Nigeria..............	....	....	117	106	110	....
Gold Coast.........	118	125	99	97	96	98[r]
Sierra Leone.......	....	....	136	141	108	....
Gambia............	....	....	....	....	90	....

* Dorjahn, *African Polygyny*, Table 196, p. 226. Since in many cases primary sources were unavailable, most sex ratios were computed from data in Kuczynski, *Demographic Survey*, Vol. I–II. Other sources of data used include the following:
 [a] Union of South Africa, *Population Census* (1949), pp. 1096–99, 1171.
 [b] Swaziland, *Swaziland Census* (1946).
 [c] Shaul and Myburgh, "Provisional Results," Appendix, Table 1.
 [d] Tanganyika, *African Population of Tanganyika Territory, 1948* (Nairobi, 1950), p. 1.
 [e] Kenya, *African Population of Kenya Colony and Protectorate, 1948* (Nairobi, 1950), p. 4.
 [f] Uganda, *African Population of Uganda Protectorate, 1948* (Nairobi, 1950), p. 3.
 [g] A. Rutten, "Démographie Congolaise," *Congo*, II, No. 2 (1921), 4.
 [h] P. Ryckmans, "Notes sur la Démographie Congolaise," *Bulletin de Séances de l'Institute Royal Coloniale Belge*, II, No. 2 (1931), 261–62.
 [i] G. Trolli, "Contribution a l'Étude de la Démographie des Bakongo," *Bulletin de Séances de l'Institute Royal Coloniale Belge*, V, No. 2 (1934), 303.
 [j] Neesen, "Quelques Données Démographiques," p. 1012.
 [k] Angola, *Censo geral da população* (Luanda, 1941–43), I, 3.
 [l] Mozambique, *Anuario estatístico*, 1950 (Lourenço Marques, 1952), pp. 22–23.
 [m] A. Carreira, "Guiné portuguesa: Censo da população não civilizada de 1950," *Boletim cultural da Guiné portuguesa*, VII, No. 28 (1952), 736.
 [n] *L'Encyclopédie Coloniale et Maritime* (1950), V, 101.
 [o] French Cameroons, *Rapport Annuel sur l'Administration sons Mandat des Territoires du Cameroun* (Paris, 1926), p. 49.
 [p] G. LeFrou, *Le Noir d'Afrique* (Paris: Payot, 1943), p. 307.
 [q] Kuczynski, *The Cameroons and Togoland*, p. 413.
 [r] Gold Coast, *Census of Population, 1948: Report and Tables* (London, 1950).

forces the conclusion that more males than females are born alive but that this difference may be less than is indicated by the extensive Euroamerican data. Far more data from Africa are needed, however, before conclusive proof can be given for any such difference, which to all indications would be small. The excess of males continues throughout childhood, judging from the scattered studies containing material on age and sex composition, and is transformed into an excess of females during adulthood as a direct result of a sex differential in mortality. It is impossible to determine at what age this reversal of the sex ratio occurs, primarily because adequate material on age- and sex-specific death rates is lacking. Probably the age at which females first predominate varies considerably in different parts of Africa in response to disease, nutrition, housing, sanitation, and occupational hazards. Male infanticide is not extensively practiced by any African population and may be dismissed as a mechanism producing a female surplus.

The sex-selective action in mortality, through wars, raids, and feuds, has been of minimal importance during the past few decades since the establishment of European administration. With a few exceptions there is also reason to doubt that such activities meant a decimation of the male population, since African patterns stressed the taking of captives as much or more than the slaughter of enemy warriors.[50] It must thus be assumed that the indicated higher male mortality at all ages except the childbearing years is brought about by their relative physiological and biological weakness and greater susceptibility to disease, compounded by the greater mortality risks entailed in such predominantly male economic occupations as industrial labor, plantation work, and mining. While hunting, house-building, canoeing, and cutting the upper limbs off trees may not always be dangerous, they are more often fatal than preparing food, hoeing gardens, and carrying produce. Moreover, labor recruitment may expose male workers to a combination of disease, poor nutrition, temporary shelter, unsanitary living conditions, and unfamiliar patterns of subsistence work.

Even a cursory comparison of the data on the sex ratio in Table 5 with those in Table 3 on the number of wives to one hundred husbands demonstrates that the "natural" surplus of females is by no means sufficient to account for the incidence of polygyny found in the various parts of Africa. It is thus necessary to reject the hypothesis that polygyny is possible because there are more women than men in the various African territories, though the data indicate that a part of the requisite surplus of women is provided by this biological mechanism.

It is evident that, in a population where the numbers of females and males of marriageable age are relatively equal, for every celibate male there is a surplus female available for a polygynous marriage. Each celibate female reduces the surplus by one; hence, the size of the surplus provided by differential rates of celibacy can be easily determined. We are justified in speaking of a female surplus, for though a female deficit is theoretically possible, the African data show that the number and percentage of celibate males exceeds the number and percentage of celibate females.[51] Once again, however, this mechanism is insufficient in itself to account for the surpluses of women necessitated by polygyny on the scale indicated in the literature (Table 3). It is not a fact, as laymen sometimes assume, that many men go through life unmarried so that a few can be polygynous.

The size of the female surplus in a given population is not measured by the sex ratio of adults defined in terms of age, as "fifteen to fifty," but rather by the "sex ratio" of those of marriageable age as this is defined by the cultures in question, for example, females aged fifteen to fifty to males aged twenty-four to fifty. Differences in the mean age of first marriage for males and females have been noted by many writers, though

[50] Harry H. Turney-High, *Primitive War* (New York: Columbia University Press, 1949), p. 30.

[51] Dorjahn, *African Polygyny*, Table 202, pp. 288–90; Table 203, pp. 292–93.

few have indicated an awareness that this produces a surplus of women of marriageable age.[52] Throughout Africa, as in Europe and America, women marry at an earlier age than men for a variety of reasons. The effect is that of excluding men in the younger age brackets from the pool of marriageable individuals while including the women in these same age brackets, say nineteen to twenty-four years where the mean ages of first marriage are nineteen for women and twenty-four for men. This factor alone can produce a surplus of women of marriageable age even where the sex ratio of the adult population shows a male predominance.

Thus the cultural mechanisms[53] of celibacy and the differential mean age of first marriage, which arbitrarily exclude certain persons of each sex from the pool of marriageable individuals, together with the mortality differentials considered above, are what make polygyny possible. Since this exclusion or inclusion is arbitrary, it will vary from population to population in accordance with the patterns of their cultures.

POLYGYNY AND FERTILITY

For most African groups polygyny is a method of providing more children per husband or per household, and what quantitative data exist substantiate this view. However, the final hypothesis to be considered, *that polygyny has a lowering effect on reproduction*, refers to fertility on a per wife basis and is thus more directly connected with the over-all picture of reproduction for any chiefdom, ethnic group, or country. Most writers, both official and unofficial, who take note of the relationship between polygyny and fertility agree that this practice results in fewer children born.[54] Thus Boelaert cites a statement by Ledent, who has studied the demographic problems of the Nkundo-Mongo peoples of the Belgian Congo for more than 10 years: "Les femmes des monogames sont toujours plus fécondes que les femmes de polygames, et, plus une population est prolifique, plus la fécondité des femmes de monogames l'emporte sur celle des femmes de polygames. Du point de vue de la natalité, la monogamie doit donc toujours être favorisée."[55] Gessain, the French demographer, is apparently strongly convinced of the effect of polygyny on reproduction when he states: "L'on peut se demander si les méthodes de la démographie entièrement basées sur l'hypothèse mono-

[52] Among those cognizant of this result of a differential mean age of first marriage were: George H. L. Pitt-Rivers, *The Clash of Culture and the Contact of Races* (London: G. Routledge, 1927), pp. 116 f.; Sonnabend, "Demographic Samples"; G. Gordon Brown and A. Bruce Hutt, *Anthropology in Action* (London: Oxford University Press, 1935); William R. Bascom, unpublished lectures, 1939.

[53] Dorjahn, *African Polygyny*, pp. 269–309.

[54] *Ibid.*, pp. 310–70.

[55] Boelaert, *La Situation Démographique*, p. 44. No reference is made to any specific publication of Ledent.

game pourraient s'appliquer à une société polygame."[56] On the other hand, Culwick and Culwick feel that polygyny, at least on a small scale where a man has two or three wives, has no effect on fertility:

A specimen count of the children of nearly 500 women, 237 who had always been monogamous and 235 who had always been polygamous belonging to the same places and age grades, gave a fertility rate of 2,300 per 1,000 for the former and 2,430 for the latter, a difference in favor of polygamy but far too small to be of statistical significance whatever. We therefore conclude that polygamy has no effect on the birth-rate.[57]

Primarily because of the difficulties in ascertaining age in African populations, a wide variety of ratios is found in African demographic studies. Pregnancies, all births, all live births, or the number of children living at the time of the investigation may be related to all wives, all fertile wives, or even all husbands. In some cases an attempt is made to limit either group in terms of "children who haven't reached maturity," "juveniles," "women thirty-five years and older," or even "old women." All of these are attempts to approximate the true fertility ratio (number of children zero to five years to the number of women fifteen to forty-four years), and while the differences inherent in the various measures render comparisons between different populations precarious, each is valid for comparisons between the monogamous and polygynous segments within a given population.

Of the twenty-three studies analyzed[58] previously, only five show the polygynously married women to have been as fertile or more fertile than the monogamously married segment. The published data thus indicate that the hypothesis is true and that polygyny does have a lowering effect on fertility. Unqualified confirmation, however, cannot be given on the basis of these fragmentary data, since this formulation of the question masks a number of important variables. It is possible that the fertility differentials indicated by the data may be the result of differences in divorce frequency, sterility, age differentials between spouses, or abstinence rather than the coitus rate differential (per wife per year) which logically follows from the rotational system for wives in polygynous households.

Fertility, measured per woman over a given period of years, decreases as family instability increases; hence any tendency for divorce to be more frequent in the polygynously married segment of a given population than in the monogamously married segment would create a fertility differential to the detriment of the former and the population as a whole. Un-

[56] Robert Gessain, "Anthropologie et Démographie," *Population*, III (July, 1948), 493.

[57] Culwick and Culwick, "Study of Population," p. 379.

[58] Dorjahn, *African Polygyny*, Table 229, p. 368.

fortunately, quantitative data are lacking, though Boelaert[59] and others state that polygynous unions are less stable.

Another possible source of difference is the question of whether or not the monogamous and polygynous segments have comparable sterility rates. The ethnographic data suggest the presence of at least two factors in many African groups: a tendency to take a second wife if the first proves to be infertile, and more frequent extra-marital intercourse in polygynous households—hence an increasing probability of contracting venereal disease which soon spreads throughout the household, bringing at least partial sterility.[60] Isolated statistical studies[61] seem to indicate that polygynously married women as a group have a higher percentage of sterility, and statements by medical officers[62] also express this belief; yet confirmation must be withheld, as in the case of divorce, since there is no indication that the two segments are comparable in age composition and in duration of marriage. That they may not be comparable is suggested by the tendency in many areas for older and wealthier polygynous males to marry young women; younger and poorer men are then forced to marry older women or widows who can be obtained for less bride-wealth. Fertility is relative and shades off with the biological process of aging; therefore, any tendency to link younger, more fertile women with older, less fertile men, and vice versa, will lower the fertility of the group as a whole.

Widespread patterns of abstinence from a woman for a more or less extended period of time after she has given birth are found in many African areas. As an ideal, this is equally important for the monogamously and polygynously married, but there is some evidence that monogamous couples more often fall short of this ideal. Talbot and Herskovits, to name but two, have stressed this difference in behavior with respect to the ideal.[63] Carr-Saunders expresses no doubt as to the operation of the factor of abstinence in lowering fertility:

> The relatively low birth rate [i.e., of tropical Africa] is due to the maintenance of an ancient custom which keeps the family small . . . the custom of abstaining

[59] Boelaert, *La Situation Démographique*, p. 41.

[60] A contrary tendency, indicated below in relation to abstinence, is that monogamous males seek sexual satisfaction with prostitutes while the abstinence prohibition bars relations with the wife after childbirth, thus increasing their chances of contracting a venereal disease and so reducing the over-all fertility of the monogamous segment. No estimation of the net effect of these two tendencies can be attempted at present.

[61] G. Olivier and L. Aujoulat, "L'Obstétrique en Pays Yaoundé," *Études Camerounaises*, XII (December, 1945), 38.

[62] Sierra Leone, *Report of the Census for the Year 1931* (Freetown: Government Printer, 1931), p. 12.

[63] P. Amaury Talbot, *The Peoples of Southern Nigeria* (London: Oxford University Press, 1926), Table 13, pp. 378–87. Melville J. Herskovits, *Dahomey* (New York: Augustin, 1938), I, 268.

from intercourse until the child has been weaned, and weaning may be postponed for a long time. The length of time differs from tribe to tribe, but the practice does effectively keep the successive children spaced out and makes large families of living children impossible. Increased child mortality might up to a point be compensated for by an increased birth-rate; for intercourse would be resumed on the death of a child.[64]

The practice of abstinence also operates to offset the differentials in coitus rates between monogamously and polygynously married women, since it permits the polygynous male to drop pregnant and nursing wives from the rotational cycle. There is also a possible connection with sterility, in that when the wife of a monogamist is pregnant or nursing, the husband tends to seek sexual gratification elsewhere, especially if the sanctions of the abstinence taboo are strong. In recent times at least, these husbands risk contracting venereal disease through relations with prostitutes.

It may be concluded that polygyny and the sociobiological complications it brings seem to have a lowering effect on fertility, but no reliable estimation of the size of this apparent reduction in fertility can be made on the basis of the available quantitative data.

Definitive, problem-oriented research is clearly needed to assess the roles which traditional African demographic patterns such as polygyny are playing in the population dynamics of sub-Saharan Africa today. The necessity for collecting both quantitative data and the ethnographic material which provides the setting for such statistics and gives meaning to them must be systematically stressed. What is needed is an approach which uses the methods and theory of both demography and anthropology—what might be called, for lack of a better name, ethnodemography. A significant pioneer attempt has been made by Monique de Lestrange,[65] who has championed a "sociodemographic" method. Further research is required, however, to ascertain the feasibility of age calendars, for example, and to determine the contribution to be made by anthropological field methods. The development of such a method should immeasurably help to overcome some of the obstacles and so to provide more valid data upon which to determine the demographic position of sub-Saharan Africa.

[64] A. M. Carr-Saunders, *World Population* (Oxford: Clarendon Press, 1936), pp. 302–3.

[65] Monique de Lestrange, "Pour une Méthode Socio-Démographique," *Journal de la Société des Africanistes*, XXI (1951), 97–109.

6. Ethnohistory in the Study
of Culture Change in Southeast Africa

Southeast Africa affords a rich body of historical data, only partially exploited, in the records left by early Portuguese explorers of the African
coasts. These include the writings of priests, traders, navigators, and
government officials dating from the end of the fifteenth century. The
quality and time depth of these documents vary for the different sections
of Africa. In some places little or nothing is known of the African societies before the arrival of European colonists in the past century, but in
areas where the Portuguese attempted early alliances and subsequent
occupation, historical documentation is available. This is particularly
true of the area now known as Mozambique, as well as the British and
South African territories immediately adjacent to it.

Among the southeast African Bantu sufficient historical data can be
consulted to trace the history of culture change for some societies from
the fifteenth to the twentieth century, and its use should correct much of
the conjectural reconstruction of African history and ethnography which
has been based upon surmise rather than fact.

Neglect of the historical evidence from this area has numerous examples, even among scholars who have known its existence. Posselt, in discussing the disputed "Kingdom of Monomotapa," which sixteenth-century Portuguese visitors had described as Karanga, dismisses their
writings. He denies the possibility of the Karanga branch of the Shona
having dominated the scene, and on the basis of sources which he does
not name, claims that "all the Native evidence shows that the Barozwi
were the rulers until their overthrow by the Swazi in 1830."[1] While little
is known of the Rozwi Shona, in either historical or contemporary studies, the sixteenth-century records and subsequent writings of the Portuguese, as well as the traditions of the Lovedu in Transvaal and the
Gwambe and Makwakwe in Mozambique, frequently refer to the Karanga, who are known as an old and continuing Shona people. Modern

[1] F. W. T. Posselt, *A Survey of the Native Tribes in Southern Rhodesia* (Salisbury:
Southern Rhodesia Government, 1927), p. 9.

African traditions and historical records alike associate the Karanga and Monomotapa. In this conjecture Posselt merely follows a tradition of disbelief, for many writers, including Theal, have contended that there never was a kingdom such as Monomotapa save in the minds of the Portuguese.[2]

Caton-Thompson repeats a point of view common in South African literature. "No unaided native mind, pure negro or Bantu, devised the use of metal alloys," she writes, in spite of finding bronze in the rock structures of Southern Rhodesia which she says were built by Bantu workers. Although she says that the Bantu of this region have no capacity "to think for themselves," she considers them to have been the builders of the Zimbabwe stone fortresses, terraces, temples, and other structures, explaining their decadence as due to the successive waves of "migratory Bantu Hordes." The modern observer finds it difficult to fathom how a segment of the migratory Bantu found time to stop long enough to erect the architecturally well-planned and ruggedly constructed rock buildings which Africans and Europeans generally concede must have taken many people many ages to build even in peace, as Caton-Thompson suggests, yet inspired by some unknown danger, "wild beasts, wilder Bushmen," or other.[3] An acceptable solution to this Zimbabwe riddle must depend upon careful study of the pertinent documents of the sixteenth century as well as archeological data and the survey of relevant traditions of Bantu whose ancestors migrated from this area uniquely known for its use of rock buildings.

Theal, a renowned South African historian, not only attributed the Karanga and Monomotapa to Portuguese imagination but also treated as fraudulent the cartographical reports of the early explorers. Like others he reacted against the glowing accounts which the Portuguese carried to Europe. Nevertheless, Theal published these reports among other writings of European explorers in a nine-volume work, *Records of South Eastern Africa*, which is of inestimable worth to the ethnohistorian interested in southeast Africa.[4]

Among these records are sixteenth-century accounts of shipwrecked sailors, providing ethnographic descriptions of the coastal peoples. Ac-

[2] George McCall Theal, *Records of South Eastern Africa* (9 vols.; Capetown: Cape Colony Government, 1898–1902), II, 9.

[3] G. Caton-Thompson, *The Zimbabwe Culture Ruins and Reactions* (Oxford: Clarendon Press, 1931), *passim*.

[4] Theal, in *Records of South Eastern Africa*, published reports of Portuguese, French, German, English, and Dutch nationals who recorded their experiences and reactions on the southeast African coast. These appear in the languages in which they were originally written, usually with English translations. In spite of copyists' errors, some debatable translation, and a lack of critical precision, this work provides Africanists with a starting place for ethnohistorical research to which European and South African scholars have been much indebted.

counts of the material culture of the peoples in Pondoland, Zululand, Swaziland, and the plains from Delagoa Bay northward to the Zambezi make these reports significant to an ethnohistorical approach to the cultures represented in this area.

The elder Junod called attention to these records and treated their relevance to the study of the Thonga peoples about Delagoa Bay.[5] Later, his son indicated that these materials and other historical documentation demonstrated the continuity of cultural development among peoples inland from Beira and points farther north.[6] He added to the sources mentioned by his father other early Portuguese references to the inhabitants of Mozambique and neighboring territories.

In the eighteenth century Gomes de Brito gathered the original chronicles of shipwrecks, describing the contacts of the sixteenth-century survivors with indigenous peoples from Natal to northern Mozambique.[7] In 1609 Friar João dos Santos described the people of this country as he himself observed them or as he had heard about them from contemporary explorers.[8] Both these works were reissued at the turn of the present century, and Paiva e Pona published a collection of writings describing the missionary efforts of Portuguese priests among the tribes of the Monomotapa federation or kingdom about the same time.[9]

Later Portuguese historians, including Botelho, Montez, Alberto, and Toscano, have used these and other materials, and their writings provide a working index to many of the sources which the ethnohistorian may investigate for himself. Fr. Luiz Feliciano dos Santos, a Portuguese priest, used these records of earlier centuries. In spite of an obvious antipathy for Junod and a disdain for other students of the Bantu language and culture in Mozambique, he has used their findings to prove his theory of the Shona origin of the Chopi peoples.[10]

Axelson, combining the interests of historian and archeologist, searched the records in Portuguese archives in studying the early history of Southern Rhodesia and the movements of Bartholomew Dias, who doubled the Cape of Good Hope in 1488. Through these reports he was able to identify the location of the Dias beacon on False Island, ending the dispute as to its existence and the authenticity of the various chron-

[5] Henri Alexander Junod, "The Conditions of the Natives of South Africa in the 16th Century: Report to the South African Association for the Advancement of Science," *South African Journal of Science*, Vol. X, No. 6 (February, 1914).

[6] Henri Philippe Junod, *Os indígenas de Moçambique no século XVI e começo do XVII* (Lourenço Marques: Imprensa Nacional, 1939).

[7] Bernardo Gomes de Brito, *História trágico-marítima* (Lisbon, 1904–5).

[8] Fr. João dos Santos, *Ethiopia oriental*, ed. Luciano Cordeiro (Lisbon, 1891).

[9] A. de Paiva e Pona, *Dos primeiros trabalhos dos Portugueses no Monomotapa* (Lisbon: Sociedade de Geografia de Lisboa, 1892).

[10] Fr. Luiz Feliciano dos Santos, O.F.M., *Gramática da língua Chope* (Lourenço Marques: Imprensa Nacional, 1941), Introduction, pp. 9–20.

icles referring to it. Of special importance to the historian and the ethnohistorian are Axelson's annotated bibliography and report on the archives and libraries containing primary sources significant in the study
of peoples in southeast Africa.[11]

During his investigations Axelson discovered the hitherto unnoticed
report of António Fernandes, a confidential agent for the king of Portugal between the years 1514 and 1517, which had been kept secret by the
Portuguese monarchy. This document, describing ethnic groups in central Mozambique, Southern Rhodesia, and Nyasaland, provided new
knowledge of the people composing the kingdom of Monomotapa early
in the sixteenth century.[12] It confirms both earlier and later reports from
this area and conforms largely to the present-day knowledge of the geography and ethnography of the area.

Through minute attention to detail the Junods located the Tembe,
Nyaka, Mabota, Manhica, Inhampula, Gwambe, Panda, Tonga, and
Zavara, not to mention peoples north of Inhambene. That these people
occupy approximately the same countries that those bearing their tribal
names inhabited four centuries ago is sufficient evidence to challenge the
opinion expressed by Theal: "It would serve no useful purpose to give the
names of the tribes about Delagoa Bay and northward as placed on record by the Portuguese writers, for even if those names were accurate at
the time, the communities that bore them have long ceased to exist, and
never did anything to merit a place in history."[13] Not only do these people occupy the same areas, but they also are found to possess most of the
features described by the early observers.

The younger Junod suggests six conclusions based on the ethnohistorical study of the broad area covered by his research:

1. Tribal and geographical names are much the same now as they were in the
   sixteenth century, and the distribution constant.
2. The people of Mozambique have retained essentially the same basic
   language over the past four centuries.
3. The techniques of manufacture and use of the marimba, finger harp, horn

[11] Eric V. Axelson, "Discovery of the Farthest Pillar Erected by Bartholomeu
Dias," *South African Journal of Science*, **XXXV** (1939), 417–29; "Finding of a
Bartholomeu Dias Beacon," *South African Geographical Journal*, XXI (1939),
184–297; *South-east Africa, 1488–1530* (London: Longmans, Green, 1940), pp. 184–
297.

[12] Hugh Tracey, *António Fernandes: Descóbridor do Monomotapa, 1514–1615*
(Lourenço Marques: Imprensa Nacional, 1940). Articles on this material discovered
by Axelson and critically reviewed include: W. A. Godlonton, "The Journeys of
António Fernandes," in *Proceedings and Transactions of the Rhodesia Scientific
Association* (Salisbury, 1945), Vol. XL; J. F. Schofield, "The Journeys of Antonio
Fernandes," in *Proceedings and Transactions of the Rhodesia Scientific Association*
(Salisbury, 1949), XLII, 84–95.

[13] Theal, *South Eastern Africa*, II, xxxl. The same opinion is expressed by the
British Naval Intelligence in *Manual of Portuguese East Africa* (London, 1920), p. 98.

trumpet, hemp smoking equipment, and other details of material culture are distributed much the same now as they were in the sixteenth century.
4. Agricultural products have undergone little change, and farming methods appear to be the same as earlier.
5. Little change in social organization is to be noted.
6. Religious beliefs and practices as described in the sixteenth and seventeenth centuries are typical of the modern native living in the traditional way.[14]

The persistence of culture is indicated by the similarity of twentieth-century traditions of origin and the sixteenth-century reports of alleged tribal migrations, and of modern genealogies and the records of actual chiefs. For example, the followers of Gamba were reported to have migrated before 1560 to the land of the Tonga, where they lived across the river from the descendants of Panda, a situation which in mid-twentieth-century traditions would be reported thus: Gamba came from the land of Tobele and Mujaji (northern Transvaal) and dispossessed the Tonga, who moved eastward; the country of the Gwambe is separated from that of the Panda people by the Inhassune River. The houses peculiar to the Zulu, Thonga, and Tonga peoples were described in the sixteenth century with the same characteristics which distinguish one from the other now. The ways in which the Africans at Delagoa Bay fortified their villages, hunted, traded, married, treated their sick, and buried their dead have remained constant for more than four centuries. They eat the same kind of seed cakes, wear the same dress at military dances, follow the same pattern of symbolic dancing, live by the same type of social organization, and practice the same economy that characterized their different groups when the Portuguese first encountered them. Distinctive tools, musical instruments, and diet continue with the ethnic successors to peoples who displayed different tastes and habits four hundred years ago.

These facts contradict the oft-repeated South African assertion that the Bantu entered this part of the continent after the Europeans had discovered and occupied it. The concept, popular among the Europeans in South Africa, has been perpetuated despite the evidence compiled by Junod from the early records. It continues to describe the Bantu as savage marauders and never-resting nomads from the north who came into a country almost devoid of culture.

The Junod studies and conclusions concerned the peoples in the region from Natal northward to the Zambezi. The Gwambe, one group of the peoples mentioned, are examined here to illustrate the validity of Junod's conclusions and the applicability of the ethnohistorical method to the study of a restricted cultural unit.

The Gwambe live some ninety miles southwest of Inhambane, north of

[14] Junod, *Os indígenas de Moçambique*, pp. 81–88.

the Inharrime and east of the Inhassune River. They trace their legendary ancestry to Gamba, a chief described in the letters of two Portuguese priests who wrote of baptizing Gamba and his family in 1560 during a two-year missionary occupation of the Gwambe capital. Their present habitation, in relation to rivers, neighboring peoples, and other documentable data, remains relatively unchanged in four centuries.[15]

Three periods in Gwambe history have been analyzed, the first two on the basis of historical documents and the last on the basis of anthropological field work.[16] Historical records provide background material from the first entry of the Portuguese late in the fifteenth century to the present. The records of explorers, traders, officials, priests, and settlers were searched for descriptions of customs and material culture to be compared with contemporary data. This body of material offered leads for further ethnographic investigation in the field and was used to check contemporary verbal traditions about persons, places, and events.

The first period, in the sixteenth century, followed the migration of the Gwambe from the Karanga highlands to the coastal plains of Mozambique. Gwambe culture was modified so that their customary way of life might be pursued with accommodation to their new land, Wutonga, after leaving their mountain home.

The second period, at the end of the nineteenth century, followed three and a half centuries of occupation of Wutonga, during which there were relatively constant but evolving relationships with other Bantu groups and occasional brief, voluntary trade arrangements with Europeans at the ports. Change was limited to linguistic accommodation, selective borrowing and reinterpretation of artifacts and technology of neighboring cultures, and shifting economy dependent upon the changing conditions of commerce. This period serves mainly to help in determining when change occurred and to confirm the stability of cultural elements which remained unchanged.

The third period, the first half of the twentieth century, follows sixty years of Portuguese political control, European missionary education, and modern industrial participation. It represents the most marked changes in the conditions under which the Gwambe lived, including the depletion of natural resources, mass labor migrations to the Transvaal, substitution of colonial rule for indigenous autonomy, universal acceptance of a cash economy, indentured labor, controlled agriculture, taxation, and participation in alien religious, educational, industrial, recreational, and medical activities. It has been marked by the efforts of the

[15] Charles Edward Fuller, "An Ethnohistoric Study of Continuity and Change in Gwambe Culture," (Ph.D. dissertation, Department of Anthropology, Northwestern University, 1950), pp. 6–20.

[16] *Ibid.*, pp. 145–205.

Gwambe to maintain continuity in their way of life in a changing historical situation.[17]

The approach taken here will be to discuss first the Gwambe culture as it is presented to the contemporary observer by its people and then as it was described in the sixteenth century. The use of the ethnohistorical method in this investigation illustrates its applicability to the study of cultural continuity and change.

THE CONTEMPORARY PERIOD

Two Gwambe tribes and the Nkumbi occupy a country known as Wutonga or Wunzonge,[18] which lies between 24° and 24° 30' south and 34° and 35° east. Great Gwambe, ruled by a chief named Jacob, is domiciled in the western third, along the Inhassune River; Small Gwambe, whose chief is Joseph, inhabits the central section; and the Nkumbi live in the eastern region, from which their chief, Jubane, rules has Paramount over the entire area. Though the Portuguese discovered the country in the sixteenth century, they began effective rule only about 1890. The Gwambe do not accept the European view that they live in Chopi country. Wuchopi, they say, is south of the Inhassune-Inharrime river valley; Wupanda, the country of the Panda, is west of the Inhassune River; and the lands of the Tswa and Hlengwe are clearly stated to be to the north. Claiming Wutonga as their own land, they do not admit its relationship to the Tonga people, whom they call "Makhoka." The Nkumbi are the latest arrivals in Wutonga; the Chopi probably entered the southland in extended waves of migration, but the Gwambe and all the other peoples mentioned have occupied their present lands since the sixteenth century or earlier.

The Gwambe share many traits of culture with the Chopi. They make the marimba (*timbila*), manufacture bark cloth, and carve various vessels of wood like their southern neighbors. Like them, they use the bow and arrow, until recently not used by other inhabitants of southeast Africa. Many Chopi women have married into the local families, introducing their own peculiarities of speech among the Gwambe, who call their own language "Nzonge." Their religious customs, largely centered in ancestor worship but involving spirit possession, are much like those of nearby tribes.

[17] *Ibid.*, pp. 206–52.
[18] The land described as Wutonga or Wunzonge is known by many variants of these names, according to the dialect used. "Otongwe" and "Nzongwe" are commonly heard. The sixteenth-century priests from Portugal recorded their impression of the name as "Tongue," which in their orthography was probably the equivalent of "Tonga," the value of the final vowel being relatively high. The prefix *wu-* or its alternate, *o-*, before the name of an ethnic group denotes its use to describe the country of that society. However, now, as in 1560, the Tonga people do not occupy the country known by their name.

There are marked differences, however, between the Gwambe and their neighbors. Their pride in industry, cleanliness, strong and neat buildings, agricultural success, and good grooming leads them to look disdainfully upon the Khoka and Chopi. They eagerly point out differences between their language, Nzonge, and ShiChopi and Gitonga (of the Chopi and Khoka peoples). While some use Chopi dugouts and boats, they obtain them by purchase or rental. The Gwambe, unlike the Chopi, would not leave a meal or a discussion of genealogies or politics at the sound of a marimba orchestra; and unlike the Khoka, they do not eat fish, although edible fish are plentiful in their rivers. While they do fine agricultural work, they do not share the enthusiasm of the Nkumbi and others immediately northeast for the culture of fruit trees.

Their discussions are frequently preoccupied with sex, and ritual intercourse is important in almost every crisis faced by clan or family. The initiation of a girl is painful; the initiate is forced to dance while inserting a wooden doll in her vagina, and she climaxes the ceremony by having relations with a man designated by her sponsor. Her experience is called *Shikundla na Mwari*, which means "Rendezvous with Mwari." Mwari, appearing with Mujaji in most Gwambe genealogies, is no more than an ancestral name to them, though the Shona peoples worship Mwari as a high god to whom they dedicate similar sexual rituals.[19]

Boys among the Gwambe and Nkumbi are circumcised at puberty. Like their neighbors, they look upon the accompanying songs and dances more as games than as ritual. Nevertheless, women and girls have customarily been barred from the circumcision camp and are subject to rigid taboos at home. It is strange, then, that in 1946 a Christian African nurse was able to persuade the chiefs in Nzonge to permit her to perform all the circumcisions with modern implements and medicines and to teach the boys songs with a Christian motif. One wonders how fully male circumcision was assimilated by the Gwambe and Nkumbi as an indigenous rite. The elders are divided in their opinion, but many say that their ancestors did not practice the rite. Among them it has had not the educational social emphasis found elsewhere but a stress on sex per se, which has been modified by the influence of Christians.

Traditions of the Gwambe mention many cultural changes. The great famine in which thousands died late in the last century led people to eat foods they had formerly avoided, including pork. Tales about former days describe the woman grinding corn and cassava with stones, while the present-day woman uses a wooden mortar and pestle.

Genealogies and oral history point to the west as the origin of the Gwambe, some of the elders claiming that their ancestors came from the Vesha (i.e., Venda) in northern Transvaal. A few stress the Mujaji and

[19] Fuller, "Ethnohistoric Study," pp. 128 ff.

Mwari or Muhari elements of their genealogical tables, indicating that these belong to their ancient history. They do not, oddly enough, connect Mujaji in their ancestral line with the neighboring Khoka (Gitonga) word *mujaji*, meaning "rain," nor with Mujaji, the Rain Queen of the Lovedu. Neither do they admit understanding a relationship between the ancestor Muhari and the name found in the women's initiation rite. The acuteness of their traditions makes them speak with intimacy of persons too far removed to have been known even by the oldest among them, and though their genealogies would clearly indicate the passing of centuries, their historians narrate events which happened to their remote ancestors as though from the viewpoint of eyewitnesses. It is little wonder that investigators have sometimes gained the impression that the migration from the land of the Vesha and Karanga took place in the last generation.

The Gwambe play a game common to the entire area occupied by Chopi, Khoka, Tswa, and Northern Shangaan. The children choose one or more persons to be "it." Then they gather about "it" and begin a chant: "Where, oh, where is Gwambe?" Suddenly, to the apparent surprise of "it," all the other children run off into the woods, crying, "Gwambe's children are scattered everywhere." This game is a favorite of the Mukhambi people, usually termed "Tswa" and most commonly speaking the Tswa language. "Khambi" differs but little from Gambi, a variant of Gwambe. The Mukhambi historians likewise claim Vesha as their traditional home, and the location of seven widely distributed habitations called "Mukhambi" suggests a circuitous river valley route from the northern Limpopo River south to Wuchopi, thence northeast past Wutonga into the country of the Tswa north of Inhambane and Massinga. Everywhere these people settled, they chose a live spring of water in a location with rock outcroppings, leaving the vast sandy areas to others and avoiding the sea. Like the Gwambe, they never became fishers. Where the climate permits, they have fine herds of cattle.

In viewing Gwambe tradition, it is necessary to exerpt a few essential details from scores of genealogies. From a council of subchiefs sitting with Jacob, the chief of Great Gwambe, a complete family tree was derived from the important genealogies. These were reviewed and tested, and the lines of thirty-one adult males were traced back to common ancestry.

The chief of Great Gwambe, now in his late nineties, is the son of Nyasanani. He survived eleven brothers who died without succeeding to the chieftainship successively held by three of his eldest brothers. Nyasanani had never been chief, being the fourth son of Chief Matane; the second son, Chief Kohunu, survived his younger brother by a few days, passing the chieftainship through six brothers and cousins before it returned to the eldest son of Nyasanani. By the most conservative estimate, Chief Kohunu was reigning at least before 1860, and probably more than ten years earlier. It was in this period that the rebellions fostered by Maeueua and Muzila, sons of Manicusse, drew Portuguese troops into the center of Gwambe territory, where they later established a military post named "Cogunu" in honor of Kohunu. Matane, the father of Kohunu, probably reigned between 1820 and 1850. The lines converge here, and most Gwambe genealogies agree in tracing their descent from Matane, through Nyapilo, Naynunge, Gamba, Tobele, Mujaji, and Muhari. The last six names are constant, though their order varies.

Parallel genealogies derived from the families of Small Gwambe, with a separate chieftainship, go back to the same series through Lishuke, apparently a brother of Matane. Gumundu Zavala, a so-called Chopi chief of the Zavala area, traces his lineage back to Zavala, whom he calls the grandson of Tsuvawura, son of Gamba. Tradition thus injects at least two generations between Zavala and Gamba.

An independent body of tradition maintained among the Guilundu of Shilundweni suggests that the Gwambe line is abbreviated. A well-established lineage leads to Tanya, who, battling with the decendents of Zavala about 1840, called upon Portuguese soldiers from Inhambane to help him in his war. The clearly defined line of Tanya runs back over at least nine remembered generations to Shilundu, the ancestor who, according to oral history, left Nkosa, a country to the west, and took up residence at the seacoast. Shilundu must have lived well before the eighteenth century, for the country already was known by his name before 1708, when De L'Isle published a map with the name "Querunde" where tradition says Shilundu reigned.[20] The middens of an old kraal in which Shilundu is said by his descendents to be buried were traced by information provided by Guilundu historians, the site being that indicated on maps of 1708 and 1720 as Querunde.[21] Guilundu, Gwambe, and Zavala traditions link Shilundu with Gamba.

THE SIXTEENTH CENTURY

Within this area no tradition mentions any contact with Europeans except in reference to warfare of the past century. However, Portuguese sources document a sixteenth-century contact of significance. In 1559 a Portuguese priest at Mozambique baptized a youth who claimed he was the son of King Gamba from Inhambane. The following February a Jesuit, Fr. Gonçalo da Silveira, agreed to go to the boy's home to try to convert his father and his court. For the next two years he and his assistants, Fr. André Fernandes and Fr. Andrade da Costa worked for the

[20] G. de L'Isle, in Tracey, *António Fernandes*, p. 74.
[21] Tracey, *António Fernandes*, pp. 74–78.

conversion of Gamba's people. The letters of these missionaries are full of ethnographic notes about the Gwambe and their Tonga neighbors.

Missionaries soon learned that Gamba was the chief not of Inhambane but of a country they called "Tongue" (Wutonga), ninety miles inland from the port of Inhambane. The geographical description makes it clear that the capital was not far from the junction of the Inharrime and the Inhassume rivers. Along one route to this place there were many fat cattle in a valley which was probably the Inhanombe, the "River of Cattle." En route they passed areas where citrus fruit was abundant and whence it was frequently brought to sell to the missionaries at Tongue, which had little fruit or agricultural products except beans and ground nuts. Tongue was apparently near what is now called "Cogunu," and the agriculturally fruitful neighboring land was that occupied by northern Thonga between Tongue and Inhambane. These circumstances continue to the present except for changes brought about by European occupation.

Descriptions of the people likewise are applicable in the present. The people occupying Tongue were called the people of Gamba, who were said to have come from Mocaranga, located in what is now northern Transvaal and Southern Rhodesia. It has already been noted that the Gwambe now call their country "Wutonga" or "Wunzonge" and that they and the Makumbi call their common language "Nzonge." The priests were intrigued by the fact that the country of these Karanga Shona people, under Gamba, called their country "Tongue," while the Botonga were a different people, living between Tongue and Inhambane. The Tonga (i.e., Khoka) group inhabits the area east of Tongue today, a confusing fact to moderns. Father Gonçalo, writing of Inhambane inhabitants, says: "These are Botongas, and those of Tongue Mocarangas, so that *sine baculo transivimos Joranem et ecce cum cuabus turmis regredimus.*"[22]

In these early descriptions the Gwambe are said to have come from the west, leaving the country of the Karanga Shona because of a dispute in the royal family. They had taken over the country from the Tonga. The missionaries said that the Gwambe were cleaner, more industrious, and in many ways superior to their "Botonga" neighbors. They liked beef, but they had to buy cattle from the neighboring tribes. Their sons were not circumcised as were the "Bongas" or "Botongas" who made up a large percentage of the coastal population. Peaceful except when drunk, they drank considerably although they claimed to be more sober than most people in the land. Their drinks were either a liquor of cashew fruit or of *kanye* nuts or a milder brew of grain, much the same as at present. The *empombe*, a drinking bout, is a term still known among the Gwambe.

[22] Theal, *South Eastern Africa*, II, 87, 93.

These descriptions are as readily applied to the Gwambe in the mid-twentieth century as when written four hundred years ago.

The Gwambe, according to these missionaries, lived near great supplies of fish but did not bother to catch or to eat them. They seemed not at all interested in utilizing the rivers along which they lived, unlike the Tonga neighbors whose economy was linked with fishing. Four centuries have not changed this situation, in spite of the fact that neighbors on all sides, and the Chopi wives of the Gwambe, purchase dried fish and shrimp peddled by the Tonga or Chopi from the coast. Their love for the darker forest spots for residence was noted then and still persists. The way in which women worked in the fields more than men is little changed. Then as now, anyone could persuade a group of men to go out with their dogs and weapons to hunt. The elephant trap, methods of killing hippopotamus, buffalo, and other game, motions and dress of men in war dances, divination procedure, cures for diseases, diet, funeral customs, and judgment by ordeal were all described in terms familiar to one acquainted with Gwambe life in the present century.[23]

Certain customs related to sex and marriage, although misunderstood by the missionaries, are sufficiently indicated to demonstrate their similarity to modern ways of the Gwambe. The widow of a man is still "inherited" by his nephew, and an unsatisfactory spouse is returned by her husband to her parents, with an appropriate rebate of bride-wealth or the substitution of another wife. Other patterns which persist include polygyny among the elite, negotiations pertaining to the unfaithfulness of a wife, and the removal of ritual uncleanness of death or infidelity by sexual rite. Shocked to the point of mentioning his inability to describe some "unspeakably vulgar customs," the priest indicated that at the time of sickness, death, or crisis the Gwambe used a rite "too ugly to describe" in order to cleanse away the dangerous and infectuous uncleanness.[24] To hear a modern Gwambe tribesman describe ritual intercourse, the collection of the semen, and its mixture into a medicine with which to anoint the big toe of every villager in order to ward off evil could well explain the timidity of the missionary writing to his fellow priests.

When the sixteenth-century Portuguese said that oaths were made by blowing on the face of the person to whom a pledge was made, he apparently referred to the ritual by which a Gwambe, making an oath in the traditional way, tosses a bit of sand into the air and blows the sand toward the person to whom he is speaking.

A description of the bark cloth and its method of manufacture as well as the mode of its use as clothing fits perfectly the procedure followed

[23] *Ibid.*, II, 58–98. Cf. Fuller, "Ethnohistoric Study," pp. 83–86.
[24] Junod, *Os indígenas de Moçambique*, pp. 15 ff. Cf. Fuller, "Ethnohistoric Study," pp. 57, 69 ff.

among the Tonga and some Gwambe until the first part of this century. The manufacture and use of the marimba (*timbila*) by Gwambe and Chopi men remain unchanged. Their extreme love of music is noted, and among the Gwambe and Chopi the prestige attached to the *timbila* is unrivaled.

Early Portuguese missionaries recorded two songs and their interpretation. Neither is understandable in the language of Tonga, Tswa, or Chopi, but Gwambe's memory of Shona words, such as *gombe* (cow), *fuka* (to fall), *ambuze* (goat), *c(h)apana* (to be absent), and *virato* (sandal), indicates not only applicability to the Gwambe but also some affinity for the Karanga dialect of the Shona language. Such terms as *milandos*, meaning "civil disputes," *motro* for the "poison ordeal," "mouth" for the bribe paid the chief and his council to hear a quarrel, *muzimo* for the "spirit of an ancestor," *songos* (ŋanga) for the "diviners of witches," and other words recorded by the priests are not strange to the Gwambe listener, who interprets them as they were reported in the letters written between 1560 and 1562.[25]

In 1589 Diago do Couto, writing the record of the wreck of the "S. Thomé," narrated the account of the survivors' journey up the coast. Naming chiefs of the Delagoa Bay area that are familiar now—Nyaka, Manhica, and others—he mentions Inhampula, near the country of Zavala, located where the descendents of the Inhampula people live now. The Inhampula chief suggested a route that led the company overland to a great river to the north which the survivors said was "the size of the River of *Ouro*, which is at the latitude of 24-1/2°, and which divides the kingdoms of Panda and Gambe." Do Couto says that, "passing to the other side, they went to the city of this king Gambe, who would be a league and a half from the river."[26]

The capital of Great Gwambe today is situated across the Inhassune River from the kingdom of Panda. In 1952 informants at Inhampula advised that to reach Inhambane without using the modern European road and ferries, one should travel by a northerly route, where no hills or rivers need be traversed, coming to the junction of the Inharrime and Inhassune rivers. There one would cross and, passing Gwambe, follow either the Inhassune River or a series of lakes leading to the Inhanombe River, thence to the Bay of Inhambane. The old Gwambe village would be right in the way of this route.

Diago do Couto mentioned the hospitality of King "Gambe" and related how the two Portuguese priests had baptized him and his sons, naming them all after St. Sebastian and giving them all the surname of Sá. Although Sá (saint) is not retained as a surname in its original sig-

[25] Junod, *Os indígenas de Moçambique*, pp. 14 f., 81 ff.
[26] Theal, *South Eastern Africa*, II, 218–19.

nificance, it appears to be perpetuated by the Gwambe in an indefinite term used between men and boys much as Americans use the words "pal" or "chum."[27]

These sources make clear that the land of Tongue occupied by Gamba in 1560 and 1589 is the Wutonga of the Gwambe in the twentieth century. Ironically, Theal, who published these documents, overlooked their value and concluded that there was no continuity between the tribes of those early days and our present ethnic groupings.

The historical records, together with tribal traditions, lead to other discoveries. At several points along the juncture of the Inhassune and the Inharrime there are old middens on which modern Gwambe claim the ashes of many generations have been cast and where the bones of some of their past chieftains rest. In one of these was found a grinding stone, though Gwambe informants did not recognize it as anything more than a stone that was worn smooth.

The word "Mwari," known as the name for God in the religion of the Shona and the Rhodesian Matabele appears both in the contracted form and its longer variant, "Muwari" and "Muhari," in most Gwambe genealogies. To most informants its meaning is unknown, and it is not connected with the female secret initiation rite, *Xikundla na Mwari*. Few confess knowing anything about this rite, which men are prohibited from witnessing at the cost of their lives. Details of the ritual, with its emphasis on the female genitalia and its suggestion of sexual intercourse, are similar to ceremonies found among some of the Shona tribes. A Shona woman was asked if she recognized the name *Xikundla na Mwari*, and while she disclaimed having seen the rite herself, she described it in terms similar to those used by the Gwambe, denying, however, that the initiates were forced into relations with men at the climax of their initiation. The functions of this rite, either as sexual education or as a physical preparation for marriage, are less significant here than its explanation as a symbolic relationship with Mwari, the paramount of Shona ancestral gods. Why should the Gwambe, with Mwari as an "ancestor," use a Shona rite and its Shona name without connecting it either with their own ancestral name or with the Shona high god?

There is ample justification for the view of Henri Philippe Junod[28] and Fr. Feliciano dos Santos[29] that the vocabulary of Chopi, Gwambe, and others in this district have much in common with various Shona dialects. Where the language used by the Gwambe differs from the neighboring Tswa or Gitonga, it frequently approaches the usage of the Shona, es-

[27] Fuller, "Ethnohistoric Study," pp. 19, 210. Cf. Theal, *South Eastern Africa*, II, 182 f., 218 f., and Junod, *Os indígenas de Moçambique*, pp. 43–44, 50–52.

[28] *Ibid.*, pp. 14–22.

[29] Dos Santos, *Gramática da língua Chope*, pp. 9–20.

pecially when related to the interests of men. Similarities do not stop with vocabulary or other linguistic factors; they are very pronounced when it comes to proverbs, riddles, folk tales, and omens. Moreover, names of places and persons in Gwambe, Zavala, and Guilundu nomenclature which defy local explanation are given logical explanation in Shona.

THE IMPORTANCE OF ORAL TRADITION

It is not intended here to prove a relationship between the Gwambe, who have apparently occupied Wutonga for the past four hundred years, and the Shona or any other particular group of people, in spite of the intriguing fact that Shona influence was felt keenly among the Lovedu and the Venda of northern Transvaal. The primary purpose is to indicate the importance of oral tradition and recorded history to a thoroughgoing study of any African group. A secondary purpose is to note other avenues of approach which are needed to corroborate or correct the information offered by oral tradition. Native tradition, rightly examined and subject to adequate controls, should be able to yield at least five main contributions to history:

1. As in the case of the Gwambe, and also as in an investigation of the Africans of the Delagoa Bay and those Sofala areas, it is clear that tradition can help set the confines of cultural continuity. Gwambe traditions reported in the sixteenth century, corroborated by historical documentation, and tested by ethnographic studies of contemporary traditions and culture combine to identify the Gwambe as a society with a continuous history from about 1500 to the present in the same geographical location.

2. It has been found that tribal historians, with their memory primed by reference to a recognized genealogy, can recall oral tradition which traces the relationships of the tribe at many points in its history. This type of history is subject to error and may be suspected of interpretation in terms of modern knowledge. Nevertheless, with due allowance for the play of imagination and post-rationalization, tradition indicates peoples with whom a culture has had contact and reveals the terms of those relationships.

3. Retentions of obsolete words, idioms, or proverbial expressions give clues to linguistic development and relationships. Proverbs are injected at different points in most genealogies in southeast Africa, expressing cryptic messages about the people or periods concerned. Two informants may give the same proverb differently, one in the archaic form and the other in the mold of modern language and thought. Some of the phrases, inexplicable in the language of the person whose genealogy is being given, find explanation in a foreign tongue.

4. Careful study of tradition should give some understanding of the changes taking place in cultural traits. As the tribal historian recounts the exploits of his ancestors, he resorts to the repetition of stereotyped phrases which he has learned as a child and uses memorized descriptions of customs as they were when these stories were first introduced to oral history by contemporaries of the events described. Thus an insight into former days may be gleaned, but ever with the knowledge that the old may be interpreted consciously or unconsciously by the teller of the story in terms of his own experience.

5. If sufficiently documented by history, tradition sometimes reveals the relative strength and weakness of various aspects of the culture involved. For example, the Gwambe, according to the Portuguese priests, did not practice circumcision, whereas all their neighbors did. The Shona, from whom they are supposed to have come, still lack this rite, but the Gwambe today have circumcision ritual, though using a foreign vocabulary. Their permitting a woman nurse to assist them in their rites in recent years, introducing Christian songs, suggests that while the Gwambe borrowed circumcision from their neighbors, they had not taken it so seriously as to let its normal taboos become intrenched. Many other patterns of Gwambe behavior described in 1560 have stubbornly resisted change, including their distaste for fish and their preference for forest homes.

CONCLUSIONS

The use of oral tradition, checked against historical documents and compared with contemporary customs observed through anthropological field work, has provided a picture of change and stability in Gwambe culture with considerable detail and unusual time depth. Changes have occurred as a result of a migration from a mountain to a coastal region, with the adaptation to a new habitat and new neighbors, and they are occurring today as the result of European contact. But the striking fact which emerges from this study is the degree of stability in Gwambe culture despite the forces which have impinged on it during this period of four hundred years.

Various disciplines can contribute to a more complete reconstruction of Africa's past. Archeology, although perhaps overconcerned with man's prehuman ancestors on the one hand and the spectacular ruins of Zimbabwe on the other, can throw considerable light on cultural development in southeast Africa by investigating the numerous other stone buildings in Southern Rhodesia, the widespread rock paintings often ascribed to the Bushmen, the middens along the coast of Mozambique, and other sites. Linguistics, through analyses of the relationships between Bantu languages, can add to our knowledge, while in return the ethnohistorian may aid the linguist in recovering vocabularies of some Bantu languages recorded over a period of several hundred years. Geography can help in two ways. The study of the cartographical record of Africa for significant changes in maps should extend our record of outside contacts by revealing when new information about given regions was supplied by explorers. The study of geographical changes may tell when and why mountains covered with complicated terraces became too arid for cultivation or when one lake emptied into another, an event used to date tribal movements in places as distant as Inhambane in Mozambique and Luluaberg in the Belgian Congo.

These and other disciplines may provide data not available in historical documents, either because they were not recorded or because they antedate European contact. Yet the contribution of ethnohistory has just begun to be made. Both Henri A. and Henri P. Junod pioneered in reclaiming history from the documentary sources, but with a disappointing lack of persistence. Axelson's careful scholarly work is buried in a published thesis which was not distributed as widely as it deserved. It provides materials which have not been adequately interpreted, while the thousands of microfilms of the documents and manuscripts he uncovered in Portugal still lay unused in the archives of Southern Rhodesia in 1957. Despite errors in transcription and interpretation, Theal's vast collection of manuscripts with their laborious translations are at least a starting place for anyone who is unacquainted with the French, Dutch, Portuguese, and German documents on the discovery and exploration of South and East Africa. As anthropological field work and other investigations of contemporary African cultures are correlated with the systematic use of historical records, we can expect a more complete and more reliable understanding of the factors of change and stability in African cultures.

7. Ibo Receptivity to Change[1]

The Ibo are a sedentary agricultural people dwelling mainly in the tropical forest areas of southeastern Nigeria. Members of this cultural and linguistic grouping, consisting of about five million persons, live slightly inland from the coast and are separated from it by Efik, Ibibio, Ogoni, Eastern Ijaw, and other peoples who share with them many similarities in culture and in contact experience.

Before direct European contact the Ibo consisted of more than two hundred independent territorial groups, each composed of one or more villages or of dispersed residential groupings. The internal organization of these territorial groups was based on patrilineal clans and lineages. Though there was some trade and intermarriage, each group had its own government and was relatively independent of the others. Hostility and small-scale warfare between neighboring units was common. There were no large political groupings—no states or kingdoms—to unite these groupings and provide them with an over-all unity of social structure and culture.

The Ibo are probably most receptive to culture change, and most willing to accept Western ways, of any large group in Nigeria. Hundreds of thousands of them have migrated to other parts of the country as a result of culture contact following the British conquest of their country between about 1860 and 1915. The majority of them have moved to urban centers such as Zaria and Kano in northern Nigeria, Calabar in the southeast, and Lagos in the southwest.[2] Cities, which were nonexistent in the Ibo area previous to European contact, in the last fifty years have developed rapidly around transportation, trade, and administrative headquarters. Many Ibo have migrated to these centers, such as Aba, Port Harcourt, Umuahia, Onitsha, and Enugu. Despite their rural back-

[1] This is a revised version of a paper read at the Northwest Anthropological Conference, held at the University of Oregon, Eugene, Oregon, May 11–12, 1956.

[2] Nigeria, Department of Statistics, *Population Census of the Northern Region of Nigeria, 1952* (Lagos: Census Superintendent, 1953), pp. 26–29; *Population Census of the Eastern Region, 1953*, Bulletin No. 6: *Calabar Province* (Lagos: Census Superintendent, 1954), p. 79; *Population Census of Lagos, 1950* (Lagos: Government Printer, 1951), p. 10.

ground, the Ibo find urban life stimulating and rewarding. Urban Ibo sometimes speak of their rural counterpart as "bush people," or "primitives," in a manner reminiscent of that of some British in Nigeria in the early part of the present century.

Ibo hold many of the white-collar and domestic positions in Nigeria and are employed in the government and in private firms out of all proportion to their total number. Ibo traders are active throughout the country, and while they do not dominate the African trade in Nigeria, they play an important role in it. Throughout Ibo territory there has been an incessant demand for schools and education. Largely as a result of this, a program of compulsory education was begun in southeastern Nigeria in 1953,[3] though it has yet to be fully implemented. Where missions and the British administration have been unable or reluctant to build schools, local Ibo communities have often done so themselves, hiring their own teachers. Educated Ibo are noted for their rejection of agriculture as a way of life, many preferring poverty in an urban area to rural farm life at home.[4]

Traditional leadership within local groupings, which was largely in the hands of the elders, has changed in many areas so that younger men with schooling, prominent traders and businessmen, and professional people now play important roles in local government. For many years the Ibo have been in the forefront of the nationalist movement in Nigeria and the most active ethnic group in national politics; they have been largely instrumental in the formation and success of the National Council of Nigeria and the Cameroons, long a major Nigerian political party. In recent years other peoples, notably the Yoruba of southwestern Nigeria, have rivaled their prominence in political and nationalistic affairs, yet their position is still crucial. Ibo politicians tend to be anticolonial but not pro-traditional or antagonistic to western European culture; they believe that they can become Westernized more rapidly if freed from British rule.

Other significant changes in Ibo culture are also occurring. The larger unilineal descent groups, so characteristic a feature of Ibo society, are becoming less important as lineage and clan members leave home on a temporary or permanent basis, as traditional agriculture—normally under lineage and clan control—comes to play a less vital role in Ibo economy, and as belief in ancestral spirits gives way to Christianity. In turn, the importance of the smaller family groupings as social and economic units is increasing. These changes in kinship organization are most

[3] Nigeria, Eastern Region, *Policy for Education* (Eastern House of Assembly, Sessional Paper No. 6, 1953 [Enugu: Government Printer, 1953]).

[4] George Cockin, "The Land and Education in the Ibo Country of Southeastern Nigeria," *International Review of Missions*, XXXIII (1944), 274–79.

noticeable in the urban centers but also are occurring in rural areas. Missionaries have had considerable success in converting Ibo to Christianity, though many conversions are not total, elements of traditional religious forms survive, and some nativistic Christian churches have come into existence. Traditional art, notably wood-carving, is declining, and in some areas traditional artists are rarely found. To some extent new art forms, such as thorn carvings and small wood and horn animal carvings have developed, largely to meet the interests of the more acculturated Africans and of the Europeans in Nigeria.

Why, then, have the Ibo, living in small, relatively independent groups with a sedentary agricultural way of life, been willing to accept new conditions and to change so rapidly? Four factors need to be examined: the influence of the European slave trade on the Ibo, the nature of direct European contact following the slave trade, the nature and organization of Ibo culture, and the high population density in Ibo country.

THE SLAVE TRADE

From the seventeenth to the middle of the nineteenth century the southern coast of Nigeria was subject to intensive European slaving activities. Several million slaves were probably taken from this area. A great deal of trading occurred in the region from the Niger River eastward to the Cross River, perhaps more than in southwestern Nigeria. Many Ibo were involved in this trade, some living in the small trading towns that developed in non-Ibo areas on the southeastern coast and some acting as agents from Aro Chuku, an Ibo group near the Cross River whose men moved relatively freely about large parts of Ibo country and dominated much of the internal slave trade.[5]

Many Ibo were taken as slaves to the New World, but we have very little information on the effect this trade had on the Ibo. We do know that slavery was also an indigenous Ibo practice, that many Ibo willingly co-operated in the trade, and that they obtained European goods, particularly iron, guns, ammunition, cloth, and liquor. We also know that some Ibo communities were destroyed in the course of the trade, particularly by Aro Chuku agents or their allies, and that a complex system of major trade routes, particularly in a north-south direction, developed in southeastern Nigeria. It is also clear that no large centralized state system evolved in Ibo country as a result of this trade, as occurred elsewhere in West Africa.[6]

[5] K. Onwuka Dike, *Trade and Politics in the Niger Delta, 1830–1885* (Oxford: Clarendon Press, 1956), pp. 28–29, 30–41.

[6] Daryll Forde, "The Cultural Map of West Africa: Successive Adaptations to Tropical Forests and Grasslands," *Transactions of the New York Academy of Sciences*, Ser. 2, XV, No. 6 (April, 1953), 217–18.

Since many Ibo were exported as slaves, we might expect that the population decreased considerably during this period. However, their population density is high today and appears to have been so from the earliest direct British contacts within the area in the second half of the nineteenth century. Either it was already high before the period of the slave trade, thus attracting the European traders to the southeastern coast, or it increased as a direct result of European contact. Several writers have indicated their belief that the latter might have been the case,[7] and certainly the immediate coastal area of Nigeria seems to have had a low density until the slave trade attracted people to this region.

It seems likely that new crops introduced from the New World during the slave trade period, such as maize and cassava (manioc)—particularly the latter, which is easy to grow, survives in relatively poor soil, and can be harvested at any time of the year—made possible a higher density of population than previously. Again, the slave trade brought members of other cultural groups into Ibo territory and probably led to an expansion of the Ibo frontiers. The period of the European slave trade was thus one in which important social, economic, and demographic changes occurred, and was not a period of static conditions.

BRITISH CONTACT

Most of Ibo country did not come under British control until the early 1900's, later than some other parts of Nigeria. This was accomplished largely through small military patrols which caused little physical damage and did not effectively change most native institutions. Administrative control has not been more intensive than in many other sections of Nigeria, though the type of administration has differed. In northern and southwestern Nigeria, where native states and kingdoms were found, the British for years administered the country through the traditional rulers by a system known as "indirect rule."[8] Among the Ibo, where large-scale political groupings were lacking, they appointed a chief for each local group. This practice was unpopular, the chiefs often having little real authority with their own people. Leadership by single individuals was rare, since the authority of a group of influential elders, perhaps with a few dominating leaders, was a common pattern. As a result, conflict developed between the appointed chiefs and the traditional leaders, culminating in the Aba riots of 1929 and the reorganization of the native authority government in the 1930's and 1940's on the basis of village and village-group councils of traditional rulers—the elders. By

[7] Glenn T. Trewartha and Wilbur Zelinsky, "Population Patterns in Tropical Africa," *Annals of the Association of American Geographers*, XLIV, No. 2 (June, 1954), 153.

[8] Margery Perham, *Native Administration in Nigeria* (London: Oxford University Press, 1937), chap. v.

this time it was too late to develop a system of indirect rule based on traditional authority, since educated and acculturated Ibo were already demanding a place in local leadership. Since the Second World War local government councils and administrations have been further developed to give these new leaders a dominant place in local and regional affairs.

Thus, because of their previous and successful experiences with indirect rule in northern Nigeria and their lack of awareness of the true nature of Ibo authority and leadership, the British failed to stabilize the traditional system of government within the framework of the colonial administration. The traditional system of control was weakened, and confusion arose as to who possessed authority. These factors helped to permit the rapid rise of the new educated and acculturated Ibo into positions of authority. If the British had from the first crystallized the traditional government by the creation of councils of elders, the rise of new leaders would probably have occurred more slowly.

A second result of direct contact is economic production for export. Each of the three major areas of Nigeria produces important export products, placing it on a cash-economy basis and tying it closely to the world market.[9] In the north, the major products are groundnuts (peanuts), cotton, and tin; in the southwest they are primarily cocoa and secondarily palm oil and palm kernels; and in the southeast—the Ibo area—they are mainly palm oil and palm kernels. With the exception of tin production, which is restricted to certain local areas of the north, there do not seem to be any marked differential changes brought about by the production of any one of these products when compared to the others. In each case, production has been by African individuals or small groups, mainly in their home areas; a complex system of markets and middlemen between the producer and the European buyer has evolved; and the production of traditional crops and goods has continued, though specialists who do not grow subsistence crops are also found. There seems to be nothing unique about the production and distribution of palm products in the Ibo area compared to that of other export crops elsewhere in Nigeria, so that this factor cannot account for the receptivity of the Ibo to change as compared to other peoples.

Nevertheless, economic differentials exist. In southeastern Nigeria, the trade in palm products replaced the slave trade in the middle of the last century, keeping channels of cultural interchange at a high level. In southwestern Nigeria, the Yoruba were engaged in warfare among themselves and with the Dahomeans until 1890; before the development of cocoa as an export crop early in the present century there was little production for export, and European trade was not highly developed in this

[9] Daryll Forde and Richenda Scott, *The Native Economies of Nigeria* (London: Faber & Faber, 1946).

area. In northern Nigeria, where the European slave trade had never been as important as in the south, the development of export products for European markets on a large scale has occurred only in recent times.[10] What is unique about the economic relations between the Ibo and Europeans is that they were intensive, continuous, and of long duration. Through trade, first in slaves and later in palm products, the Ibo acquired many new items of material culture, new wealth, and new standards of values and prestige.

During the slave trade the Ibo who had migrated to the coast and the Aro Chuku Ibo within Ibo country were most affected by economic contact, and they became influential politically as well as economically. Following the change from trade in slaves to trade in palm products, the influence of the coastal Ibo declined, and after the British military expeditions into Ibo country during the first decade of the present century the Aro Chuku influence on trade was destroyed. The production and distribution of goods for export became anybody's business, and economic contacts between European and Ibo were established on a broad basis.

The particular features of colonial administration and the length and intensity of economic contact are the most striking differentials in British contact between the Ibo and other peoples in western and northern Nigeria. A third factor, missionary influence, must be considered.

Missionaries are important in Nigeria, as in other parts of Africa, not only because they have introduced new religious beliefs and practices but also because they have provided most of the schooling. There seems to be nothing unique about missionary work among the Ibo as compared with other sections of Nigeria, though it began slightly later in Ibo country than in the southwest. In northern Nigeria, because of Moslem influence, Christian missionary activity has never been very widespread, but it has been very influential throughout southern Nigeria and about equally so in the southwest and southeast. Mission work has been intensive among the Ibo and has had profound effects on their culture; many converts have been gained and much education has been provided. However, Ibo receptivity to missions is not explained by anything distinctive in mission work among them; instead, it is related to certain general features of Ibo culture which will be discussed below.

A negative factor, important throughout Nigeria, should also be mentioned. The British have never had a large European administrative staff in the country; they have not permitted European colonization; and, in fact, most of the country does not appear to be attractive to colonists. These factors have prevented the development of a permanent European population, with its own culture and a social and political hierarchy ex-

[10] Dike, *Trade and Politics*, chap. vi, and pp. 99–101. Forde and Scott, *Native Economies*, pp. 8–9.

cluding Africans except for limited contacts through trade and menial labor. The presence of such a group in Nigeria might have greatly impeded the recent developments and changes in Ibo culture. It is instructive to compare the Ibo with the Kikuyu of Kenya in this respect.[11] Both share many similarities in culture and in social organization. Both have reacted to direct European contact by migration to urban areas, rapid assimilation into jobs under Europeans, strong demands for education and political freedom, and so on. But the presence of permanent white settlers near the Kikuyu has lead to increasing tensions through the blocking of Kikuyu demands for rapid change and the assimilation of European culture. This has not occurred in Ibo country. The British have rarely for long blocked Ibo aspirations in the direction of culture change, greater control over their own affairs, and advancement toward higher, more influential positions in the colonial administration.

IBO CULTURE

There is little in the *formal* outlines of Ibo culture[12] to explain the reasons for rapid culture change. The village and local territorial groupings are largely composed of patrilineal clans and lineages which are corporate residential groupings controlling land and trees. These patrilineal groups have religious features, notably patrilineal ancestral spirits and the deity of the earth (*ala* or *ale*) which are concerned with crop fertility and human welfare. Many other spirits serving a variety of purposes are found. In some areas, age grades are well developed; secret societies and village men's societies are important in some regions; and title societies[13] are also of some significance.

But if we examine the traditional culture more closely, we see that there are elements of social behavior which help to explain the tendency toward change. The Ibo are a highly individualistic people. While a man is dependent on his family, lineage, and residential grouping for support and backing, strong emphasis is placed on his ability to make his own way in the world. The son of a prominent politician has a head start over other men in the community, but he must validate this by his own abil-

[11] John Middleton, *The Kikuyu and Kamba of Kenya* ("Ethnographic Survey of Africa, East Central Africa," Part V [London: International African Institute, 1953]). Jomo Kenyatta, *Facing Mount Kenya* (London: Secker & Warburg, 1938). Louis S. B. Leakey, *Mau Mau and the Kikuyu* (London: Methuen, 1952).

[12] Daryll Forde and G. I. Jones, *The Ibo and Ibibio-speaking Peoples of Southeastern Nigeria* ("Ethnographic Survey of Africa, Western Africa," Part III [London: International African Institute, 1950]). C. K. Meek, *Law and Authority in a Nigerian Tribe* (London: Oxford University Press, 1937).

[13] A title society is a group which one joins by paying a set fee and feasting the members. The members split the fee, and the title-taker becomes a member for life, entitled to share the entrance fee of others when they join. In addition to its being a financial institution, in some areas its members hold (or formerly held) political power, and it is everywhere a prestige grouping.

ities. While seniority in age is an asset in secular leadership, personal qualities are also important. A secular leader must be aggressive, skilled in oratory, and able to cite past history and precedent. A man gains prestige by accumulating the capital (formerly foodstuffs, now largely money) required to join title societies and perform other ceremonies. Much of the capital necessary for these activities is acquired through skill in farming and ability to obtain loans. Successful farming is a matter not merely of diligently using the proper agricultural techniques but often of a person's ability to obtain the use of the land resources of his friends, conjugal relatives, and his own unilineal groups. The ability to secure loans readily is a reflection of a person's prestige, the respect granted him, and the effectiveness of his social contacts. In all these activities a person receives support and guidance from his family and lineage.

The possibilities of enhancing status and prestige are open to virtually all individuals except descendants of certain types of slaves and are not restricted to members of particular lineages, clans, or other social units. Ibo society is thus, in a sense, an "open" society in which positions of prestige, authority, and leadership are largely achieved.

Following British conquest, the Ibo quickly recognized the superior authority and influence of the new rulers, and though they objected to it, they did not completely reject it. Rather, the acquisition of this power and authority became one of their important goals. The task was not merely to control the British influence but to capture it. Education was quickly seen as an avenue to white-collar jobs with government, posts in the native authority system, and positions in the British administration itself. Though traditional techniques for seeking prestige and leadership changed, basic goals of the control of power and influence did not; they expanded to include the sphere of the British.

The situation of culture contact has, of course, accentuated and expanded other possibilities of individual achievement. Trade has increased greatly since the cessation of traditional intergroup warfare. Some individuals have emigrated outside Ibo territory and obtained land which they now farm successfully. New avenues of achieving prestige have opened up, such as sending children through school and acquiring European clothing and material equipment. Culture contact has given impetus to the well-developed pattern of individualism within the traditional culture.

Group achievement is also stressed in Ibo culture. Villages, unilineal groups, and other social units are often competitive in terms of size, wealth, and influence. Individuals are conscious of the relative status of the groups with which they are associated. The relative social position of these units is not static but is constantly changing. The history of Ibo villages and other groupings shows their continual rise and fall in population, prestige, wealth, and influence.

European culture, essentially competitive even in its colonial form, has given these traditional group rivalries new dimensions. Villages compete to build the first or the best school, village groups to improve their markets. Many social groups strive to push some of their "sons" ahead in schooling and to obtain scholarships in competition with other groups. Individuals who acquire schooling, wealth, or political influence are expected to use their new social standing to benefit the groups with which they are associated.

A number of alternative paths lead to success and prestige. A successful man may be a wealthy farmer or trader, in some cases a fisherman, an influential priest, or an important secular leader. He may—though he need not—combine two or more of these social positions. Religious leaders are sometimes quiet, thoughtful elders, people who are withdrawn socially, in contrast to the more aggressive and vocal secular leaders. There is room for the achievement of prestige in leadership for two strikingly different personality types.

In addition to some freedom in selecting a career, there are other alternatives. Individuals have some choice in which title societies to join, and in what order. In the field of religion, a person can sometimes choose from a variety of spirits those with whom he wants to be associated and to whom he wishes to make sacrifices. He may consult a diviner as to which spirit he should approach for a particular purpose, but he is not obliged to accept the diviner's advice and may choose the spirit himself.

A variety of judicial techniques are used to settle disputes. The nature of the dispute may determine which judicial agent will be sought, but often the disputants and their relatives have a say in determining where to present the case. The judgment may be made by patrilineal elders, the elders of the village or a group of villages, one of several famous oracles, or by swearing innocence to a spirit which is believed to kill those who lie to it. Which judicial agent the disputants decide to use depends to some extent on their personal contacts and resources and upon their estimation of their own ability to win the case before the judicial agents available to them.

Ibo culture thus provides alternatives which the individual must decide upon in terms of his own skill and knowledge. Their significance for the individual is that he rapidly develops experience in making decisions in which he must estimate his own position and opportunities for success.

The alternatives open to the individual have been increased by the situation of culture change. In addition to those already mentioned in reference to individual achievement, the development of a British system of courts, which in some areas now operate alongside the traditional ones, has given the individual an even wider range of choice. The introduction of Christianity has given greater religious choice, and, characteristically, many Ibo have accepted Christianity without rejecting all their traditional religious beliefs. The whole pattern of culture contact by its very nature introduces new cultural alternatives. Although this is usually the case, the Ibo—traditionally accustomed to thinking, acting, and making decisions in terms of a range of alternatives—are more at home in the culture contact situation than members of other societies with different orientations.

Another factor of importance is that in Ibo society secular leadership is generally in the hands of groups of elders. While individualism is important and certain members may strongly influence decisions of the group, there is a strong emphasis on leadership, whether it be that of the elders of a lineage, clan, village, or group of villages. Traditional leadership is, however, not strongly authoritarian, and consensus on a given matter may develop slowly. One result is that though the elders tend to represent traditional points of view, they have not always been able to agree on how to deal with British authority; they have frequently been unable to hold their own people to traditional viewpoints—particularly the younger men who have had considerable contact with European culture—in much the same way that they were never able to organize effective resistance to the small British military patrols which conquered them group by group.

Group leadership has also helped to prepare the Ibo for the introduction of national and regional legislative councils. Traditional local hostilities as well as antagonisms arising out of the development of a Nigerian political system are mirrored in the hostility of the Ibo representatives toward one another in the regional and national councils. The attempts of influential representatives to seize power in these councils have been counterbalanced by the techniques of group leadership that the Ibo have brought from their traditional culture.

Most Ibo are familiar with organizations which are independent of kinship, a feature characteristic of European culture but not of importance in some African societies. Associations based on residence include age grades, secret societies, men's societies, co-operative work groups, and title societies. Some of these are voluntary groupings, and others are compulsory. The experience gained in these traditional associations has undoubtedly eased the transition to such new voluntary groupings as improvement unions, trade organizations, labor unions, and political associations.

When we examine Ibo culture closely, we notice a remarkable variety of cultural forms underlying a similar broad pattern. In a few village groups, double unilineal descent systems exist, but in most regions descent is patrilineal. The social and economic independence of women is much greater in some areas than in others. Secret societies are important in some regions but absent in others. While a variety of religious spirits are found in each local group, their functions and rituals differ from group to group. There is also considerable difference in residential patterns in different regions of Ibo country. To some extent these variations can be explained in terms of the large population of Ibo country, the lack of a single centralizing force, and adjustments to different ecological factors. Beyond this, the Ibo for a long time have willingly incorporated small numbers of other peoples with different cultures into their social groupings. Strangers are readily adopted and provided with land; new religious shrines are acquired by trade and purchase; new forms of title societies and religious ceremonies are readily incorporated. The Ibo had been accepting new cultural forms and new personnel for many years prior to European contact.

POPULATION DENSITY

There has also been a continuous pattern of settlement and resettlement of small groups, particularly families or individuals, either within one local group or from one to another. There are few histories of large-scale migrations or movements of whole territorial groups. The history of any single local group is one of numerous movements of small numbers of persons into and out of the community. This pattern provides precedent for individuals and small groups to move within Ibo country or out of it today. Not only are Ibo enticed by the possibilities of accomplishment in other areas, but they are accustomed to this kind of mobility.

The high population density of parts of Ibo country undoubtedly is a basic factor in this mobility today and probably was in the past as well. Agricultural communities in certain central areas, such as Owerri and Onitsha, cannot support the local population,[14] and many Ibo, particularly younger sons, turn to trade, crafts, urban livelihood, and employment in the colonial administration or European firms for survival. Although the causes of the high density have never been adequately explained and are in need of study,[15] its effects seem to be physical mobility, particularly of younger family members, and adaptation to change.

[14] Forde and Scott, *Native Economies*, p. 78. G. I. Jones, "Ibo Land Tenure," *Africa*, XIX, No. 4 (October, 1949), 309–23.
[15] Pierre Gourou, "Géographie du Peuplement en Nigéria Méridionale," *Bulletin de la Société Belge d'Etudes Géographiques*, XVII (1947), 58–64.

CONCLUSIONS

Certain elements in Ibo culture thus play an important role in culture change. Some of these are present in southwestern and northern Nigeria as well, but with differences. The state systems of the west and north make for more centralized authority, acting as a conservative force; there is less emphasis on individual achievement; the court system is more hierarchical; and leadership tends to be inherited rather than achieved. The presence of urban centers and the physical mobility in Yoruba country in the southwest facilitate change, but the over-all pattern differs from that found in Ibo society.

Change is a function of the kind of external cultural forces which a society encounters and of its existing framework of organization. It is unlikely, for example, that the Ibo would readily accept a strongly centralized, hierarchical, autocratic state system of the kind existing in northern Nigeria. British colonial culture may at first have appeared to the Ibo to have many characteristics of an autocratic society. The British conquerors were obviously a powerful, though small, political group which formed a distinct social class apart from the Ibo. But the Ibo also perceived that British colonial culture provided them with new avenues of individual enterprise and of social and physical mobility, in terms of a cash economy and new types of labor and skills. They recognized that it was possible to use a variety of techniques gradually to lessen the power of the colonial government, which was not, after all, rigidly inflexible.

Ibo culture can thus be characterized by its emphasis on individual achievement and initiative, alternative prestige goals and paths of action, a tendency toward equalitarian leadership, considerable incorporation of other peoples and cultures, a great deal of settlement and resettlement of individuals and small groups, and considerable cultural variation. Some of these attributes are characteristic of what have been designated "loosely structured" or "flexible" societies.[16] However, the Ibo differ from some such societies in that they have clearly defined, well-organized, and effective social groupings, particularly unilineal organizations but also age grades, village societies, and other associations. The "flexibility" in Ibo culture does not lie in any structural weakness in these groupings but in individuals' ability to work through and across them to achieve desired goals and in their freedom to select alternative activities. Furthermore, these groups support the individual in his ac-

[16] John F. Embree, "Thailand: A Loosely Structured Social System," *American Anthropologist*, LII, No. 2 (April–June, 1950), 181–93. Bryce F. Ryan and Murray A. Straus, "Integration in Sinhalese Society," *Research Studies of the State College of Washington*, XXII, No. 4 (December, 1954), 179–227. Social Science Research Council Summer Seminar on Acculturation, 1953, "Acculturation: An Exploratory Formulation," *American Anthropologist*, LVI, No. 6 (December, 1954), 976–77.

tivities, and his achievement in turn brings prestige to them. An individual who takes a series of titles is supported by his family and unilineal groupings. The rising young political leader receives support from these groups, from other kinship groups, and from age grades and other associations.

How these patterns of Ibo social and cultural behavior came into being is not known. Our discussion of the "traditional" culture is based mainly on studies made since 1900; whether it existed previous to the earliest European contacts in Nigeria in the fifteenth century is not known. Nor is it certain whether the emphasis on individual achievement, alternative choices, and other features which facilitate culture change developed out of the slave trade or not. Unless archeological evidence should eventually provide sufficient information on the period before the slave trade, we will never know whether Ibo culture ever tended to be more static, less open to achievement and choice, than at present. All that we can say is that the "traditional" aspects of Ibo culture, as we view them today, show certain characteristics which help to explain why the Ibo are changing rapidly.

Yet, paradoxically, of all Nigerian peoples, the Ibo have probably changed the least while changing the most. While many of the formal elements of the social, religious, economic, and political structure, such as lineages, family groups, age grades, and secret societies, have been modified through culture contact, many of the basic patterns of social behavior, such as the emphasis on alternative choices and goals, achievement and competition, and the lack of strong autocratic authority, have survived and are a part of the newly developing culture. But basic patterns of social behavior, of interpersonal relationships, have changed little,[17] though new symbols of success replace old ones and new goals appear.

The major factors underlying Ibo receptivity to change are clear. The high population density has affected physical mobility and adjustment to new conditions. Ibo culture is itself a changing one, and it is particularly adapted to certain aspects of European culture. The Ibo have had constant contact with Europe, first indirectly and then directly, for over three hundred years, and it would probably be an error to consider that their culture was relatively static before the period of direct British contact. The early European contacts were relatively friendly and co-operative despite the horrors and tragedies suffered by individuals who died or were carried away in the slave trade. Trade in palm products effectively replaced this earlier trade. The British conquest caused little internal disorganization, for, with the exception of the destruction of the dominant position of small groups of Ibo traders (an action which many Ibo

[17] The most striking exception is probably the decline in respect for seniority of age.

welcomed) and some changes in religious and political matters, they did not initially destroy Ibo culture or its indigenous system of leadership. On the other hand, this leadership deteriorated to a considerable extent because of the British failure to crystallize it within the colonial administration, leaving the way open for new types of leaders to arise.

8. Pakot Resistance to Change

The marked resistance to European innovations which the Pakot (or Suk)[1] of western Kenya have maintained despite deliberate European attempts to induce change on three broad fronts—political, economic, and religious—presents a challenging problem. That this conservatism is, however, not restricted to the Pakot, who number fifty-five to sixty thousand, is apparent when we consider the other Nilotic[2] peoples, who number over three million.[3] The resistance to cultural change which characterizes the Nilotic people as a whole becomes the more striking when it is contrasted with the acceptance to change among neighboring Bantu peoples of East Africa, so that any attempt made to isolate the factors which explain these strikingly different reactions to Euroamerican culture may be profitable.

POLITICAL ORGANIZATION

Like most other Nilotic peoples, the Pakot have never had leaders with well-defined authority. Their political organization is segmentary

[1] The name "Suk" is of doubtful origin, probably Masai. The people call themselves Pakot (or Pokot), the singular form being Pachon. The Pakot inhabit three administrative districts, all bearing the name "Suk": West Suk District of west central Kenya; East Suk, a northern subdivision of Baringo District of Kenya; and Kara Suk, which is administered as a part of Uganda although it belongs to Kenya and which contains a mixture of Pakot and Karamojong. Little is known of the few Pakot outside of West Suk (and they are consequently not the subject of this paper), except that they inhabit hot, dry lowlands fit only for herding, but there is good reason to assume that, despite their political separation, all Pakot are basically alike in culture.

[2] This group is usually divided into "Nilotes" and "Nilo-Hamites," a distinction based on alleged linguistic differences and a hypothetical "Hamite" invasion. Since the support for this rests principally on debatable linguistic evidence and since Greenberg has shown both "Nilotes" and "Nilo-Hamites" to be linguistically related as members of the Eastern Sudanic section of the Macrosudanic language family, both will be referred to hereafter simply as "Nilotic" (J. H. Greenberg, "Studies in African Linguistic Classification: VIII. Further Remarks on Method: Revisions and Corrections," *Southwestern Journal of Anthropology*, X [1954], 405–15; see, however, the rejoinder by G. W. B. Huntingford, "The 'Nilo-Hamitic' Languages," *Southwestern Journal of Anthropology*, XII [1956], 200–222).

[3] Based on figures in M. A. Bryan and A. N. Tucker, *Distribution of the Nilotic and Nilo-Hamitic Languages of Africa* (London: Oxford University Press for the International African Institute, 1948), *passim*.

and acephalous, and their sense of unity rests on bonds of commonly accepted customs and laws and on various economic and social ties. What delegated authority exists is vested, not in the heads of lineages or clans as is so often true of African peoples, but in adult males in general, and particularly in the older men (*poi*), who are greatly respected—especially those who show ability in leadership and are of high moral and ritual status.

Except for a few small trading settlements of recent origin, peopled by Indians, Somalis, and a few Bantu entrepreneurs, the Pakot have no villages. They are scattered over the plains and mountain ridges in homesteads consisting of circular grass- or manure-roofed houses attached to corrals where cattle are kept at night. A group of homesteads within an area defined by a ridge or other natural feature constitutes the "neighborhood." Each neighborhood is a largely autonomous political unit, within which the old men play a prominent role in directing community activities of a secular and religious nature. Each articulates with other neighborhoods through the common culture, social and economic ties, and "courts" which settle disputes between members of different neighborhoods. The method of articulation in some respects resembles the situation Evans-Pritchard describes for the Nuer,[4] which he characterizes as opposition of lineages; but one of the chief differences between Nuer and Pakot is that these local groups among the Pakot are not lineages but are based principally on voluntary association. Apparently neighborhoods never engage in physical combat; all disputes are settled by lawful processes, and even individual self-help is strongly discouraged. The composition of the neighborhoods is somewhat unstable, since a member can leave at any time to settle in a new area, usually to avoid drought or cattle diseases, though he usually returns when conditions have improved.

The only individuals who managed to command any high position of power were the "chief diviners" (*werkoi*), whose counterparts are to be found among most of the southern Nilotic groups, for example, in the *laibon* of the Masai. These men were virtuosi both in divination by dreams, which the Pakot believe to be the best method of foreseeing the future, and in the use of magic, which is universally recognized as a medium of both social control and private revenge. They do not seem to have been numerous at any time, and the Pakot are exceedingly reluctant to discuss them, but some were evidently more respected than others.

The most famous chief diviner about whom we have any extensive

---

[4] E. E. Evans-Pritchard, "The Nuer of the Southern Sudan," in *African Political Systems*, ed. M. Fortes and E. E. Evans-Pritchard (London: Oxford University Press, 1950), pp. 281 ff.

information is Erimat, who became prominent just before 1918.[5] He was able to coerce most Pakot to the ends he desired through his dreams and magical power. Among other things, he foretold impending attacks by the enemy, the propitious time for Pakot raids, and whether the rains would come or not; for his services he received payments of stock or a share of the loot taken in raids. However, Erimat was neither a king nor a real political leader in the usual sense, because his motives were allied not with government but with the welfare and procurement of cattle, the most valuable possessions of all Nilotics except the Anuak.[6] According to legend, Erimat tried to establish a hereditary line by having his son succeed him when he died, as Masai *laibons* do, but there are no signs of this today, nor does any person wield the power that he or any other chief diviner was supposed to have had. If the legend has any foundation in historical fact, this instance may represent an unwillingness to give any authority carte blanche; this would be in accord with the Pakot world view. Diviners and workers of magic continue to operate, divination now being directed, at least on the surface, away from cattle raiding, which the British colonial government forbids.

Besides the elders and diviners, there are "community leaders" or "arbitrators" (*kiruokintin*), men chosen for their wisdom and skill in making decisions and in arbitrating disputes. They are selected by the elders of a neighborhood to preside at discussions.[7] Because they have no clear-cut authority, their role is difficult to define; the only excuse for their existence seems to be the occasional need for some focus for discussion and arbitration. They are said to organize such community projects as irrigating fields and community defense; but they cannot command, and their word is never law.

Of these three groups, the old men generally possess the core of authority and respect, although the Pakot do not show much deference to anyone. The old men dominate discussions of important matters, lead debates in the courts, and render the final decisions as a group. When the occasion demands, they act as priests and leaders in other kinds of ceremonies. It is from their ranks that diviners of stature derive, and they choose the community leaders.

[5] Information about Erimat was obtained from unpublished historical material in the government files at the West Suk District headquarters in Kapenguria; the information was recorded by Juxon Barton during his tenure as district commissioner and was graciously made available by the district commissioners in 1951–52.

[6] The Anuak, according to Butt, call themselves "bead people" and do not prize cattle (see Audrey Butt, *The Nilotes of the Anglo-Egyptian Sudan and Uganda* [London: International African Institute, 1952], p. 32).

[7] In the center of West Suk, around Ortum, where much of this information was gathered, the men spoke of the community leaders as being chosen by the elders. Peristiany, in his paper "Pakot Sanctions and Structure" (*Africa*, XXIV [1954], p. 18), suggests a different reason for their position, namely, long residence in the area.

An elaborate system of age sets, which stratifies all males, partly compensates for the lack of both political centralization and organized kinship groups by creating groups in the society to which various roles can be assigned. Crosscutting the clans and neighborhoods, the age sets constitute convenient units to which men can rally for defense, raiding, or ceremonies; but their function is less clearly evident than among the Nandi and Masai, where age sets act as actual divisions in a standing army. As Gulliver has argued for the Jie,[8] the age sets of the Pakot are not really military groups but status-gradings of adult men. The members of each set are bound to one another by lesser obligations and privileges. The oldest men receive the best helpings of meat and are seated in the position of honor in the semicircle of the ceremonial feast at which cattle are slaughtered, while the other age sets are ranked between them and the youngest men. These neighborhood feasts are held at irregular intervals for various purposes: to pray for the sick, to appeal for relief of drought and disease, to initiate a young man into adulthood, or simply for recreation and to consume meat. Together they constitute one of the most important integrative rites.[9]

Clans and lineages are to some extent responsible for the activities of their own members, regulating marriage, defending those in difficulty, punishing, and even executing those who commit serious crimes. However, ties with neighbors are in some ways as strong or stronger than those of the clan, and a group of neighbors usually joins in the defense of one of their number who is in conflict with someone from another neighborhood. This seems to arise from the fact that all fines for crimes are paid in livestock; the loss of cattle by any member is a loss to all, since milk and cattle are commonly shared within the neighborhood, and a feast is possible only when there are sufficient cattle to justify killing a steer. No more strict ordering of society than this seems to have been necessary for the seminomadic, individualistic, and equalitarian life of the Pakot.

This diffuse political organization was the first facet of Pakot life to come into conflict with the policies of the British rulers. In 1905, after the initial exploration of this area by such men as Teleki, Thompson, and Peters[10] and after what is now Kenya Colony was acquired by the British in 1890, colonial rule was extended into the Pakot area. Meanwhile, the Masai were being moved from their rich grazing lands in the

[8] P. H. Gulliver, "The Age-set Organization of the Jie Tribe," *Journal of the Royal Anthropological Institute*, Vol. LXXXIII (1953), *passim.*

[9] For more information on feasts see H. K. Schneider, "The Subsistence Role of Cattle among the Pakot and in East Africa," *American Anthropologist*, LIX (April, 1957), 278–300.

[10] Their experiences are recounted in L. von Höhnel, *The Discovery of Lakes Rudolf and Stephanie* (1894); J. Thomson, *Through Masai Land* (London: Sampson Low, Marston, Searle & Rivington, 1885); C. Peters, *New Light on Dark Africa* (London, New York and Melbourne: Ward, Lock & Co., 1891).

Rift Valley around Nakuru and resettled farther south; the Nandi, Kipsigis, and others were being subjugated and confined to reserves. It was customary for the government to send a district commissioner into a newly opened area to set up a camp, begin collecting taxes, and try to bring about a cessation of raiding among the pastoral people. Not much more than this was possible.

The first headquarters for the Pakot was established at Lake Baringo in the Rift Valley, and after at least two subsequent moves it was finally located in 1930 at Kapenguria, a center that has become widely known as the site of the Kenyatta trial. The district commissioner had jurisdiction, at the beginning, over the huge Baringo area, which included the territory of the Pakot and the Turkana, but later the Pakot were separated and subdivided into the three administrative units that now exist.[11]

Contrasted to the Turkana and Karamojong to the north and the Nandi to the south, who had to be subdued by force, the Pakot originally had the reputation of being quiescent and tractable. Why they did not openly resist is not known, but it has been suggested that they were glad to exchange a few goats and sheep as taxes in return for British protection from the Turkana and other marauding people who had so often defeated them. Avoiding the payment of taxes became their form of resistance; but taxes, the major innovation of the new government, did not seriously disturb them, and they were partly compensated by being invited to participate in British-sponsored raids against their enemy, the Turkana.

The first intensive attempts at political reform were probably undertaken about 1918 by Juxon Barton, who seems to have been a man of great ambition for reform. Neither the pattern of his innovations nor the impetus for them were original with him, but he was the first active agent of their introduction. Unlike Crampton, one of his predecessors who lived close to the Pakot and whose main task seems to have been organizing them to help subdue the Turkana, Barton undertook to create a new government like those which were being set up all over east Africa.[12] The Pakot reaction to these two men is indicated by the fact that "Karamdi," as they call Crampton, was remembered with affection after more than forty years, while Barton has either been forgotten or is remembered only as one of the stream of Europeans who have tampered with their culture.

Barton's predecessors, recognizing the position of the elders, had tried

[11] All information about the early history of contact and experiences and reactions of government officials was obtained from unpublished annual reports and other records made available by the district commissioners at Kapenguria.

[12] Discussed historically in detail for all of Kenya in Lord Hailey's *An African Survey* (London: Oxford University Press, 1938), pp. 382–93.

to work through them—without success. Barton began by ascertaining as accurately as possible the major Pakot social and political districts before contact; Cheptulel, Lomut, Masol, WeiWei, Riwa, and several other districts, each consisting of a group of neighborhoods, were officially gazetted as "locations." To each location a "headman," later called a "chief," was assigned, presumably following the principle that if one is to apply indirect rule, a society must have chiefs. Barton also reasoned that it would be easier to control a nomadic people if their periodic migrations were stopped; therefore individuals were forbidden to leave their native locations.

Barton recognized the impossibility of using the chief diviners, because their functions were closely associated with warfare and therefore essentially incompatible with the *pax Britannica*. Among the Masai, Nandi, and other southern Nilotics it had been found necessary to remove diviners from power or to exile them.[13] Following this pattern, Barton set about hunting Erimat; he failed to apprehend him, but according to all indications, Erimat fled from Kenya to Uganda and died about this time. More than thirty years later the Pakot still expressed their resentment of the government for having "killed" Erimat.

In later years the government separated the judicial power from the executive, a principle formerly unknown but easily applied because of the general lack of well-defined indigenous governmental structures. In fact, when Barton and his successors had finished, they had created all three of the branches of government familiar to the Euroamerican world —executive, judicial, and legislative. A court system of native tribunals was instituted for each location in 1923 with a chosen elder, or group of elders, heading it. A native council[14] was formed in 1925 with the "chiefs" acting as representatives, and later an elected representative from each location was added. Thus the structure of the new Pakot government became basically that created for all other aboriginal peoples in Kenya.

Throughout this period life went on without much change. The Pakot paid no deference to the new chiefs and ignored orders not to cross location lines, while government officials could do little to enforce their decrees.

The new governmental structure has continued with some revisions. In 1952 there were eleven locations in West Suk, each of which had a chief, and a twelfth was being proposed. Formerly each location had its own native tribunal, but these were reduced to three courts in different

[13] For a discussion of this see G. W. B. Huntingford, "The Orkoiyot," in *The Nandi of Kenya* (London: Routledge & Kegan Paul, 1953), pp. 38–51. See also H. A. Fosbrooke, "An Administrative Survey of the Masai Social System," *Tanganyika Notes and Records*, No. 26 (1948), pp. 25 ff., for a discussion of the *laibons*.

[14] Shortly after 1952 the Kenya government changed the names of these institutions to African courts and African district councils.

parts of the district, each of which met once a week to hear civil and criminal cases (as distinguished by the British). The native council, composed of twenty-two men, met quarterly with the district commissioner, who acted as president and directed most of its decisions.

Of all the new political institutions, only the tribunals achieved any degree of acceptance, probably because they resembled the traditional Pakot "bush courts," which the Pakot still conduct. The power of the elders who preside over both of these has been limited, and crimes of a serious nature, if discovered, find their way to the district commissioner, who is the first class magistrate, or to higher courts of the colony. The native tribunals are occupied chiefly with cases of theft, violation of contract, extortion, and the like (usually involving women and cattle), and with offenses against the bylaws imposed by the native council at the government's behest. However, even the native tribunals cannot be said to have achieved more than limited success, as evidenced by the fact that the records of the most popular one list only 162 civil cases for the year 1950, many of which involved aliens residing in the district. This court had 114 criminal cases listed for 1951, but crimes—except assault—are usually violations of bylaws with action brought by the colonial government officers. Most litigation continues to be carried on in the traditional bush courts.

It is thus apparent that the democratic structure introduced by the colonial officials does not actually function and that the Pakot are in fact still administered by direct rule. Their antipathy to this system is readily observed, and confirmed by an examination of the annual reports of the district commissioners over the years. From Barton's report in 1920 that the chiefs were evading their responsibilities to Flynn's, in 1945, that as far as he could see after thirty-four years of administration West Suk was one of the most "backward" districts in Kenya, little seems to have changed. At a native council meeting in 1951, the district commissioner offered the budget which he had prepared and introduced all other important matters. Except for one or two individuals who were products of the government or mission schools, the chiefs and representatives confined themselves to irrelevancies and obstruction, showing a marked lack of interest in the proceedings.

The chiefs have not acquired a higher social position from serving in their new capacities, and their lack of interest in council meetings stems at least in part from a fear of retaliation by their constituents should they actually propose any new measure. In meetings held in their own locations they are freely contradicted and even insulted, for they often owe their positions (and accompanying salaries) to the elders who proposed them as candidates, or they are viewed merely as the equals of others present. They are expected to serve, not to lead, and if they become "abusive"—i.e., if they try to enforce their commands—magic may be used against them. Their hands are tied.

THE ECONOMY

Pakot economic life centers on herding. Farming, which varies in importance depending on the nature of the land, takes second place in esteem if not always in fact. Livestock consist of zebu cattle,[15] fat-tailed sheep, goats, and a few donkeys. All male stock, except for a few kept for breeding purposes, are castrated, and the resulting three types of cattle have different functions. Cows are all-important as providers of calves and milk, essential to the diet; because of the expected yield of calves, cows are looked on as particularly valuable capital goods. Bulls are kept for breeding but, like cows, are eaten when their usefulness is ended. Steers are prized above all for their beauty but are actually less valuable than cows from an economic point of view. Steers are slaughtered for various rituals, for which they are exclusively used, and also serve as media of exchange to secure grain. Cattle are too valuable and too scarce to be slaughtered indiscriminately, so sheep and goats are more often killed for entertaining visiting clansmen or best friends and on other occasions. In the end all stock, except those which are for some reason inedible, are eaten whether they are intentionally slaughtered or die unexpectedly.[16] Livestock provide milk, meat, and blood, while the dead animals are a source of hides, horns, and other by-products used for shoes, clothing, and accessories. The economic uses of cattle for all Nilotics are highly important, but the cattle are more than mere economic goods. They are a subject of focal interest in the lives of the people, as is indicated by the aspects of beauty attributed to them and the identification with and affection for them that is felt.

The Pakot knew only two crops before the British came, eleusine, or "finger millet," and sorghum, or "millet."[17] Both are held to be desirable because they are hardy and can grow under adverse conditions with comparatively little attention. Furthermore, the best "beer" is made with them, and beer is an essential component of social interaction. Farming is generally concentrated in the rainy season from about April to August, when fields of an acre or two in size are cleared on the slopes; they are used for a season or two and then abandoned after their fertility has diminished. Fortunate individuals can grow two crops a year, harvesting in both the dry and rainy seasons, by practicing flood irri-

---

[15] To be distinguished from the long-horned cattle which are characteristic of the Hima-dominated Bantu people to the south and west of the Nilotics.

[16] See Schneider, "The Subsistence Role of Cattle."

[17] As is implied here, the term "millet" does not refer to the plant of the same name in the western hemisphere. Specifically, these two plants are *Eleusine coracana* and *Sorghum caudatum*.

gation.[18] This is particularly true in WeiWei location, which has the largest network of canals in the reserve. As the amount of land available for farming is limited and in great demand, concepts of ownership are more clearly formulated for it than for any other land. Pastoralists dwelling on the edges of the hot, low plains can obtain a crop during the rains by planting eleusine, the hardiest crop. Those who have few cattle can live on the slopes or along the sides of the mountains where farming is possible but pastures restricted, and some can manage large herds and farms together.

The Pakot are linked together by three levels of economic dependency. On the lowest level there are the homesteads which produce enough to satisfy most of their needs, except for such imported items as beads and other decorative goods—and in recent times some maize flour, which is sold by alien traders. To achieve maximum production, members of each neighborhood band together in co-operative labor and lending of goods, this co-operative tendency being ritually reinforced by periodic communal cattle feasts. Beyond this, at the third level, the Pakot are tied together by symbiotic relations allowing those who have little grain to trade meat and cattle for others' surplus grain. The two main groups of people are distinguished as the "cattle people" (*pipatich*) and the "grain people" (*pipapagh*).

Another type of exchange which is important in cementing relations resembles the custom[19] of the Kipsigis, Nandi, and other east African peoples of depositing cattle with neighbors and friends. By distributing cattle far and wide, they insure that only part of their herds will be lost in the event of cattle raids or disease in the home area and so guarantee that they will not be left destitute. To this widespread practice the Pakot have added a variation in their institutionalized trading partnership (*tilia*) between men. The person receiving a cow must give to its owner a steer, or sometimes grain or goats and sheep. Subsequently, the new possessor of the steer may use it as he pleases, usually for bride-wealth, a feast, or to trade for grain. The new holder of the cow keeps it as long as it lives but must make small gifts to the former owner and periodically transfer to him one of its calves. After the cow dies, no further debt is owed. Frequently, the holder of the cow fraudulently claims that it has died so that the burden of continuous payment may be lifted from him. This is in part responsible for the many civil cases relating to cattle mentioned above.

[18] Also practiced by the Marakwet and Elgeyo to the south of the Pakot on the Rift Valley escarpment and among the Lango of the southern Sudan.

[19] Called *kaptich* by Nandi and *kimanagan* by Kipsigis. G. W. B. Huntingford, *Nandi Work and Culture* ("Colonial Research Studies," No. 4 [London: Colonial Office, 1950]), p. 38; J. G. Peristiany, *The Social Institutions of the Kipsigis* (London: George Routledge & Sons, 1939), pp. 150–52.

Beginning about 1930, the British undertook economic reforms because of a desire to raise the standard of living, to increase the Pakot contribution to the economy of Kenya, and to preserve its resources but also, it would seem, because of a conflict of cultural values and a lack of understanding of pastoralism. Certainly British criticisms of Pakot economic practices suggest that there is something unnatural about a people whose interests are restricted to herding cattle and something wrong or wasteful in an economy which does not value work for its own sake but allows men to loll in the shade.

Through the early years of contact the government was too occupied with other things to concern itself with Pakot economic activities. Barton commented in 1920 that the Pakot were not much interested in adding maize to their crops. In 1926 another district commissioner described them as a "very lazy tribe at any time," who made no attempt to increase their cultivation or to grow better crops.

Economic reform actually began, not as the result of official policy, but as the avocation of G. H. Chaundy, the principal of the government school at Kapenguria from 1930 to 1943. He instituted a curriculum heavily biased toward "good" farming techniques in the hope that the pupils would disseminate the knowledge they gained. Hoping to induce the Pakot to leave their pastoral life, he established demonstration plots throughout the reserve in order to show them the advantage of diversifying their crops and to give them experience in handling new crops, including cassava, cashews, kapok, tomatoes, potatoes, bananas, papaw, beans, oranges, lemons, sugar cane, limes, and peppers. Good land was selected for these plots where cultivation could usually be aided by irrigation, and the government required adult men to devote a small amount of labor each year to their upkeep.

Only the introduction of maize was moderately successful. Some farmers grow it voluntarily, and in Seker location, where there is indication that the people were initially forced to plant it, it is consistently used. Maize, it would seem, is acceptable mainly because it is not unlike millet and finger millet in appearance and method of cultivation. Its disadvantages are that it requires more attention and better growing conditions than the traditional crops and special equipment to grind it, so that most of it is traded to the Turkana or to Indian shopkeepers or taken to the shops to be ground in the mills of the Indians.

In 1943 Chaundy stated in print that resistance had been broken down and that an agricultural "revolution" had been accomplished in the area.[20] Aside from the limited acceptance of maize, however, his work met with strong resistance, despite his sincerity, good intentions, and

[20] G. H. Chaundy, "The Agricultural Education of a Primitive Tribe: The West Suk of Kenya," *East African Agricultural Journal*, VIII (1943), 1–11.

zealous efforts. He tried to eliminate the erosive practice of planting on steep slopes but finally had to introduce ordinances requiring farmers to place contour ditches in all fields to reduce the wash-off of earth and to stop further slope-planting. As late as 1940 he was told by the chief of Seker location that because of a famine, many families had migrated down to the Malmaltai River to gather wild plants. Chaundy replied that the shortage of food was due to their own indolence, that he had warned them the previous year that locusts were coming and that they should plant white and sweet potatoes, and that he had even given them seeds to do so. The chief answered that the people did not want to plant these crops which required too much labor and only wanted to grow their traditional crop, eleusine. The Pakot like many of the new foods Chaundy introduced and eat them when they can get them, but they have offered various excuses for not raising them, the favorite being that their cows would dry up if they did so.

The frequent result of the ordinances relating to farming was that the African agricultural instructors, who were assigned to enforce them, began accepting bribes to overlook illegal cases so that planting of steep slopes is still widespread.

After World War II, when Chaundy had gone, the Colonial Development Corporation provided funds for permanent livestock and agricultural officers in the area and attempted to establish groundnut (peanut) growing in West Suk. This scheme failed and, to 1952, the officers had had no more success than Chaundy. Mnagei location, where the government headquarters and school are situated, has been considerably changed; some farmers are using plows instead of the traditional short-handled African hoe, but many, if not all, are aliens or people living under the eyes of the government.

The campaign to establish new agricultural methods was accompanied by an attack on methods of animal husbandry. For many years it has been widely agreed in Kenya that the pastoralists overgraze their land, destroying it through erosion. The Carter Land Commission of 1932 estimated that the Pakot had over three hundred thousand head of cattle for a population of little more than twenty thousand, but an accurate census by the livestock officer in 1952 gave a total of slightly more than one hundred and ten thousand head of cattle for West Suk, with an equal number of goats and thirty seven thousand sheep for a population of about forty thousand.

Short of destocking the area forcibly, a policy that has been instituted in some other places,[21] the only feasible suggestion for reducing the herds was to promote the sale and export of cattle to other areas. The Pakot

[21] C. I. Meek, "Stock Reduction in the Mbulu Highlands, Tanganyika," *Journal of African Administration*, V (1953), 158–66.

sell stock among themselves and trade cattle in the *tilia* system, but they object to selling cattle to foreigners largely because the mutual long-term obligations for help and support secured through cattle-sharing and trade are lost in outright sale. Since the early days they have disposed of some stock to pay taxes, and even today steers are sold to Somali traders[22] to obtain cash, but they prefer to use the animals in the traditional manner and sell the hides, of which a large number are exported annually. Their resistance to selling cattle has been reinforced by the fact that European settlers have agitated for quarantines on the reserve. Their reasons include the fear that the export of African cattle would adversely affect the prices of their own cattle on the market and that cattle diseases endemic in the reserve would spread to their own herds. Quarantines have been in effect for long periods of time, but in 1941, when such considerations were of secondary importance, the Pakot exported three thousand head of cattle. After the war the quarantine was reinstituted.

Pakot reaction is that the government wants to keep them poor. They ask why individual settlers are allowed to keep large herds, while they themselves are discouraged from doing so. The enormity of proposals for the reduction of stock is best seen when we examine their value system, which leads them to look upon a man with a hundred head of cattle as rich, one with ten head as poor, and one with no cattle as "dead."

With the attempt to decrease the total size of herds, Chaundy sponsored bylaws which established restricted grazing areas and were designed to improve the condition of the range. The Pakot had grazed cattle both on the plains and in the mountains, where the grass is always lush, but the plains people resorted to the mountains only during conditions of drought. They had, in fact, an indigenous plan whereby areas of termite-resisting grass in the neighborhoods were closed for grazing except during droughts and in the dry season of the year, and fines were imposed on those who trespassed. Some groups have continued this procedure, but there is no record that the government was aware of it in 1939 when some ninety square miles were set apart under the bylaws and guards posted over them. The Pakot have resisted the imposition of this new system, and one of the most frequent "crimes" judged in the tribunals is violation of these restricted grazing areas. However, the underlying principle is familiar, and they have co-operated to the extent of building thornbush fences around the grass reserves.

The Pakot argue that the government exaggerates the problem of erosion; even though there are large patches of exposed red earth on the plains, they maintain that the area has always been that way. They

[22] Somalis usually have the permits to trade in hides and stock, while Indians have the concession for milling maize.

regard government officials as perennial pessimists who constantly complain that the land is being washed into the rivers, and they ignore these warnings because their cattle continue to be fat and sleek.[23] They are unmoved by arguments that they should protect the land for posterity; one man said, "My sons will have to solve their own problems."

Propaganda about "improving" the breed of cattle has fallen on equally deaf ears. The trading partnerships, the frequent necessity of slaughtering cattle for feasts and food, the use of cattle feasts to establish reciprocal obligations, and other factors make it necessary for a man to have many cattle. For these reasons the idea of breeding one superior animal to replace three or four inferior ones is not understandable; moreover they are not convinced that their own cattle are inferior.

It is apparent that most of the changes in economic life have been minor. The development of a market for hides is perhaps an exception but does not affect them to any great extent, while the growing of maize is not widespread and when it occurs has been incorporated into old patterns. Most economic changes have been forced on the Pakot by new laws which specifically prohibit burning grass throughout most of the year, cutting trees in forests at the heads of streams, violating restricted grazing areas, and cultivating without contouring. Trading areas have been delimited in the reserve in which the traders offer a variety of goods for sale, but the Pakot have taken to few of these. Their major purchases are imported ground maize, sugar, beads and wire, long iron knives (like machetes), cotton sheeting, and a few other minor consumption goods. The long knife or *panga* has largely replaced the traditional long knife which was made by indigenous blacksmiths. These innovations could probably be eliminated with little effect on the Pakot; certainly they could still adjust to a situation in which the innovations did not exist.

One activity which might be mistaken for a marked change in custom has developed since the advent of the British. Many young men leave the reserve to work as herders and field hands on nearby European plantations after they have passed through the rigorous puberty circumcision ceremonies; after a few months or a few years they return home to be initiated into adulthood in an elaborate feast (*sapana*). This is not an entirely new pattern, as young men have traditionally gone away from home before initiation to work for wealthy herders, usually on the plains. They were paid in livestock for acting as herdsmen, acquiring some cattle with which to start their own herds and impressing their fathers with their diligence so as to encourage them to provide the steer for the initiation feast and the cattle for the wedding payments. Young men are

[23] Visitors often express surprise at the healthy, fat cattle which contrast sharply with the seemingly sparse grass.

forbidden to marry before initiation but usually take their first wife immediately afterward. The work on European plantations and the money wages are the only new elements in this practice, and no overwhelming number of Pakot leave the reserve to work.[24]

EDUCATION AND RELIGION

Traditionally, formal education is provided during circumcision ceremonies—at meetings near the circumcision hut, which is set off by itself in the bush—when young boys from a number of nearby neighborhoods receive from three to five months' training and instruction in traditional lore and morality. In addition, children learn the system of values and techniques of life in informal groups and by precept at home. Education is designed to instil an appreciation of the value of their way of life and of cattle in particular. Knowledge of animal husbandry and other techniques is acquired through participation in the economic activities of the home.

In religious life the Pakot, like most Nilotics, lack a systematic verbalized cosmology, although under the surface there seems to be a complex system of beliefs about the nature of the universe.[25] They believe in a high god and creator, Tororut, who seems to be a paternal guardian and disciplinarian and who manifests himself in the sun, the stars, the rain and thunder, and other natural phenomena. Prayers are addressed to this deity or to his manifestations for aid in times of sickness, drought, and other misfortunes. The ancestors, who play such an important role in the religious life of the Bantu and some Nilotics, are much less significant. The only spirits thought to continue to exist after death are those of adult men (and on some occasions adult women also) who have families and who have achieved some degree of wealth and ritual, moral, or social status. These spirits intervene in the affairs of the living, and prayers for help are sometimes addressed to them; but the Pakot seem to regard death as the greatest of evils and consider it a breach of etiquette even to mention the names of those who have died or to talk about death. The ancestral spirits are looked upon for the most part as malevolent, irritable, and vindictive; they are blamed for misfortunes that befall their former homesteads. Little knowledge of the afterlife, of the ancestral spirits, or of their high god is admitted. The Pakot are to some degree fatalists, taking misfortune as it comes, pleading with their god and the supernatural forces to help them in times of need but never assured that they will do so.

[24] For example, six hundred went out in 1932 and about 500 in 1947.
[25] A more thorough discussion of Pakot moral and religious beliefs is to be found in H. K. Schneider, "The Moral System of the Pakot," in *Encyclopedia of Morals*, ed. Vergilius Ferm (New York: Philosophical Library, 1955), pp. 403–9.

They also seem to feel that the traditional way of life is most acceptable to Tororut, that he created it and desires it to continue, in fact, that it is the best conceivable life. An upset in the balance of metaphysical forces explains much, but not all, evil that occurs. A man whose life has been free of evil deeds is ritually pure; but through certain acts or by involvement in situations charged with danger of social disequilibrium he may become "unclean," and misfortune will descend on him. A man who becomes ill often interprets this as a result of his behavior, as do his neighbors. During all of the major transitional periods of life, including birth, circumcision, and death, "uncleanness" is present—at birth in the mother, at circumcision in the boy, and at death in the surviving spouse and children of the dead. Most criminal acts, including murder and the practice of malevolent magic for private ends, produce this ritual uncleanness, but it does not relate directly to illegal acts, as is seen in the case of the mother at the birth of a child. That a warrior who kills a member of an enemy tribe is also made unclean, even though his act is praiseworthy, is further illustration of this principle. Unclean persons are isolated from the rest of society until they can be cleansed through appropriate ceremonies, such as sprinkling them with the blood of a goat or washing them with the contents of its stomach. Uncleanness is clearly a transitional social state, a period of change of status which is a period of tension precisely because some shifting of the normal equilibrium of the group is in process. The cleansing ceremony is a device for smoothing that transition. The net result of the system is to encourage equilibrium and to alert the group to special precaution to preserve it during those times when it is most liable to disturbance.

Magic, which is so important in the religious and moral life, is probably the most effective means of social control. It may be used by individuals in authority and by the community as a whole to achieve their ends or by those who have been insulted or injured against those who have offended them. It may also be used by evil persons who wish to injure others for personal reasons, but this is generally condemned, and those who use magic in this way are considered to be congenitally evil and deserving of the most extreme punishment. Privately practiced magic is equated with murder or worse. One of the most important tasks of the diviners is to identify workers of magic so that they can be brought to justice.

Magic makes it possible for the elders and members of a community to punish criminals who are unknown, while the ever-present danger of being killed magically by a person one has injured makes the Pakot hesitate to offend each other in any but a few socially acceptable ways. One middle-aged man said that he would not even like to have an unusually large herd of cattle because his neighbors would envy him and someone would cast a spell on him. Magic may also be used by the community to punish a deviant, so that most persons are careful not to transgress the accepted ways even if they should be so inclined. Because magic is accepted as a stern reality, deviation is rare and undoubtedly carefully considered.

This brief summary sketches only the main outlines of Pakot belief, but it serves to give a setting for a discussion of their reaction to the third major assault on their way of life. This began about the time Chaundy inaugurated his work, in the combined areas of education and religion. Education was not left strictly to the missions, as was true in so much of Africa. A government school was established in 1928, three years before the Bible Churchmen's Mission Society obtained land and constructed a mission and school.[26] Both organizations subsequently established small elementary "bush schools" throughout the district to introduce local boys to schooling. By transferring to the main schools at the mission at Nasokol or at government headquarters at Kapenguria, they could continue their studies. In 1951 it was possible to obtain an education up to Form II.[27]

The schools and missions have succeeded no better than other innovations. Both schools have drawn their students mainly from the more aggressive alien peoples, such as Kitosh, Kony, and Sapei, who have come into Mnagei location, where the main schools are situated. Attendance in the bush schools has always been poor, and the district commissioners have had to cajole Pakot fathers into sending their sons to them. A bush school serving one of the most populous Pakot locations in 1951 had only about ten students, and they attended classes irregularly. In 1948 the district commissioner complained that the government school at Kapenguria had only 102 pupils, less than half of whom were Pakot; classwork, he added, was very poor.

Pakot arguments against schooling are clear. First, small boys assist in herding small stock, and putting them in school makes this impossible. Second, they see no value in learning reading, writing, or arithmetic; they do not envy European ways and have no desire to emulate them. Another factor undoubtedly is the permissiveness of childhood, which makes it an enviable period and does not create the strong conflicts that would lead children to desire emancipation.

Resistance to Christianity is also based in part on simple indifference. There seems to be nothing in Christianity to appeal to them, and their own beliefs seem to have been sufficient for their needs. Such a reaction to Christianity in Africa is not surprising. It is almost axiomatic today

[26] At Kongolai-Kacheliba, later moved to Nasokol, near Kapenguria.

[27] There are six standard grades and after those two Forms in the school system in the district.

that converts are secured largely through the monopoly of educational facilities by missions. Since the Pakot desire no education, the church cannot use its most effective proselytizing device. In 1952 the head of one mission station stated that he could count on the fingers of one hand the number of Pakot he thought had been converted in the twenty-five years he had been in the area, despite his diligent efforts.

But reaction to missions is based on other things as well. In West Suk conversion means going to school, and the criticisms of education hold for both mission and government schools. Furthermore, to worship in a Christian manner, one must live a sedentary life, reside near other people and the church, recognize a religious leader with authority, abandon polygyny, and refrain from circumcising the young, all things held to be undesirable if not impossible. The missions have made their task no easier by refusing to compromise and in some cases by demanding abstention from certain rites for no apparent reason. For example, a young boy must choose between baptism and circumcision, despite the fact that except on the western border of the district circumcision is a *sine qua non* of Pakot life. An uncircumcised man is scarcely considered a man and certainly not a true Pakot.

In summary, the Pakot today persist in the old ways. The women wear their indigenous costumes of goatskin skirts and capes. The men wear hardly any clothes at all. They carry their eight-foot spears, wear elaborate clay headdresses which designate them as initiated adults, tend their flocks, cultivate their crops, and drink great quantities of their all-important millet or honey beer. They conduct their government as far as possible as they have always done in the past, paying as little attention as possible to the government (*serkali*) and, when necessary, countering its moves with passive resistance or active obstructionism, including the use of magic against those who are tempted to deviate. They continue to provide all the education and religion needed for this life in the community and remain unconvinced of the alleged benefits of government schooling and Christianity. Their herding life provides all they need and all they want, and they have found almost nothing in Euroamerican culture that will entice them to abandon their old ways.

OTHER NILOTIC PEOPLES

The Pakot's determined resistance to British pressures is based upon their satisfaction with their traditional culture and their feeling that it is superior to and more desirable than Euroamerican civilization. Associated with this conviction is an attitude, which varies from simple indifference to contempt of all other people, that makes ethnographic work among them difficult, especially when the attitude is coupled—as it is—with the suspicion that outsiders' attempts to learn about Pakot culture are motivated by a desire to change it. Suspicion, reserve, indifference, contempt, and the feeling of superiority are all related to their desire to resist change and maintain their culture as it is. Reactions of this kind, however, are not restricted to the Pakot but have been noted among other Nilotic peoples by a number of observers.

Audrey Butt has summarized the impressions of those who have had dealings with the peoples of the northernmost Nilotic area, conventionally known as the "Nilotes," to whom we refer as the Nuer-Shilluk group:

All who have come into contact with the Nilotes have remarked on the proud, individualistic and truculent behavior which they display towards each other and particularly toward foreigners. They consider their country the best in the world and everyone inferior to themselves. For this reason they despise clothing and scorn European and Arab culture, and are contemptuous and reserved with foreigners, so that it is difficult to get to know them. Their attitude toward any authority that would coerce them is one of touchiness, pride, and reckless disobedience. Each determines to go his own way as much as possible, has a hatred of submission, and is ready to defend himself and his property from the inroads of others. They are self-reliant, brave fighters, turbulent and aggressive, and are extremely conservative in their aversion from innovation and interference.[28]

The core of this conservatism is the feeling that they are inferior to no one and superior to all. Evans-Pritchard encountered this conservatism while working with the Nuer and has described graphically how difficult it was even to persuade a man to tell the name of his lineage.[29]

Of the Bari-Lotuko or "northern Nilo-Hamite" group,[30] who are still largely isolated, too little is known to comment, but within the Karamojong-Teso or "central Nilo-Hamite" group[31] Gulliver notes that conservatism and suspicion make for the greatest difficulty in getting cooperation and information. The Turkana had to be subdued with considerable armed force, which has left a legacy of hostility toward

[28] Butt, *The Nilotes*, p. 41. This subgroup includes the Nuer, Shilluk, Anuak, Acholi, Lango, Dinka, Burun, and Bor Belanda of central Sudan and northern Uganda and the Luo, part of whom are in the Sudan and part in southwest Kenya.

[29] E. E. Evans-Pritchard, *The Nuer* (London: Oxford University Press, 1940), p. 12.

[30] G. W. B. Huntingford, *The Northern Nilo-Hamites* (London: International African Institute, 1952). This group includes the Bari, Kuku, Kakwa, Marshia, Mondari, Pojulu, Nyangbara, Nyepu, Lokoya, Kotuko, and Lango of the southern Sudan and northern Uganda. What information we have on the Bari-Lango is summarized in this source and shows that although almost all are predominantly pastoralists in outlook, some have lost most of their cattle through the slave raids of the last century.

[31] P. Gulliver and P. H. Gulliver, *The Central Nilo-Hamites* (London: International African Institute, 1953). This group includes the Karamojong, Teso, Kumam, Jie, Dodos, Turkana, Toposa, Donyiro, and Jiye, among others, of northeast Uganda and northwest Kenya.

whites; but when their attitudes are compared to those of other Nilotics, it is apparent that they come not from this reason alone. Although they are still quite isolated from Europeans and therefore have had little opportunity to borrow from them, it seems that they are also proud, satisfied, and unwilling to change.[32]

The Nandi-Masai or "southern Nilo-Hamite"[33] group have been in contact with Europeans most intimately, but the pattern of conservatism continues. Huntingford indicates that the Nandi are proud and intensely conservative. Writing about them in 1950, he said:

> Their pride in themselves and their tribe, their contempt for all who were not like themselves, and their dislike of foreigners remain to this day, though modified; but in the early days of the British administration these feelings were intensified by the attempts of a foreign people to interfere in their affairs. Their first estimate of the Europeans was "they are women, these Europeans, because they tie themselves up with clothes" and though they confess to some fear of the firearms used by these "women" they stood up to them for nine years. Added to this is their intense conservatism, and their preference for their own way of life and their own methods which are still strong enough to resist the lure of civilization as offered to them through the media of trade, government, missions, and colonization.[34]

The Kipsigis, who number seventy thousand and are probably the largest of the Nandi-speaking people, are also conservative and hostile to innovation, partly because of the ill feelings generated toward the whites who used force to subdue them. Peristiany saw the family being affected by the young men leaving to work on farms, with or without their fathers' permissions, but on the whole they have also remained quite stable in the face of contact.[35]

Some of the Pakot's closest neighbors on the eastern Rift Valley escarpment to the south have the same attitude as the Pakot. Hennings speaks of the Elgeyo and other Nandi-Masai as follows:

> The pastoral tribes show no . . . indecent haste to abandon their old way of life. On the whole khaki shirts and shorts, felt hats, cigarettes, bicycles, and football mean little to the Elgeyo and their kindred tribes, and their cousins, the Masai and the Samburu. . . . Some people, I know, will call this a life of stagnation, implying that anything old and unchanging is stagnant. I think that both premiss and conclusion are open to question. The Elgeyo herdsman has as

[32] P. Gulliver, *A Preliminary Survey of the Turkana* ("Communications from the School of African Studies, University of Capetown," N. S. No. 26 [Capetown, 1951]), pp. 5–12.

[33] G. W. B. Huntingford, *The Southern Nilo-Hamites* (London: International African Institute, 1953). In this subgroup, the Nandi, Kipsigis, Dorobo, Elgeyo, Kamasya, Sapei, Kony, Pakot, Marakwet, and Barabaig in western Kenya and northern Tanganyika are commonly distinguished as the "Nandi-speaking peoples," and the Masai, Samburu, and Njemps in Kenya and Tanganyika as the "Masai-speaking peoples."

[34] Huntingford, *Nandi Work and Culture*, p. 108.

[35] Peristiany, *Social Institutions*, p. 4.

good food or better, as good or better housing, and a generally more healthy life than millions who live in the industrial towns of Europe. Unemployment and poverty, those spectres of western civilization, have no meaning for him. He is at one with his environment, a pastoralist with his cattle on the high equatorial pastures of Africa; and because he feels himself a part of his Cosmos, his heart is at peace and he is carefree and happy in a way that millions in Europe never know.[36]

As this passage shows, the life of the pastoralists appeals to Europeans as well as the Nilotics, so much so that many Europeans, like Hennings, succumb to its charm and are spoken of as having the "disease" of "Masaiitis." As its name suggests, it was first manifested among officials assigned to the Masai who sometimes became so enamored of Masai ways that they lost their effectiveness as administrators and had to be transferred.

The Masai, in the eyes of east African settlers, are the prime example of pastoral stolidity; many writers have commented on this, among them Elspeth Huxley:

> In this modern world of blackboards, committees and demagogues, these obstinately conservative nomads, wandering with their enormous herds from pasture to pasture, seem like dinosaurs or pterodactyls, survivors from a past age with a dying set of values—aristocratic, manly, free, doomed. Like everything else in nature that will not or cannot conform to a changed environment, they must perish or merge; only the shield of British administration stands today between them and the historical fate of the nomad caught by the relentless and mounting pressure of the teeming cultivators.[37]

Fosbrooke confirms their conservatism but interprets it more approvingly:

> If by soul erosion is meant a deterioration in obedience to existing moral standards, a falling off in observance of organized religion, a lack of purpose in life, then the Masai are amongst the least affected of peoples. Ever since their original contact with Europeans, more than half a century ago, they have as a people most courteously defined their attitude, more by deeds than words, that they are satisfied with their mode of life and intend to adhere to it. Certain adaptations and concessions they have made but only after critical examination and slow absorption, not by unreasonable apeing.[38]

No culture remains static and changeless, however, and the Nilotic cultures are no exceptions. Some Nilotic peoples have been prone to changes which reinforced their pastoralism, and all have borrowed from each other, sometimes extensively. Much has been borrowed from the Masai by their neighbors, and the Pakot have borrowed from the Karamojong and Turkana to the extent that they have become atypical of

[36] R. O. Hennings, *African Morning* (London: Chatto & Windus, 1951), pp. 166–67.

[37] Elspeth Huxley, *The Sorcerer's Apprentice* (London: Chatto & Windus, 1949), p. 89.

[38] Fosbrooke, "Administrative Survey," p. 50.

the Nandi-speaking people. There are some examples of accepting traits from the Bantu and from Europeans. Prins has shown that there is still some debate about where the age-grade systems of east Africa originated, some suggesting that they are Bantu in origin, though he believes they derive from the ancestors of present Ethiopians.[39]

With a few exceptions, such as the Kony, Sapei, and perhaps the Kumam, Teso, and Karamojong,[40] resistance to Euroamerican tradition seems to be the rule; but these exceptions do exist. A possible explanation for the Sapei, Kony, Kumam, and Teso is that they have become "Bantuized" through conquest by the powerful Bantu of Uganda and so have become more prone to borrowing from Europeans. These deviations, however, only make the general pattern of Nilotic conservatism stand out more sharply.

NEIGHBORING BANTU PEOPLES

The conservatism of the Nilotics and the associated attitudes which support it also stand out in relief when contrasted to the receptivity to innovation of the neighboring Bantu peoples of Kenya and Tanganyika —such as the Kikuyu and the related Kamba, Teita, Nyika, Taveta, and Pare,[41] and the Abaluhya or Bantu of Kavirondo, who include Tsotso, Vukusu or Kitosh, Kakamega, Maragoli, and others.[42] Although not many of these Bantu peoples have been studied from the point of view of culture change, and although not all may be equally receptive to it, the available evidence suggests a far greater degree of adaptation to Euroamerican culture and willingness to depart from the traditional patterns than is to be found among the Nilotics. Speaking of east Africa in general, Huntingford has stated:

It is probably among the pastoral tribes that resistance is most common and most active. . . . In general it may be said that the pastoral tribes are the most and the agricultural tribes the least, resistant to new forms of culture,

[39] A. H. J. Prins, *East African Age-class Systems* (Groningen: J. B. Wolters, 1953), p. 121.

[40] Gulliver is the only person who has written much about these people, and this qualification is based on his comments. According to him the Kumam and Teso were changed some time ago by an invasion of Baganda, who set up an administration in the country. The Karamojong, he also says, have taken to plows to some extent and show a few other changes. How extensive these changes are he does not say, and beyond these few remarks there is no other information (Gulliver and Gulliver, *The Central Nilo-Hamites*, pp. 11–12). In a private communication, Walter Goldschmidt has said that the Sapei were likewise conquered by the Baganda.

[41] See A. H. J. Prins, "Provinces Culturelles en Afrique: Essai d'une Classification Justifiée," *Kongo-Overzee*, XIX (1953), 289–305, for a discussion of the relationship of these people.

[42] For a discussion of the relationship of these people see Huntingford, *The Nandi of Kenya*, p. 2.

though it must be understood that this is but a generalization, and may not be found to fit all cases.[43]

The agricultural people listed by Huntingford include Bantu groups such as the Kikuyu of Kenya and the Chaga, Ngindo, Pogoro, and Bena of Tanganyika, plus a few of doubtful classification. The pastoral groups are Nilotics except for the Somalis and Gala, the so-called Hamites. A third group described as "both pastoral and agricultural" are all Bantu. Despite their cattle, this third group probably still places most emphasis on agriculture.[44]

While the Nilotics have been criticized for their "stagnation," the Bantu have been criticized for "aping" Western ways. The Bantu have taken to European culture to the extent that they constitute a potential threat to the security of the settlers through their political activities, trading, and persistent desire to achieve a comparable standard of living. Government schools almost identical to those among the Pakot have taken deep root among the Kikuyu. Many years ago they established the first independent school system in Africa, modeled on the European pattern. The Kikuyu, who constitute the largest indigenous society in Kenya, have become very active in politics and have flooded the labor market, becoming the most numerous people in the domestic service, government, and trading. Their frustration when their aspirations for change could not be achieved has been held to be largely responsible for the Mau Mau uprising, which also partly came from their eagerness to borrow certain aspects of European culture; during the process, changes unavoidably occurred in group solidarity and in aspects of culture that they had wished to preserve.

CAUSES OF NILOTIC CONSERVATISM

Attempts to derive the causes for the different degrees of receptivity to acculturation among the Nilotics and Bantu are difficult because of a lack of clear understanding of how these processes work. However, some tentative conclusions are possible. Initially, one is tempted to attribute the Nilotic conservatism purely to the fact that they possess the cattle complex, which has been defined[45] as an intense devotion to cattle and a permeation of this value into all other aspects of culture. It could be argued that the cattle complex would make Nilotic cultures incompatible with those of Europeans; but since the Bantu of East Africa also possess the cattle complex, such an answer is inadequate.

[43] G. W. B. Huntingford and C. R. V. Bell, *East African Background* (2d ed; London: Longmans, Green, 1950), p. 83.

[44] *Ibid.*, pp. 55–57.

[45] M. J. Herskovits, "The Cattle Complex in East Africa," *American Anthropologist*, Vol. XXVIII, Nos. 1,2,3,4 (1926).

The cattle complex, nevertheless, seems important when combined with an essentially pastoral way of life; together these two factors seem to give a partial answer to our question. The Kikuyu, Abaluhya, and other Bantu peoples of East Africa are traditionally sedentary agriculturalists who value cattle highly and, like the Bantu of southern Africa, share the cattle complex, but among them cattle are of less economic importance than among the Nilotics. Agricultural products are basic to the subsistence economy and are recognized as the staff of life, while cattle function mainly in the prestige economy or as a supplement to agriculture. The aboriginal Kikuyu had few cattle and were not dependent upon them for food. The Abaluhya could not raise many cattle, although the Vukusu are described as predominantly pastoral by Wagner,[46] who, in fact, speaks of all the northern part of the Abaluhya area (north and south Kitosh) as predominantly pastoral. Huntingford, in his classification cited above, does not include a single Bantu group under the heading of truly pastoral.

That the cattle complex must be considered together with pastoralism in assessing reactions to change is evident when we examine its position in these two groups of cultures. While the cattle complex is the focus of Nilotic cultures, among the Bantu of East Africa it seems to be in competition with other values which may represent the central values of an ancient Bantu culture type before the cattle complex was diffused. Among Pakot and other Nilotic peoples it is the central, all-encompassing value; among the Bantu it seems to have been modified by the values of trading, agriculture, education, lineage solidarity, and other pursuits. Pastoral life can provide security when it is possible to accumulate many animals, as the Nilotics generally do. Even though devastating cattle plagues have been known, cattle are less affected by drought and disease than are crops in the usual Nilotic habitat, since cattle can be moved but crops cannot. More important, as far as the Nilotics are concerned, is the fact that cattle, sheep, and goats increase "by themselves" and need comparatively little attention.

Two other factors to be considered are the degree of adaptation of Nilotic culture to the habitat, to which Henning refers in speaking of the southernmost Nilotics as "at one with their environment," and the degree of cultural integration. In Nilotic cultures, as exemplified by the Pakot, all the diverse elements seem to be mutually compatible and to function with a minimum of friction. A change in any element might produce a chain reaction of adaptation with the culture, and the Pakot have succeeded thus far in resisting innovations which would have this result. Among the Bantu, on the other hand, one may regard the very

[46] Gunter Wagner, *The Bantu of North Kavirondo* (London: Oxford University Press, 1949–56), II, 39.

desire for change as an expression of a lesser degree of cultural integration.

In his discussion of Bantu and Nilotics, Huntingford mentions only a few warlike Bantu peoples, while all the Nilotics valued warfare because through it losses to their herds could be recouped, wealth could be increased, and young men could be provided excitement and a means to achieving fame and fortune. The Nilotics have traditionally been the terror of the Bantu people, and they willingly attacked each other. While some old men welcome peace, occasional cattle thefts by the young men still occur. All these factors combined to develop pride among the pastoralists, feelings of well-being and superiority over other people, and a fierce desire to maintain a life that made these possible. The Bantu of this area are not described in these terms; they have usually been on the defensive, bound to the soil, and imitative of the Nilotics, whose culture they seem to view as possessing much of value to them.

9. The Dynamics of the
Ngombe Segmentary System

The Ngombe are a Bantu-speaking people, numbering some hundred and fifty thousand, the majority of whom live in swampy forests on either side of the Congo River between Lisala and Coquilhatville in the northwestern part of the Belgian Congo. Their major interest lies in hunting game in these forests; agricultural pursuits, yielding principally manioc and plantain, are considered less important and are relegated to women. This subsistence pattern admirably suits their segmentary social system in which a local kinship group subdivides into two or more parts upon reaching a certain size or generation depth. Segmentation was formerly accomplished through actual spatial separation, but this process is impeded by the government policy of enforcing permanent village settlement. In time this policy will have an adverse effect on the traditional social structure, according to which only those bound by patrilineal ties occupy common territory. When groups which no longer feel united by common lineage are prevented from achieving geographical separation, the traditional system of regulating social relations will not suffice.

The Ngombe peoples are widely dispersed over most of the Ubangi district as a result of the operation of segmentation as well as more general migrations and warfare. They cannot properly be termed a tribe, for there is little interaction between different groups. Any group which recognizes descent from a common ancestor is called a *libota*, whether this is a nuclear family whose father is still living, a village whose founding ancestor lived three or four generations ago, or a grouping of villages whose patrilineal genealogies lead to a common ancestor ten or more generations previous. The present study concerns itself for the most part with one *libota*, some five thousand descendants of the ancestor Gonji, most of whom live just north of the Congo River near its confluence with the Mongala.

Europeans and Americans are accustomed to terms for social and political units which suggest their level in the structure (as with town, county, state, and nation), but the language of the Ngombe does not make such distinctions. *Libota* denotes a patrilineal group regardless of size. The term *ngando* may similarly apply to an individual household, a section of a village, or an entire village, wherever a geographic locus is associated with a kinship group. This failure to distinguish terminologically between the levels of segmentary structure which we regard as significant does not mean that the Ngombe do not recognize the organization in which they live. Rather, it indicates that they view their system as an eternal process and not as a static structure, emphasizing the growth of families and not concerned with abstract structural principles.

It is of utmost importance to a Ngombe man that his name live in the memory of the generations after him. To assure this, he should marry several wives and father many children who in turn will produce offspring. This whole group would then be known by his name following the prefix *Boso-*, as in "Bosogonji," meaning "the *libota* or *ngando* of Gonji." Since the individuals composing this group also desire to leave their names for posterity, each tries to found his own *libota* or *ngando*, and there is the theoretical possibility of segmentation in every generation. If Bosogonji, in our example, segments into smaller *ngando* or *libota*, all of those segments together would still be referred to as Bosogonji; however, as the group grows larger and its segments drift apart territorially, the *Boso-* prefix is dropped, though the group is known always as "the children of Gonji," "the *libota* of Gonji." Both the prefix *Boso-* and the term *ngando* imply a geographic locus which is absent at the higher levels of the Ngombe social structure and which is not implied in the term *libota*.

It is unnecessary for the Ngombe to distinguish between the various levels of segmentation in the abstract, but for a description of the organization and function of these social units it is a prerequisite. The terminology suggested for segmentary systems by Evans-Pritchard,[1] while useful in part, is not entirely appropriate because his two terminal elements, "maximal lineage" and "minimal lineage," connote a finitude not compatible with the Ngombe system, which has a continuity almost without beginning and without definite end. The Ngombe do not have a clan organization which one could define as a maximal lineage; as more generations pass without forgetting the name of their ancestor, their lineage becomes deeper and wider.

The social units of the Ngombe are designated in this study in these terms: immediate family, extended family, *etuka* (plural *bituka*), village, major lineage, subtribe. Each broader and deeper grouping includes several units at the next lower level. The Gonji subtribe embraces at least five major lineages sharing the ancestor Gonji. Gwenjale, a major

[1] E. E. Evans-Pritchard, *The Nuer* (London: Oxford University Press, 1940).

lineage, includes five villages all kin through the family of Gwenjale. Bosomboko is a village composed of five *bituka* descended from Mboko. One of these is Bosomboli, which in turn is segmented into four extended families with the common ancestor Mboli. The extended families, like that called Bosobusilimo, are made up of patrilineally related immediate families. These various levels are shown in Figure 7.

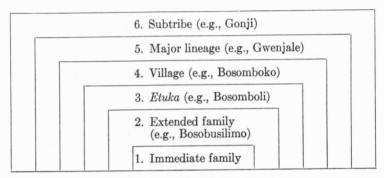

Fig. 7.—The social units of the Ngombe

The process of segmentation is not governed by rigid principles but is dependent on unformalized factors such as group size, propinquity of habitations, and freedom of migration. Accordingly, segmentation may occur more often in some lineages than in others, and occasionally one finds a social unit which appears to lie between the levels just distinguished. One such is the subvillage, a group of several *bituka* which lack the autonomy distinctive of a village; another is the extended family which fails to reproduce sufficiently in several generations, so that it continues to function as an extended family when its generation depth suggests that it could be an *etuka*. One further point in the way of exceptions should be made here: while membership in any group is patrilineal, occasional individuals or families attach themselves to the lineage of their mother, in which case they and their descendants are considered as continuing the *patrilineal* line of their maternal grandfather or maternal uncle.

The functioning of Ngombe social units can best be analyzed by working down from the subtribe through the intermediary units to the extended and the immediate family.

THE SUBTRIBE

The subtribe composed of the descendants of Gonji is a lineage with a depth of some ten generations. Gonji is an actual, not a legendary, ancestor, for his descendants have identified themselves as the *libota* of Gonji since he first fathered a family. Aside from its name and the fact that the genealogy descending from the ancestor is known, there is little recognition of kinship and few communal bonds among the five thousand members of the subtribe, at least among those whose lineages meet only at this extreme point in the structure. One such member would call another *mwangwambi* (brother),[2] in contradistinction to a person who is not a descendant of Gonji, in much the same way as the Ngombe call all Africans "brothers" to distinguish them from all Europeans.

No privileges or duties derive solely from membership in the subtribe, nor does this unit affect marriage or warfare. It is neither endogamous nor exogamous, and wars have often been fought between villages of the same subtribal group. The subtribe holds no land, and there is no territorial bond except in so far as the various subgroups which make it up occupy contiguous territories. Several of the lineages descended from Gonji are on the south side of the Congo River, far from the major section of their subtribe. Were it not for the administration's restriction of village movements and warfare, the traditional pattern of Ngombe migrations might well have scattered the group even more widely.

Although it may have begun as a smaller group with considerable functional significance, the subtribe has no social, political, or economic importance either in traditional Ngombe life or in the eyes of the Belgian administration. Because it lacks a *raison d'être* and because the process of segmentation demands a constant rising in the level of structure to make a place for the newly forming segments below, the particular grouping which is a subtribe at a given time must eventually pass into oblivion, the name of its founder forgotten or disregarded. As this occurs, the unit just below it in the social structure, the major lineage, moves to the class "subtribe."

THE MAJOR LINEAGE

The major lineage has the positive characteristics which define a subtribe, but the fact that its founding ancestor is from a less remote generation makes for a much stronger feeling of kinship among its members. This unit includes the descendants of the patrilineal ancestor whose name it bears, and its members call each other "brothers" in distinguishing themselves from members of any other major lineage—that is, when the frame of reference is at this level. Because interaction among members of different major lineages is much more common than that among members of different subtribes, the name of the major lineage is more often spoken and the brotherhood of its members more often

[2] Literally, *mwangwambi* means "child of my mother," but it is used in this patrilineal society to indicate a sibling in any sense.

affirmed. Membership in a major lineage, as in a subtribe, involves no limitations on marriage, but the closer degree of kinship manifests itself in other ways.

Warfare, commonly waged among segments of the major lineage, was the object of several proscriptions. Village chiefs (*bakumu*, singular, *kumu*) did not participate in such intragroup warfare and had no need to protect themselves. The supernaturally protected warrior leaders (*bilombe*, singular, *elombe*) normally did not participate because they disapproved. No administrative authority is recognized over a major lineage, although the chief of the senior village, descended from the oldest son of the founder of the major lineage, is said to have the right to forbid any junior segment to establish a chieftainship or to replace a deceased chief. If it actually exists, this is the only power which a traditional chief possesses over a major lineage, the segments of which are politically and economically independent. Under Belgian administration, however, a unit called a *sous-chefferie*, often identical in membership with a major lineage, is under an appointed *chef du groupement*.

The major lineage manifests greater spatial unity than a subtribe. Its segments more often occupy contiguous land, even though exceptions are observable. While some informants talk of a boundary (*mweya*) surrounding the land of a major lineage, defining the area within which all members share hunting and fishing rights prohibited to outsiders, this does not make of the major lineage a corporate land-holding body, for control of land remains the responsibility of the local group, and transgression of territorial rights is seen as a threat to the individual village rather than to the major lineage. A village can give outsiders permission to use its land without referring the question to the major lineage, which has no means to approve or disapprove, being devoid of any administrative apparatus such as a council or chief. It is thus that Bosomboko, a village of the major lineage Gwenjale, allows Mombangi, a non-Ngombe village, to fish in its swampy forests, without reference to other villages of Gwenjale.

Rivalry and consequent quarreling among the segments of a major lineage show its lack of cohesion. So much jealousy exists between Bosomboko and Bosodengasia that it is said that the members of these two villages cannot meet without fighting. This tension was increased some years ago when the administration removed the office of *chef du groupement* from Bosodengasia and appointed a man from Bosomboko. Among other villages, *chefs du groupement* have been seen to prohibit villagers from participating in a mock battle, as part of funeral ceremonies for an important man, on the ground that it might lead to an actual fight.

THE VILLAGE AND SUBVILLAGE

The village is a community of one hundred and fifty to three hundred members who inhabit contiguous plots along a road or forest path, with the continuity broken only between the several segments, *bituka*, of the whole. Like all other Ngombe social units, the village is composed of the agnatic descendants of the ancestor for whom the group is named, although, as at other levels, some few may trace descent from the founder through a female link. Upon marriage a woman moves to her husband's place of residence, but since most marriages unite members of the same village, most women live their full lives in the village of their birth.

Co-operation among villagers is most notable in hunting and warfare, the former, as has been indicated, having been the most important economic activity of the Ngombe and the latter their most important political activity. This co-operation manifests itself frequently in the *botai* hunt, in which all the men of the village set up a huge circle of nets in the forest and drive the animals from the center to the perimeter, where they are killed by the men stationed at the nets. Aside from this obvious demonstration of joint action, a successful hunt implies the supernatural concordance of the village ancestors, on the one hand, and, on the other, of the village *bemba*, persons with innate supernatural powers for both good and evil.[3] To avoid overemphasis of the village unit in the economy, it should be noted here that these co-operative hunts are often carried out at the level of the *etuka*, when in order to augment the number of hunters affinal or matrilineal kinsmen are invited to assist.

Warfare, for the most part, was an intervillage institution, requiring co-operation among villagers. Crucial in this respect was the warrior leader (*elombe*), whose strength, courage, and invulnerability were assured by the ancestors and by the supernatural powers of the *bemba*. Should the leaders suffer injury or death in a battle, the men would assume that the battle was lost and scatter to save themselves in the forest. Even the women of a village played some part in warfare, for they are said to have remained close to the combat, shouting encouragement to their husbands, brothers, and sons. While it was only by special arrangement that two villages allied themselves against a common enemy for a specific engagement, the segments of one village were perpetually so allied, as much by kinship as by geographic location.

Aside from the fact of kinship, the major element in bringing about cohesion of the village group is the existence of the traditional chief

---

[3] The importance of *bemba* is more fully treated elsewhere. See A. W. Wolfe, "The Institution of Demba among the Ngonje Ngombe," *Zaïre*, VIII (October, 1954), 843–56.

(*kumu*), who is elected by the unanimous choice of the villagers and endowed with supernatural powers by the ancestors. This office is not strictly hereditary, though it normally remains in one lineage, either an *etuka* or an extended family of the village. Though his supernatural powers are extensive, behavior toward the chief is governed by few rules of etiquette other than those which apply to any elder. His rank is indicated by distinctive insignia consisting of a necklace of leopard's teeth, a leopard-skin hat topped with gray and red feathers, and an iron or brass bracelet with a semilunar bell. He wears this ensemble only upon visiting or receiving important persons or when he dances the secular dance (*mbela*) reserved to the chief himself, one of his wives, and an appointed dancer.

The chief must work as hard as, if not harder than, his fellow villagers. He receives no assistance from them in preparing his gardens or building his houses; nevertheless, he is expected to be generous in providing food and tobacco to all who visit him and to provide lodging for overnight visitors. Because of the extra work forced on his household, the Ngombe say, "A chief must have at least three wives." He does receive from the villagers a degree of respect, of which the only material evidences are the certain rare animals given, in whole or in part, to him: the leopard, the python, a certain species of bird, the tail of a crocodile, and the trunk of an elephant. These gifts, material symbols of respect and deference, are so seldom received, however, that they cannot be considered as economically significant and certainly in no measure compensate for the chief's constant expenditures in entertaining fellow villagers and strangers.

The chief has at his command certain supernatural sanctions. If the villagers fail to heed his decision on such subjects as warfare or the moving of a village, or if they fail to show him due respect, he may cause the ancestors to withhold all good things from the village—game, offspring, or success in war. These sanctions are not applied to individuals or, apparently, even to particular segments of the village but only to the whole community. The fusion of kinship and "political" organization is quite apparent, for though the election and functions of the chief are "political" in nature, he is in reality a surrogate for the elder of his kinship group. His sanctions are the very ones which any elder may apply to his own group or to any individual thereof. Further, the generosity a chief is expected to display toward his people duplicates the ideal pattern between an Ngombe father and his children.

Before the Belgian administration introduced other agents at the village level, the maintenance of public order depended largely on the traditional chief, assisted in some respects by another officer, the "speaker" or "judge" (*mowe*). The selection of a speaker is dependent on his being blessed by the elders as a young boy so that the ancestors foster in him traits of leadership, wisdom, and the ability to "speak straight." By this combination of personal ability and supernatural assistance, recognized by all the villagers, a man comes to be recognized as "he who knows tradition," and his position as speaker is unchallenged.

When invited to arbitrate, the chief and speaker had jurisdiction in cases of adultery, theft, and homicide involving members of different segments of the village. For example, a husband discovering another man with his wife would try to kill him immediately; failing this, he would let it be known that the adulterer's life was in danger. After some time, the adulterer could petition the chief and speaker to attempt to re-establish peace, either by simply assuring the husband of his fear of the proposed punishment and of his future good intentions or by offering the husband an indemnity. Disrespect for the chief, exemplified in one instance when a woman killed a young crocodile and failed to bring the tail to him, gave rise to a judicial proceeding in which the speaker acted both as prosecutor and as judge.

The village chief and speaker function in relations with other villages as well. While it was the warrior leader who directed warfare, a peace pact between two villages was concluded by the chiefs at a ceremony involving the execution of a slave. Peaceful visits of one village to another for purposes of entertainment, an institution called *eloki*, offered opportunities for the speaker to exercise his function for the village and for the chief. It was he who determined the length of stay and the value of the gifts to be exchanged. The speaker's opinion was also important in deciding whether a village site was to be changed, an event occurring, in pre-European days, every few years.

The regulatory functions of the traditional leaders have in large measure been usurped by the local officials appointed by the Belgian administration. These are the *chef du secteur*, whose jurisdiction may correspond to a subtribe; the *chef du groupement*, whose sphere of authority may be a major lineage; and the various *capitas*, who supervise work demanded of a village or segment thereof. The degree to which traditional functions have been taken over by these appointed officials depends on the local situation. A *chef du groupement* will often be called upon to adjudicate differences concerning adultery, theft, and bride-wealth arising in his own village, whereas in other villages under his jurisdiction such differences will more often be arbitrated by the traditional leaders. In general, the people prefer not to rely upon outsiders for the settlement of intravillage disputes; each village is an autonomous kin group which prefers to regulate its own affairs.

The existence of these two parallel organizations, the traditional and the appointed, may demand some explanation, especially in view of the fact that the Belgian policy is one of indirect rule. Formerly, the administration appointed the traditional chiefs to the official posts of *capita* and *chef du groupement* almost ex officio. The unwillingness of these traditional leaders to give up certain traditional patterns considered incompatible with the Belgians' "civilizing mission"—such as polygyny and the trial by poison ordeal for certain kinds of offenses against society —brought about their gradual replacement by individuals who are Christians and monogamists. Commonly, the appointed official is from the same family as the traditional chief, a factor which in part explains why no instance of rivalry or jealousy between the two kinds of officials was observed. Another reason for their apparently good relations is that any show of jealousy or greed is avoided as a manifestation of evil, but a further, perhaps more important, explanation is that both see their work as lying in different spheres. As a traditional chief verbalized his relation to the headman appointed by the government: "I stay in the village with the people; he manages the affairs which concern the white man."

Normally a Ngombe village is composed of a simple grouping of *bituka* segments, but in some an intermediate grouping, to which the term "subvillage" may be given, is found. A subvillage has many characteristics of a true village: a traditional chief and speaker, one or more warrior leaders, a considerable population segmented into different *bituka*. Yet it, like any single *etuka*, is considered part of the larger unit, the true village. The village of Bosomboko, for example, includes five *bituka*, three of which are grouped together to form a subvillage, while the other two are not. The subvillage may be viewed as a transitional stage between *etuka* and village in the ideal growth of the progeny of any Ngombe man from a simple family, to extended family, to *etuka*, to village, to major lineage, to subtribe. Through population size and generation depth, the subvillage has "outgrown" the distinctive characteristics of an *etuka*—exogamy and leadership by its senior member— but it has not dissociated itself from the other segments of the village sufficiently to achieve the geographic separation and political autonomy characteristic of a true village.

Very likely this transitional stage between *etuka* and village was seldom of long duration before the Belgian administration restricted migration, prohibited warfare, and registered individuals by village for taxation, labor, and public health purposes. Previously, separation would have been accomplished without ceremony, as with all segmentation, by gradual drifting apart territorially, economically, and socially. The chief of the village from which such a group seceded would think of the new village as his ward, but the effectiveness of his sanctions, in so far as the new village was concerned, would be decreased proportionately with the geographic distance between their two settlements and the number of generations they were removed from a common ancestor.

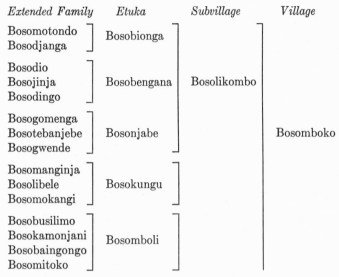

| *Extended Family* | *Etuka* | *Subvillage* | *Village* |

FIG. 8.—The structure of Bosomboko village. The left-hand column names all the extended families of the village in the order in which they are found within a distance of one mile. The adult male population of the village is ninety-seven: Bosolikombo, sixty-three; Bosokungu, fifteen; Bosomboli, nineteen.

Figure 8 shows the structure of a village, Bosomboko, which includes a subvillage, Bosolikombo. Several details of this structure illustrate the fluidity of the Ngombe system. Likombo, the person whose name is perpetuated by the subvillage, was actually a woman, the sister of Kungu and Mboli. Her children, having met with difficulty in their father's village, returned to their grandfather, Mboko, who sheltered them. Their descendants proved to be so prolific that Bosolikombo is now greater than the combined populations of the other segments of the village, Bosokungu and Bosomboli, who are the true patrilineal descendants of Mboko. The larger population, more than descent from Mboko through a female, gives Bosolikombo that degree of self-sufficiency which marks it as a subvillage.

THE ETUKA

The *etuka* is the next unit in order of size, consisting of a kinship group numbering less than thirty men with their children of both sexes, as well as their sisters who reside elsewhere with their husbands but remain members of the *etuka* of their birth. The bonds of this group are closer and more secure than those of the village group, based as they are on common descent from an ancestor who is seldom more than four generations removed from the youngest member. Although the Ngombe themselves sometimes use the term *etuka* more loosely, it is here restricted to units of this level where exogamy and leadership by seniority rather than election demonstrate the close kinship ties.

While in the larger groupings we have seen that members call each other "brothers" in a general way, within the *etuka* this is impossible, since distinctions of generation must be made. Any member of one's own generation is brother (*mwangwambi*), but a member of his father's generation is father (*sangwambi*), and a member of either one's grandparents' generation or that of one's grandchildren is *tatambi*; one's own child, or any *etuka* member of that generation, is *mwambi*. The intimate relationship between members of an *etuka* is thus clearly reflected in and supported by the kinship terminology.

Organized co-operation by members of the *etuka*, as in the case of the village, is found only in hunting and in warfare, but a high degree of solidarity is nonetheless manifest in ordinary life. A day seldom passes when any *etuka* member does not see every other one, with the exception of the married "daughters" living in other villages. The children play together; the women work with each other and go together to fetch water. The men visit each other, accompany one another in hunting or other forest activities, share each other's food, and drink palm wine together. The fact that all waking hours are spent outdoors, under the shade of trees or in open-sided shelters, maximizes the opportunity for intercourse among *etuka* members. There is not, nor could there be, much that is private or secret within the *etuka*.

The *etuka* head (*mosuku o ngando*) is normally the oldest man in the oldest generation.[4] Though senility may make him incapable of active leadership, either in temporal or spiritual matters, it is seldom that a senior man yields this status. An exceptional instance in which a junior held the title of *etuka* head was in Bosoameya, an *etuka* of the village Bosongindola; there the true elder recognized his own unsuitability not so much because of the state of his health or mind but because he had no wife or children. In other words, he had not been blessed by his elders and ancestors, while his younger brother manifestly enjoyed supernatural favor and deserved the title of *etuka* head, since his descendants composed the largest extended family in the *etuka*.

Actually, the responsibilities of the *etuka* head are nominal. He has no exhausting duties but is simply the oldest living father, recognized as

---

[4] The term *mosuku o ngando* denotes not only the elder of an *etuka* but also the elder of any extended family. As a further illustration of the wide meaning of *ngando*, it may be noted that the full title of village chief is *kumu o ngando*.

having considerable influence with the ancestral spirits whom he will soon join and as having more wisdom than the others because he has lived more years and "has seen the village before." His importance, or lack of it, is directly dependent upon his willingness to assert himself, on his youthful accomplishments in warfare and hunting, and on the number of offspring he has fathered. That his willingness to assert himself is to a degree dependent upon these other factors is without doubt, for both are criteria of a successful man. His functions are limited by the organization of Gonji Ngombe society in that inter-*etuka* relations are within the purview of village officers, while the important affairs of marriage, division of game, and supplication of ancestors are for the most part performed at the level of the extended family. A good *etuka* head is one who tells about ancient times, "the good old days" when the Ngombe were warriors, "before the Europeans made us into women."

Unlike the village chief, the *etuka* head has no badge of office, and what meat he is offered from outside his own extended family is more a gift than a tribute. What he receives is respect, a commodity difficult to measure. He is often greeted with the more formal *mbala-o* in lieu of the now-popular *mbote*. He is offered a chair when he approaches; a pipe of tobacco is prepared for him; and when he speaks, all listen.

Respect for age in general is an understandable sentiment in view of the proximity of elders to the ancestors, yet ambivalence is suggested in some behavior. The head of an *etuka* is most likely to live in the most dilapidated hut because he is not strong enough to build himself a new one; the Ngombe ideal that each man should build his own house is not set aside even for such venerable men as this. The importance of ancestral blessing by elders is continually stressed, but children who make a game of stealing food from a half-blind *etuka* head are not severely reprimanded by their parents. The man who respects the views of an elder on tradition may say of him, in other matters, "He is growing old, becoming like a child." These several evidences of seeming disregard for the aged, however, do not invalidate the evidence that, in essence, the elder is privileged· and respected.

THE EXTENDED FAMILY

The *etuka* is divided into two, three, or four segments, each composed of three to eight adult males with their children and their sisters, which may be termed "extended families." These may include only the families of siblings, or they may be more extensive, including the families of sons of siblings. Not the actual biological relationship nor the depth of generation but the size of the group, its ingroup solidarity, and its functions relative to other segments within an *etuka* define the extended family of the Ngombe. A lineage group which has only a few adult males, even though their common ancestor may extend four generations back may be but an extended family, not an *etuka*, because it plays precisely the same role as other extended families of lesser depth in the exogamous *etuka* to which it is attached. In Figure 8, above, the *etuka* of Bosomboli is shown as composed of four extended families, one of which is Bosomitoko. According to the normal segmentary pattern, all the members of Bosomboli should be descendants of Mboli. In this case, however, Mitoko, the founding ancestor of Bosomitoko, was the *elder* brother of Mboli, and his descendants, reduced to two adult males beyond the age of reproduction, find themselves attached to the *etuka* founded by a man junior to their own founder. The group is relegated to the status of an extended family because of its loss of numbers.

The members of an extended family recognize the leadership of the eldest male member, who may be called by the same title as the *etuka* head (*mosuku o ngando*) or simply "our father" (*sangwasu*). His position is vital both for the group as a whole and for its individual members, for it is he who petitions the ancestors to give the group a successful hunt or success in other ventures, and it is likewise within his power to curse or bless any individual in the name of the ancestors. The duties of the elder of an extended family are clearly defined. When game is killed, it is not to be cut except with his sanction and under his supervision. The first shares are divided among the families of his own group and then, if possible, among the other extended families of the *etuka*. Decisions relating to marriage are his responsibility, though he receives considerable advice from the immediate family involved. If physically capable, he himself undertakes discussion of the problems posed by marriages, especially bride-wealth requests. His real influence, however, depends a great deal on the degree of his seniority and on his qualities as leader. As with the *etuka* head, personal exploits approved by the ancestors enhance his authority.

Sharing of economic goods plays an important role in preserving the bonds of the community in the extended family. The distribution of game and of incoming bride-wealth is the most manifest aspect of this pattern, which asserts itself in any number of ways. A wife serves fish from her season's first catch to every elder member of her husband's extended family. An artisan who sews, repairs bicycles, or does carpentry applies his skill gratis for an extended family "brother." A demand for a gift or loan from the extended family is almost assured of positive response, and theft within an extended family is theoretically impossible, according to Ngombe definition.

Because both families of siblings and families of sons of siblings may be included in one extended family, there may be a generation of "grandfathers," a generation of "fathers," and a generation of "sons." Where this is the case, one may ask whether the families descended from one "grandfather" do not form a unit which excludes the families descended from other "grandfathers." This is quite true, especially where the extended family has a considerable population and where more than one lineage is producing offspring. However, no special functions are reserved to the senior male of such a grouping, who in order to assert himself would have to take over the functions of the head of the extended family with regard to bride-wealth and division of game. Where these functions are assumed, the grouping is considered an extended family in its own right; where they are not, the grouping is significant only in the relations between children and their father's brothers, not in the relations between families as units.

THE IMMEDIATE FAMILY

The father shares his position as head of an immediate family with his brothers, for among the Gonji Ngombe siblings are so close that it is difficult to exclude the father's brother from this unit. Of either man one says, "He fathered, but really fathered, the children," even though a man does not have sexual access to his brother's wife. To understand this, one must visualize a group including not father, mother, and children but *fathers*, mother, and children. This conception is based on more than the mere fact of classificatory terminology. When a boy kills his first animal, he presents it to a brother of his father, never to his real father, regardless of seniority. When a boy takes a wife, one of his father's brothers, with the elder of the extended family, is chiefly responsible for producing the necessary bride-wealth; conversely, upon the marriage of a girl, a brother of her father is chiefly responsible for and retains the greater portion of the bride-wealth.

This orientation of siblings toward their common interest exists not only in their roles as fathers but in every aspect of their lives, having been learned from childhood. Many of the tales they are told as children emphasize the interdependence of siblings, often portraying the death of one who did not heed the advice of his brothers. Proverbial references to these stories are used as admonitions. Children have no private property, unless it be clothing. Elder siblings show responsibility for their juniors even when it is not given them as a specific duty. A man calls his older brother's wife "my wife" because he may "inherit" her upon the death of his senior. The wife of a younger brother, however, is always addressed as "sister-in-law," and a man would never marry his younger brother's widow.

There is reason for the Ngombe man to state, "Brothers never fight, for the younger fears his older brother as his father." To the status differential based upon generation, by which the interaction of fathers and sons is patterned, is added the principle of seniority within each generation, so that all members of a given generation within the extended family are not categorically equal. Upon the death of the father, or the last "father," the senior son becomes the head of the group, his position sanctioned by the supernatural ability to bless or curse his younger siblings in the same manner as his father had done. He may even "inherit" his father's wives, the mothers of his siblings, making his position as elder the more evident. At the death of a man who is survived by both a younger brother and sons, his personal property is shared by all survivors, but his wives will usually marry the brother in preference to the eldest son.

Though the lasting solidarity of sibling groups tends to overshadow the immediate family in its strict sense of a husband and his wife or wives and their unmarried children, certain distinctions set this group apart from collateral units. Despite the almost complete economic union among siblings, housing and gardening permit little co-operation. Each married woman occupies a house or a separate room of a polygynous household which she shares with her husband and children. The Gonji Ngombe are firm in their conviction that a man must build his own house, or houses for each of his wives, without help from his brothers. Now, since larger houses are replacing the former low, rectangular, ridged huts, a brother is often called upon to help put up the ridgepole, but his assistance is kept to a minimum.

Further, each married man is supposed to have exclusive gardening rights on all the land "in front of" and "behind" his house or compound. Since the houses of siblings are often contiguous or connecting, this principle of land tenure yields a narrow strip often less than twenty feet wide. Because the administration imposes gardens fifty paces wide, the traditional ideal of land tenure is impossible, and gardens are placed wherever land is available. The sufficiency of land and the lack of interest in agriculture make this potential problem currently unimportant. Each man clears the gardens for his wife or wives without co-operation from his brothers, and, correspondingly, each wife works in her own gardens. Housing and gardening patterns, then, stand in contrast to the co-operative or collective patterns in other areas of Ngombe life.

CONFLICTING EUROPEAN AND NGOMBE PATTERNS

In its essential structure the organization of Gonji Ngombe society is not yet changed despite a half-century of European contact. However, the areas of conflict between European ways and traditional Ngombe patterns enlarge as Christian missionary work expands, as the demand for European material goods rises, and as the Belgian administration increases its control over local affairs. Nor is there reason to assume that the rising trend of these three factors will be reversed. The incompatibility of European and Ngombe patterns becomes apparent in a consideration of three basic principles which underlie the Ngombe segmentary system. The first of these is that any grouping is composed of individuals descended from a common patrilineal ancestor and, conversely, that only individuals or groups so related develop among themselves an ingroup attitude. The second, closely related to the first, is that authority is based on lineage and seniority and that the regulation of relations between individuals and between groups conforms to this pattern. The third principle is that of village autonomy.

So fundamental is the patrilineal basis of all social groups that the Ngombe find almost inconceivable the idea that Europeans in their own homeland do not form villages upon this pattern and that brothers may even live permanently in different localities. Exceptions to this rule are found among the Ngombe where individuals or families join a group to which they are related through a woman, but in such cases the matrilineal nexus is not stressed, and the descendants of a woman are considered as continuing the patrilineal lineage of her father. Uterine ties are recognized and are important for the individual, as in regulating marriage, but they do not serve as a basis for forming lasting groups.

A corollary is that the degree of Ngombe social identification depends on the patrilineal connection. The significance of this for administration on a European pattern is manifest. Administrative units, to be efficient, must be larger than the groupings traditionally integrated in the Ngombe lineage system. Conscious of this, the Belgian government has attempted, at least since the administrative reorganization in 1933, to group for purposes of administration those Ngombe villages which are patrilineally related, such as a major lineage, and to appoint a representative of the senior lineage segment as *chef du groupement.*

In the Congo-Ubangi region to the north of the Gonji area are found some Ngombe villages composed of unrelated segments. These exceptions to the pattern described above result from political disturbances created with the coming of Europeans into the area. When they first made contact with the Africans along the Ubangi River some fifty years ago, the explorers and traders made agreements with certain "chiefs," who promised their co-operation in exchange for guns and ammunition. Villages benefiting from such arrangements soon demonstrated their power, sometimes almost exterminating other groups. A certain Ngombe village, Bososama, followed this pattern, and its leader is said to have become the most feared man in the surrounding countryside. While there is no evidence of actual conquest and subjugation, unrelated groups decimated both by war and by a smallpox epidemic came to live with the people of Bososama, thereby coming under the leadership of the Bososama chief. Some years later, when the Belgian administration organized the region, at least one of these groups, Bosomosibo, was still living with Bososama, and the situation was thus crystallized by the administration. With this, however, also came the end of the warfare and epidemics, so that Bosomosibo no longer needed the protection it had sought from Bososama, and its members are still petitioning the administration for permission to establish their own village. The important point here is that while the need was present, integration of unrelated groups existed, but even after several generations the one group retains consciousness of its separateness and of a desire to assert itself as independent.

The second principle, that authority and the regulation of relations rest on the lineage and seniority, is firmly reinforced by the confidence that lineage ancestors share a continuing interest in the affairs of the living and have the power to implement their will. Despite years of missionary activity and the growing number of Ngombe who are baptized as Christians, no decline is seen in the traditional faith that the ancestors sanction the authority of the senior member of any local lineage group. Success in founding a village, fathering a large family to perpetuate one's name, or in any other venture which is highly valued depends upon the blessing of the living elders and the deceased ancestors. The answer, "Our ancestors did it this way," is considered sufficient to explain a particular behavior pattern because the ancestors are the ultimate authority. The traditional chief regulates the affairs of his village by the same means as are at the disposal of the elder of an *etuka*, of an extended family, or of an immediate family—the granting or withholding of ancestral blessings in the way of successful hunting and procreation. The position of the chief with respect to the village is analogous to that of a senior brother with respect to his younger siblings after the death of their father.

In the light of this system of authority, consider the problem of administration on a European pattern where physical force or its threat is the major sanction. That grave difficulties are encountered is apparent in the fact that of the more than eighty men living in one village, all but one had been imprisoned by the Belgian administration at one time or another. Punishment on such a scale comes to be viewed as just another unfortunate circumstance of life in these times. A young man who had been nominated by the elders to fill the office of speaker of the village was sentenced to imprisonment for five years for having stolen money from a European merchant. Neither the evidence of his dishonesty— and none doubted his guilt—nor the fact that he would be out of touch with the village for so many years dispelled faith in his ability to function as speaker in judging traditional affairs after his release. The two areas of activity, traditional and European, are isolated, as was indicated previously in the statement of a traditional chief vis-à-vis the functions of his government-appointed counterpart. How long such ideological compartmentalization can defer conflict is a question involving the most complex variables.

The third principle of the Ngombe social system bearing upon the problem of European administration concerns the lack of any traditional administrative authority above the level of village. The major lineage and subtribe have neither chief nor council. Each village is traditionally autonomous, and its relations with other villages depend on the degree of patrilineal relationship and the ties established by intermarriage. While peace was the normal relation between villages of the same major lineage even before Belgian administration, warfare might be felt necessary to avenge the abduction of a wife, the unprovoked murder of a villager, or some other wrong. Peace with villages outside the major lineage was established only by a ceremony in which the two village chiefs took part, and it was valid only in so far as it was sanctioned by these chiefs independently. No super-village authority existed to insure observance or to apply sanctions in the event of violation of the pact.

The Belgian administration attempted to follow the patrilineal principle in grouping together related villages and to follow the principle of seniority in selecting the *chef du groupement* from the senior village of the group. Yet, because of the pattern of village autonomy, this officer is viewed not as an extension of traditional authority but as the representative of an administration whose justification is force, not tradition.

A subjective barrier between the Ngombe system and certain European patterns to which it has been exposed may thus be seen as contributing to the stability of Ngombe culture in its present situation. Because some of the demands of the Belgian administration must, if continued, eventually undermine the traditional system, it cannot be maintained indefinitely. The restriction on migration especially will adversely affect the segmentary system, for with the passing of time and generations the degree of kinship within each village will lessen, but its composing segments will be unable to set up new villages. This effect will be more severe if there is an increase in the birth rate, presently abnormally low, or if the mortality rate declines, for an expanding population would increase the strain toward segmentation.

The agricultural program, under which each man must cultivate a prescribed acreage of a market crop, dilutes tradition in devious ways, the effects of which are felt only gradually. Agriculture is an activity in which lineage ancestors have very little interest and in which there is almost no co-operative activity on the part of lineage brothers. Increasing emphasis on agriculture entails a corresponding decrease in the time and energy devoted to hunting. Hunting and the ceremonial activities which accompany it involve the whole lineage community and support traditional Ngombe culture, while agricultural activities have the opposite effect.

In conclusion, the segmentary social system of the Ngombe is marked not only by its internal consistency but by its consistency with other aspects of Ngombe culture, by the stable and effective way in which it organizes individuals and groups to accomplish the goals they themselves establish. Dissociation between traditional and imposed activities has served to maintain the appearance of consistency after fifty years of European contact and more than thirty years of actual Belgian administration. Nevertheless, the effects of the impact of acculturation appear to be cumulative in areas which will undermine the basis of the segmentary system, though it is difficult to predict the nature of the adaptations that must eventually occur.

ROBERT A. LYSTAD

10. Marriage and Kinship among the Ashanti and the Agni: A Study of Differential Acculturation

The Gold Coast[1] under British colonial administration and the Ivory Coast under French colonial administration provide a situation well suited to *post hoc* controlled comparison of social processes. In this part of West Africa, as in numerous other sections of the continent, indigenous societies have been in continuous contact, under varying degrees of intensity, with the peoples of Europe since the early fifteenth century. The special characteristic of the acculturative complex in this region, and that which gives it particular importance for the analysis of cultural change, is the manner in which, in adjacent areas, peoples with identical cultures have come within the spheres of influence of two varieties of Western culture and systems of colonial rule.

In order to exploit the analytic potentialities of this "laboratory" situation, two groups, living on either side of a colonial boundary line, have been selected for comparison. They are the Ashanti of the Ahafo area of western Ashanti in the Gold Coast and the Agni of the Indenie area in the Ivory Coast. The comparability of these two groups is evident in the social and physical characteristics they share and in the distinguishing features of colonial policy which have differentiated them during the course of their recent cultural history.

The factors common to each of these populations may be outlined as follows:

A single precontact culture.—Both the Ashanti and the Agni are Twi-speaking, Akan peoples. The Indenie-Agni have a known culture origin which, allowing for slight regional variations and separate political organizations (though identical political institutions), is spatially and temporally identified with that of the Ahafo-Ashanti.

[1] Despite the adoption of the name "Ghana" when it became independent on March 6, 1957, the designation "Gold Coast" has been retained here, since this was its name when the research on which this paper is based was done. The "ethnographic present" is used throughout, although the time referred to in the paper is 1950.

Similar natural habitat.—Goaso and Abengourou, the administrative centers of Ahafo and Indenie, respectively, are within sixty miles of each other, in tropical rain forest areas, with similar climates, topographies, and soils and with similar flora and fauna.

Similar demographic features.—The two groups have been selected not only for their spatial contiguity and cultural affinity but also for the similarities they manifest in population size and distribution. Each has a population of approximately twenty-five thousand, living in towns and villages that range between two hundred and twenty-five hundred people, with a median town population of about one thousand.

Similar distances from the centers of greatest acculturation.—Neither the Ahafo-Ashanti nor the Indenie-Agni live in such urban centers as Kumasi and Accra or Abidjan. Both, though linked by telephone or telegraph and by first class roads to centers of contact, are relatively remote from them. Kumasi is about 90 miles or six hours' journey by truck from Goaso, and Abidjan is about 125 miles or twelve hours' journey from Abengourou.

Similar numbers of permanent or semipermanent European residents.— There are only forty Europeans in Indenie and ten in Ahafo. In both regions the social distance between Africans and Europeans is such as to minimize the differences in the effect of contact.

Similar economic structure.—The precontact production of subsistence goods by shifting cultivation and hunting has been altered in both regions by a reduction of hunting to a submarginal status and of food-crop farming to a marginal activity, with the introduction of cash crops as the basis of the economy. In Ahafo the cash crop is cocoa; in Indenie, cocoa and coffee. The production per capita appears to be approximately equal.

During the last sixty years, the Ahafo-Ashanti and the Indenie-Agni have been subjected in similar degree of intensity to the colonial policies of Great Britain and France. British policy may be characterized generally as one of "indirect rule," French policy as one of "assimilation through direct rule." Theoretical statements of these policies suggest greater differences than are witnessed in the daily interaction between local colonial administrators and colonial subjects in specific administrative areas like Ahafo and Indenie, and a brief description of the two operational points of difference between them is, therefore, in order.

The first of these differences is in the degree to which local Africans participate in local government. The Ahafo-Ashanti do so in greater degree than do the Indenie-Agni, through two principal agencies of government, the native authority and the advisory committees. The first agency has long given authority, though carefully limited by the British, to chiefs, village headmen, and their African staffs. The second, instituted in 1944, has extended the possibility of participation in local government to persons other than traditional royalty on the basis of recognized skills and interest in local government. The committees are consulted in matters of town management and development, education, and finance, and their activities culminate in the writing and approval of the district budget, which is presented for open, public debate at the annual budget meeting. Although the broad determination of resources and their expenditure is beyond their control, the Ahafo nevertheless are consulted in the initial planning stage, may offer suggestions for subsequent minor alterations, may voice disapproval, and are asked to vote final approval of the budget.

No similar participation occurs in the French territory, where interest in local government is confined simply to responses to policies, programs, and budgets announced by the government to the area through the chiefs. Participation in the traditional, pre-European forms of government in the areas of activity in which Africans are permitted to operate is no less intense in Indenie than in Ahafo. Indeed, the attempt to maintain the old rules of succession to the chieftainship precipitated a riot in Indenie in 1948, but this kind of interest is peripheral to actual participation in the effective colonial system of government.

The second operational difference between the British and French policies is in the degree of formal education or schooling available to the two groups. So striking is the difference between the two areas in this respect and so similar are the remaining aspects of local colonial administration that it may almost be concluded that this factor alone constitutes the independent variable.

Four senior schools (ten years of schooling) have been established in Ahafo. Indenie, in contrast, has no schools at this level. Twenty schools provide six years of formal education for Ahafo children; Indenie has but one school at this level. Most of the towns and villages located on the road system in Ahafo provide at least three years of schooling; Indenie has but one school at a comparable level. The two schools serving the entire population of Indenie are located in Abengourou; Ahafo's twenty-four schools of comparable or superior level and its undetermined number of three-year schools are widely dispersed throughout the area.

There are 333 students enrolled in the two schools in Goaso, a town of 1,000 inhabitants; 129 of the students are in classes beyond the sixth year. Six hundred students are enrolled in the two schools in Abengourou which serve all of Indenie's 25,000 people; only 43 of these students are in the sixth and final year of classes offered in these schools. Of these 43, only 7 plan to take examinations qualifying them for further education in schools located in other cities outside the Indenie area.

The two school systems do not appear to differ greatly in curriculums, in quality of education, or in facilities. The differences are found, rather, in the extent and intensity of schooling; Ahafo greatly outranks Indenie in breadth of distribution and in duration.

There have, of course, been agencies operating in the acculturative situations other than those which implement colonial policy through the enlistment of African participation in local government and through formal education. Agricultural, medical, and other governmental services, the Roman Catholic and the Protestant missions, the commercial firms, the Europeans themselves, the acculturated Africans from other areas, and the transportation and communications systems all play their roles. Impersonal factors also influence culture change in West Africa; the Second World War interfered with programs of development, especially in the Ivory Coast; world market prices for cash crops affect the availability of money; and internal and international political problems create tensions in the governing countries which affect the colonies. These factors, and others, are relevant to the understanding of culture change in these areas, but they can better be analyzed in other contexts. Because they have impinged upon the precontact cultures of both these regions to a similar degree, furthermore, they may here be treated as constants.

In this chapter, therefore, differing colonial policies, reflected in differential degrees of participation in local government and in differential degrees of formal education, are regarded as the independent variables. The dependent variables to be considered are the social institutions of marriage, family, and kin groups, and the patterns of social stratification and of attitudes toward formal education.

MARRIAGE

The institution of marriage has undergone relatively little change among the Ahafo-Ashanti when compared with economic, political, and, to a lesser extent, religious institutions. Precontact ideals continue to be expressed and, in the main, practiced, although certain tendencies must be noted as exceptions to this generalization.

Possession of a minimum of six years of formal education—more years are preferable—has been added to the qualities traditionally desired in a husband and son-in-law. Although the cash income of an educated man is not superior to that of the uneducated farmer in Ahafo, his prestige is considerab y higher. He is in a position to communicate readily with Europeans; non-literates are dependent upon him in economic and political transactions requiring literacy; and he is qualified for a greater variety of jobs, particularly the prestige-laden clerical jobs in government or business, and for business-managerial or independent retailing jobs. The prospect of superior marriages thus functions as an incentive to young men to continue their schooling and as a means by which the social and economic position of a woman's family may be reinforced and enhanced.

A similar degree of schooling is not essential for a prospective wife. Few women have attended school beyond the third year, since doing so is not regarded as of any particular benefit to them. Those who have completed secondary school or have qualified themselves for skilled occupations are desired by young men of comparable education, but the bride-wealth asked by their families is likely to be nearly prohibitive for all except the unusually prosperous. The number of educated women in Ahafo, furthermore, is too small to affect the traditional marriage pattern.

A second tendency to change may be noted in the relaxation of the rules of sib exogamy consonant with the decreasing awareness of sib definition. Many men profess not to know the sib affiliations of either themselves or their wives, and when intra-sib marriages are discovered, they are justified on the grounds that the sib members are now so numerous that the traditional rules no longer need apply. Extra-sib marriages, however, continue greatly to outnumber what traditionally would have been regarded as incestuous alliances. No cases of intra-lineage marriages have occurred in Goaso, and the old rules of exogamy are intact with respect to persons descended from a known or nearly known common matrilineal ancestor. On the other hand, the incidence of cross-cousin marriages, a pattern once highly preferred, is low, and this kin relationship is seldom mentioned as a criterion for selecting a mate.

The payment of the bride-wealth remains a necessary, ritualistic, token payment guaranteeing the stability of the marriage. Despite the increase of wealth in Ahafo, there has been no increase in the amount of the bride-wealth except in the case of the well-educated girl. A new payment, however, which may be called the "courtship payment," is now expected by the young woman's family; it is offered early in the courtship period as a token of the serious intentions of the suitor. Like the bride-wealth itself, this payment is small in value, is frequently paid in money, and in no way acts to force postponement of marriage by a young man.

Young people of both sexes exhibit an increasing tendency to initiate courtship and marriage without consulting their parents. This is a trend deplored by older parents and grandparents, but the absence of sanctions against it indicates gradual acceptance of the pattern. If the selection of mates has become more largely the province of the young, family approval is nevertheless desirable, and it is unlikely that a proposed marriage would be pursued if bitterly opposed by the family. Evidence for the persistence of the old pattern, in spite of its modification, is to be found in the continuing large number of marriages between persons from the same or neighboring villages.

Only a small proportion of the marriage ceremonies are conducted in either of the two Christian churches in Goaso. The two reasons given for the retention of the traditional, non-ecclesiastical marriage pattern are the greater cost of a church ceremony and the restriction it imposes upon subsequent polygamous marriages. In view of the wealth of the Ahafo region, the latter is probably the more important reason. In cases in which church ceremonies are held, the groom is likely to be a person with at least ten years of schooling and with a clerical job.

The changing patterns observable in Indenie are similar to those in Ahafo. A minor exception is the absence of the courtship payment which has become characteristic of Ahafo marriage. A more notable exception to the general similarity is the incidence of marriages in Indenie which were considered irregular in the traditional culture.

Agni informants estimate that at least 50 per cent of the marriages in Abengourou are of the type called *soma*, without the payment of bride-wealth. One of the reasons advanced for such irregular unions is the increased economic independence of women. Because they now own productive farms worked by hired labor, women no longer seek the security of marriage; they prefer the freedom of liaisons which may be permanent or temporary according to the desires of the partners.

This explanation is plausible enough except that women are probably no more economically independent in Indenie than in Ahafo, where such irregular unions occur infrequently. Rates of divorce and the dissolution of irregular unions appear to be about the same in Indenie as in Ahafo, and both groups attribute their "high" rates to the greater economic independence of women. The Ahafo, however, do not countenance irregular unions, and the explanation of their frequency must be sought in other factors.

Two such factors are evident. The first is the greater availability of hired labor in the Abengourou area than in Ahafo. The differences between the two regions in this respect are not sufficient to warrant treatment as separate, independent variables; they do, however, represent a small degree of variation within the economic constant. Agni informants interpret this labor phenomenon as one which frees the husband from dependence upon a wife for farm labor and makes him less eager to acquire a wife for her labor value. They also view it as a factor which enables a woman more easily to exploit land which she has acquired.

The second and more important factor lies in the area of family and lineage stability. The authority of the parent and of the family head in Ahafo has weakened, but in Indenie it is even more debilitated. The incidence of irregular marriages is but one reflection of an underlying change in attitude toward family organization. Whereas such marriages are accepted—though not encouraged—in all strata of society in Indenie, they are to be found only among persons of low prestige in Ahafo. And whereas such unions do not appreciably decrease the prestige of the partners in Indenie, they are adjudged not only irregular but also deplorable in Ahafo. The presence in Ahafo and the absence in Indenie of the courtship payment may also indicate the relative strength of the family in the two regions.

The greater weakness of the family and the lineage in Indenie, a weakness which prevents enforcement of traditional rules of marriage, is attributed to the greater political weakness of family and lineage heads in Indenie government. The reduction of their authority in political affairs has been accompanied by a reduction of their authority in matters of the family and marriage. It is the judgment of Agni informants that a restoration of greater political authority to family and lineage heads would result in a restoration of control over marriage. In the present social situation, however, the traditionally irregular marriage has acquired such respectability that few Agni are disturbed by it.

Changes in attitudes and behavior are not evenly distributed throughout the populations of Ahafo and Indenie. In both areas the youth and young adults are more accepting of change than is the older generation, which is comparatively more ready to denounce the changes and more anxious to adhere closely to the traditional patterns.

FAMILY

Changes in the patterns of family organization in Ahafo must be viewed against changes in certain other institutions which influence them. Ahafo is an area which is economically attractive to its residents. An underpopulated region with underdeveloped cocoa resources, its population is gradually increasing through migration from other Gold Coast areas and by natural growth. The youth and the young adult men tend to remain in the village of their birth, although some few young men move to urban areas in search of clerical jobs or secondary school educations upon completion of their tenth year of schooling. The proportion of these is small, for the attraction of a cash income from cocoa is sufficient to overcome the superior prestige of urban employment. The uncertainty of finding urban employment, furthermore, reduces the desire to migrate to the larger towns and cities, and the difficulties of finding placement in the crowded secondary schools discourage primary school graduates from leaving.

Patterns of family residence have, in general, undergone relatively little change. There is a tendency for newly married couples to take up a patrilocal residence, although this is by no means a new pattern. If a change is to be noted in this respect, it is that of a movement away from the widespread traditional pattern of bi-local residence, in which the husband and wife reside in the households of their respective family heads. The implication of this tendency is that the father-child relationship is assuming somewhat greater importance than it previously had in a society which strongly emphasized the mother-child relationship. This implication is reinforced by the pattern adopted for the division of children in the case of a separation or divorce; the sons are likely to remain with their father, the daughters with their mother. Conclusions cannot be clear cut, however, because the traditional patterns allowed for a multiplicity of arrangements in all these situations.

What does appear with greater clarity is the change in the sanctions for whatever alternative residence arrangement is adopted. The traditional prime consideration of the relative weight of the father-child relationship as against that between a mother and her children is yielding to economic considerations. The major determining factor now is the comparative economic attractiveness of the regions in which the two families live. The importance of this factor is also revealed in the way in which a son may be encouraged to take up residence in an urban area away from his family or families when his education has qualified him for work there or when he feels that such a move will improve his position. When the Ahafo advisory committees on education and finance offer scholarships for secondary education, they even insist that the student has no obligation to return to Ahafo if his chances for success are greater elsewhere.

The frequency of village exogamy is increasing. This pattern is encouraged by parents seeking economically advantageous marriages for their children, and it is also facilitated by the degree to which young men from other areas, attempting to enrol in the less crowded upper-primary or secondary schools in Ahafo, take up temporary residence in Ahafo towns. There is a tendency, therefore, for young married women to establish new homes in towns other than those of their birth and, more specifically, in the towns and households of their husbands' mothers. Marriage between residents of neighboring villages is an old pattern in Ashanti culture, but its frequency and the frequency of marriage between persons from more distant villages has increased since contact.

There is evidence of the weakening of the traditional pattern of moving to the home of their mothers' brothers by boys at about the age of puberty, although the degree of change is difficult to assess because of the probable disparity between the traditional ideal and traditional practice. In any event there is increasing acknowledgement by the father of his responsibility to rear and educate his son well into the adolescent years during which the boy attends school. This is an extension of his former responsibility both in time and in expense, and it is one which the father now readily accepts. The mother's brother is theoretically obligated to assume the burden of extended education during the adolescent years, but the frequency with which he actually does so is low. Only in the instance of the father's defection from his new educational obligations is the matrilineal uncle likely to assume responsibility for his nephew, and even then he is likely to ignore or to limit his traditional obligation to his nephews in favor of his newly acquired obligations to his own sons.

The father's obligation to his son is strongly encouraged by the Christian missions and taught by mission-trained teachers. When attendance at a local school is precluded by overcrowding, however, a boy may establish residence with a matrilineal uncle in a town in which schooling is available. The earlier pattern has by no means been eradicated.

The composition of the extended family household has not altered appreciably, except for the addition of unrelated boys boarding in a town in order to attend the school or of laborers working on the farm of the head of the household. These, however, are transient residents and affect but little the operation of the household.

A major change in the functioning of the traditional household is the removal of school children from the labor force. This, of course, is a corollary of the father's assumption of the obligation to educate his children in school. Increased wealth has made possible replacement of the children by hired labor, and the new pattern, therefore, has not diminished the value of the farm production. What has occurred, however, is an apparent increase in the degree of emotional attachment between father and child as against mother's brother and child, and this has been accompanied by a change in their economic orientation. The rules of inheritance provide the most vivid evidence of this change.

Although there is no overt alteration in the traditional pattern of matrilineal inheritance, the desirability of a change to patrilineal father-to-son inheritance is much discussed by the Ahafo-Ashanti. The difficulties such a shift would engender in polygynous families in which the sons are members of various lineages are, at least in part, recognized. About 75 per cent of the immediate families are monogamous, however, and for them the patrilineal inheritance of property does not appear to raise insurmountable problems. Among the remaining 25 per cent of the families are to be found the older, somewhat wealthier men, who usually resist the notion of so radical a change in inheritance patterns.

In general, the principle of patrilineal inheritance is most strongly supported by the generation of young men who are unmarried or who have but one wife. Adult men in the role of father also seem inclined to prefer this European pattern because of their increased emotional and economic investment in their children. On the other hand, in their role of matrilineal uncle and nephew, men tend to support the traditional principle of matrilineal inheritance. Most adult men and young men thus simultaneously play potentially conflicting roles; they are at once fathers, sons, matrilineal uncles, and nephews. In the traditional society this situation created tensions which had to be resolved by balancing obligations between matrilineal and patrilineal kin groups. In the modern society the basic ambivalent attitudes toward the two families and lineages in which the individual participates are heightened by the increase in wealth and the desirability of its inheritance. At the present time, the conflict is resolved by retention of the traditional pattern of matrilineal inheritance and succession, by a more intensive recognition of the reciprocal emotional and economic obligations of the father-son relationship, and by nearly endless discussion of the advantages of patrilineal inheritance.

The division of labor by sex within the family has been altered, particularly in the production of the cash crop, cocoa. While women retain their obligations to produce food crops on their husbands' lands for consumption by their immediate families and households, their role in cash-crop farming on their husbands' property is limited largely to the operation of removing cocoa beans from the pods, a family-and-friends co-operative enterprise. Many women may also assist their husbands in the care of the growing cocoa trees, but in the majority of families this work is performed by the husband and by his hired laborers.

Further change is noticeable in the reduced importance of the pattern of having women produce surplus food crops for cash sale in either the local or the city market. The decrease in surplus food-crop production has been accompanied, however, by an increase in cash-crop production by women on land provided either by their husbands or by their lineages. Since women retain control of the income from both their cash-crop and their food-crop surpluses, they have gained a larger measure of economic independence from their husbands and within their lineages while at the same time strengthening the economic position of their own extended families and lineages.

Women have not, to be sure, become either large-scale landowners or a leisured class, although a few female heads of families in Ahafo may approach such status. By and large, the wife's major economic role is still that of laborer on her husband's farm, producing food crops for consumption by the immediate family or household. To a greater degree than previously, however, she receives independent economic benefits.

This modification of her role has been stimulated by the colonial policy of encouraging cash-crop production and has been accepted in a culture in which all members of a kin group traditionally may contribute to and benefit from its wealth and prestige through economic production.

In Ahafo this increase in the wife's economic independence has not generally been accompanied by an increase in authority within the immediate family, where the locus of authority continues to reside in the husband. The pattern of schooling reinforces this feature, for attendance at school is terminated at an early age for all but the exceptional girl, while boys continue in order to gain the social, economic, and political advantages afforded by further education. The pattern of political participation also reinforces this feature; few women have as yet achieved positions even in the lowest ranks of the governmental agencies at any level.

The incidence of polygyny appears to have neither increased nor decreased despite the injunctions of schools and churches against it. Approximately 25 per cent of the Goaso families are polygynous; the number of wives range from two to six, two or three wives being the most common. Strong arguments against plural marriage are heard, however, from those whose ideal standard of living has been raised and who have accepted the additional obligation of education for their children. Since their salaries are frequently incommensurate with their added obligations, they feel that birth control and monogamy are necessary. Such attitudes are held by only a few of the clerical workers and teachers in Ahafo who have had the most schooling, whose incomes are inferior to those of many farmers, and whose ideal standards of living more closely resemble those of the Europeans. Even for these few, polygyny remains a desirable institution in spite of the difficulties incurred in its practice.

The position of the extended family approximates that of the immediate family. It is subject to the same strains but has retained its essential cohesiveness. This can perhaps best be illustrated in one feature of its economic activities. Individual production of cocoa cannot be determined by an examination of the receipt books of the cocoa buyers, because most individuals submit at least part of their produce through the head of their extended family. The subordination of the immediate family to the extended family and to the lineage is still a major characteristic of Ahafo-Ashanti social structure; the persistent pressures working toward closer father-son identification are not yet sufficient to rupture the old matrilineal institutional patterns.

A comparison of the relationship between the family and certain other social institutions in Ahafo-Ashanti with the counterpart of this relationship in Indenie-Agni reveals certain similarities and differences in acculturation. There is little noticeable difference between the two regions with respect to such factors as the economic incentives to remain in Indenie, the lack of emigration, the maintenance of the traditional rules of residence in regular marriages, the frequency of village exogamy, the composition of the household, the division of labor by sex, the increasing economic independence of women, the incidence of polygyny, and the general subordination of the immediate family to the extended family and lineage. Certain other factors, however, are sufficiently different to warrant examination; these are the relationship of the irregular marital unions to family structure, the status of women in the family, and the retention of matrilineal uncle-nephew identification.

The woman who is partner to an irregular union remains in her mother's home, and her children remain with her. Although her mate is expected to provide for their support, he may do as he wishes, and the woman has no recourse if he does not. Father-child ties are hence tenuous, and the primary burden of rearing the children falls upon the mother and her matrilineal family, thus fortifying the traditional uncle-nephew relationship.

The schools are administered either by the government or by the Roman Catholic church, and the church itself attempts to strengthen the ideal of father-son obligation. But fewer children attend school, and they do so for shorter periods of time than in Ahafo. The school, therefore, exerts less influence on the father-son relationship and is unable to alter significantly the uncle-nephew relationship, which is supported by tradition and reinforced by the more recent pattern of the irregular marriage. In effect, there is no recognized need for change, and the old position of the mother's brother remains unmodified; residence with the mother's brother during adolescence is more frequent than in Ahafo, and the principle of matrilineal inheritance remains unquestioned.

These characteristics apply to the families in regular marriages as well as to those irregularly married. Indeed, were it not for the frequency of irregular unions and the increasingly independent economic status of women, it would appear that in principle, at least, family structure and function are but little altered in Indenie. The appearance of these two phenomena, however, indicates a tendency toward an increasing individualism in practice which belies the apparent stability of the structure. It is an individualism expressed within the basic structure of the traditional family, whose framework remains. Within this framework the authority of the family and lineage heads has diminished, but the old patterns have by no means been completely disrupted.

Thus the differential acculturative factors operating in Ahafo and Indenie, as they bear on the institution of the family, have made for a similar direction and intensity of change. In one of the two aspects in which noticeable differences have occurred, matrilineal uncle-nephew relationships remain stronger in Indenie than in Ahafo, although in both regions the authority exerted by the family head is diminished, and in Indenie it is the acknowledged principle rather than the practice which is most evident. The other aspect, the principle of matrilineal inheritance, still accepted in practice in both regions, is less often considered a "problem" in Indenie than in Ahafo. Nonetheless, despite its apparent greater retention of these two traditional patterns, family organization in Indenie appears to be somewhat weaker than in Ahafo.

KIN GROUPS AND ASSOCIATIONS

Matrilineal kin groups in Ahafo-Ashanti are yelding their traditional importance as regulators of behavior to various types of voluntary associations. Lineages, composed of those kin living within a relatively restricted area but wider in their membership than the extended family, are still recognized, and a strong sense of lineage cohesion still remains. This is particularly apparent in those areas of political authority retained by the Ashanti, such as the selection of chiefs and village headmen and the control of landed property, and in such crises of the life cycle as birth and death. The somewhat diminished control exerted by kin groups in the institutions of marriage and the family has already been noted, but it is in the aspects of economics, politics, religion, and education that the weakened position of the kin groups and their replacement by associations are most clearly revealed. Kinship remains an important factor in regulating behavior, but associational groupings are progressively arising and expanding their spheres of influence in such a way as to undermine traditional kinship functions.

Within the economic structure, the kin groups wield a decreasing influence in the distribution of goods and services and in the control of wealth. Five features of the economy of Ahafo-Ashanti particularly demonstrate the direction of this change. The first of these, the questioning of matrilineal rules of inheritance, has previously been discussed; the rules remain, but the sanction for them has been shaken.

The second is the shift from the traditional payment of tribute based on kinship and residence to the payment of rates and taxes. Some of these are imposed directly by the national government; others are imposed by the citizens through their local government agencies solely on the basis of residence. Considerations of kinship are excluded from the determination of these taxes. Payments of the traditional type have not been completely abolished, but they have in large measure been replaced by the impersonal system of taxation.

The third feature of the changing economy is the increasing dependence upon the managers of European cocoa firms, professional moneylenders, and the cocoa co-operatives for cash loans; this is tending to re-place the traditional dependence for economic aid upon members of the kin group. The fourth feature is the growing popularity of affiliation with the recently introduced, government-sponsored cocoa-buying co-oper-atives on the basis of individual rather than extended family or lineage membership. Apart from the traditional craft-guild organizations, no such associations existed for the producer of food or cash crops in the old economic system.

Finally, there is the diversification of economic enterprise into non-agricultural crafts and into retailing, wholesaling, and transportation occupations, all pursued competitively by individuals rather than by kin groups. These five developments, of which only taxation is prescribed by the government, indicate the weakening of the economic solidarity of the kin group and portend even more radical changes in the direction of indi-vidualistic enterprise and dependence upon associational rather than upon kinship groupings.

Impressive evidence of the weakening of kin groups in the sphere of politics is to be found in the rise to popularity and power of a national political party, clearly an associational grouping. The Convention Peo-ple's Party won a majority following in Ahafo without appeals to kinship solidarity and has stimulated a national consciousness without reference to kin groupings. Indeed, its leaders are reported to have ridiculed the institution of the chieftainship—a political institution in which kinship affiliation is crucial—without apparent damage to its own power posi-tion.[2]

On the levels of national, regional, and local government, the right of associational governmental agencies to govern is unquestioned. The in-stitution of the hereditary chieftainship is still defended—though it is not without many serious critics—but there is no desire to return to a seg-mented political system in which power is vested primarily in kin groups. The responsibility for initiation and maintenance of government on all levels is increasingly placed on individuals and committees elected, ap-pointed, or qualified through civil service examinations on the basis of their rationally pertinent skills. Kin group affiliations may not be com-pletely ignored, and they remain basic for the selection of personnel to fill traditional offices, but in no instance are they used to the exclusion of

[2] Since 1950 the Ahafo-Ashanti have shifted their national political support from the Convention People's Party to the National Liberation Movement, a political association which draws its major support from Ashanti. Although the N.L.M. is predominantly a regional rather than a national movement and is not without some of the features of a broadly defined kin group, it is, nonetheless, an association, and its aspirations are those of a political association rather than of a kin group. Its appeal lies as much in the discontent of an economic class of farmers and of minority political groups as in its ostensible support of the institution of rule by chiefs.

considerations of an educational, economic, civic, and personal nature.

The traditional religious aspect of Ahafo-Ashanti culture has also been altered by the introduction of associational groups into the once kin-oriented religious groupings. The various branches of the Christian church, with which perhaps 50 per cent of the population are affiliated in one way or another, have not eradicated the kin groups' control over behavior and attitudes, but they have raised doubts about certain aspects of the religious sanctions which support the kinship structure and about the efficacy of certain traditional rituals which affirm kin-group solidarity. Church membership is adopted and church administration is conducted without reference to kinship, and participation in the church provides an avenue for upward social mobility within the Ahafo community. This cuts across kin boundaries to such an extent that even the Christian descendants of slaves may merit the most elaborate funerals and the homage of royal lineages.

The greatest change in social institutions which has contributed to the weakening of the kin group, however, has occurred in education. Formerly a function of the family and lineage, it has become predominantly a function of the government and of the churches. The European innovation of the school has so altered the process of enculturation as to create a class of persons who are literate and vocal in their criticism of authority exercised both through the traditional patterns of kinship and chieftainship and through the recent European patterns. The demand for educational facilities leaves no doubt of the acceptance of the school either by the younger generation, which benefits most directly from it, or by the older generations, whose status quo would appear to be most threatened by its influence. Schooling, especially for men, has become a value in itself.

The consequences of this development for a social organization which formerly was oriented toward the kin group are significant. The new institution, formal education, operates in an acculturative setting which, under colonial rule, has come to include both the undermining of traditional patterns of political control based on kinship and the opportunity for individuals to acquire greater wealth through the production of cash crops. These factors together have contributed to the emergence of new criteria for class differentiation and new patterns of social intercourse.

The precontact division of society into royal and common strata still exists in Ahafo, but both commoners and royalty, particularly those with only remote opportunities for the acquisition of real political or economic power, are highly critical of the division. Sufficient change in attitudes has occurred among members of both social strata to warrant the placing of schooling and wealth alongside kinship as criteria of social class. It may still be said that there is no completely adequate substitute for proper descent—that is, membership in a royal or prestige-laden kin group—and there is still no mobility across royal kinship boundaries. Nevertheless, it is possible for competitive individuals to gain power and prestige over others, including those of royal lineage, through education and economic success. The man with schooling is nominated for the chieftainship before those who stand ahead of him in direct line of descent, and the commoners, whose vote ultimately determines chiefly succession, approve such a nomination. The chief who lacks the qualifications of schooling and wealth becomes increasingly dependent upon those who have them, and his position as lineage and as political head thereby becomes increasingly insecure.

French colonial policies, a reflection of which is the relative lack of schools, have induced changes in kin-group organization among the Indenie-Agni which may be characterized as similar in direction but generally less intense in nature. This is not intended to imply that kin groups in Indenie are stronger than in Ahafo, for the shared factors in the acculturative process have had similar effects in both regions. Voluntary associations, however, have not arisen to carry out diminished kin-group functions in Indenie in the same degree to which they have in Ahafo.

There are two institutional areas in which the degree of change in Indenie exceeds that in Ahafo. The first of these, the reduced control of the kin group over the marriage of its members, has previously been discussed. The second is in the institution of religion. The Roman Catholic Church has replaced the traditional religious structure more extensively in Indenie than have the various Christian churches in Ahafo. The Church has done so largely because of the colonial government's former proscription of precontact religious ritual, a policy regarded as consistent with its assimilationist aims. Similarly, consistent with the aims of "indirect rule," the British have not proscribed traditional religious practices, and these have been retained in greater degree than in Indenie.

In the economic aspects of culture, however, associational groupings comparable to those in Ahafo have not developed. Controls by the kin group over behavior in these respects have weakened, but its place has not been taken by organizations other than those within the structure of the colonial government. As in Ahafo, the payment of traditional tribute has been partially superseded by national government taxation. There are, however, no self-imposed taxes, since the Indenie-Agni do not participate in local government in the same capacity as that enjoyed by the Ahafo-Ashanti. There is greater dependence upon kin for the extension of credit than in Ahafo; there is no role of professional moneylender in the economic system. There is comparatively little diversification of economic enterprise outside of cash-crop production, and there is complete dependence upon European firms in cash-crop transactions and upon the firms or non-Agni ethnic groups for consumer goods. Associational group-ings like the Ahafo producers' co-operative have not developed.

In the sphere of national politics, the Indenie-Agni are characterized by a lack of national consciousness, although a few individuals are ex-ceptions to the general rule. There is little identification with the national political associations which are active in urban areas in the Ivory Coast and indirectly influential in all its regions.[3] Instead there is an intense, almost nativistic desire to keep intact the chiefly symbols of precontact political authority based on kinship, even though the real political au-thority of traditional offices has been drastically restricted.

The school, as an educational association, is accepted in the degree to which it has been offered by the Europeans, but the attitude toward it is one of relative indifference. Teaching by family or kin members in the traditional pattern remains the norm in education. There is, furthermore, little evidence of new criteria for class stratification; membership in the kin group retains its pre-eminence, however weakened, in this area of behavior.

With respect to the replacement of kin groups by associational groups as regulators of behavior, therefore, the differential acculturative situ-ations have produced certain differences in the degree of change in Ahafo and Indenie. In kin-group control over marriage and the acceptance of Christian religious patterns there has been greater change from the tra-ditional culture in Indenie. Lesser change has occurred in certain eco-nomic, political, educational, and stratification patterns. In each in-stance the differences are related to the way in which colonial policies have been implemented in the two regions.

SUMMARY

In this discussion, emphasis has been placed primarily upon evidences of change in social institutions, and this tends to obscure evidences of stability. In no sense need either the Ahafo-Ashanti or the Indenie-Agni societies be characterized as disorganized. The indexes of social break-down—delinquency, crime, riot, rebellion, mental illness, unemploy-ment, poverty, emigration, diminishing population—do not appear to be appreciably higher than before contact. There is unrest, to be sure, par-ticularly where social institutions impinge upon political institutions, where seats of authority shift from family and kin groups to associations, but this unrest should not obscure the gradual and essentially orderly character of the changes. Indeed, the over-all impression one obtains from these two societies is one of acceptance and adaptation of social

[3] There is evidence of heightened national political interest and activity since 1950, but at the time of this research there was little evidence of positive partic-ipation in national political movements.

institutions to changing conditions, whether imposed from outside the culture or emerging from within in response to other changes. To be sure, there are individuals and groups who resist change more firmly than does the majority; there are those who accept it more readily. As has been shown, change also occurs more rapidly in some aspects of culture than in others, and within a single aspect or institution patterns change at variable rates. For the most part, however, acculturation in Ahafo and Indenie has not been accompanied by social disorganization.

It is clear that varying degrees of change in social institutions have arisen among the two peoples living under conditions of contact with European cultures which are similar or identical in most respects but dissimilar in one, colonial policy. In general, the British system of colonial administration by indirect rule, encouraging greater and more widely distributed participation in government and in other associational groups and implemented by more extensive and intensive formal education, has fostered greater and more rapid change than has the French system of assimilation through direct rule without the implementation of intensive formal education. The consequences of these policies seem to have been more rapid development in Ahafo of a capacity for self-expression along certain newly accepted cultural lines and of a capability for immediate control of the cultural future.

11. The Changing Economic Position
of Women among the Afikpo Ibo

In the history of the British administration of Nigeria, Ibo women have
constituted a unique and unforgettable human force. When they
changed almost overnight from apparently peaceable, home-loving
villagers into a frenzied mob of thousands who in December, 1929,
attacked administration authorities while their men stood passively
by, they brought about a sudden interest in the previously little-
known Ibo-speaking peoples. This uprising,[1] precipitated by an un-
founded rumor that Ibo women were to be taxed by the government,
arose from uneasiness on the part of the women concerning their economic position, which had already suffered from the world depression
and which they envisioned as being further threatened, as well as from
other non-economic grievances. Though order was soon restored following the disturbance, which became known as the Aba riots or women's
riots, the administration realized that the policy of government by indirect rule, which had been introduced to Ibo territory after it had
proved successful in northern Nigeria, was ill suited to the Ibo, and various programs for the study of Ibo culture were set in motion.

The Ibo-speaking peoples, numbering over five million, live in independent and politically autonomous groups covering a large part of
southeastern Nigeria. They have a non-hierarchical type of political organization and have been referred to as "ultra-democratic" in their values.[2] The component groups of Ibo speak differing dialects and show
considerable cultural variation. Though they share many linguistic and

[1] For an account of this disturbance see Nigeria, *Aba Commission of Enquiry:
Minutes of Evidence* (Lagos: Government Printer, 1930); *Report of the Commission
of Enquiry Appointed To Inquire into the Disturbances in the Calabar and Owerri
Provinces, December, 1929* (Sessional Paper of the Nigerian Legislative Council,
No. 28 [Lagos: Government Printer, 1930]). A brief summary of the uprising is
given in Margery Perham, *Native Administration in Nigeria* (London: Oxford
University Press, 1937), pp. 206–20.

[2] Daryll Forde and G. I. Jones, *The Ibo and Ibibio-speaking Peoples of Southeastern Nigeria* ("Ethnographic Survey of Africa, Western Africa," Part III [London:
International African Institute, 1950]), p. 24.

cultural traits, the Ibo have only recently begun to think of themselves as a unified people.

Afikpo, a village group covering an area of 64 square miles on and near the west bank of the Cross River about 90 miles north of the Atlantic coast, consists of 23 villages bound together by a common government and numerous social, ritual, and economic ties. The total population of Afikpo is 26,305,[3] and the people live in villages ranging in size from around 125 to almost 3,000 inhabitants.

The Afikpo are classified by Forde and Jones[4] as belonging to the Eastern or Cross River Ibo group. They share many cultural characteristics with Ibo communities to the south and west but differ from the main body of Ibo peoples particularly in their double descent system, compact village residential pattern, strongly developed system of age sets, and village men's societies. They show some cultural similarities to the Yakö, a non-Ibo people who live directly to the east of the Cross River.

THE ECONOMY OF THE AFIKPO

The Afikpo economic system is based on agricultural subsistence but also includes a well-developed system of internal exchange and some elements of an external exchange economy.[5] A network of indigenous markets meeting on successive days of the week exists in and within walking distance of Afikpo. This network is part of the larger system of local markets spreading across Ibo country which is related to Afikpo by traditional bonds of friendship[6] and modern ties of trade. Before British occupation, market trade was less important in Afikpo than in other Ibo groups situated along the major slave-trading routes.

The agricultural staples are root crops, the most important of which is yams. Cassava and coco yams are secondary crops which are heavily relied on during the season when yams are not available. Farming is the prestige occupation for both men and women, while fishing is an important source of income among the men of a few villages along the Cross River. The palm-products industry is of minor importance, in contrast to many Ibo communities to the south and west.

Local trade in markets in or near Afikpo is conducted by both men and

[3] Nigeria, Census Superintendent, *Population Census of the Eastern Region of Nigeria*, Bulletin No. 4: *Ogoja Province* (Lagos: Government Statistician, 1953), p. 25.

[4] Forde and Jones, *The Ibo*, p. 51.

[5] This is essentially the type of economy found in most rural areas of southern Nigeria, as described by Forde. Internal exchange here refers to the exchange of goods and services within Nigeria, while external exchange refers to that between Nigeria and other countries (see Daryll Forde and Richenda Scott, *Native Economies of Nigeria* [London: Faber & Faber, 1946], p. 32).

[6] The ruling elders of Afikpo do not permit the people of Afikpo to trade at the market of neighboring Amaseri village group, a traditional enemy of Afikpo.

women. Men sell yams, meat, fresh and dried fish, and various kinds of European imported goods; women sell their surplus farm crops, pots of their own manufacture, dried fish, poultry and eggs, salt, rice, cooked foods, and sometimes European goods such as kerosene or soap. Long-distance trade in pots, fish, and yams from the Afikpo area and European goods from the seaports and other cities of eastern Nigeria is the exclusive province of men. Afikpo women are discouraged from engaging in this trade, and the few who have attempted it have stopped after a short time. This seems to be associated with women's lack of wealth for trading capital, the restrictions placed on their mobility by their household economic responsibilities, and controls exerted over them by the men of Afikpo.

Division of labor is chiefly by sex, and men and women rarely work together. There is little full-time specialization, and there are no formal craft associations or guilds, though there is a society of diviners and native doctors to which both male and female religious and medical specialists belong. Except for women's pot-making, there is little indigenous craft work. In agricultural production, men grow only yams, the prestige crop of Afikpo; yams are associated with various supernatural sanctions, they are symbols of human fertility, and they represent wealth in ceremonial activities. Afikpo women grow cassava (manioc), coco yams (taro), maize, and "small crops": gourds, groundnuts (peanuts), squash, beans, and various leaf crops.

Responsibility for the support of the household is divided between husband and wife. The husband is supposed to provide sufficient yams for the needs of his wife and children during the period when yams are plentiful, from September through January or February, and to give her meat or fish at the time of festivals. The wife is supposed to provide the staple root crops from approximately February to September and salt, palm oil, peppers, and other vegetable crops throughout the year. Within the polygynous family, the division of labor is according to the component elementary families; economic co-operation between wives of the same husband is minimal. Not only do husband and wife farm their crops separately, but each owns the crops he produces. The wife's right to keep the profits from her own production and trade over and above her contribution to the maintenance of the household is of basic importance to the economic status of women generally. Though the Afikpo say that a husband may demand that his wife give him her market profits, this seldom occurs.

The policy of separation of the sexes, a common African pattern true of the Ibo generally, seems to be especially strict among the Afikpo, where relations between men and women are characterized by strong male domination. The ideal of the innate superiority of men over women is backed by men's controls over land and the supernatural and by sanctions of the village men's society, one of whose admitted purposes is to "keep the women down."[7] Though Afikpo women now have greater physical mobility and economic independence than they had in the days before British occupation, they are still more limited in these respects by restrictions imposed by their husbands than are the women of many other Ibo groups.

THE ECONOMICS OF AFIKPO WOMEN

The predominant pattern of economic activities among Afikpo women is one of farming, pot-making, and market trade, usually of agricultural surplus and pots. The four days of the Ibo week alternate between farm and market days, and almost all women both farm and buy and sell in the market. There is a considerable range of variation in both the scale of farming and the extent of market trade. Both depend on the amount of farm land available to a woman and on individual factors such as physical strength, skill in farming and trade, personal ambition, and childbirth.[8] Her rights to the use of farm land are obtained through her husband,[9] since her crops, with the exception of cassava, are grown on the edges of and between the mounds in which her husband's yams are planted. Cassava is either planted in yam heaps after the yams are harvested or grown in separate plots devoted to that crop alone. The amount of farm land a woman may use during a given season is largely a function of her husband's standing in relation to landholding groups with which he is associated and his personal initiative in dealing with them. A woman may farm more land than has been assigned to her by her husband if she can afford to rent it. Some husbands rent land for their wives' cassava crops, but they are not under obligation to do so.

Since it is not customary for a man to give his wife money with which to start trade, a woman usually begins trading with the slender margin of her agricultural surplus, and perhaps from pots she has made. Only after patient toil and saving does she acquire sufficient trading capital to buy goods wholesale to sell retail. The large-scale woman traders found in some Ibo groups do not exist in Afikpo, and it is generally only the older women, largely freed from the duties of child care and with time

[7] The village men's society, in which membership is compulsory for all Afikpo men, is similar in this respect to the *Mmɔ* societies in Nsukka Division as described by Meek, but the existence of secret societies is not typical of the Ibo as a whole (cf. C. K. Meek, *Law and Authority in a Nigerian Tribe* [London: Oxford University Press, 1937], pp. 66–79).

[8] Mothers of young infants do not farm or go to market; their economic needs are cared for by their husbands, relatives, and co-wives.

[9] Since girls marry at around the age of fifteen years, the only unmarried women are widows and divorcées, who are supplied with farm land by their own kinsmen.

to acquire wealth, who are able to trade on anything except a very modest scale. Nevertheless, market trade is of great importance in the eyes of Afikpo women. Not only does it represent a means of acquiring economic independence and possibly wealth—both of which are highly valued by the Ibo—but also market day is a welcome break from the toil and monotony of farming and household tasks.

Though there do not seem to be any Afikpo women who are full-time traders, able and ambitious women may increase their market profits by taking advantage of price differentials within the local market network. One central market serves all the Afikpo villages and the surrounding area, while several smaller markets meet on different days of the week. In addition, there are a half-dozen or more central markets of neighboring village groups and other smaller markets within a radius of ten or fifteen miles of Afikpo. In certain of the outlying ones, products such as yams, cassava, and rice cost less than in Afikpo, where prices tend to be slightly higher because of the presence of the government headquarters of Afikpo Division. Certain products are obtainable only in one place and sell for a higher price elsewhere—for example, a type of chalk used for body-marking which comes from nearby Edda. In the central Afikpo market, six miles away by bush path, the chalk retails for three times the price it fetches in bulk at Edda market. At Okpoha, six miles from Afikpo in another direction, the chalk fetches four times the bulk price. A type of seeds used to thicken soup can be bought in Edda and sold at Okpoha at a 100 per cent profit.

Certain products, either grown on farms or purchased in a market, are processed for sale by Afikpo women. These include prepared foods, the most important of which are cassava meal (*gari*), peanuts grown or bought in bulk and roasted and salted, rice bought wholesale in an area where it is plentiful and then winnowed and sold locally, and tobacco bought in "ropes" and ground into snuff. In both these types of trade the profit is obtained at the expense of considerable exertion: carrying loads long distances, processing the materials to be sold, or both.

Another method of profiting from market sales is the purchase of goods in quantity for resale in small amounts. Chili peppers, calabash seeds (*ɛgusi*), dried crayfish, and *iyaya* (a small dried fish used in soup), are bought by the sackful and resold by the English cigarette tinful—a fairly standard measure for Nigerian markets—or by the measure of the lid of the cigarette tin, as in the case of *iyaya*. Such trade requires a greater initial outlay and is thus closed to women who do not have the resources to buy goods in quantity. For example, in 1952 a sack of dried crayfish bought in Afikpo from men traders who obtained it in Calabar sold for from £3 to £4; retailed in the central Afikpo market it fetched roughly twice this price. Some women may be helped to undertake this type of trade by a husband or a male relative who is a professional trader, or several women may pool their resources to buy a sack of crayfish.

As in the case of farming, the factors of physical strength and personal ambition are important to a woman trader's success. Since the only practical means of travel between Afikpo and most of the neighboring markets is on foot and since goods are transported in head loads, both these qualities are necessary to success. Though most Afikpo are accustomed to walking distances of fifteen miles or more in a day, they live in hilly country, and some of the terrain is rugged—particularly that between Afikpo and Okpoha, which seems to offer some of the better trading opportunities. Though opportunities for the acquisition of wealth are available, there is no short cut to success.

Success or failure of market trade may depend on other factors. One is the trader's choice of commodity and the markets at which she will buy and sell. Though the prevailing prices of the different goods in the various markets within walking distance of Afikpo are well known, an alert trader may take advantage of seasonal variations. For example, during the dry season when oranges are scarce, they sell ten for a halfpenny at Edda, while at Afikpo they sell at four for a halfpenny. Another factor is the effectiveness of a trader's salesmanship and of her interpersonal relations in general. Since many people may be selling the same commodity in the same market at the same time and at the same price,[10] personal ties such as friendship and membership in the same kinship, residence, or association group may also be important in a buyer's choice of which seller to patronize.

Unlike some West African societies, the Afikpo do not seem to have any well-developed system of holding food products until a period of scarcity. There is little doubt that the advantages of such a practice are understood by women traders, but they emphasize quick turnover of commodities bought and sold. During the "famine" season ($\ominus nw\ominus$), from the time when the yam supply from the previous season is exhausted until the new yam crop is harvested (roughly mid-May to September),[11] rice is sold for 50 per cent more than during the season when yams are plentiful; yet no trader interviewed made a practice of buying rice[12] when the price was low and holding it until the price went up.

However, a number of Afikpo women sell cassava meal at Okpoha and

[10] Although there is no formal system of price-fixing in Afikpo, prevailing prices for most commodities are well known by sellers and buyers alike and are generally held to. During periods of scarcity or of great demand, such as the times of important festivals, sellers may agree informally on a minimum price for a given commodity, but no action will be taken if a trader undersells his colleagues.

[11] Before the introduction of cassava and other supplementary crops hunger was often acute during this period.

[12] The Afikpo do not grow rice but buy it from people in the Okpoha area and resell it locally.

Aba Omɛgɛ, where the market for it is better than in Afikpo during the famine period.[13] One woman maintained that she went to Aba Omɛgɛ each market day during this period because she was "hard up and must earn food money then." Yet the records of the market trading activities of seventy-three Afikpo women show that while seven women sold cassava meal in these markets regularly during the "famine" season, twenty-one women sold it at the same markets only during the dry season, when yams were available. Though this may seem uneconomic, there are several reasons for it. First, the season at which the highest prices are obtainable for staple foods is also the season of greatest farming activity. Since frequent weeding of crops is necessary, and a woman must cultivate her own crops and also weed her husband's yams, the burden of heavy farm work, plus the necessity of walking as much as six or seven miles each way between village and farm, precludes active participation in market trade. Second, the rains make the bush path between Afikpo and Okpoha very difficult during this time, and the Asu River at Okpoha is sometimes too high to cross if there has been a heavy rain. Finally, lorry traffic to Okpoha and Aba Omɛgɛ from the north and west provides a ready market for prepared food such as cassava meal throughout the year.

Pot-making is a third major economic activity of Afikpo women, though this craft is found only in scattered Ibo communities. Afikpo women do not learn to make pots until after they marry, but thereafter the majority spend much time making pots during the dry season, when farming duties are relatively light. Motivation is almost wholly economic. One old woman, when asked why she made pots, replied, "So I will not die of hunger." Another explained, "Hunger forces me to do so." However, some younger women do not make pots, giving various reasons for this: having lived away from Afikpo during the time when they would ordinarily have learned to make them, failure in their attempts to learn pottery techniques, or the feeling that they can earn more from other activities.

Aside from the few pots that they keep for household use, women usually sell their best pots wholesale to long-distance traders for resale in Calabar and other towns on the Cross River, retailing the poorer ones in nearby markets. The central Afikpo market and those at Edda and Okpoha, where pots are not made, are their chief local outlets. Some women sell their pots as soon as they are made, while others save some as a reserve fund for emergencies. Prices in the Afikpo and nearby markets are informally controlled by a long-standing ruling of the village-group fe-

---

[13] Trade in cassava meal does not involve holding from the time of harvest until a period of scarcity, for cassava can be left in the ground until it is needed and can be harvested at any season.

male elders which regulates the number of pots of a given size that a woman may take to any local market on any one day. This ruling, made originally to keep the price from falling, is still carefully observed, for the elders can enforce it by fining offenders.

Other sources of income are wage labor, such as carrying goods between local markets and the Cross River for traders or carrying building materials and smoothing mud on the walls of houses for building contractors,[14] dressmaking and patching clothes by machine,[15] and midwifery. Since a woman becomes a midwife-diviner, ɔgwϴ (medicine), only through a complex process of supernatural revelation, few women are thus employed. This occupation is more rewarding in prestige than in financial remuneration, though a midwife is likely to have more money than most Afikpo women.

A prestige economy involving second funerals in honor of deceased parents and membership in title societies, highly developed among men, is found to a lesser extent among women. The importance of titles and second funerals is reinforced by numerous social and religious sanctions, and though traditional values connected with these activities are in some cases being altered as a result of European contact, the principles underlying the prestige economy of Afikpo have been little changed.

The economic activities of the few women who have been to school or have lived in the larger cities of Nigeria while their husbands were employed there tend to follow European patterns more closely than those of Afikpo tradition. Information was obtained from eleven of the twenty-odd Afikpo women who had completed elementary school (Standard VI certificate)[16] by the beginning of 1953.[17] Of these, two who were still in school and one who had just finished secondary school were unmarried, six were married, one was a widow, and one a divorcée who had not remarried. Most of them lived away from Afikpo for at least part of the year, at school or in the cities where their husbands worked. Two were teaching, one had taught before marriage, and another planned to teach when she finished secondary school. One had just been graduated from nurse's training in London and was about to begin a course in midwifery

[14] House-building is traditionally done by voluntary co-operative labor, but a recent trend is for some persons to hire contractors to build semi-European houses. Also, many Afikpo women have been hired as laborers in connection with the building of schools and missions in Afikpo.

[15] Since a sewing machine is still a comparatively rare luxury, the number of women doing this type of work is small.

[16] One woman who had gone only through Standard IV was included in this listing because she was widely traveled and highly acculturated and had through her own effort advanced her learning considerably beyond the level she had attained in school.

[17] The number of females age fifteen years and older in Afikpo village group was given as 8,211 in the 1953 census; it can be seen that these represent a small proportion of the Afikpo women (*Population Census of the Eastern Region of Nigeria*, p. 25).

there. Her sister in Afikpo had just finished secondary school and was waiting to enter a nursing school in Nigeria. Four women worked as dressmakers, two of them having other posts, one as a teacher and the other as the supervisor of the Native Authority reading room of the Afikpo Government Station. Only two engaged in farming; two traded in the market or sold at home, dealing only in cooked foods and European goods; and none made pots. Three were not working regularly.

Since there was very strong resistance to the idea of schooling for girls in Afikpo until the late 1940's,[18] most of these women are the daughters of men who worked in Nigerian cities. Though they speak of themselves as Afikpo, only four of the eleven have lived a substantial part of their lives there, and some have been there only on visits.

There is little communication between the schooled and unschooled women of Afikpo. Not only is there little similarity in their economic orientation, but the former are "strangers" as far as social life and the religious system are concerned. Aside from the obvious fact that most women who have been to school lack training for intensive farming and pot-making,[19] the factors of prestige and practicality are operative in their economic activities. They reject pot-making as being both wasteful of effort and socially inappropriate.[20] They criticize both men's and women's title-taking, considering it a bad financial risk and preferring to spend their money on the education of their children and other family members. These women are also set off from most other Afikpo women by their European clothes and Europeanized style of life at home. There is little understanding or empathy between schooled and unschooled women in Afikpo.

Of the married Afikpo women with schooling interviewed, all had Afikpo husbands with a similar education. In contrast to the preference of some Ibo men for wives without schooling mentioned by some writers, Afikpo men who have been schooled are said to have an overwhelming preference for educated wives, since in their social life they would be embarrassed by untrained wives who did not know how to entertain their husbands' guests in European fashion.[21]

---

[18] In contrast to parts of Owerri and Onitsha provinces, where there have been both boys' and girls' mission schools for half a century, there has been little mission influence in Afikpo until quite recently. As a rule, Christian missions have been the pioneers in girls' education in eastern Nigeria.

[19] Both farming and pot-making involve carrying heavy loads for long distances, a form of physical exertion for which educated women have not been trained.

[20] One woman said, "The people of Afikpo respect me as an educated woman, but if I made pots they would consider me an equal."

[21] In polygynous families in which there is one educated wife, it is she who helps her husband entertain European and educated African guests, while the other wives are not seen. No cases were recorded of a man who had more than one wife who had been to school.

CHANGE IN THE ECONOMIC POSITION OF AFIKPO WOMEN

Before the establishment of the British Government Station in Afikpo in 1902, a woman was literally in a position of physical and economic dependence on her husband. She could go neither to farm nor to market without an armed escort, for slave-raiding and warfare between village groups made travel outside a person's own village perilous in the extreme. The men's crop, yams, comprised a larger proportion of the diet than now, and the economy was one of meager subsistence, with a small margin of surplus. Though markets existed, the scale of trade was small and restricted to the cluster of friendly villages which they served.

A man did not permit his wife to trade in the market for five years or more after marriage, and when she did start trading, she sold on his behalf for the first few years. He kept all the profit from the trade, feeding and clothing her in return. It was some years until he let her begin trading for herself. Major limitations of women's trade in precontact times were the narrow margin of economic surplus and the lack of a form of currency in small enough denominations to be used in women's exchange. Since women's trade consisted largely of the barter[22] of surplus vegetable crops, it was difficult for a woman to amass wealth in a non-perishable form to be used at the most advantageous time.

Following British occupation, several changes in the Afikpo economy occurred which may be summarized under the following headings: a marked increase in physical mobility as a result of the cessation of the slave trade and intergroup warfare, an increase in resources with a consequent rise in the standard of living, and a growth in the economic independence of women. Outlawing the slave trade deprived some men of an important source of income. Though this had a detrimental effect on their economic status, it widened the scope of both the men's and women's economies by giving them greater freedom of movement. New sources of income for men developed with the expansion of trade and fishing following the freeing of the Cross River from the control of hostile groups and with the establishment of the Afikpo Government Station.

For women the major source of economic change, which occurred at about the same time as the British occupation, was the introduction of cassava from a neighboring Ibo group.[23] The Afikpo consider cassava a woman's crop, beneath the dignity of men. This attitude is associated with supernatural sanctions concerning the cultivation and consumption of yams, their traditional position as the prestige crop, and preference for

[22] Manillas and cowrie shells seem never to have been used for currency in Afikpo, though cowries were sometimes used for personal adornment. The traditional form of money, brass rods, was in denominations too large for use in women's trade.

[23] The Afikpo say that the Ibo first learned of cassava from the Yoruba of western Nigeria.

them as food.[24] Women's acceptance of cassava has meant not only the alleviation of the traditional famine period preceding the yam harvest but also a profound alteration in the economic and social relations between husbands and wives. In precontact days if a woman's husband did not give her food, she was in a sorry plight; now it is possible for her to subsist without the aid of her husband. In the words of an elderly Afikpo woman:

Nowadays women do not care if the husband doesn't give them any food, for they can go to the farm and get cassava. If a woman has any money she buys [rents] land and plants cassava. The year after she does this she can have a crop for cassava meal, which she can sell and have her own money. Then she can say, "What is man? I have my own money!"

Whatever the validity of the impression given by the contention that women have been liberated from a state of subjugation and dependence, it is undoubtedly the case that the events of the past fifty years have brought a real improvement in the standard of living for all Afikpo through the virtual ending of the famine period, a rise in the nutrition level, introduction of clothing on a large scale, the building of some larger houses in a semi-European style, the use of carpentered furniture, and the schooling of some children.

Though wealth has long been an index of personal importance and distinction for both men and women, a change has been occurring in their economic aspirations in recent years. Men wish to achieve and maintain a high consumption level, exemplified by having European clothes, metal-roofed houses, wooden furniture, and certain European food and smoking habits, but they still regard title-taking as the most valid means of investment.[25] While many women agree that title-taking represents the best disposition of wealth, a number of them, both schooled and unschooled, give first consideration to a standard of living including clothing and adequate nutrition and the education of their children, which until the introduction of an education rate as a part of the tax in 1953 involved both the payment of school fees and the purchase of uniforms. The decline in the number of titles taken by women since the mid-1940's, during a time when business conditions were good, corroborates this trend. Women say that formerly a woman would be willing to live for years on a near-starvation diet and wear one cloth until it fell to shreds in order to save as much as possible, to be able to show her wealth and importance by taking a title.

The present-day attitude of many women is expressed in the words of

[24] The Afikpo are well aware that yams are higher in food value than cassava.
[25] When a person joins a title society, he pays a fee which is divided among the title-holders. Thus, if he lives long enough after taking a title, he may receive more in new members' fees than he spent in joining the society.

one woman, "Taking titles is good, but not if you let yourself go dirty. When one does not eat in one's house and takes unnecessary titles it is bad." Women with schooling have little sympathy for title-taking. As one said, "Titles have no benefit, for if one performs title today he may depart from this world next month and all will be lost." This statement refers to the actual case of a man who died a month after he had taken the highest men's title in Afikpo at the cost of £200, leaving his sons, who were in school, destitute. This incident made a much stronger impression on women than on men.

Men's interest in title-taking continues much as in the past. A number of men's titles associated with the village men's society are compulsory for all Afikpo men. Because all men participate in the activities of the village society regardless of the extent of their acculturation and schooling, the society validates title-taking as an economic activity and reinforces the ties between Afikpo men and the traditional culture. Although a few men have questioned the values and goals of the society, their social conformity has been achieved through strong pressures brought to bear on them. There is no equivalent binding force between the traditional culture and contemporary life in the case of women.

There are several basic differences between men's and women's titles. While there are more than twenty men's titles, ranging from inexpensive ones taken in boyhood to costly ones taken in adulthood, there are only two titles for women, both of which are taken late in life and which involve large expenditures. Men's titles, at least in the early stages, are a necessity, but women's have always been luxuries. Because they were less firmly lodged in the enculturative process, they have been more readily subject to reinterpretation, being replaced by forms of expenditure which are more meaningful and satisfying today in terms of everyday existence and the realities of the more modest women's economy.

A raised standard of living and the schooling of children are coming to be spoken of as titles in themselves. One hears remarks such as, "I put two of my children through school," or, "I bought myself a Singer sewing machine," instead of comments on title-taking. And while a considerable number of traditionally oriented women in Afikpo say that they wish to take titles when they are able, the trend seems to be for women to concentrate on being able to "give their children voice" through education. Thus the traditional women's title system appears to be canceling itself out through lack of participation. Yet, despite the rapid change in the women's prestige economy, the principle underlying the old and new forms is the same: the achievement of distinction and prestige, and sometimes profit. Most Ibo think of schooling first as a means of obtaining prestige positions with high pay. Many Afikpo consider the education of children a very real investment, for it is their children who will support them in their declining years. The implications of reinterpreting a sewing machine as a "title" are similar, for dressmaking is a profitable activity throughout Ibo country.

The changes in the relative economic positions of men and women since British occupation must have taken place very gradually. While acculturative processes such as schooling and contact with Europeans were first experienced by men and still have had little direct effect on most Afikpo women, the economic position of women seems to have undergone a greater change than that of men. Though the women of Afikpo have less wealth than those of some other Ibo groups, their emancipation from dependence on their husbands is very significant. Most of them do not question men's traditional position of superiority in almost every field, but a few of the more acculturated women are beginning to do so.

The increase in self-esteem women have experienced since British occupation has been further bolstered by ideas about the position of women propounded by European missionaries, teachers, and government administrators. Most Afikpo men regard these attitudes as appropriate for Europeans, whose women seem uniformly weak and helpless, and they do not share them for their own wives; but Afikpo women recognize the potentialities for improving their own positions. In addition, their contribution to their children's economic prospects and prestige through financing their schooling is not only an important basis of their self-respect, but it gives them a more advantageous position in dealing with their husbands and children.

Thus, while men have been concerned with maintaining the status quo, women have used culture change as a means of improving their economic position. For though respect for men was a deeply ingrained trait of traditional Afikpo culture, the idea of improving one's position was also strongly emphasized. Moreover, cassava must have had a special appeal for women as a means of alleviating the press of the famine season, when they were responsible for the household food supply. Men's rejection of cassava was logical enough, for in Afikpo thought yams represented wealth;[26] they were the ultimate in a staple food for human consumption;[27] and they were a supernaturally sanctioned crop vital to survival in both the sacred and secular realms. Women, being economically insecure and, so to speak, having nothing to lose, were in a very different position. In the realm of economic attitudes, paradoxically, men have had the greatest degree of direct acculturative experience, but women have changed the most.

[26] They were traditionally, and still are, used in the payment of fees in title-taking.
[27] An Afikpo, on being told that yams did not grow in the United States, asked, "But then how can your children grow up?"

A COMPARISON WITH OTHER IBO GROUPS

There are three basic types of economic community among the Ibo. The first is the rural group subsisting chiefly by agriculture, of which Afikpo is an example.[28] This type is relatively self-sufficient in food and other household needs, and though some of its members may be long-distance traders or may work as migratory laborers in other areas, such activities are not essential to its survival.

A second type is the semi-agricultural rural community marked by high population density, soil exhaustion from overfarming, and often by extensive development of the palm-products industry. They are common in the "palm belt," extending from Benin to Calabar and including most of Owerri Province and part of Onitsha Province. While agriculture is still an important activity in these communities, it is no longer the basis of subsistence, and much of the food supply must be imported, the standard of living being maintained by the export of laborers to urban centers and less densely populated agricultural areas. Jones has termed them semi-urban or suburban groups which are no longer true agricultural communities but rather "reserves of labour."[29] They are generally characterized by a longer period of direct European culture contact and a higher incidence of schooling and conversion to Christianity than communities of the first type. Where oil-palm products are stressed, market trade is important among both men and women and is practiced on a larger scale than in communities such as Afikpo. The scale of trade is related to the source of money income—palm products—to the proximity of European trading firms, and to such other economic institutions as the availability of credit with European firms and savings associations known as contribution clubs or *mikiri* (from the English word "meeting").[30]

[28] Other similar Ibo economies are discussed in J. W. Wallace, "Agriculture in Abakaliki and Afikpo," *Farm and Forest*, II (October, 1941), 89-93, and Forde and Scott, *Native Economies*, pp. 64–71.

[29] G. I. Jones, "Ibo Land Tenure," *Africa*, XIX (October, 1949), 323. Examples of this type of community are Nguru, discussed in Sylvia Leith-Ross, *African Women* (London: Faber & Faber, 1939), pp. 135–83; Oko, in A. T. Grove, *Land Use and Soil Conservation in Parts of Onitsha and Owerri Provinces* ("Geological Survey of Nigeria," Bulletin No. 21 [Zaria: Nigerian Government, 1951]), pp. 59–73, and "Soil Erosion and Population Problems in South-east Nigeria," *Geographical Journal*, CXVII, Part III (September, 1951), 291–306; Umuɛkɛ Agbaja, in M. M. Green, *Ibo Village Affairs* (London: Sidgwick & Jackson, 1947); and Umunna, in Jones, "Ibo Land Tenure," pp. 311–12.

[30] There are men's *mikiri* in Afikpo, but the only such group ever organized for women was discontinued after a short time because of internal dissension. For a discussion of men's and women's *mikiri* in a semi-urban group in the palm belt, see Shirley G. Ardener, "The Social and Economic Significance of the Contribution Club among a Section of the Southern Ibo" (Annual Conference, West African Institute of Social and Economic Research, Sociology Section; Ibadan, University College, 1953), pp. 128–42 (mimeographed).

The third type is the true urban center, modeled substantially after European economic patterns. Ibo cities such as Onitsha, Enugu, Port Harcourt, and Umuahia have grown up around European commercial and administrative centers and are mainly dependent on money earnings for subsistence.

The economic position of Afikpo women differs from that of the women of semi-urban communities in several respects. In the semi-urban groups of the palm belt, a woman's income is usually larger than in Afikpo, and hence the scale of her trade is larger. However, except for a few wealthy women traders, these women are, like the Afikpo, restricted by farming and household duties to the area close to their homes, though the controls exerted over them are not so strict as in Afikpo and though transportation to and from the cities by lorry is easily available. They obtain their income chiefly from farming, the processing of palm products, and market trade. While they have, like the Afikpo, adopted cassava and expanded the scale of their market trade since British occupation, the significance of these changes from the precontact economy is different.

In Afikpo cassava is a symbol of women's independence and potential wealth, that is, a surplus good,[31] while in the more densely populated communities it is of importance chiefly as a consumption good;[32] for the overfarmed infertile land does not permit the cultivation of yams as the chief staple, as in Afikpo. In these communities income from the palm-products industry and market trade is used to import a large proportion of the food supply, whereas in Afikpo most of the food supply is home-produced. Since the prosperity of the palm-products industry is dependent on the vagaries of the world market, an element of uncertainty is always present in the economy of groups depending heavily on this source of income.[33] Thus, while the women of semi-urban Ibo groups may be richer than Afikpo women, the modest economy of the latter appears to make up in stability what it lacks in wealth.

The vocations of city women are divided into occupations of educated and uneducated persons, with some overlapping of the categories. The largest proportion of women who are gainfully employed work as market traders.[34] The scale of trade is variable, ranging from small quantities of cloth, soap, salt, palm oil, or foods to the large-scale trade of the "big"

[31] Cassava is eaten by the Afikpo, but its main economic importance is as a commodity for sale.

[32] Leith-Ross suggests that in periods of economic depression women's burden of farm work is proportionately heavier in such communities—where the chief food staples, cassava and coco yams, are grown by women—than in the less densely populated areas where yams are the main staple (cf. Leith-Ross, *African Women*, p. 144).

[33] One of the contributing factors in the Aba riots was a sharp fall in the price of palm products in the autumn of 1929.

[34] Discussions in the literature give no indication of the degree to which city women traders may have been schooled.

woman trader who buys commodities such as cloth wholesale and may have several assistants in her employ.[35] Urban women work also as middlemen in the fish and yam trade and as moneylenders and pawnbrokers. Dressmaking is a lucrative calling, in which both schooled and unschooled women are employed. A source of income which is said to have increased greatly since British occupation is prostitution, which, though it occurs in rural areas also, seems to have a higher incidence in cities, where more money is available and fewer traditional controls can be enforced. Though most city women do not farm, they are expected to contribute to the support of the household.[36] However, men often bear a larger share of household expenses than in rural Ibo groups. Although some men are said to complain that their wives become lazy after moving from the country to the city, much of the data concerning the work activities of urban women do not support this contention.

A type of women's economic position which crosscuts other classifications is that associated with rural-urban residence. Some men from rural areas who work full-time in cities have their wives divide their time between home and city, returning home for crucial parts of the farm season to attend to their crops.[37] This occurs both with densely populated semi-urban groups and with subsistence agricultural groups such as the Afikpo, a number of whom are employed as laborers or professional workers in Nigerian cities. The wives of such men take their places in the society of their home village as they do in the city, though they are usually a part of the more Europeanized element of the home community. Nevertheless, for their fellow women at home they are an important link in the acculturative process of the remoter rural areas.

A factor which is related to women's economic position is that the tradition of a man's paying bride-wealth at marriage has survived to the present day throughout Ibo territory, regardless of the acceptance of Western schooling and Christianity. In both semi-urban and urban communities there has been a drastic inflation in the amount of bride-wealth, which varies with the amount of formal education a girl has had, for it is believed that a father is entitled to a return of the investment he has made in his daughter's schooling.[38] The payment has become increasingly

[35] For a description of urban women's trade, see Leith-Ross, *African Women*, pp. 339–40.

[36] Sylvia Leith-Ross, *African Conversation Piece* (London: Hutchinson & Co., 1944), p. 44.

[37] Leith-Ross, *African Women*, pp. 273–74.

[38] In Owerri Town in 1955 the bride-wealth was £100 for a girl with no schooling, £200 for one who had finished elementary school, and as high as £300 for a certified teacher, nurse, or midwife (Nigeria, Eastern Region, *Report of the Committee on Bride Price* [Enugu: Government Printer, 1955], p. 6). Leith-Ross reported that in Owerri Town in the mid-1930's the bride-wealth ranged from £10 to £30 (*African Women*, p. 204).

difficult for most men, and as a result there has been a decrease in polygynous marriage and an increase in common-law marriage and prostitution, with both men and women marrying at a later age.[39] This change has tended to weaken the economic position of men in relation to that of women. In Afikpo the bride-wealth is fixed at £5; the difficulty men experience in marrying and the consequent social disruption which have been reported for some Ibo groups have thus not occurred.

Type of residence is not necessarily a determining factor in women's vocations. Though farming and the processing of palm products are rural occupations, women who practice them may also be urban residents during part of the year. Market-trading and dressmaking are common to all types of Ibo communities. Except for dressmaking, these are traditional activities antedating British occupation. The factor responsible for the most fundamental change in the economic position of Ibo women—as has been true also for men—is schooling, which in most cases draws an irrevocable status line in the women's relations to members of their community, be it rural, semi-urban, or urban. Though the occupations of educated women are not determined by residence, they are practiced chiefly in cities, where there are more opportunities for such work than in rural areas. The most common of these occupations are teaching, nursing, welfare work, midwifery in accredited maternity homes, and dressmaking. A few openings in these professions occur in rural areas as well as in cities, and it can be expected that their number will increase. The attitudes of educated Afikpo women toward their own economic status in relation to others of their community can probably be taken as typical for women who have had enough schooling to become professionally qualified.

However, in areas such as parts of Onitsha and Owerri provinces, in which there has long been schooling for girls, there is an intermediate stage between the schooled and unschooled women of Afikpo: that of women who have had three or four years of schooling but are unable to qualify for professional vocational openings. This does not yet exist in Afikpo because until recent years the opposition to girls' education was so strong that only girls who were strongly motivated attended school, and most of them have completed elementary school. Though little information is available on the economic position of semi-schooled women, they appear to follow the occupations of marketing and skilled trades such as dressmaking but to do little farming, since most Ibo who have been to school consider it a low-prestige occupation, and it is a skill which girls who have attended school usually do not learn in childhood.

Among the Ibo generally, women's schooling has important impli-

[39] *Report of the Committee on Bride Price.* J. S. Harris, "Some Aspects of the Economics of Sixteen Ibo Individuals," *Africa*, XIV (April, 1944), 325.

cations for their economic and social position. The idea, found particularly in cities, that an educated woman should not work after marriage lest she endanger her prestige has made it difficult for many girls to find husbands after leaving school, since most men are unwilling to pay the high bride-wealth asked for schooled girls, only to marry a wife who will not be an economic asset.[40] Many prefer to marry uneducated and semi-educated women because they cost less to marry and are thought to be better workers. Like many young men in Nigeria, young women who have had some schooling but not enough to qualify for professional and semiprofessional posts, yet who are unwilling to take up the traditional economic pursuits of their home communities, face a difficult problem in finding a means of support congenial with their training and personal preferences. For women marriage provides at least a partial solution to the problem of economic support, but even this is proving difficult in some communities.

SUMMARY AND CONCLUSIONS

The economic activities of Afikpo women consist chiefly of traditional pursuits: farming, pot-making, and market trade. These have been expanded by increased physical mobility and by the introduction of British West African currency as well as cassava. As the result of European contact, women's attitudes toward the traditional prestige economy are changing in the direction of immediate practical considerations rather than long-range ventures yielding uncertain returns. In contrast, the prestige economy of Afikpo men has largely maintained its orientation in the direction of traditional values. In the face of culture change affecting the relative economic positions of men and women, men's interests have been channeled toward maintaining the status quo, while women's have benefited by the acceptance and exploitation of new culture elements.

Factors such as extreme population pressure, uncertainties of the palm-products industry, and the inflation of marriage costs have had little effect on the Afikpo. Though Afikpo resembles the overpopulated semi-urban areas in having a considerable incidence of labor migration, the movement of Afikpo men toward the cities seems to be in the interest of vocational advancement rather than a requirement for subsistence.

The economic activities of schooled Afikpo women are similar to those of educated women of semi-urban and urban communities. The wide gap between the interests and experience of schooled women and the unschooled majority of Afikpo men and women serves to maintain a social distance between them. However, it seems probable that as girls' schooling becomes more common, economic and social positions intermediate

[40] Leith-Ross, *African Women*, pp. 259, 264–65, 266.

between present professional occupations and traditional pursuits will develop.

Although economic change in Afikpo has not had the disruptive effect on social relations between men and women that has been described for communities where there has been extreme inflation in marriage costs, there has been considerable change in the relative positions of husbands and wives. The ending of warfare and the slave trade deprived men of a certain measure of prestige as head-hunters and as defenders of their families and villages, at the same time weakening their controls over their wives because of the lessening of the wives' dependence on them for protection. The economic opportunities afforded women by culture change further increased their economic independence and self-esteem and made it possible for them to subsist without the support of their husbands.

In this transition two traditionally approved ideas, the high value set on individual enterprise and industry and the right of wives to ownership of any profits of their productivity over subsistence needs, combined to produce a result which is incompatible with traditional values: wives' flaunting of their husbands' authority over them. Thus, Afikpo men's rejection of cassava, in itself a culturally valid action, has weakened their position of authority as husbands. However, uncertainty about the proper respective positions of men and women exists chiefly on the domestic rather than the general level. Men's position of religious, moral, and legal authority is in no way threatened. In other words, though change in the relative economic positions of men and women in Afikpo has contributed to conditions of instability in relations between husbands and wives, it has not altered the traditional division of economic responsibility for the maintenance of the household, upon which the survival of the family and the society depends.

12. Wolof Co-operative Work Groups

The solution of problems by communal effort, which is common in Wolof life, is exemplified in the activities of the groups which provide mutual aid in labor and economic "insurance" for their members. This kind of group is usually referred to as a *kompin* (probably derived from the French *compagnie*); only the old men still use the traditional Wolof term (*xamba*). It has commonly been referred to as a "co-operative work group" in the literature on western Africa, but it also provides entertainment, mutual aid in production, and "insurance" here as among other West African peoples. It is difficult to determine whether its economic or its social functions are more important in the eyes of the Wolof, a question which is also raised by the fact that the term *kompin* is used by those who live in Bathurst, the capital and port city of the Gambia, to refer to a variety of clubs and societies which have no co-operative work functions. In any case, the term "co-operative work group" is appropriate for the institution in its rural setting because of the paramount significance of its function there.

The Wolof, who are predominantly Moslem, number about seven hundred thousand, of whom six hundred and sixty-six thousand reside in the French territory of Senegal and thirty thousand in the Gambia under British administration.[1] This study is based on work in the Gambia, primarily in the villages of Njau in Upper Saloum and Ballangar in Lower Saloum and in neighboring Senegalese villages.

The Wolof are basically cultivators, although the well-to-do ones raise some cattle. The cultivation of the staple food crops, millet and guinea corn, is the responsibility of the men, who are also the chief producers of peanuts, by far the most important cash crop. The younger men, especially, have devoted themselves to the production of peanuts to a point where food staples have had to be imported from abroad. Where the

[1] *Report of the Census Commissioner for Bathurst* (Bathurst: Government Printer, 1944) and *Annual Census of the Protectorate* (Sessional Paper No. 5, 1949 [Bathurst: Government Printer, 1950]). Also, *Afrique Occidentale Français: Encyclopédie Coloniale et Maritime* (Paris: Éditions de l'Union Française, 1949), I, 114.

Wolof live near the river, the women grow rice in the mangrove swamps and marshlands along its banks, a practice which has only recently spread to Upper Saloum. Ordinarily the Wolof woman cultivates a few vegetables on the compound land, and perhaps also a small field of peanuts. Unlike the neighboring Mandingo, the Wolof readily move to better land when they have exhausted the soil.

Farming is made difficult by a short rainy season which permits only one annual crop and by the variation in the amount of rainfall from year to year. Because of variable rainfall, substandard soil, and the neglect of food crops in favor of cash crops, periods of food scarcity frequently occur, especially in Lower Saloum, where much of the soil is exhausted.

Cloth-making is by far the most important craft. Men participate in its production by growing cotton and women by spinning it into the thread. Then it is woven by the male *jam*, who are members of a social class composed of the descendants of slaves. Other male craft specialists are leather workers, blacksmiths, and basket makers; of these crafts only basket-making is not restricted to certain classes in Wolof society. Pottery is made by women.

Wolof society is a rigid hierarchy. Membership in each stratum is inherited through the paternal line, and those who belong to the various classes are prohibited from marrying outside their own level. From high to low, these groupings are the *jambur* (composed of persons of freeborn descent); the *jam* (descendants of *jambur* slaves); the *tega* (blacksmiths) and the *ude* (leatherworkers) who can marry the *tega;* the *jam* or "slaves" of the *tega* and *ude;* the *gewεl* (minstrels); and, lastly, the *jam* of the *gewεl*.

The largest kinship unit with which each individual identifies himself is the *χaskan*. This is a large sib whose members have the same surname and are believed to be descended through the male line from a common ancestor. Though the sib no longer proscribes endogamous marriages, its totemism and self-consciousness suggest that it once may have done so, perhaps before contact with Islam. The sib is divided into subsibs, extended patrilineages, and patrilineages, of which the first two groupings seem to have little functional significance except in the selection of chiefs in the "royal" sibs. Rules of exogamy are found only at the level of the patrilineage, which, unlike the larger groupings, includes one's actual relatives in the male line but seldom traces relationship back farther than the great-great-grandfather. The patrilineage in any given locality is headed by its eldest member, who should be consulted about all affairs of the group, especially land distribution, marriage, and disputes.

The Wolof also recognize the matrilineage, known as *mεn* ("mother's milk"), which like the patrilineage seldom traces its relationship back farther than three generations but which has different functions. Though it is through the patrilineage that one inherits status and property, a person goes to the matrilineage, where he knows he will be affectionately received, for advice and economic aid; and children are frequently sent to their maternal grandparents shortly after weaning to be trained.

The patrilineage, plus the wives of its male members, comprises the extended family. This may be made up of several compounds, consisting typically of the eldest male, who heads the group, his wives and children and the families of his younger brothers and of his sons, some tenant farmers, and occasionally *jam*. The extended family is thus the primary group in Wolof society, functioning in the production of necessities, the control and inheritance of land, the regulation of marriage, the settlement of disputes, education, and the general enforcement of socially sanctioned behavior.

The traditional political organization of the Gambian Wolof exhibits little complexity compared to many in the same west African culture province. Villages, usually made up of several distinct patrilineages or sibs, are small in the Gambia, with an average size of 135 in Upper Saloum between 1947 and 1951, though they were somewhat larger in Senegal. The basic political unit is the headman and his council of elders, who administer the everyday affairs of the community. The chiefs who formerly ruled aggregates of villages ordinarily had little to do with village administration. They were looked to primarily as military leaders, though verdicts of local law courts could be appealed to them and though they occasionally sent representatives to the villages or came in person to recruit soldiers or to exact tributes of food or property. In any case, the whole of the kingdom of Saloum, including the chieftainships of the Gambia River region, did not have the massive pyramid of authority, the total population, or the stability of the great western Sudanese kingdoms such as those of the Mossi and Hausa. Nor were there any urban centers like Timbuktu and Kano.

Under British administration, district chiefs are selected from the sibs of the traditional chiefs within the kingdom. Although their authority has been curtailed, they still have enough wealth and prestige to keep alive a series of mutual rights and obligations in relation to their people, including those associated with the co-operative work groups.

COMPOSITION AND STRUCTURE OF WORK GROUPS

Co-operative work groups are organized by sex and, roughly, according to age. The typical female group is made up of young unmarried women and of young married women who have not gone to live in their husband's compound or have not yet given birth to a child. Young married women who have children make up a separate work group in the village, and girls who have not reached the age of puberty sometimes another. The male group is made up for the most part of unmarried men ranging in age from boys of twelve who have been circumcised to men over thirty. Because bride-wealth is high and marriage ceremonies expensive, men seldom marry before they are twenty-five. A few young married men who are not yet "masters" of their own compounds are allowed to join the group while they work for their father, paternal uncle, or older brother, who feeds them and their families from his granary. Because of the wide range of age of its members, there is usually only one male co-operative work group in a village.

The number and variety of these groups increase with the size of the village. While smaller communities cannot support even one, Ballangar, the largest "pure" Wolof community in the district of Lower Saloum, with seventy-five compounds, supports four: one for little girls, another for adolescent girls, a third for young married women, and one for young men. Elderly informants state that work groups were larger during the tribal wars of the nineteenth century, when villages were larger because of the need for defense.

Any young man is eligible to join a male work group when he is old enough to do a man's work. There are no class restrictions on membership and participation, except that the children of the chief (*dɔm i bur*) often feel that it is beneath their dignity to belong to them. In general, however, the co-operative work group cuts across lines of both class and lineage. There is no formal election or initiation; a new member simply joins in its activity when it meets.

Each male and female group has its leader, called *botal*. The leader of the men is customarily an older married man of the class descended from slaves. He is selected by the members, but on the basis of several qualifications. Most Wolof will agree that he must be married, the head of a compound, wise, honest, generous, and energetic. In addition, as a former leader said, "He should be respected—he must be an elder to them all and be able to lead people." The young men of Njau village deposed their *botal* because he "used the work group for himself"; he kept most of the fruit of its labor and was ungenerous in distributing food at its feasts and dances. Much the same qualifications are used for selecting the *botal* of each of the co-operative work groups of women.

When the young men wish to form a new group or to select a new *botal*, they meet in the village square to decide whom they should choose, after which they go to his compound with drums beating. They urge him to accept the post and stipulate that "if anyone goes against your wishes, you can speak to him harshly, because we have all decided on you as our head." This offer is rarely refused, because it is both an honor and an opportunity to accumulate wealth. If the candidate agrees, he accepts the gift of kola nuts which the members offer him. If he has a goat, he provides a feast for the members which is followed by dancing. The feast is in recognition of the honor that has been bestowed upon him and a public announcement of the formation of the group.

Young men also choose a "team captain" from among their own numbers, who is often called *bur* (chief). He is a member of the freeborn class "who is not afraid of hard work," because he must always set an example to the others when the group is working. He also acts as intermediary, informing the *botal* of the group's wishes. Whoever wants the group to work on his farm first approaches the *botal*, who relays the request to the *bur* for approval; if this is given, it is the duty of the *botal* to summon the group by beating a drum and to announce the task to be done. The relationship of the *bur* and *botal* seems to be patterned on that of the district chief (*seif* or *bur*) and his slave-descended assistant (*farba* or *jalige*), but the *botal* has probably more authority than was possessed by any slave in the nineteenth century, when slavery was still in force. He is the effective head of the group, since the freeborn leader rarely exercises his authority and is seldom referred to in discussion. The female co-operative work groups also choose a freeborn *bur*.

ECONOMIC FUNCTIONS

These groups play an important role in the agricultural activities of the Wolof, who hold that group labor is easier and more efficient than individual labor. They make up in manpower for their inefficient tools. Lacking even the typical West African hoe, they cannot cultivate— much less plow—before planting, and they must therefore engage in long, arduous, and frequent weeding. A variety of informal groupings, other than the formally organized *kompin*, do farm work on a reciprocal basis. Most important in the everyday economy is the patrilineal and patrilocal family or extended family plus migratory tenant farmers who lodge in the compound. Other co-operative groups are made up of more distant kin, "best friends," and their families.

From the Wolof point of view, the male work group is most useful because it enables its members to meet heavy obligations of work for their fathers-in-law. Part of the marriage contract usually involves labor on the fields of the father-in-law: harvesting peanuts, weeding a field of guinea corn or millet, or clearing a new field before planting time. Or a man may be called on to build a new house or repair thatched roofs and fences in his father-in-law's compound. When a member is not well, he can also enlist the aid of his work group to work his own fields.

The large fields of the district chiefs are weeded or harvested annually by the groups of young men from the larger villages of the district. Sometimes, one of them will work for a revered holy man to get his blessing (*barke*), which prevents misfortune and promotes prosperity. A male group often cultivates a field of grain or peanuts of its own, reserving the yield for a dance and feast, the food for which is prepared by a young women's group.

Before the British established the protectorate, public works were the responsibility of the *kompin*. They were under the direction of the *botal*, who was instructed by the village headman and the elders to call out the members whenever a task needed to be performed for the community. Today, under British control, its responsibility is less clear, but all able-bodied men, whether members or not, join to construct and repair the resting place in the village square and the village well. The work group still forms the nucleus of the labor force on these projects, but the work is considered to be a community responsibility. In larger villages the work group weeds the village square and clears bush paths to neighboring villages. Sometimes it assumes such new responsibilities as constructing and repairing motor roads for the government.

Both the male and female co-operative work groups work annually on the fields of their *botal*, in return for which this officer is expected to supply a goat and to contribute a large part of the food and money for feasts. The male and female groups help each other in many ways. Whenever the men work the fields, the women bring food and water to them; the men clear land for the women, build fences around rice fields to prevent the wild animals from injuring the crop, assist with their harvest, and transport their grain to the village.

One work-group practice of interest is that known as "stealing the field" (*sach i tɔl*) or "making mischief" (*tɔny*). Without the knowledge of its owner, the work group simply goes to a field early in the morning and weeds or harvests it for him. Faced with a *fait accompli*, even a parsimonious man must kill goats or a cow for a feast and present the *botal* with gifts if he wishes to keep face in the community. To avoid disappointment, however, someone known for his wealth and generosity is usually selected as a "host."

Every host whose field is worked, whether chief, noted holy man, father-in-law or kinsman of a member, is expected to supply food, kola nuts, and cigarettes. If he were to refuse, the group would simply quit and go home. In addition, the host often gives money or goods or both to the *botal*, who may distribute them or hold them in trust for some future expenditure of the group. Frequently, the host also makes a handsome gift to the "champion" worker of the day. None of these gifts is stipulated or bargained for, either before or after the work is done, nor is it considered payment for the services rendered. In 1950, wealthy men and women commonly hired men to work their fields at two shillings per half-day, plus lunch; but there was no wage labor before contact, when wealthy men had slaves.

The work of the young women's co-operative group is similar to that of the men's. It works the fields of its *botal*, of a chief's wife, or of a member who is ill. It may "steal" the field of a wealthy woman, and it cultivates a field of its own to build up a reserve for feasts.

When a member of a female group marries or holds a naming ceremony for her first-born child, its members help prepare food, sing, and dance. They also help to prepare food for visitors from other towns who attend *rites de passage* for a member of the district chief's family, when even the work group of little girls prepares a small bowl of food. When the food is ready, each female group parades through the villages to the compound of the chief, preceded by several male drummers and by its own colorful flag of trade cloth.

Observation confirms the Wolof belief that a man works harder with his group than alone. The rapid, unrelenting character of group work is shown by this description of the co-operative work group of the village of Leba harvesting peanuts.

The first man arrived about 8:30 A.M., and others rapidly followed until by nine o'clock there were twelve men digging. Ten minutes later three more men, the last of the group, came. All worked in a stooped position—never standing erect—moving in a more or less regular line down the length of the field. They worked amazingly fast. In this work short-handled spades (*χiler*), made by African blacksmiths, are grasped in one hand, and with these several quick jabs are made at the base of the peanut plant. The *χiler* has a thin iron spade-shaped blade about five inches across, with a sharp edge to cut the roots of the peanuts, which is manipulated with the convex side up. The handle, fitted to the blade, is about eighteen inches long, with a sort of pistol grip that gives the leverage necessary for the jabbing stroke.

Several loosened plants are collected in the other hand and thrashed about, or the backside of the shovel is swung against the roots to free dirt and sand. The plants are then thrown to one side and left scattered about the field to dry. Later they are brought together in a big pile in the center of the field.

The pace of the work is rapid and sustained. Occasionally, a man drops out of line to smoke a cigarette or sharpen the blade of his *χiler*, but only one seemed to take unnecessary advantage of these opportunities to exert less effort. All worked until 10:35, when about half stopped for a drink of water but immediately returned. They continued until 11:45, when they stopped to eat the food provided by their host, the son of the chief. By 12:05 half were back at work again. One man started singing Moslem hymns while another across the field repeated each verse. Soon the rest joined in and continued in leader-and-chorus response style. They had not brought their drums along because of the distance from their village. By 12:10 they were all back in the field, working steadily until they finished the field by *Tisibar* (midday prayer, 2:00 P.M.), which is the usual time to quit work at this time of year, just after the rains, because the sun becomes extremely hot. The size of the field was one hundred by ninety-six yards.[2]

[2] From field notes on file at the Department of Anthropology, Northwestern University.

There are a number of reasons why group work is efficient and productive. Working with one's companions, joking and singing, is obviously less tedious than solitary labor. Singing and drums are important; in fact, drumming is so important that the work group of Njau village was inactivated for several months when the best drummer in the community was in mourning for a close relative. Working rhythmically to the beat of the drums, the stifling heat, the dust, and the monotony are minimized.

Perhaps more important in stimulating production is competition between the workers. As elsewhere in West Africa,[3] the Wolof co-operative work group involves dramatic competition when a large group of young men weeds a millet field for its chief. This occasion is considered a sort of sporting contest, attended by the community as a whole and preceded for several nights by a ceremony called *wɔngɔ* held in the village square. This ceremony formerly preceded battles, which have been replaced by working contests.

Accompanied by drums, each young man paces back and forth in a dignified manner within a circle formed by the villagers, holding in one hand a long stick which, it is said, has replaced the spear of former days. He boasts of the work he will do on the chief's field, no doubt much as in former times he would have boasted of how well he would fight in battle. Placing the "spear" on the drum to silence it, he declares, "Tomorrow I will be among the young men like a lion when he enters a herd of cows," or "Tomorrow I will work from dawn to sunset without tiring," or "If anyone likes to drink sweat like water, he should come tomorrow and get it off my back." Young men often represent themselves as brave and strong, "like a lion," and try to live up to their boasts.

The elders, small boys, and girl friends of the young men turn out to watch the contest. Groups from several villages are ranged on all sides of the field, and their members work furiously without stopping in a narrowing circle until they converge in the center. Young women sing praise songs for their favorites and fan them with their wrap-around skirts. If part of the circular line lags, girls and drummers stand behind the laggards and urge them to work faster. Each group has its own cheerleader or praiser, who encourages his group to work harder.

The best worker is given a large hock from the cow butchered by the chief, and often also money, clothing, or some other gift. Such a champion is highly regarded in the community and usually has little difficulty in marrying the girl of his choice if she is a member of his social class. Since prestige attaches to hard workers in most agrarian societies, it is not surprising to find that hard work is part of the threefold behavioral ideal of the Wolof, along with religious piety and respect for one's elders.

[3] Melville J. Herskovits, *Economic Anthropology* (New York: Alfred A. Knopf, 1952), p. 108.

That slackers are rarely encountered in the co-operative work group is due in great part to pride (*jɔm*), in this context, the desire to have the good opinion of others. A person who knows no shame is said to have no pride—as when one ignores some social convention and pays no attention to criticism. The importance of this value in group work was pointed out by the *botal* of the Ballangar co-operative work group: "Boys do not become members of our group until they have developed a sense of pride which would prevent them from resting while the older boys are working. If a man is old enough to be a member, he will not quit while the others are still working, even if he is very tired and hungry." Because of pride, the *botal* rarely has to rebuke members for absenteeism or indolence.

Wolof concern with pride affects another function of the co-operative work group, its "insurance" or mutual-aid function in alleviating the heavy burden of ceremonial expenditures. Most Wolof would rather be poor but proud of their conspicuous display and consumption of wealth than rich but shamefaced. Marriage costs are high—higher than those of any other kind of ceremony. The bride-wealth alone amounted to as much as, if not more than, the average annual income (£15–£20) of the adult males in the relatively prosperous village of Njau in the years 1946–48.[4] In addition, other expenditures of a bridegroom average about £10.

The co-operative work group aids its members only at a first marriage, subscribing money, livestock, grain, or kola nuts to reduce the financial burden. Naming ceremonies, especially those for the first-born child, also entail considerable expenditures of grain, livestock, and money. If the child is born between June and December, the members subscribe to a fund to buy a sheep or a goat, and in such cases the co-operative work group of both the father and the mother of the child contribute. The amount that an individual member subscribes differs according to social class and age. Those who are freeborn may contribute something like one shilling or four cups of grain; persons of slave descent, sixpence or two cups of grain; the younger members, three pence or one cup of grain; the members of the entertainer class may contribute nothing but will draw all of the water for the ceremony.

A member forced to pay a heavy court fine or faced with other emergencies is also aided by his group. These functions are important, since few young men, even with the help of their kinsmen and close friends, can cope with the heavy burden of emergency or ceremonial expenditures.

[4] David P. Gamble, *Contributions to a Socio-economic Survey of the Gambia* (London: Colonial Office, 1949), pp. 104–7. Gamble estimates that about one-fifth of the total expenditures of the adult males of the village of Njau went for marriage payments.

SOCIAL FUNCTIONS

In addition to increasing production, providing protection comparable to insurance, and furnishing what William James has called a "moral substitute for war," the co-operative work group also has a major function in organizing entertainment. Aside from the feasting, joking, drumming, and singing which accompanies work, the male group often joins that of the young women simply to have a party. Parties, with feasting, wrestling, and dancing to drums in the village square, are held at night, often immediately after the harvest season.

When it decides to have a feast and dance, the male group uses money or food from its common fund or makes up a special fund to buy a goat or a cow and pay the drummers. Rice, guinea corn, or millet is supplied by the *botal* of both the male and female groups and is cooked by the young women. The men provide the drummers and give presents to the women, who sing their praises and dance for them. Groups from neighboring villages are invited and are expected to reciprocate some other year. Villages compete to see which can give the best feast—the criterion being the amount of food consumed. For example, the co-operative work group of the village of Ballangar took pride in a three-day feast held for visitors from neighboring Senegalese villages in which "eight goats were slaughtered and eaten," and the guests were so pleased that they gave their hosts £8 before departing.

During the harvest season the male and female work groups also serve as hosts to visiting drummers, wrestlers, and female impersonators (*mbandakat*),[5] with the men again providing the meat and the drummers and the women doing the cooking.

The co-operative work group of the young unmarried women sometimes visits other villages. Singing, and with drums beating, they arrive at the outskirts, where the young men who come out to greet them are asked for gifts. They kill several goats, while the young women of the village prepare a feast in honor of the visitors, followed by customary singing and dancing. After a visit lasting from two days to a week the girls start back home, usually accompanied by the young men and traveling at a leisurely pace, playing drums and singing. When they reach their own village, the young women give a feast to repay the young men. These parties provide an opportunity for the young people to meet potential marriage partners, though in theory only the parents arrange marriages. The fact is that many marriages and some illegitimate children result from these visits.

[5] *Mbandakat*, who are usually of Lebou or Serer origin, perform in elaborate feminine costume and coiffure. They dance and sing well, make amusing comments while dancing, and teach the girls new songs by singing with them in the leader-and-chorus response style.

The bride's co-operative work group has a recognized place in court-ship and marriage rituals.[6] A suitor must give a large bundle of kola nuts to the work group of the young woman whom he is courting; this serves to make public announcement of their engagement. Thenceforth the girl may not receive any other male visitors. When she transfers her residence to her husband's compound, the bride's group, in addition to her close female kin, often accompanies her on the journey, singing and dancing along the way. Later it returns to her home, carrying all her possessions to her husband's compound, where the singing and dancing continue to entertain and honor the bride. The group helps in the preparation of at least one of the meals but, like the bride herself, it leaves most of the work to the female kin of the bridegroom.

If the bride is proclaimed a virgin, both the male and the female work groups share in an additional feast. Ideally, every day during the festiv-ities the elderly women of the husband's compound must go into the hut where the bride has slept to see whether she has had intercourse with her husband and whether there is evidence to demonstrate her virginity. If this is found, the festivities will be on a grander scale, for the bride can ask for anything she wishes as a reward for her virtue. On occasion, the husband waits until the feasting and dancing are finished and the guests have gone home before having intercourse. In this case, the girl takes the bloodstained bed cloth to show her kinsmen, and her cross-cousins then take the cloth to the husband, demanding a goat, money enough for a second goat, twelve handfuls of grain, and two bottles of palm oil. These are taken to the house of the *botal* of the bride's co-operative work group, where a feast is prepared by the young women to which members of the young men's *kompin* are invited. On any Moslem feast day after this the bride sends a dish of food to the *botal* of the unmarried women's work group. A song refers to this gift: "May any bride who does not do this never have a child to send on errands."

Occasionally a young man may arrange with his *botal* to have the members of his group abduct a girl whose parents refuse to allow her to come to his compound, even after all of the bride-wealth has been given. The men hide near the well from which she customarily draws water, capture her, and transport her on their shoulders or on horseback to her husband's village. The girls of her village, though usually pleased, follow them half the way shouting mock protests. A message is sent from her husband's home to inform the bride's parents that she has been stolen but that, if the parents insist, she will be returned to her home. "Bride theft" of this type usually occurs when the parents delay their daughter's

[6] For additional background on Wolof courtship and marriage see David W. Ames, "The Selection of Mates, Courtship and Marriage among the Wolof," *Bulletin de l'Institut Français d'Afrique Noire,* Vol. XVIII (January–April, 1956); "The Eco-nomic Base of Wolof Polygyny," *Southwestern Journal of Anthropology,* Vol. XI (Winter, 1955).

departure to her husband's compound because they have not purchased the clothing and miscellaneous household articles which she is expected to take with her.

FUTURE POTENTIALITIES

The functions of the co-operative work group thus range from its primary activities in food production to marginal and relatively minor ones such as bride "abduction." Despite the fact that the Gambia was one of the first areas of sub-Saharan Africa to experience contact with Europeans, the group resembles other rural Wolof social institutions in that there have been no fundamental changes in its form or functions. As has been indicated, it has survived mainly as a recreational group in the urban situation of Bathurst, but in the country side it is still a viable economic institution, though it has already made certain minor adjustments to the changes which have taken place since contact. Thus, the group assists today in the payment of fines imposed by the British organized courts, as it presumably did with those imposed by the traditional Wolof courts, and it contributes to the production of peanuts, introduced since contact from America, as well as of the traditional subsistence crops.

The question which remains to be considered is how the work group could further contribute, if properly utilized, to the solution of the contemporary problems of the Gambia. Among these are the need for the increased production of both foodstuffs and export crops, the subsidiary problem of the perennial indebtedness of the farmer, and the periodic seasons of hunger.

Because of its small size and limited resources, there has been less intense economic and political penetration of the Gambia than of other parts of British West Africa. Nevertheless, European contact has resulted in a shift of emphasis from subsistence food crops to the cash crop of peanuts. The younger men especially have devoted themselves to the production of peanuts to a point where food staples have to be purchased from the traders who import or buy locally at harvest time, reselling at enormous profits when food is scarce.

Where land is scarce and exhausted, there is an annual food shortage during the rains, just when most energy must be expended in farm labor. It is then, also, that the majority of the farmers borrow from the traders at high rates of interest to buy food and other necessities.[7] The farmer

[7] This is most often the case among the Wolof in the district of Lower Saloum who are indebted to the "big" traders at the river port centers. Even in Upper Saloum, where the Wolof farmers are more prosperous, most of the men are constantly in debt to petty traders in the villages, who charge 100 per cent interest on loans. In one list of creditors kept by one such trader, loans ranged from 10s. to £6, with a mode of £3. For a more extensive discussion of indebtedness, see Gamble, *Socio-economic Survey*, p. 108.

has a never-ending burden of debt. When he sells his peanuts to the trader, the loan and interest are deducted from the money due him. After purchasing a few essentials in the trade store, he often does not have enough money to take care of the wants of his family until the next harvest season.

Clothing, made for the most part with European-manufactured cloth, is today the major item purchased by both sexes.[8] It has a high prestige value, and all self-respecting family heads try to keep their families properly clothed. The Wolof also purchase sugar, kola nuts, tobacco, perfume, kerosene, mosquito netting, knives and machetes, iron pots, bicycles, sunglasses, sun helmets, and liquor disguised as a "medicine" for Moslem customers. Even if they were willing to give up their newly acquired tastes for goods of European manufacture, many of which are now regarded as essentials, it is of course impossible for the Wolof to isolate themselves from the modern world and to return to their pre-contact way of life. The economy of the Gambia has become inextricably linked to the outside world. The poverty of natural resources rules out any well-balanced, relatively self-sufficient economy, and it is probable that the Gambian dependence on foreign trade will continue to increase while her economy remains almost entirely agricultural.

The immediate need in the Gambia is therefore to increase agricultural production. Subsistence crops must be expanded and diversified to provide a better diet for the population, and the techniques of producing and marketing cash crops must be improved to raise the standard of living of the Gambian farmer. The increased production of subsistence crops would alleviate the period of hunger; the increased production of cash crops would reduce the farmer's indebtedness.

The co-operative work group is already making a marked contribution in the production of both cash and subsistence crops, but it has obvious potentialities for increasing them further. Its "insurance functions" could be expanded to give increased protection against large expenditures for emergencies and ceremonials, and, like European co-operatives, it could provide modern credit facilities and alleviate the burden of debt.

If the economic role of the co-operative work group were broadened, as Little has suggested,[9] the standard of living could be further raised. Group purchase of cattle herds could both enrich the village diet by supplying meat and dairy products and increase the production of staple grain crops through manuring the fields, which are nearly exhausted in many areas. Eventually, co-operative stores and marketing facilities might be established, and mechanized farm equipment might be introduced.

[8] *Ibid.*, p. 104.
[9] Kenneth L. Little, "The Organization of Communal Farms in the Gambia," *Journal of African Administration*, I, No. 2 (April, 1949), 81.

Among neighboring ethnic groups in the Gambia, similar work societies have already been utilized to expand production.[10] The scheme was initiated in 1946 in some Mandinka, Serahule, and Fula villages in the Upper River Division by a Wolof, Rev. John Faye, M.B.E., with the assistance of his associates in the Anglican mission. The leadership and organization of the traditional group has been largely retained, and its competitive spirit and local pride have been effectively utilized by offering small cash prizes to the groups which produce the most in relation to the size of their farms and labor force.

Among the Wolof the *kompin* is the only village-wide association that bridges all of the local kinship groupings and social classes. The value of mutual aid and the efficiency of group labor are recognized, and the group has an established *esprit de corps*. The co-operative work group is an indigenous institution well suited to make a significant contribution to the solution of some of the pressing problems with which the Wolof today are faced. Economic problems must be solved within the framework of indigenous social institutions. To be accepted, cultural innovations must be psychologically meaningful, and to be meaningful, they must be related to established institutions and traditional patterns. As Little has said: "It is generally agreed that social development of the British West African territories depends very largely upon the adoption and use of up-to-date methods of economic production and distribution. The great problem, however, is how to increase the earning power of the peasant without divorcing him too rapidly and too completely from his traditional way of life. The only sure way is to base the new ideas and the new technical practices as far as possible on existing institutions. Progress in the economic field, as much as the social one, will be made not by disrupting the established tradition but by modifying it to suit the modern requirements of commerce and industry."[11]

[10] *Ibid.*, pp. 76–81.
[11] *Ibid.*, p. 76.

13. Economic Change and Mossi Acculturation

Some five thousand Mossi from the kingdom of Yatenga in the Upper Volta have been resettled on the newly developed lands of the Niger Irrigation Project in the French Sudan. Removed from a cultural setting which has been relatively undisturbed by the influence of European civilization, they are required to adapt themselves rapidly to an economic situation structured and directed by Europeans. Economic organization being the variable involved, a study of their adjustment provides an opportunity to examine some of the cultural problems and processes related to economic development in underdeveloped areas.

Yatenga is the northernmost of four Mossi kingdoms located in the Upper Volta. It is a sub-Saharan savanna land of red earth, low rainfall, gently rolling plains, and low hills. Ouahigouya, the capital, gives its name to the French administrative unit, the Cercle de Ouahigouya, which has governed the kingdom from its headquarters in this ancient city since its conquest in 1895.[1]

To distinguish themselves from the people of the neighboring kingdoms of Ouagadougou, Fada-N'Gourma, and Tenkodogo, the Mossi of the Yatenga sometimes speak of themselves as "Yadise" (those of Yadiga). This name refers to the fact that they regard themselves as being descended, as a nation, from Naba Yadiga, the half-mythical warrior-prince from Oaugadougou who broke away from his father's dynasty to form the separate political entity, Yatenga, which bears his name (*ya* for "Yadiga" and *tenga* for "country"). The Mossi have not always been numerically and culturally dominant in the Yatenga, as they are today. They recognize that their ancestors came from the south, from Mamprusi and Dagomba in the northern territories of Ghana.

Highly organized politico-religious states representing the cultural amalgamation of native and foreign populations and institutions are characteristic of the Voltaic region of West Africa. Acknowledging that we "owe to Rattray the discovery that these central Voltaic tribes are

[1] Capitaine Noire, *Monographie du Cercle de Ouahigouya* (Ouahigouya, 1904), p. 15.

composed of two major groups of communities," Fortes goes on to describe this pattern succinctly:

> On the one side are those that claim to be descendants of immigrants from parts of the country other than their present habitats. On the other side are communities that claim to be the autochthonous inhabitants. . . . Many of the immigrant communities claim descent from forbears of the Mampuru ruling stock. Though now wholly amalgamated with the alleged aboriginal inhabitants, they have certain ritual observances and a system of chieftainship similar to those of the Mamprusi. . . . The institution distinctive of the autochthonous communities is the office of "Custodian of the Earth." This ritual office, involving priestly functions in connection with the cult of the Earth, is found among many West African peoples from the Senegal to the mouth of the Niger. In the Voltaic region it is the exclusive prerogative of the autochthonous communities.[2]

The inhabitants of the Yatenga at the time of the arrival of the Mossi were the Kurumankobe, or Fulse, as they are called by the Mossi. Their descendants recognize their indigenous origin but have become almost wholly acculturated to the Mossi. While most Mossi bear the sib name Wedraogo and maintain political control in the Yatenga, the descendants of the Kurumankobe usually have the sib name Savadogo and are excluded from the exercise of political authority. They have retained the custodianship of the earth, and the elders of their lineages and sibs are the Mossi's *Tenga Soba namba*, their "earth custodians," charged with propitiating the supernatural forces of nature.

POLITICAL AND SOCIAL ORGANIZATION

The present king of the Yatenga, the *Yatenga Naba*, is a lineal descendant of the first ruler, Naba Yadiga. The members of the lineage of the king are called "those who maintain themselves upon us" (*riim namba*). Directly subordinate to the authority of the Yatenga Naba are his four grand ministers, each of whom has authority over a particular province (*solum*) of the Yatenga.[3]

The province over which each of the grand ministers presides as lord is divided up into a number of cantons (*tense*), each of which is ruled by a chief who is the central political authority both of the village in which he resides and of the villages within the canton. Like the province, the concept of the canton is not precisely territorial. Some villages may owe

[2] Meyer Fortes, *The Dynamics of Clanship among the Tallensi* (London: Oxford University Press, 1945), p. 6.

[3] These provinces refer not only to geographical areas of the kingdom but to particular categories of the population. For example, the *Balum Naba* has direct authority over the southern regions of the Yatenga and indirect authority over the cantons of Riziam and Zittenga, political entities which have never fully recognized the central authority of the *Yatenga Naba*. This same minister is also especially charged with maintaining liaison with certain of the more important earth custodians throughout the Yatenga.

their allegiance directly to the *Yatenga Naba* for historical reasons or because their chiefs are related to the royal lineage and superior within the social hierarchy to the local nobility (*nakomse*) to which the canton chiefs belong.

Subordinate, in turn, to the canton chief, is the village chief (*Tenga Naba*), who is the central authority in the aggregation of "quarters" (*sakse*) of which a Mossi village is composed. These quarters are the dwellings of patrilineal extended families and lineages (*boodoose*). Such a residence is called a *saka* if it contains the house of the lineage elder (*sak kasama*) or a *yiri* if it represents only a junior segment. In either case the dwelling of the oldest male in the group is surrounded by the separate houses of his wives, his younger brothers and their wives, and his sons, nephews, cousins, and their wives and children. Each adult individual has a separate house within the *saka*.

The smallest unit within the residence of the lineage is the nuclear family (*zaka*) composed of a man, his wife, and their children. If a man has more than one wife, the term *zaka pedere* (*zaka* half) may be used when the man's relationship with one of his several wives is being considered. He himself is called *zaka soba*. As a young man's family grows, each of his new wives is provided with a house adjoining his. In addition to his house and the houses of his wives, each man's household contains several granaries used to store the produce from the millet fields he has been assigned by his lineage. It is with the members of his own household that a man is in most frequent social and economic interaction. The fields he works with their assistance are the principal source of the food supply for the nuclear family unit.

The *yiri* is the next largest social unit within the *saka*. The term refers to the extended family dwelling inhabited by a man, his wives, his male children, and their wives and children. It may be composed of as many as fifteen separate nuclear families. While its inhabitants usually consist of the married sons of an older man and their nuclear families, it may also be composed of a man, his wife and children, and his younger brothers and their wives and children. Since its members are closely related within the lineage, there is greater social and economic interaction among them than there is with the other lineage members. As the *zaka soba* is the principal and final authority within the *zaka*, the *yiri soba* is most important within the *yiri*.

Composed of the nuclear and extended family dwellings of its members, the Mossi residential unit is typically inhabited by all of the local representatives of the sib. In addition to the dwelling of the lineage elder, it contains the altar (*kiemserogo*) where the ancestral spirits of the lineage are worshiped. The lineage elder has authority over everyone living within his *saka*. As counselor to the village chief and intermediary with the ancestral spirits, he is the principal political and religious authority within his lineage.

The single term *boodoo* is used to refer to three separate groups: the sib, the lineage, and the local residential kin group described above. Aside from formalized recognition of patrilineal descent and inheritance, the lineage functions most significantly as a local residential kin group in which the economic and social participation of the female non-members is as important as that of the men. Although the men are most prominent in the direction of its affairs, their wives have a considerable, if somewhat indirect, effect upon decisions made. Even in the relationship of the members of the lineage to their ancestral spirits (*kiemse*), the women play an important part in preparing the food and the libations to be offered. They give birth to the members of the lineage, nourish them until weaning (usually at the age of two), and provide them with guidance and training for their ascribed roles. In the education of the female members of the lineage the wives play a more important part than the men. But it is in their economic activities that the significance of the women's role is best seen. In addition to their farm work, they co-operate fully in repairing roofs, flooring the courtyards, and even assisting in the brick-making which precedes house-building. The economic and social contribution of the wives is of equal importance with that of the husbands and sons, and it is more important than that of the daughters, since females born into the lineage marry and leave just as they become fully productive members of their fathers' households.

Daughters, however, serve their lineage in a different way. As they are successful in winning for themselves a good name in the households of their husbands, so the bond of economic and social co-operation established between the two lineages at the time of marriage is strengthened. When they mature, they return to assist the members of their lineage with ritual obligations to the ancestors. If they are left childless at their husband's death, they may return to their father's household to reside.

Separated from one another by millet fields and the public way, the dwelling of each Mossi kin group has the appearance of a small walled village. Each round mud house with its thatched roof has a separate courtyard which is usually contiguous to the courtyards of the other houses in the residential unit of which it is a part. The individual dwellings are constructed in such a way—the wall of each house or courtyard being contiguous to that of the nearest neighbor—as to form a circular wall whose exterior is closed at all but two points. The dwelling of each kin group has a small exit and a large open entrance way just within which is located a thatch-covered sun shelter (*zande*) where the men of the lineage gather to rest, to work at small crafts, and to talk. Guests are received, gossip exchanged, and social and ceremonial obligations discussed in its shade. Here also, the men of the lineage take their meals, brought out to them from the kitchens of their wives and set before them by their sons, who first attend their fathers and then dine on what remains.

A few paces away is the grinding platform (*nere*) where the women gather to prepare the grain for their families' meals. This great circular mud table, some twenty feet in diameter, is raised about three feet from the ground. Its surface is beaten hard and worked over with cinders and manure to make it rainproof. Each woman has her assigned place at this platform where she keeps her pestle and where she stations herself at dawn and again at dusk to grind her millet and learn the news of the day.

Frequently found at the outer perimeter of the dwelling of the Mossi kin group is the house of the son of a lineage woman who has returned from his father's household to live in the benevolent presence of his mother's family, with whom he enjoys an especially permissive relationship. The house set aside for the residence of the young unmarried men of the lineage is also located on the outer edge of the compound dwelling.

A recent addition to the traditional pattern of village organization described above is the independent households of socially ambitious individuals who have chosen to separate themselves from the residences of their lineages in order to profit from their own economic or religious enterprises. Many have become independently wealthy through successful commercial ventures; others, as a result of conversion to Islam, have gained prestige through religious authority and wealth through the tuition and services provided by the Koranic students. Often these people are much younger than their lineage elders, not in line for the inheritance of political or religious authority through traditional channels, and unwilling either to accept the authority of their seniors or to share economically with the less prosperous members of their lineages. They are deviants, in conflict with the communal patterns of consumption and with the emphasis on accepting established authority which characterizes the traditional social organization of the Mossi.

THE TRADITIONAL ECONOMY

Much agricultural endeavor is necessarily co-operative. Each farmer is dependent on the assistance of his kinsmen to get his fields seeded, cultivated, and harvested in the short time during which each of these operations must take place. However, the yield from his field remains his own, to be shared only with his own wives and children. Members of the lineage also work in the fields under the specific control of the lineage elder. Although the harvest from these fields is stored in the granary belonging to him, he can be relied upon to share with the members of the lineage if this should be necessary.

Capital goods in the form of houses, granaries, and fields are the property of the lineage. Individual rights are limited to temporary use and custodianship but are passed on to others when a general shift in residence and role follows the death of a senior member of the lineage. Although property is passed on in accordance with the rules of descent in the lineage, part of the property redistributed represents the product of the labor of the lineage as a consanguineal kin group. For, as has been indicated, the labor of the wives, who are not lineage members, is as important as that of their husbands and children.

The lineage head discusses the coming year with the other elders, and an over-all production plan is made out. They decide what fields are to be left fallow, what ones are to be planted to cotton and the varieties of millet, what lands may be used by individuals desiring to plant a cash crop, and what, if any, land may be loaned to neighboring lineages or to in-laws. With the approach of the first rains, all economically active men and women go to their fields to prepare them for planting, leaving behind in the village only the old people and the children who are still too small to assist in the fields or tend their fathers' animals.

A considerable portion of the land within the limits of a Mossi village is under the direct control of the village chief (*Tenga Naba*) and the earth custodian (*Tenga Soba*), the local representatives of political and supernatural authority. This land is used for the public way, for the market place, and for burial grounds and latrines. Except for that which is too poor for any purpose, all available land within several miles of a village is put under cultivation.

Ki is the generic name which the Mossi give to the millet, which is the basic product in their economy and which receives the largest single allocation of land and labor of any Mossi economic activity. Two kinds of millet are planted, a large-grained variety (*kenda*) and a small-grained variety (*kazua*). Millet is the first crop to be planted after the rains have begun. Small- and large-grained millet seeds are frequently mixed and sown in the same field. Small-grained millet may also be sown in the same field with a white bean (*benga*). A "tired" field may be left fallow for five, ten, or fifteen years. When it is first replanted, it will be seeded to millet for the first three years. The fourth year it may again be put into millet, but if the previous crop was not good, cotton will be planted. Usually, a Mossi farmer plants cotton for two years, millet for three, then groundnuts, more cotton, then two more years of millet. It is believed that cotton renews the soil because of the intensive cultivation required: the earth is brought up into hillocks and turned over; after picking, the plant may be turned under and left to enrich the soil.

Apart from the co-operative cultivation of fields under the proprietorship of the lineage elder, each farmer works for himself. He aids his relatives, and they in turn assist him with his work, but the results of their communal effort are not shared. This applies not only to the work of planting but also to cultivation and harvest. The decision about what is to be planted in a particular field and how it shall be cultivated rests finally with the individual farmer.

Communal or co-operative effort is much more characteristic of the work of cultivation than of the planting period, when everyone is in a hurry to get his own seeds into the ground and requests for assistance are not welcomed. A strong note of competition is evident at this time. A man takes pride in his efficiency as a farmer, and there is a race to see who can get farthest along with his work. In the earliest phase of preparations for the approaching rainy season it is the individual's best friend upon whom he relies most for assistance. He is the first person to be called on for assistance in clearing the field for planting. If a Mossi farmer is unmarried, he may also ask the other unmarried men of his lineage for help. If a long day must be spent in the field in order to clear and clean it properly, his mother will offer the helpers the midday meal, which is carried out to them as they work.

Naba koba (chief's cultivation) is the name given to the work which the villagers do in the fields belonging to the village chief. A village elder is charged with announcing when and where work in the chief's fields is to be done, and each lineage head relays the news to his kinsmen. This contribution of labor is no longer obligatory, as it was formerly, but only a question of social pressure and recognition that individual well-being and the welfare of the village "depend on the chief."

Every Mossi is an agriculturist. Although agriculture is the principal source of income, everyone also engages in crafts, particularly during the dry season when the work in the fields is finished. However, there are no full-time crafts specialists. Even the African functionaries in the European administration and the teachers, clerks, and merchants all work in their fields part of the time during the rainy season. The activities of the blacksmiths, leather workers, butchers, wood workers, herbalists, and small merchants are carried out on a much smaller scale and are fitted into the routine established by the rains and the growth of their millet. Only elders whose age keeps them from the fields might be thought of as specialists who do not participate in agriculture, but their land is worked by younger members of the family, and they take a keen interest in the course of its cultivation. The village chief, the earth custodian, and certain other elderly and important members of the community do not cultivate; this is because of their position and age rather than because they are so exclusively occupied with political or religious duties. In every case, they own fields and are dependent upon their produce for an important part of their subsistence.

Each Mossi village in the Yatenga holds a market every third day; markets operate in nearby villages on the intermediate days. There are few full-time merchants; men usually market their wares themselves and trade in items of European manufacture. Except for the sale of meat, it is a man's wives who sell farm produce. For marketing her husband's surplus millet, a woman receives a gift when the market closes.

Markets are most active in the early hours of the morning when meat and farm produce are fresh. By afternoon only a few merchants stay on, trying to sell their remaining produce to late-comers at greatly reduced prices. Social satisfactions derived from participation in the market are greatly valued; it provides an opportunity for meeting friends and kinsmen and for exchanging gossip and observations on one another's dress, the crops, and current political developments. The market is a place for making loans and receiving small gifts from kinsmen and friends, for flirtations and the arrangement of rendezvous, and for that casual sort of social interaction which is one of the principal pleasures of life in the Yatenga.

The Mossi farmer is dependent on the co-operation of the members of his lineage both for the success of his individual economic endeavor and for their support if his crop should fail. To be assured of this support, he must contribute generously to the maintenance of his position in the intricate network of rights and obligations which describes the relationship of the individual to his kin group. A constant exchange of visits and presents, ceremonial and economic assistance, and presence and participation in the affairs of the lineage are necessary to maintain his status within this group.

The nature of the social, economic, and emotional dependence of the individual on his kinsmen, his affinal relations, and his neighbors is such that his social well-being and economic success may properly be regarded as depending as much on his skill in manipulating this complex web of relationships as on his specifically economic endeavors. When a man decides to forego a second weeding of his fields in order to prepare presents and make the journey to the funeral of a kinsman, he is making a choice which, considered in the total context of the culture, is realistically in accord with his own economic best interest.

The farmer feels equally dependent on the deceased members of his lineage, the ancestral spirits (*kiemse*). If he feeds them a chicken, they may steal the soul from a neighboring stand of millet and bring it to enrich his own field. If properly treated, they can be depended upon to protect his shea nut trees from the high winds which might otherwise destroy the yield. And, depending on his attentions to them, they can give or take away the good health necessary to carry him through the arduous activity of the rainy season when work is hardest, the granaries nearly empty, and food in short supply. Separate ancestral spirits look out for different aspects of the well-being of the individual. Satisfying their various sacrificial requirements is both expensive and time-consuming, but their good will is essential to the success of the farmer, and it is in his own best interest to be attentive to their needs.

THE EARTH CUSTODIANS

A close relationship exists between the control of the water supply upon which the agricultural economy depends and the authority of the earth custodians in their role as intermediaries with the several manifestations of Wennam, the Mossi deity. The deity itself is somewhat aloof from the affairs of men, but through his specific manifestations and with the intercession of the earth custodians (*Tenga Soba namba*), descendants of the indigenous inhabitants of the Yatenga, the individual propitiates Wennam in order to control the various forces of the natural and supernatural environment upon which the success of his economic or social endeavor is dependent. Tenga Wende, his terrestrial manifestation, and Tido Wende, which gives life to the vegetable kingdom, are the aspects of Wennam which are most frequently evoked; but Siguiri Wende, the deified first ancestor of the Mossi; Ki Wende, the millet god; and Saga Wende, the rain deity, are also frequently called upon for help.

Each Mossi village in the Yatenga is divided into one or more areas, each of which is in the "command" of one of the village earth custodians. Each of these areas contains both the dwelling of the Savadogo lineage of the earth custodian and the residence and farmlands of various "true" Mossi lineages. The head of each lineage maintains the good will of the terrestrial manifestation of the deity through the intercession of the earth custodian who "commands" his land. In some instances a lineage may own land under the authority of two different earth custodians; in this case offerings must be made at the shrine (*tenga*) of each.

The good fortune which may be secured through obeisance to the terrestrial manifestation of the deity (Tenga Wende) involves both sacrifices and gifts of money to the earth custodian and abstention from acts offensive to the earth. For example, sexual intercourse may take place only in a private courtyard or within the house. Violation of this rule defiles the land and must be expiated through a special sacrifice and the payment of a fine to the earth custodian. Any lost object found in the public way or in the bush is in the custody of the earth deity and must be turned over to the earth custodian to await the inquiry of the proper owners. If such objects are unclaimed, they are given to Tenga Wende by being placed on his altar, where they become part of the earth symbols (*tiinse*). As a result, these altars are piled high with old sardine cans, bicycle parts, remnants of clothing, unusual stones and scraps of metal, baskets, wooden implements, and weapons, which are left there to decompose slowly and return to the earth. Travelers in a strange village need never fear that their property will be stolen if they deposit it near the altar of the earth custodian.

When a farmer wishes to clear a part of the bush which has previously been unused, he must first ask permission of the earth custodian and make a present to the earth deity. If he wishes to use the land again the following year, the request and the gift must be repeated. Such a field may be passed on to his descendants, who have a right to the land so long as they acknowledge each year the authority of the earth custodian. If a new well is to be dug, his authorization must be requested, and his advice may also be asked for the proper place to seek water. The wise Mossi farmer consults the earth custodian frequently about his agricultural activities. He also reports anything that he may have done to alter the condition of his farmlands or the surrounding bush, not because each individual act is of such great importance, but because maintaining good relations with the custodian of the earth is in the interest of his own economic security.

OTHER ASPECTS OF RELIGION

Other descendants of the original inhabitants of the Yatenga, the Bogoba, are especially charged with the propitiation of Tido Wende, the vegetal manifestation of Wennam. In addition to the many manifestations of Wennam and the complex organization of priests and ceremonial designed for his propitiation, many other forces inhabit the unseen world of the Mossi. Indeed, to the observer their number and variety might at first seem to be almost as great as the number of Mossi with whom he may discuss these beings. Each man's description of these supernatural beings varies in terms of his subjective reaction resulting either from direct experience of them or from stories he has heard concerning their behavior. In contrast to Wennam, whose disposition is essentially benevolent so long as he is properly propitiated, these lesser supernatural beings are more frequently malicious and always more difficult to control. Perhaps for these reasons they are not worshiped. The Mossi's concern is not to propitiate them but to neutralize their evil intentions by the use of protective charms (*tim*).

The "bush," the unused land lying beyond the farms, is the least-known aspect of the Mossi natural environment. This is especially true of those far areas of the bush where even the authority of the earth custodians does not extend and where unknown spirits dwell. For although the bush is included in the orderly universe which the Mossi have fabricated, it exists at the periphery and is a thing to be feared. The name of this unknown and unowned part of the bush is synonymous with fear. Dreams in which an individual sees frightening images are called "bush creeping up" (*weogo doore*) or "bush traps you" (*weogo n'yoko fo*). These phrases are also used to describe the emotional shock, the feeling of fear, elicited by the unexpected sight of a frightening object like a corpse or a lion.

Most important among the supernatural beings inhabiting the bush are the twin spirits (*kikirdisi*). Living in pairs or in larger groups, they inhabit the bush, caves, baobab trees, and certain dense thickets of underbrush. While specific details vary, it is generally conceded that they are small, about a foot tall, black like the Mossi, and of both sexes. Their social organization is like that of men: each group is ruled over by a twin spirit-chief (*Kikirdisi Naba*).

Twin children are always regarded as the emissaries of the twin spirits. Shortly after the birth of twins their mother takes a present of food to a place where the twin spirits are known to dwell. Leaving the gift and expressing her thanks, she also makes it clear to the twin spirits that if they have any sort of malicious intent in sending her their children they might as well take them back immediately, since she will tolerate no foolishness. If, through her new children, they plan to torment her, they should save their efforts and desist at once. While the twin spirits are frequently mischief-makers, they are more frivolous than malicious and essentially neither good nor evil. The death of newborn twins is accepted with relief, for it is believed certain that the twin spirits have been thwarted in their mischievous intent and have conceded defeat.

THE ECONOMIC AND CEREMONIAL CYCLE

A brief description of the economic cycle and the ceremonials which mark its phases will serve to illustrate the way the Mossi perceive their relationship to the forces of their natural, supernatural, and social milieux and the methods by which they seek to assure their well-being through control of these forces. The year is usually divided into twelve moons whose names refer either to the principal economic activity of the season or to a ceremonial which accompanies it.

The first moon of the Mossi year is called "Gambo" after the name of the village which celebrates its first rain-making ceremony (*Tengana*) at this time. Although the rains are still five or six months away, this ritual marks the beginning of the new economic cycle. Each household which possesses land controlled by the earth custodian sends one of its young girls with an offering of millet gruel to place at the altar of Tenga Wende, the terrestrial manifestation of the deity. The earth custodian advises

Tenga Wende of the desire for a good growing year and gives each girl a small part of the wet earth near the shrine; this represents the now sanctified soul (*shiga*) and is placed under the granary from which the millet seeds for the new crop will be taken.

Then those who possess land controlled by the earth custodian organize a hunt for his benefit. The following day, the earth custodian visits each lineage which possesses fields in areas of the bush under his custodianship. He is given calabashes filled with millet gruel, which he pours as a libation on the earth, asking Tenga Wende to grant good health, heavy rains, and a successful harvest to the household. As the libation is poured, the women try to catch a little in their own calabashes of gruel, which they then pour as their sacrifice. Because the millet from the granaries of good harvests is lucky, other women want to try to catch a little of it in their own offerings; thus the libations spill from one calabash into another as they fall on the earth.

The second moon is called "Bega" after the ceremonial which coincides with the first labor in the fields, the clearing and burning which precedes planting. After making a sacrifice at his own altar, the earth custodian goes to the residence of the neighboring priest (*Boga*) specifically charged with the propitiation of the vegetal manifestation of the deity. This visit symbolizes the interdependent relationship of the two priests and the supernatural powers which they control. The *Boga* then repeats the libations made during the previous ritual, but this time the offerings of millet gruel are made to Tido Wende, the force which gives life to the plants, rather than to the earth.

A sacrifice to Pogo Wende, the specific manifestation of Tenga Wende which guards a farmer's fields, is usually made after they have been cleared and prepared for planting. Either before or after the sowing of the first seeds, the farmer asks the earth custodian to sacrifice a sheep or a goat to the field deity, requesting good health, heavy rains, and a rich harvest. This sacrifice (*Pogo Mande*) is the final aspect of the ceremonial preparations for the new economic cycle. It is designed to enlist the benevolence not only of Pogo Wende but also of the twin spirits which inhabit the field. If the twins are well disposed toward the farmer, they will protect the soul (*ki shiga*) of his millet stand from the twin spirits from neighboring fields who might try to steal it. Like the ancestral spirits, the twin spirits send a high wind into a field, blowing the ripening grains from the stalk and liberating their "souls" (*shiise*), which are then captured to enrich the spirits' own fields.

The third moon of the year is called "Cundiba Bega." The fourth, which usually corresponds with the European month of June, is called "unaccompanied" (Quizale), referring to the fact that no ceremonial is observed during its phase. The hard work in the fields is begun at this time. "Waraga," which means "first cultivation," is the name given to the fifth. The sixth, which appears in early September or late August, is called "Baca," meaning "second cultivation."

If the millet is not yet ripe for harvest at the appearance of the seventh moon, it is also called "Baca," since the work of cultivation must continue. This choice rests with the chief of the village of Room. The entire Mossi kingdom waits for his decision to know whether the ceremonial cycle called "Basga," which closes the economic year, is to begin or whether the harvest and its attendant ceremonies are to be put off for another month. Just behind his residence is a sacred millet field whose grains, as they mature, contain an aspect of the souls (*riim shiise*) of the dead kings of the Yatenga. When the millet in this field is ready to be cut, the next moon to appear is called "Yalem," and the ceremonial cycle which closes the economic year is begun. In the early days of the Yatenga dynasty millet from this field was used to prepare a sacrificial gruel to propitiate the deceased rulers of the newly established kingdom. When it is cut today, a first portion is taken to the altar at Room dedicated to the souls of these early kings. Two other bundles of millet are prepared from the same field. One is sent to the *Yatenga Naba* at Ouahigouya, who is the living descendant of the dead kings. The other is sent to the village of Gourcy, the former capital and the first residence of the founder of the Yatenga dynasty, Naba Yadiga.

The emissaries to the two political centers are accompanied by young people who break off stalks of millet from the fields along their way, adding these to the bundles of grain so as to include all of the farmers of the Yatenga in this offering which symbolizes the dependence of the Mossi on the benevolence of the souls of the dead kings and their living descendant. The millet taken to Ouahigouya is sacrificed at the palace altar of the former rulers. Part of the millet sent to Gourcy is sacrificed at the altar of the spirits of the former village chiefs (*nakom shiise*); the other part is sacrificed at the shrine of the former kings. At Ouahigouya and Gourcy a portion of each sacrificial offering of millet is returned to Room with stalks from the local crop at each place. These are used to make a final sacrifice symbolizing the interdependent relationship of Mossi religious, economic, and political organizations. The ceremonial cycle serves to demonstrate the reliance of the people on the benevolence of the spirits of their former kings for their social, economic, and supernatural well-being.

A ceremony called "Kom Filiga" follows. Meaning "water thanksgiving," it is the occasion for thanking the Mossi ruler, the *Yatenga Naba*, for the wise direction of affairs which has permitted the farmers to cultivate their fields in peace. All village and canton chiefs travel to Ouahigouya to salute their king and rededicate themselves to his service.

The next moon, called "Tido," is the occasion for a ceremony thanking Wennam, through his terrestrial and vegetal manifestations, for his support during the growing season and for the rich harvests that have been received. Though it is directed by the custodians of the earth, it is their auxiliaries, the Bogaba, who officiate and who sacrifice at the altars to Tido Wende. After they have finished, others may offer a chicken as thanks for successful harvests or for the birth of a child.

At the appearance of the next moon the ceremony called "Filiga" is celebrated, thanking the ancestors of each lineage for their protection during the hard months of the rainy season. The initial sacrifices are made by the village chief both at the shrine to the spirits of the former chiefs and at the ancestral shrine of his lineage. Because their offerings are made to powerful spirits, it is wiser not to refer directly to them by name. They are called *Kikirigo Na Maore*, which means "twin dance." The twin spirits, like the ancestral spirits (*kiemse*), give children. Thus, through indirection a "charged" word is avoided by calling the sacrifice after an analogous but less powerful force. The specific purpose of the first sacrifice is to ask the protection and the assistance of the spirits of the former chiefs during the dangerous period which is to follow. The ancestral spirits of the villagers are then propitiated, and individuals who fail to perform the sacrifices properly may be punished by their ancestors. It is also believed that the ancestors may try to call some of the members of the lineage to join them at this time.

The sacrifices are made by the children of the daughters of the lineage (*Yasenamba*), whose permissive relationship with their mother's kinsmen is paralleled by their relationship to the ancestral spirits of their lineage. The lineage head presents the first chicken for sacrifice. Its throat is slowly cut as it is offered to the "twin" (*kikirigo*), as the "first ancestor" of the lineage is called—again through indirection, for even if the name of the first ancestor were known, it would be presumptuous of his descendants to call him by name. A chicken is then sacrificed to the "old ancestors" of the great-grandfather's generation, to the ancestors of the grandfather's generation, and to those of the fathers' generation who are deceased. As each chicken's throat is cut, the ancestors are thanked for their protection throughout the rainy season and requested to continue to look out for the welfare of their descendants during the months of the dry season which follow. Other men of the lineage may then give chickens to be sacrificed.

The final aspect of the ritual closing of the economic year is the ceremony called "Na Poosum," or "chief's salutation." It is essentially a social occasion. The homage to the central political authority made at Kom Filiga is now complemented on the village level. The elders of each lineage go to the village chief with presents of millet and assurances of their continued reliance upon his political power and intercession with his noble ancestors, in order that the village may enjoy peace through the coming months of the dry season and early rains at the beginning of the next economic cycle.

With this observance all of the sources of power—both social and supernatural—upon which the Mossis' well-being is dependent have been thanked for their support throughout the year just ended and have been encouraged, by the generosity of their supplicants, to continue their benevolence for the year to come. The Mossi understand the nature of these forces and the manner in which they can be controlled. They know them as manifestations of a deity who will reward their observance of ceremonial obligations with the soft winds and heavy rains that bring a rich harvest. The individual is intellectually and emotionally absorbed in maintaining a balance in his relationship to a world he understands. His efforts to maintain this balance are occasionally frustrated by sorcery or the contrary will of his deity, but he enjoys, nonetheless, a very real security.

CULTURAL ADJUSTMENTS AT THE NIGER IRRIGATION PROJECT

Given the nature of these interrelationships between the organization of economic activity and the social and religious institutions of their culture, the adjustment of the Mossi who have been resettled at the Niger Irrigation Project has implications which go beyond mere technological adaptation. The settlers must, in fact, adjust to a totally changed cultural setting.

Arriving at the Niger project, they fail to find the institutions upon which they have always depended for their security; they find instead a natural environment governed by forces they do not know. Their water supply is no longer dependent on the supernatural controls of the earth custodians but comes from a dam built by Europeans. They are socially isolated from their kinsmen and their ancestral spirits in the Yatenga, and they derive little comfort from the presence of fellow Mossi with whom they have neither consanguineal nor affinal relationship.

Settlers were forcibly recruited for the Niger Irrigation Project until 1944, when forced labor was abolished throughout the French Union. Now a recruitment program brings Mossi families to the project each year; every family head receives a house, oxen, a plow, and a plot of land proportionate to the number of active workers accompanying him. Under the supervision of European agronomists, they apply modern methods to the production of rice and cotton. The project administration buys their crop for cash after deducting fees for seed, irrigation, mechanized cultivation, transportation, and processing. In theory, ten years of debt-free cultivation entitle the settler to permanent residence on the land he has been loaned.

Adaptation to the conditions of the new geographical setting in which the Mossi find themselves has been relatively rapid and easy. The Ya- tenga and the Niger project lie within the same climatic zone; the only important ecological difference between the two areas is the increased water supply resulting from irrigation. This change in the origin of the water supply, control of which provides a basic sanction of Mossi reli- gion, was less disturbing to traditional belief than might have been an- ticipated.

Rather than diminishing their belief in their own religion, it only con- vinces the Mossi colonists that the forces of the natural order are differ- ent in their new habitat and accordingly must be controlled in a different way. Finding the indigenous inhabitants of the French Sudan, the Bambara, to be zealous Moslems, the Mossi settlers have accepted Islam as the religion of their new country. Confident that their religious obliga- tions in the Yatenga will be taken care of by the elders who have re- mained behind, and with some pressure from those who have already be- come Moslemized, new arrivals rapidly embrace Islam as the system by which the supernatural forces governing their new environment can be manipulated.

Their acceptance of Islam has been as superficial as it has been rapid. There is time neither for the study of Moslem theology nor for the soul- searching which must precede the rejection of previously held religious beliefs. With a tradition which emphasizes the observance of religious form rather than intense emotional participation in ceremonial, their observance of the five daily prayers, taking of a Moslem name, deference to the marabout, and casual attention to certain dietary prohibitions should be viewed as their rational reaction to the fact of being in a strange land with an obviously different supernatural order which must be dealt with in a new way. Desire for a measure of control over this new supernatural order, pressure for conformity to the religious norms of their new social setting, and—perhaps most significantly—the permis- siveness which characterizes the West African's acceptance of the exist- ence of new supernatural forces, makes Islamization possible without the rejection of previously held religious ideas or practices.

In contrast to the relative ease of their adaptation to the natural and supernatural aspects of their new environment, their adjustment to the social situations which result from the change in economic organization has been most difficult. They must, of course, learn a new technology: the cultivation of rice and cotton by modern methods. Since the ma- chines used for clearing the land and for the harvest are operated by specially trained non-Mossi personnel, the use of irrigation, fertilizer, and the plow are their most important technological innovations. Despite their difficulty in communicating with the European agronomists under whose direction they work, they soon master these agricultural techniques. Patterns of consumption are also altered, rice taking the place of millet as the staple in their diet. After some initial illness they become accustomed to rice but suspect that it is less nourishing than their traditional diet.

Far more difficult than adjusting to either the new technology or the diet is adaptation to the changed social organization. Trying to ease this adjustment but with an imperfect understanding of traditional Mossi institutions, the project administration has tried to re-create their forms in the area of resettlement.

Despite this, the new colonist finds himself isolated among social forces he does not understand. The attempt to reproduce the traditional pattern of residential grouping is meaningless in the absence of the lineage. Separated from his kinsmen and his community, the colonist is confused by social institutions whose resemblance to those he has known in the Yatenga exists only on the level of form. He does not like or understand being housed with strangers as if they were his kinsmen. Equally incomprehensible is an approximation of the familiar political organization which, ignoring the traditional sanctions of chieftainship, has a former earth custodian, whose supernatural role has traditionally precluded the exercise of political authority, as paramount chief.

Despite the efforts of the European administration to reproduce their structural appearance, the institutions of Mossi society are so interrelated that the change in the organization of economic activity has created new needs which make alterations in traditional institutions inevitable. Rather than permitting the colonists to modify their indigenous social organization to fit these new needs, the social structure rigidly imposed by the Europeans has impeded the Mossi in their efforts to adjust their institutions to the changed situation. The delegation of authority to inept administrative appointees thinly disguised as chiefs and to the older, least adaptive members of the settler communities only complicates the problem of adjustment.

Isolated from their kinsmen and the protection of their ancestral spirits, the colonists miss the emotional and social satisfactions of extended family living as well as the security of an established position in the community in which they were born. Adherence to the traditional kinship organization, with its emphasis on obedience to the elders who have remained behind in the Yatenga, makes marriage at the Niger project almost impossible.

The young men born and raised at the project resent the tradition which requires sharing and compliance with the authority of kinsmen in the Yatenga whom they have never known. Forced to return to the Yatenga to assist the extended family there, they are frustrated in their efforts to form a permanent identification with their residence at the irrigation project. More efficient than their elders in communicating with the Europeans and in learning their techniques, they are thwarted by a social organization which denies expression to their initiative. The older men, given no share in the administration of the project and with little understanding of its objectives, believe that they are being exploited by the Europeans and that they would be more successful if they were to follow their own system of production and marketing.

The Mossi have learned that the official policy of the Niger Irrigation Project specifies their participation in administration through "indigenous agricultural associations," and even through their "collaboration" within the board of directors; but they do not actually participate in either of these. Possibly the fact that the Mossi have had no previous experience of participation in democratic forms discouraged the Europeans in their early efforts to include them in the administration of the project, but such participation implies a profound cultural adjustment and would require patience on the part of the Europeans. Whatever the case, the fact that the colonists know they have a right to participate in the administration and yet are denied it only serves to increase their conviction that they are being exploited.

Unsure of their rights to the land, unaware of the goals of the project, and inhibited by their artificially maintained tradition from forming meaningful social relationships in the area of resettlement, the Mossi make little permanent identification with the Niger project and its objectives. They say that it is like the hut a man builds in his fields during the rainy season; when the crop is harvested, he will return to the house of his fathers.

The relatively rapid and easy adaptation to the new natural setting and the supernatural forces which govern it is probably due both to the lack of European interference in this aspect of the colonists' lives and to the traditional permissiveness of West African religions. On the other hand, the greatest obstacle to adjustment seems to be just that aspect of the changed situation which was designed to facilitate it: the reconstruction and artificial maintenance of a social structure which cannot be efficiently integrated with the new economic organization. This structure has been maintained with such rigidity that it actually impedes Mossi efforts to reinterpret their institutions in terms of their new situation.

The Mossi who have returned from the Niger project have had little effect on their kinsmen in the Yatenga. Islamized colonists are often too young to be listened to seriously by their elders. If they are returning as senior members of their lineages, and since their power and prestige are dependent on the maintenance of the socio-religious status quo, they are unlikely to be innovators. For these same reasons the few changes in the social organization which have occurred at the Niger project have had little effect on the social environment of the Yatenga.

Most of the agricultural techniques acquired in the Sudan are useless in the Yatenga because of the absence of irrigation. Even were this not so, the rationale of the modern agricultural methods employed at the Niger project is not explained to the settlers; they are required to follow the instructions of the European agronomists or be penalized. As a result, the improved agricultural techniques of the Europeans are regarded as just another of the white man's incomprehensible ways and are quickly forgotten.

The response of the Mossi to resettlement at the Niger Irrigation Project shows that in a situation of rapid cultural change, retentions or changes on the superficial level of form are misleading; nor is a brief statement of the functional interrelationship between institutions sufficient. The final reality of an institution lies in its meaning for the members of the society in which it exists, and its final evaluation must be based on its capacity to fulfil the changing needs of individuals. This concept is essential to an understanding of the colonists' dissatisfaction with the effort of the Niger project administration to reproduce artificially a static model of their traditional social structure. This can also be seen in their reaction to a changed supernatural order; an analysis which failed to descend beneath the level of form would miss the significant fact that their psychological response to religion and the basic premises of their theology have remained unaffected by an "Islamization" which amounts to little more than adopting certain new propitiatory usages.

Apparently not understanding the interrelationship of cultural institutions and the sanctions which give them meaning, the administration of the Niger Irrigation Project sought to modify the Mossi organization of economic activity without referring to the traditional values to which it is vitally related. Seeming to regard the indigenous culture as little more than a compendium of savage rites upon which superior European usages need only be imposed in order to prevail, such an approach reveals a failure to comprehend both the complexity and the tenacity of the Mossi cultural heritage.

14. The Adaptive Functions of Fanti Priesthood

The primary requisite to becoming a Fanti[1] priest is possession by a deity (*obosom*) or by the "little people" of the forest (*mboatsia*). This state of possession or "call" is the supreme religious experience. It occurs when the deity "comes down on the head" and may occur at a public ceremony where drumming and singing are conducive to possession, or it may come to the individual in private—some priests maintained they were alone in the forest when first possessed.

The one who has this experience for the first time need not become a priest, but he may begin serving an apprenticeship if his family and those who are already priests agree that it is desirable. Priests may be of either sex; a male novitiate is trained by a priest and a female one by a priestess. The period of training is said to be five years, but it may be shortened for an adult or an adept student. One aspect of the training deals with therapeutic techniques, including instruction about properties of various plants and herbs and their location; but much of the instruction concerns the deity to be served by the candidate, for he will be the medium between the people and his god. Dancing, how to call his deity, and the construction and use of charms are also stressed in his training.

During this period he is not paid but is required to do any task his master sets for him. Although he is not isolated from the community, he must observe many restrictions and fulfil many obligations. He must have white clay on his face and shoulders on the days of the week sacred to his deity and wear as his primary garment the special rust-colored cloth which designates his calling. Abstention from sex relations is obligatory. He is also instructed and interrogated from time to time by other priests in the community. His years of training are concluded by a period of isolation, after which he proffers gifts to his master and takes

[1] The Fanti, with the Ashanti, Ahanta, Akim, Akwapim, Assin, Brong, Denkyira, Effutu, Etsii, Nzima, Sefwi, Twifo, and Wasaw of southern Ghana and the Agni of the Ivory Coast, constitute the grouping known as Akan, which numbers about two million. The various Akan peoples speak mutually intelligible dialects and exhibit a high degree of cultural homogeneity, so that much of what is stated here about the Fanti will also characterize other Akan groups.

part in a special ceremony at which he must perform specified feats under possession.

The phenomenon of possession is an important attribute of the priest-hood, and the term for priest (*komfo*) is a combination of *kom* (posses-sion) and *fo* (people). Possession is not limited to the priesthood; it some-times occurs among the devotees of some of the cults or on occasion at ceremonies such as burials or funerals, particularly among kinsmen of the deceased. The behavior of a possessed person is sometimes not unlike that of the epileptic, for he may twitch, jerk, appear to run or dance aim-lessly, and talk in unintelligible utterances.

Possession as it occurs among the priests is socially patterned, institu-tionalized, and even required under certain conditions. In short, it is pre-dictable behavior which is regarded as "normal" by the Fanti. When a priest summons the drummers because "his deity wishes to dance," it is assured that he will be possessed, or will affect the state of possession, and other activities can be forecast with some accuracy. He may dance vigorously or even wildly, but in spite of this apparent displacement of personality he still controls the drummers with signals from the dancing switch in his hand, and he never injures himself or the spectators. It is a procedure for which he has had years of training.

While the Fanti regard the conduct of the priest under possession as normal, it does not follow that the behavior of all priests at all times is considered as such. A priest, like any other Fanti, may be labeled insane (*abodamfo*). When this term is applied to a priest, it is not because of be-havior associated with his profession but because his manner of response to daily problems is considered deviant. It appears that minor deviations or slightly neurotic behavior on the part of a priest are overlooked, like the eccentricities of a genius in our own society.

Two other categories of medico-religious practitioners require mention, the first of which is the *obosomfo* (plural, *abosomfo*, literally, "people of the gods"). While this term is sometimes used synonymously with *komfo*, the Fanti generally use it to indicate those priests who serve deities of foreign provenience and who head cults whose popularity is based on their effec-tiveness as an antidote for evil magic.[2]

The other, the *adurnsinyifo* (singular, *adurnsinyi* or *odunsinni*), are primarily medical practitioners or herbalists who derive their name from *aduru*, the Fanti term for medicine. They also serve apprenticeships of several years but, unlike the priests, need no special qualification in terms of religious experience. Their function in the community parallels that of the priest in several respects, for they prescribe medicine and specialize in charms. Unlike the priest, they are never possessed by the

---

[2] For an example of *obosomfo*, see the Tigari cult described below in the section on new cults.

gods, and their method of divination is primarily that of casting lots, such as interpreting the fall of cowrie shells or kola nuts. However, some claim the ability to communicate with the deities, and some own objects that have the supernatural power to assist them in their practice. They are held to be superior to the priests in therapy by medication, as is indicated by the phrase often heard, "the herbalist is the master of the priest." Fanti elders state that in former times the herbalist confined his treatment to medication, in which he was reputed to be highly skilled. Today, however, some element of the supernatural or of magic is involved in the treatment of most of his cases. This course is not always chosen by the herbalist but is often requested by the patient. As one herbalist remarked, "People ask me to call a deity, and I do it just to make them happy and give them value for their money, but it doesn't change the medicine I give them."

COSMOLOGY OF THE FANTI

Before an outline of the function of the priest, a description of Fanti cosmology may be helpful in understanding the nature of the gods he serves. The Fanti believe in the existence of a high god, known variously as Nyame (or Onyame), Nyankupon, and Odumankuma, who created the world and everything in it, including the lesser deities and spirits who derive their power from him. But Nyame has no priesthood, and no ceremonies are held specifically for the purpose of invoking his good will. Yet though there is little direct worship of Nyame, it would be incorrect to assume that the Fanti are not constantly cognizant of his existence. Many proverbs, such as "the earth is broad, but Nyame is senior" and "to tell Nyame, tell the wind," are in common usage and indicate an awareness of his power. His primacy is evident in the prayers to the ancestors and the gods by both priesthood and laity, since they commonly end with the phrase "if Nyame wills it."

The Fanti world view also includes lesser deities known as the *abosom* (singular, *obosom*), who obtain their power from Nyame. Most of them are believed to dwell in rivers, lakes, rocks, or other natural phenomena. They are the primary concern of the priests, and we will return to them again shortly.

The amulets, charms, and talismans collectively referred to as *asuman* (singular, *suman*) hold an important place. They are used primarily in magic;[3] the power of some is derived from the magical formula used in their composition, while others obtain their potency from an *obosom*.

[3] The words "fetishism" and "juju," often used by Europeans and English-speaking Africans as generic terms to apply to African religious beliefs and practices as a whole, are misleading and should be avoided (see R. S. Rattray, *Ashanti* [Oxford: Clarendon Press, 1923], pp. 86–91).

The "little people" (*mboatsia*) whose feet turn backwards, who are said to be of various colors and shapes, and who inhabit the forest have great supernatural power and are important for both their benevolence and their malevolence.

The belief in the ancestral spirits (*asaman*, also *nsamanfo*, singular, *saman*), provides the sanctions for the basic unit in the social structure, the matrilineal clan (*abusua*). The individual finds security within his clan, for from it he obtains land to farm, assistance in time of need, and co-operation in propitiating the ancestral spirits; from the clan he inherits wealth and office, and by it he is given the elaborate funeral so important to the Fanti. The common ancestress from whom clan members believe themselves descended thus takes on a particular significance, as do the spirits of her matrilineal descendants who have died. The belief in the omnipresence of these ancestral spirits is made evident by daily acts as well as by periodic ceremonies. They have power to bring good fortune to the living or, if dissatisfied, to show their displeasure by causing ill fortune, sickness, or death.

Yet despite the importance of the clan ancestors, the spiritual bond existing in the exogamous patrilineal descent grouping is by no means minor. Every person enters the world under the aegis of his father's guardian spirit (*egyabosom*, literally, "father's deity"), which is usually a nature deity and may be appealed to like other gods. The individual also inherits his spirit or personality (*sunsum*) and soul (*kra*) from his father.[4] The *kra* is essentially the life-force of the individual, and when it departs, death follows. When a person is troubled or ill he may call a priest or herbalist to contact his *kra* and find out what is causing the difficulty. Then the *kra* may be rejuvenated by a ceremonial "washing," which involves a special feast so that a man may feed and satisfy his soul. The importance of patrilineal inheritance to the Fanti is also indicated by the fact that a marriage between a couple having the same *egyabosom* derived from a common patrilineal antecedent would be regarded as incestuous.

Each of the traditional Fanti states is reported to have seventy-seven gods,[5] but this number bears no relation to the actual number of sacred rocks, streams, and lagoons, which are far more numerous but designated as being associated with deities. Not every one of these is served by a priest, and a god need not be located in the vicinity in which his priest practices; some Fanti priests, indeed, stated that their *abosom*

[4] For a discussion of the Fanti clan and patrilineal inheritance see James Boyd Christensen, *Double Descent among the Fanti* (New Haven: Human Relations Area Files, 1954). The Fanti *egyabosom* and related beliefs may be equated with the Ashanti *ntoro* as outlined by Rattray, *Ashanti*, pp. 45 ff.

[5] The numbers three and seven constantly recur in Akan ritual, mythology, and secular matters.

were located in Ashanti. The deities are believed to reside at times in the body of water or in the object they are associated with, but they are also reported to move about and at times may be seen by the people. They are anthropomorphic and zoömorphic, or a combination of these, and are described as either human or animal, of unusual size and appearance, or as half-human and half-animal. Every Fanti state has deities that are especially revered and worshiped because of some act attributed to them in the past. Some are reputed to be particularly effective in accomplishing certain tasks, such as bringing a plentiful catch of fish, giving children, promoting sales in the market, or helping in warfare. A few even assist people who request help in antisocial behavior, such as aiding a thief to go undetected. The gods have personalities like humans: some are gregarious, some stern and vindictive, and most are capricious.

SACRED AND SECULAR DUTIES OF THE PRIESTHOOD

Each priest has a special room as a shrine for his deity. Here he keeps a mixture of medicines in a brass vessel or a figurine to which the god may come and which, in a sense, represents the deity, in addition to the other essential paraphernalia. The priest must put white clay on his face and body on sacred days and make libations and periodic offerings of food, including the sacrifice of a ram or fowl. He must refrain from eating food tabooed by the god and use cloth and equipment of the color identified with his deity, usually white. Because the deities love to dance, the priests whould assemble drummers for public ceremonies and become possessed. While in this state a priest talks in a low, guttural voice or, rarely, in a high falsetto, which indicates that the deity is speaking through him.

It is difficult, if not impossible, to separate the religious activities of the priest from his secular services; he functions both as a priest and as a doctor who aids or cures by manipulating the supernatural. To the Fanti, illness and death may be due to either natural or supernatural causes. Although hospitals and clinics are available, the traditional techniques remain the most popular.

There are several ways in which an individual may receive assistance in case of illness. He may appeal directly to the ancestral spirits, to his guardian spirit, or he may invoke the assistance of a nature deity by proffering a gift. He may choose to consult an herbalist for medication or go to a priest. The nature of his illness may influence the decision; there is no prescribed course of action that requires him to prefer one deity or spirit to another or to seek aid from a particular type of practitioner. The situation is not unlike that in the United States, where such factors as educational background, reputation of the practitioner, advice of friends, past experience, or religious conviction will determine whether a person sees a medical doctor, chiropractor, or faith-healer or whether he treats himself or trusts to the supernatural. The same factors are operative in the Fanti's choice of seeing a priest, an herbalist, or going to the hospital or appealing to the ancestral spirits or deities.

Even if a patient consults a priest, therapy may be strictly medicinal. Medicine may be taken orally, rubbed on the body, or administered as an enema or douche. However, the priest may, either on his own volition or at the request of the patient, consult his god and through divination ascertain the cause of the illness. The priest practices major techniques of divination, possession, and casting lots. While possession in a public ceremony is induced by drumming, in private treatment this state is usually achieved by having an assistant rhythmically beat a gong. Narcotics are rarely if ever used. The priest is a passive medium, for while he is possessed, his deity speaks through him, and on recovery he claims no knowledge of what he has said or experienced. The guttural speech of the priest is unintelligible to all but the trained assistant who serves as translator (*kyeame* or *abrafo*).

While possession is the primary technique of divination, a priest may at times cast lots, following any one of several procedures, the most common of which is interpreting the fall of cowrie shells or kola nuts. Another technique involves diagnosing the manner and position in which a sacrificed fowl dies and analyzing the viscera. Some priests also claim to have the power to communicate with the supernatural by the simple process of placing a magical mixture in their eyes and ears.

Divination usually reveals that the supernatural is in some manner involved in the patient's illness. With the very broad range of obligations to the supernatural, in the fulfilment of which the client may have been lax, and with the possibility that he is being punished for having broken a secular rule of conduct, the cause of an affliction may literally be any one of hundreds. An ancestor may be showing displeasure because the terms of his *samansew* (a will, given orally before death) were not properly observed. It may be that some personal property, such as a cherished piece of jewelry, that he had directed should be interred with him was retained by the family; a sister's son that he had designated as his heir may have been passed over in favor of another kinsman; some aspect of a required funerary rite may have been neglected. Since burial and funeral rites are public and since deviations from what is considered "proper" may be noted and are often topics of conversation, disgruntled ancestors are often said to be the cause of illness.

There is an apparent increase in the concern over evil magic, and often the diagnosis of a priest is that an envious kinsman is using this power against a client.[6] Several incidents involving the use of evil charms have been observed. In one case the brother of a sick fisherman requested that

[6] See section below on new cults.

a priest cure him. The priest became possessed and directed the villagers to dig at a designated spot on the beach. They uncovered a charm, consisting of a small bottle with quills in the top and containing a black mixture which was said to be causing the illness. The person who made the charm or caused it to be made was not discovered, but the patient did recover. In a similar case a charm in the form of an iron pot containing medicine was unearthed in a compound, and the death, sickness, and misfortune that had occurred during the past year to residents of that compound were attributed to it. Another cause may be failure to deliver a gift promised to some deity; some unethical or illegal act, such as adultery or stealing, may have been committed. In a Fanti village where privacy is rare and gossip is common, it is easy for a priest to know of misbehavior of some sort on the part of a client.

Treatment of an illness that is supernatural in origin may involve some form of medication as part of the therapy, but propitiation of the displeased or malignant spirit is essential. Though there is a wide variation in detail, this inevitably includes gifts and sacrifice. These may vary from offerings of food, drink, and animals to a sum of money given through the priest or buried at a designated spot in the forest. Though they have not been systematically analyzed, there is the possibility that some of the medicants used by the priests in treatment have therapeutic value; but there is no question that a positive psychological value is present in the role of the priest as a medium, which makes it possible for the patient to believe that he has established rapport with the powers that control the universe and contributes to his feeling of security. Although the herbs or other medication administered may be only a placebo, the belief that he is being helped through the attention of a skilled practitioner will thus have a positive psychosomatic effect on the patient.[7] Consultation with priests is not, however, limited to instances where there is illness to be cured. Intercession with the gods is constantly sought by women to allow them to have children. Appeals may be made to locate lost articles, or requests for good crops and good fishing and advice on personal problems may be sought.

Priests have often had the charge of charlatanism laid against them, and most Fanti can recount incidents where the trickery of some priest has been suspected or exposed. Skeptics doubt the need for burying money at a specified place in the forest in order to placate a disgruntled spirit or claim that an illness blamed on a charm was really due to the judicious use of poison. Some believe that the priests maintain an intelligence network that enables them to obtain information on the private life and ancestry of their patients which is then given out as if it were a result of divination or revelation. However, the exposure of a few cases

[7] Cf. M. J. Herskovits, *Man and His Works* (New York: Alfred A. Knopf, 1948), p. 374.

of deception does not cause the majority to lose faith in either the deities or the priesthood as a whole. Again, a comparison may be drawn with "quack" doctors and incidents of defection of men of the cloth in our own culture, where the fault is ascribed to the individual rather than to medicine or theology as such.

It is difficult to draw a line between the service of the priesthood to the community and the exploitation practiced by some of their number. That their activities are at times beneficial to their clients is undeniable, for the feeling of well-being resulting from knowing that the supernatural is appeased or the security obtained from protection against evil magic cannot be minimized. It has often been noted that the satisfaction which the non-literate derives from these activities may be equated with that which the Christian receives from attending church and conforming with the dogma of his particular sect. It would be an error to state that the Fanti priesthood as a whole is characterized by charlatanism, just as it would be incorrect to imply that no priest exploits his position. That many of the Fanti priests believe in their gods and their practices is evident from the fact that in time of sickness or need they avail themselves of the services of a colleague.

MAGIC AND CHARMS

Another function of the priest is to deal with magic, which may be good or evil. To differentiate between the two categories is difficult, since a magical instrument may be simultaneously benevolent and malevolent, in accordance with the principle that whatever aids one may harm another.

Asuman (singular, *suman*) is the generic term applied to objects or mixtures made for the purpose of protection, assistance, or for the punishment of some specified enemy. Their power may be derived from the supernatural beings who activate them or from the compulsive formulas used in their making. Charms for specific purposes have their own special names, which can designate either form or function. For example, *nsebe* refers to a charm that can be worn as a necklace or bracelet, whatever its purpose; *siri* is the name for any charm, whatever its form, which confuses an opponent in a court case; *kwanga* (or *kwanka*) denotes one that attracts a member of the opposite sex.

Great variation exists in the size, shape, ingredients, and manner of making charms; a few examples may be given to indicate the range in form and purpose. A personal charm to aid the owner in economic pursuits may be made by mixing shea butter with the necessary magical ingredients, the mixture being placed in a small brass vessel and often embellished with cowrie shells and needles.[8] A mixture of this sort may

[8] Such charms are often referred to as *aduru*, or just "medicine."

be given the power to speak to its owner and to impart such information as when and where to fish so as to insure obtaining the best catch. Like all magic, it will be efficacious, however, only if given proper care, including regular offerings of food and drink. For a charm to confound the opposition in court, one technique is to bind the proper ingredients tightly with a string and then to bury the charm.

As is common elsewhere in Africa, most priests maintain that they will not provide charms that cause illness and death, asserting that their "deity does not allow them" to do this. Here the theory of the nature of the criminal act as balanced against the duty of the practitioner to his client enters. In a magical system the priest must know the evil he is to combat, as well as its counterforce, if he is effectively to discharge his obligation to a client who seeks protection against the evil magic of an enemy. Hence it is understandable that priests who admitted a knowledge of evil magic would discuss this aspect of their work only in the most general terms. Indeed, of the many medical practitioners and priests with whom this matter was discussed, only one admitted that he ever used evil magic, and he explicitly stated that his deity permitted him to do this only when it was essential to assure retribution against someone who had "sinned." With the customary realism of the people, it is generally believed, however, that any priest can cause death or illness if properly approached, especially if the fee is sufficiently attractive.

Practices involved in the use of malignant magic also vary widely. One example of imitative or homeopathic magic consists of burying a box containing the body of a cat and other necessary medicine. Another, also used to kill or injure an opponent, is to pass him a drink while holding a magical mixture in the same hand, so that its power permeates the glass. Burying or hiding a *suman* is a common practice.

There is general agreement that a charm is more effective if it includes something from the body of the intended victim or something that has been in contact with him—nail parings, hair, a piece of his towel or clothing, a bit of mud from the place where he urinated, or merely some dust on which he has stepped. This is why the Fanti are cautious about disposing of hair and nail parings, which are held to be particularly efficacious. On the other hand, the power of a charm may be counteracted by protective magic, or it can be destroyed if the charm is burned or thrown into a latrine.

Despite the magic to which they may be exposed, it cannot be said that Africans live in constant fear of it or that their lives are dominated by it. Popular writers have often erroneously confused the public sacrifices and offerings to the ancestral spirits and nature deities with magic and "witchcraft." Yet charms that work evil are never publicly displayed by the Fanti; they are hidden from view. Customary law demanded the death penalty for those found guilty of working evil by the use of magic, and courts still fine or imprison those found responsible for the use of what is today referred to in legal parlance as "a noxious instrument." There can be little doubt that a majority of the Fanti believe that evil magic can kill, but their religion provides them with the protection afforded by benevolent spirits, and they can always have recourse to counteracting magical devices. Hence the average man in his daily round is no more concerned with these matters than the average person in an industrial society lives in fear of being killed by an automobile. Nonetheless, when a man learns that he has been marked as a victim by a worker of magic who is reputed to be particularly effective in his evil art, he may become ill or die.[9] Some skeptical Fanti claim that certain priests who wish to reinforce their reputation in this regard may claim responsibility for deaths which actually were due to natural causes, and they cite the proverb, "A priest recounts only his successes, never his failures."

The vast majority of the functions of the priests are exoteric, however, being carried on either in public or semiprivate and witnessed by clients and their relatives. The priesthood, indeed, serves the community in many capacities. If a woman dies in childbirth with the child *in utero*, the priest may be called upon to remove it prior to burial.[10] Warriors in earlier days were provided with charms by the priests to make their clothing impervious to the weapons of the enemy. In trials involving use of evil magic, priests still testify as expert witnesses, analyzing charms to ascertain their purpose; and before trial by ordeal was outlawed, the ordeal to determine guilt or innocence was administered by them. A major contribution, though incidental to the primary functions of the priests, is the pleasure derived from the drumming and dancing for the deities which characterize their rites.

POLITICAL AND SOCIAL POSITION OF THE PRIEST

The Fanti, like other Akan peoples, have a complex and highly developed political system,[11] with religion and the state inextricably linked. However, while in many African societies the priest may have political

[9] One need not delve into the esoteric for an explanation, since illness or death in this case may be understood as psychosomatic in causation or as a case of thanatomania. For a discussion of some of the psychosomatic factors involved in death by magic see Walter B. Cannon, " 'Voodoo' Death," *American Anthropologist*, XLIV (April–June, 1942), 169–81.

[10] Such a death is held to be suicide by the Fanti, and the child must be removed to make certain it was not an evil spirit that caused the mother to die. Suicide and accidental deaths are referred to as *otofo* and receive different funerary ritual.

[11] A discussion of the political structure of an Akan people can be found in R. S. Rattray, *Ashanti Law and Constitution* (Oxford: Clarendon Press, 1929), and K. A. Busia, *The Position of the Chief in the Modern Political System of Ashanti* (London: Oxford University Press, 1951).

power, this is not the case among the Fanti. The Akan political system is based on the matrilineal clan, which in turn is predicated on ancestral worship, the clan chief being regarded as the living representative of the ancestors. Because propitiation of the ancestors may be done by clan elders or others who are charged with performing these tasks, the services of the priests who are specialists in the worship of the gods are not required. And while affairs of state usually involve religious ritual, the chiefs and their advisers make their decisions on the basis of customary law rather than on supernatural sanction. A priest may be consulted on such a matter as the desirability of waging war, but the chiefs and elders are not likely to permit the dictates of the gods, as revealed by the priest under possession, to override what they consider the wisest course. Most often, indeed, the priest is called upon to invoke the good will of the gods after a decision to go to war has been reached.

Though the priesthood is not political, a priest can exert considerable influence through his manipulation of the supernatural, particularly if he can sway those prominent in government.[12] The position of the priests, indeed, is not unlike that of the clergy in Euroamerican societies. They may receive special considerations, but they are subject to the same laws as the laity. The relation of the priesthood to the elders is illustrated by the proverb, "The mouth (word) of the elder is stronger than the *suman* (charm)." This simple apothegm holds in practice. Cases have been observed where priests are summoned before a council of elders, where they bare their shoulders as a sign of respect and subservience and address the elders as *m'egya* (my father), an added sign of social subordination. The Fanti are very definite in their conviction of this right of the chiefs and elders to control the priests.

A note should be made of the status of the priestess. It is the general attitude of the Fanti that priestesses are not as effective as priests, although the difference is not great and exceptions can be noted. The situation is comparable to that existing in the medical profession in the United States, where it is admitted that a woman can be as competent as a man, yet where men dominate the field. A factor in Fanti culture which contributes to this attitude is the large number of taboos placed on women during menstruation, a restriction that circumscribes their daily tasks and limits their participation in ritual.[13] During her menstrual period a priestess may prescribe medicine, but she is prohibited from

[12] One priest, Komfo Anokye, was a great political leader who played an important role in the formation of the Ashanti confederation (see Rattray, *Ashanti Law and Constitution,* pp. 270 ff.). Fanti tradition recounts that a group of priests in charge of a sacred grove at Mankessim wielded considerable political influence in all of the Fanti states prior to their exposure as charlatans (see Christensen, *Double Descent,* pp. 12–18).

[13] Some of the menstrual taboos observed today are touching the tools or implements of a male, cooking food for the ancestors or a deity, participating in religious

divining or contacting her god. Hence she is seriously hampered in practicing her profession until she passes the menopause. The priestess also presents a special problem in regard to marriage; either she remains unmarried, or the unions she enters into are short lived. This, the Fanti claim, is due to her vocation rather than to the fact that she is an aberrant personality. The time spent with patients and in fulfilling her obligations to her deity seriously affects her ability to attend to wifely duties. Moreover, the husband of a priestess must be extremely cautious not to "abuse" her, lest he offend her deity and then have to appease it by a series of costly gifts. Some gods require that their devotees remain single, and certain priestesses maintain that they are "married to the deity" and consequently cannot marry a mortal.

ACCULTURATION

As elsewhere in Africa south of the Sahara, contact with European culture and conversion to Christianity have brought about many changes in the role and practices of the priests. The initial contact of Ghana with Christianity followed the establishment by the Portuguese of São Jorge d'el Mina in 1462 at what is now the town of Elmina. While the Catholic priests associated with the Elmina garrison did some proselytizing, very little was accomplished in terms of actual conversion during the fifty-odd years they controlled the town. Other European powers engaged in trade in the area from the fifteenth to the nineteenth centuries were more interested in gold and slaves than in the spread of Christianity; thus organized missionary activity did not begin among the Fanti until 1827.[14] Today the Christian groups in the southern half of Ghana have a following sufficient in numbers and educational background to permit the major portion of mission work and church administration to be carried on by Africans.

The impact of Christianity on the indigenous priesthood and worship of the deities cannot be discussed adequately apart from the change that has occurred in Fanti religion as a whole. Generally speaking, Christianity has resulted in a weakening of the autochthonous religion, but Christianity has only partially succeeded in imposing its own code of ethics and behavior. Since the time of the earliest missionaries, Africans have been taught that participation in traditional forms of worship was "fetishism" or superstition and was forbidden. Some Christians have refused to lend support to any ceremony which validates the position

---

ritual, and walking in or near a sacred area such as a tree, river, or stone regarded as a god. Formerly, women isolated themselves in a special hut or room during menstruation and could not cook for their husbands, but today isolation is not a common practice, and most women continue to cook for their husbands during this time.

[14] See W. E. F. Ward, *A History of the Gold Coast* (London: George Allen & Unwin 1948).

of the chief, since his rule is based on ancestral worship. Similarly, ceremonies intended to invoke the good will of important deities have been boycotted. Such an attitude can lead, and has led, to the social isolation of some Christians from their clan and the community, and it tends to bring about disintegration of the African culture.[15]

The Fanti believe that the annual or periodic ceremonies for the spirits and nature deities promote the well-being of the entire state, and prayers for prosperity, health, protection, and fecundity are offered during these ceremonies. To ignore the spirits, it is believed, will result in their visiting bad fortune and sickness on the living, and non-participation by any segment of the society can bring considerable ill. The denial of the power of the ancestors by some Christians has had a deleterious effect on the solidarity and collective responsibility of the clan, in which the Fanti formerly found a high degree of security. Concomitantly, there has been a decrease in the authority of and respect for the elders. The stress that Christian doctrine places on patrilineal descent is not compatible with the Fanti system of matrilineal inheritance, and a gradual breakdown of the latter is in process. The prohibition of polygyny by the missions has been a factor in the increase in adultery and prostitution, and in cases of childless marriages it conflicts with the strong desire for children.

Christianity cannot be designated as the sole cause of the rapid changes now taking place; as is usually the case in culture change, several factors are involved. European economic concepts, which stress individualism as opposed to the corporate responsibility of the clan, have increased the possibility of the development of a more atomized society. The implementation of a parliamentary form of government has undermined the power and prestige of chiefs and elders. Schooling has also played an important role, since "teaching the simple fact, for example, that malaria is caused by the bite of a mosquito, may raise doubts not only about native explanations and remedies for one disease, but also about the validity of the entire system of traditional beliefs."[16]

One of the problems in this transitional phase is the difficulty in classifying many people as either "Christian" or "pagan." Many who claim to be Christian rarely if ever attend church services, and continue to practice tribal ways. Many who are active in the various Christian groups also often participate in ceremonies for the ancestors and nature deities. The gods and ancestors require that stripes of clay be worn on the arms, chest, or back at specified times, such as sacred days or during periods of mourning, and many who classify themselves as Christian

[15] Cf. Busia, *Position of the Chief*, pp. 133 ff.
[16] William R. Bascom, "West and Central Africa," in *Most of the World*, ed. Ralph Linton (New York: Columbia University Press, 1949), p. 369.

continue to do this, sometimes concealing these markings, as well as charms, under their clothing. This is to be expected, since Fanti religion is polytheistic and pluralistic. Becoming a Christian while still retaining traditional beliefs need not conflict for the African, for adoption of a new deity does not necessarily imply negation of the old; it is rather to be regarded as an additive factor for protection against the uncertainties of life. All of the priests stated that they had Christians among their clientele. The tenacity of the indigenous religion is illustrated by the fact that several priests stated that they had been practicing Christians before their apprenticeships, and one priestess reported that her initial possession by her god occurred while she was attending a Methodist service.

Though one should not infer that there is none among the educated Fanti elite who can be classified as Christian in the Euroamerican sense of the term, even some of the Christian elite may be found participating in so-called pagan ritual. For this group, loyalty to a chief and the clan, on one hand, and to Christian principles, on the other, has been reconciled by placing the former on a secular rather than a sacred basis, with continued activity in clan affairs being viewed as the discharge of a social obligation.

The contemporary situation among the Fanti is paralleled by that in Nigeria as described by Bascom, who states that some educated Africans regard as unjustified and ethnocentric the Christian attitude that African religions are mere superstitions which must be eliminated. For one thing, these people find it difficult to reconcile the point of view that African religions are superstitions when African names are used to refer to the Christian deity in translations of the Bible. It is also difficult to accommodate the Christian concept of monotheism with the rivalry between the various Christian sects.[17] Some Fanti are confused about the Christian stand against polygyny, for in their reading of the Bible they find that it appears as a common practice in the Old Testament, while nothing specific is stated against it in the New Testament.

Some serious conflicts between pagan and Christian practices have been solved by compromise. Friday, sacred to Asaase Efua, the earth goddess, is a day when people should abstain from going to their farms, and on Tuesday, sacred to Bosompo, god of the sea, there should be no fishing. Early Christians were inclined to violate these taboos, since Sunday was held by them to be the proper day of rest. The conflict has been resolved by the adoption of a "five-day work week" by both Christians and pagans. Farmers generally abstain from work on the farm on both Friday and Sunday, and fishermen from their work on Tuesday and Sunday.

[17] *Ibid.*

Acculturation has brought about the modification of indigenous patterns of behavior toward the deities and the priesthood and some syncretism between the two cultures. In Esiam a European bell of some antiquity has taken on the status of an important supernatural being, and in Elmina a statue of St. Anthony left by the Portuguese in the fifteenth century has also been appropriated as a deity. The latter case is of particular interest because of the Christian elements retained and incorporated into the African pattern of worship, a parallel of the pattern so typical in the New World, where Catholic saints have been syncretized with African deities.[18] The deteriorating remains of this statue are associated with a god known as Ntona or Nturan, the local version of "São Antonio." The deity is served by a group of adherents known as the "Santa Mariafo," "the people (-*fo*) of Santa Maria," another retention from the Portuguese. Ntona is now accorded primacy over all other deities in the native state of Elmina, and the ritual and ceremony associated with its worship is predominantly African,[19] but elements of Catholic symbolism have been retained ever since the Portuguese abandoned it almost five centuries ago. These include the sign of the cross, the wearing of long white gowns by the officiants, the lighting of candles for the deity and upon the death of adherents of Ntona. All these elements were present prior to Christian proselytizing in the nineteenth century.[20] While other native priests also use white cloth, their skirts differ markedly in style from the long white robes of the followers of Ntona. Although the sign of the cross might have been adopted after the Portuguese were replaced by the Dutch in 1637, the Dutch predicant did not actively proselytize among the Africans but confined his work to the Europeans in Elmina.[21] The officiants for Ntona are also known as *asofo* (singular, *osofo*), a term applied by the Fanti to people who attend to or care for prominent deities. Unlike a priest, an *osofo* is never possessed, and he does not divine or practice magic or medicine. His duty is to see that the ceremonies for the gods are carried out. The term *osofo* is now applied to Christian ministers.

There has been a decline in the activity of the priests and in the propitiation of the deities throughout the Fanti area. Nevertheless, African religious practices continue to be relatively strong in some localities, with what appears to be a pronounced difference between the fishing

[18] Cf. M. J. Herskovits, *Myth of the Negro Past* (New York: Harper & Bros., 1941), pp. 218 ff.

[19] See also Ralph M. Wiltgen, *Gold Coast Mission History 1471–1880* (Techny, Ill.: Divine Word Publications, 1956), pp. 144–51. For a description of the annual ceremonies and ritual for some Akan deities see Rattray, *Ashanti*, pp. 151 ff.

[20] See E. J. P. Brown, *Gold Coast and Asianti Reader* (London: Crown Agents for the Colonies, 1929), II, 20–24, and J. S. Wartemberg, *São Jorge d'el Mina* (Elms Court: Arthur H. Stockwell, n.d.), pp. 152–53.

[21] See Ward, *History of the Gold Coast*, p. 74.

communities and the inland agricultural villages. In the former, priests are more numerous, and public ceremonies and drumming and dancing for the gods are more frequent; during slack periods in fishing they are almost a nightly occurrence. In the farming communities such public ritual is rare. Other differences in the degree of retention of the traditional culture can be noted, the least amount of change being most often exhibited in the fishing villages. The reason for the difference in degree of acculturation is not easily given, since contact with the European has been approximately equivalent. It can be explained in part by the greater dangers associated with fishing and by a general conservatism characteristic of fishing communities the world over, in part on a historical basis and by the different cultural backgrounds. The coast was already occupied by a people known as the Etsii when the Fanti, migrating from the north, occupied the area and subjugated the natives.[22] Thus the fishing villages are a merging of Fanti and Etsii cultures.

Acculturation has brought changes in the type of requests the priest receives from his clients. The usual, general pleas for health, protection, and fecundity are still made, but there has been an increasing emphasis on aids and nostrums to meet the needs of the modern world. Traditional charms to aid the traveler are now used by drivers and passengers on lorries; one priest claimed that he provided a charm to make people invisible to the police; a medicine formerly used to "tie the tongue" of an opponent in a dispute heard in the traditional manner before a chief is sometimes used by the plaintiff or defendant in adjudication before the government court; students request assistance to develop acumen or to pass an examination; and one deity was reported to be particularly efficacious in causing the football teams from other towns to stumble when playing the home team.

It is in the economic aspect of culture that the greatest amount of change in the nature of requests to the priests and the deities has occurred. Propitiation of the ancestors and the gods so that they will grant good crops or good fishing continues, but many appeals reflect the impact of European culture. Aid in securing fares is sought by the drivers of lorries and taxis; a fisherman requested help in getting a job in Accra unloading cargo from the ships; assistance in obtaining a position with the government or a trading firm is a common request; a goddess that was reputed to aid women selling produce in the market is now asked to help in buying or selling manufactured goods. In those sections of the Fanti area where cocoa is grown, deities are requested to assist in bringing about a high price for cocoa, in acquiring cocoa farms, and even in persuading the government crews who were "cutting out" diseased cocoa trees to bypass some farms.

[22] See Christensen, *Double Descent*, chap. II.

It is also held that the supernatural powers and the priests play a role in the contemporary political situation in Ghana. It was reported by several informants that Kwame Nkrumah, then leader of one of the political parties, had the aid of *obosom* and *mboatsia* during the campaign in 1950–51. Nkrumah was then in prison, but with the aid of the gods his spirit could make nocturnal visits to chiefs and people who were opposing him and persuade them to follow him. The support of the new government by the priesthood has been publicly acclaimed on several occasions, and the sacrifice of animals or libations for the ancestral spirits and nature deities are offered at official functions in many localities.

The remuneration received by the priest for his services has also undergone change, in both character and amount. Prior to the adoption of the British monetary system, his fee was paid in produce, animals, or gold dust, but today it is almost wholly in cash. A minimum consultation fee of two shillings is common, and if divination is involved, more may be required. Depending on the nature of the findings or the character of the medication provided, additional fees may be charged at the time of consultation, while a promise to provide a gift if the request is granted is also a standard requirement. When a client promises the priest that she will give his god a sheep if she becomes pregnant, it is understood by both client and priest that she will not actually present an animal to be sacrificed. In this case the term "sheep" is a euphemism for a sum agreed on for the deity.[23] And while priests are inclined to charge what the traffic will bear, experience has taught them the danger of pricing themselves out of the market. That this has long been recognized by the Fanti is indicated by their saying, "If divination fees are too high, the diviner will lack clients."

The impact of technological change is to be seen in some of the charms made by the priests. One example is the *siri*, made to confuse an opponent in court, in which the proper ingredients may be placed on a padlock and the name of an opponent pronounced as it is locked. A similar procedure may also be used to cause the death of someone, since it is believed that the act of closing the padlock "locks up his soul." In a similar vein, death could be caused by putting the required medicine on some shot and then calling the name of the intended victim as it was shot from a gun. *Kwanga*, the charm for attracting the opposite sex, is often made by using pomade manufactured in Europe, for in addition to the magical power of the ingredients added by the priest, it perfumes the wearer and improves his appearance when placed on his hair. There is a striking similarity between the claims made in European advertisements for the pomade and the results claimed by the priest for his *kwanga*. However,

[23] Though prices vary somewhat, average values in 1951 were: a cow, 1 guinea; a sheep, 12s. 6d.; a dog, 10s.; a guinea fowl, 3s. 6d.; a chicken, 2s. 6d.

the pomade is actually chosen for its consistency rather than any power of attraction the manufacturer maintains for it—it is a substitute for shea butter, an ingredient traditionally used in charms. It is also common to prepare *suman* in a glass vial that originally contained toilet water. Changes also have occurred in the dress of the priest, for a skirt made from European cloth has largely replaced the traditional raffia, and flour is sometimes substituted for white clay in decorating the body. One change in divination is the practice of some priestesses of holding their hands like an open book while they are under possession. They reveal the communication from their god "as if they were reading from a book" and compare it to a minister reading from the Bible.

NEW CULTS

The introduction of European economic, political, and religious ideologies has resulted in considerable culture change in Ghana, and the transition has been particularly rapid during the past two decades. A shifting of the population has occurred, along with urbanization, overcrowding, and an apparent increase in communicable diseases. There is also evidence to indicate that delinquency, crime, and unstable marriages are on the increase in some areas,[24] although it is difficult to measure with any degree of accuracy such aspects of social disorganization. The European has introduced new goals which can be achieved by only a small minority, while lack of achievement may lead to considerable tension. Failure in economic ventures, schooling, or almost any enterprise is sometimes blamed on Europeans or on the government, but many claim that jealous relatives or enemies are using nefarious techniques and power against them.

To understand this behavior, we must look at the phase of magic known as *anyen* (equivalent to the Ashanti *bayi*). This is usually translated by students of Akan culture as "witchcraft," and *anyenyi* (plural, *anyenfo*) as "witch"; but the terms "evil magic" and "workers of evil magic," which will be used here, more accurately describe the concept, since the word "witch" in English connotes a female, usually an elderly one, while among the Fanti the *anyenfo* are of either sex and of any age, though men who have this power are sometimes designated as *bonsam*. This power is distinct from charms or the "noxious instruments" discussed above. This is not a power which man can make but a malevolent force that is the projection of the will or soul of the individual who possesses it. A person may be born with this power or acquire it at any age. He has the ability to move rapidly through space and may attack victims by biting them, sucking their blood, or by making the spirit (*sunsum*) ill.

[24] Cf. K. A. Busia, *Social Survey of Sekondi-Takoradi* (London: Crown Agents for the Colonies, 1950).

The victims need not die but may suffer illness, sterility, or fail to achieve success or a desired position.

Traditionally this form of magical power is held to be effective only within the bounds of the matrilineal clan; if persons possessing the power of evil magic wish to harm someone outside their lineage, they must work through a colleague who belongs to the clan of their intended victims. It is not difficult to see how this association between evil magic and the clan could have evolved, for innumerable incidents could cause jealousy and antipathy in the close relations within the kin group. Friction may develop from real or imagined inequalities in allocation of land, housing, or inheritance, to name but a few of the reasons.[25]

There is no way of distinguishing an individual who has this power of evil magic unless he confesses or is proven guilty by trial. Fanti elders stated that a practice formerly employed to ascertain that death was the result of evil magic was that known as "carrying the corpse." When the casket was being carried to the grave, a supernatural force or power would cause the bearers to walk toward some person in the crowd or even to the room of the suspect if he were not present at the burial. This constituted an accusation of killing by magic, and a trial would be held to ascertain the guilt or innocence of the individual charged in this manner. Another practice was trial by ordeal, which could take several forms. One was to require the accused to drink a poison made from the bark of a tree; if he survived, he was presumed innocent. Other techniques which fall into the category of "trial by ordeal" are still used today, although they are by no means common. Both the priests and the military companies (*asafo*) follow practices designed to extract confessions from suspects, those believed guilty not only of using evil magic but of committing other crimes such as adultery or stealing. Water that has been used to wash the drum of the *asafo* and special herbs are placed in a gourd, and the accused is required to drink it. Since the drum is considered a god, if the accused does not tell the truth, the god will certainly bring about his death. Other practices used are exposure to the sun for protracted periods, rubbing irritating herbs on the skin, flogging, or placing a drum over the head of the accused and beating the drum.

Government has long disapproved of "carrying the corpse" and trial by ordeal, particularly where they involve use of poison or torture, so that these have almost disappeared as methods for establishing guilt in practicing evil magic (*anyen*) or the use of *suman* to cause illness or death. This function has been taken over by new cults that are reported to be particularly efficacious at "catching witches" as well as providing

[25] Cf. Meyer Fortes, "Kinship and Marriage among the Ashanti," in *African Systems of Kinship and Marriage*, ed. A. R. Radcliffe-Brown and Daryll Forde (London: International African Institute, 1950), p. 258.

protection against evil magic. This again illustrates the adaptability of the Fanti priesthood and Fanti religion. The large number of these new cults and their popularity suggest a growing concern about evil magic and an attempt to assuage the anxieties arising from rapid social change. They have spread rapidly over the southern half of Ghana since 1930, and some present a complex combination of African, Christian, and Moslem elements. Most of them are associated with a supernatural force or power of foreign provenience, imported from the northern territories of Ghana or from the Ivory Coast. In their original setting they were probably benevolent nature deities, similar to the deities of the Akan, but they have taken on a new meaning in the coastal area. Though they are called "deities" by a few people and are believed to function in the same manner as deities, most adherents refer to this power as "medicine" (*aduru*), an impersonal force or power, and joining the cult is to "drink the medicine," though no act of drinking is involved.

Typical of these new cults, and the most popular in the early 1950's, was one known as Tigari.[26] Tigari may be termed a "cult" in the sense that adherents pay a fee for membership, and obedience to dogma is compulsory for life, or else "the medicine will punish them." On joining, the devotee is informed of a list of regulations that must govern his conduct; these reflect Christian influence, for they appear as a list of "thou shalt nots" very similar to the Ten Commandments, though many deal with the prohibition of evil magic.[27] The Moslem element is reflected in the dress of the priest, the food taboos, and some of the ritual. Some of the Tigari priests deal in charms containing writings from the Koran. The ritual, drums and drumming, and equipment of the priest show a strong influence of the culture wherein Tigari had its origin.[28]

The pattern of religious behavior involved in Tigari cults is similar in many respects to that for the ancestral spirits and nature deities of the Fanti. On ceremonial occasions the Tigari priest (*obosomfo*) is possessed, and divination is also by possession. It is significant, however, that any devotee may be possessed and dance at the ceremonies, a practice that was common only for the priest for the Fanti deities. The procedure followed for invoking the assistance of Tigari is similar to that employed for the aboriginal gods. The devotee goes to the shrine at the house of the Tigari priest, makes an offering of one or two shillings, states his request,

[26] See James B. Christensen, "The Tigari Cult of West Africa," *Papers of the Michigan Academy of Science, Arts, and Letters,* XXXIX (1954), 389–98, for a more detailed discussion of the Tigari cult.

[27] These rules, which are retained in writing by some priests, include: thou shalt not kill, steal, covet your neighbor's wife, bear false witness against your neighbor, have any other gods before Tigari, or sleep with your neighbor's wife. Several in regard to the use of charms and *anyen* are also listed.

[28] For example, Tigari includes the sacrifice and eating of dogs, a practice never observed in the traditional forms of worship of the Fanti.

and eats a sanctified kola nut. He promises an animal as a gift when the wish is granted, but again this is understood to mean a stipulated sum of money.

Any man may become a Tigari priest, and although expensive, the training may be completed in a comparatively short time. Groups or individuals have been known to sponsor a Tigari priest and in return share in the income when he begins his practice. Many Fanti charge these cults with economic exploitation, something that is not entirely without foundation; rumors of maltreatment and excesses in exorcism and other cures are widely circulated but difficult to document.

Cults similar in ritual and practices to Tigari, including their concern with "witches," are to be found in several Fanti villages and towns. These are usually localized and are the result of individual enterprise on the part of their leaders, who bring "medicine" or a deity from some other locality, often northern Ghana. They set up shrines with themselves as priests, but unlike the Tigari priests, these cult leaders rarely serve an apprenticeship. These cults are often referred to as "Tigari" by Fanti who are not members, even though cult leaders claim no such affiliation, but "Tigari" tends to be a generic term for all cults specializing in protection against evil magic. Such cults usually have the name of the "medicine" or the deity they serve, and like Tigari priests, their leaders are referred to as *abosomfo* rather than *okomfo*, the traditional name for the Fanti priesthood.

These groups have been referred to as "new witch-finding cults" among the Ashanti,[29] and virtually every Fanti, when asked the purpose of Tigari, will reply that the cult offers its members protection against "witches" and that Tigari will "catch witches." Certainly one of the most spectacular rites of the Tigari cult is a ceremony where some participant, most often a woman, confesses to being an *anyenyi* and recounts the crimes she has committed. However, "catching witches" is only one of the functions of Tigari and similar cults, and their popularity is due not only to their power of entrapment but also to the protection and assistance they offer. The petitions heard at a Tigari shrine, as in the case of the traditional priests, reflect the changing needs of the people; many deal with securing jobs, economic gain, or protection while traveling. Not only those who fear "witches" join the cult, for many members regard it as insurance against any danger, including not only the so-called pagan but also the literates, Christians, and Moslems.

The introduction of new gods, shrines, and medicine has been a con-

[29] See Barbara E. Ward, "Some Observations on Religious Cults in Ashanti," *Africa*, XXVI (January, 1956), 47–61, for a discussion of the rise of these new cults among the Ashanti. Also see M. J. Field, *Akim-Kotoku, an "oman" of the Gold Coast* (London: Crown Agents for the Colonies, 1948), pp. 171–97.

tinuing process among the Fanti, and it in turn is accompanied by the rejection or abandonment of other gods and shrines. Deities that were once important often lose their following and pass into oblivion upon the death of the priests that served them and were not replaced. However, there can be little doubt that the new cults have increased at a rate that requires them to be considered as something more than "replacements" for defunct deities. That they are recent importations is evident from the fact that the shrines visited in the Fanti area were less than ten years old at the time. Moreover, the Fanti were unanimous in stating that such cults were new and numerous.[30]

That there is an increase in the new cults which are reputed to be efficacious against evil magic does not mean that the Fanti and other Akan groups are suffering from mass neurosis brought on by rapid social change or that everyone suspects some kinsman of being an *anyenyi*. Admittedly, the degree of insecurity existing in a largely nonliterate society is difficult to measure or evaluate, and it is difficult to positively state that it is greater or less than at some point in the past. In a society where the social structure, economy, and political system have been greatly modified and where new values have been introduced, a situation is created where uncertainties are likely to exist because the new norms are in conflict with the old. What is posited here is that increased anxiety has resulted from accelerated culture change. The new cults and their priesthood have provided a new combination of beliefs and rituals to assuage these uncertainties. In many respects they have elements of what has been described as a nativistic or contra-acculturative movement. They are not a resurgence of pure Akan religion, since they contain aspects of foreign ideologies and ritual, but they remain predominantly African. Their appeal indicates that the ancestral spirits, the deities, and the priests that serve them have not adequately met the present needs of the people; neither has the white man's Christianity. One must conclude that the popularity of these new cults which are reputed to provide a prophylaxis for evil magic reflects an attempt to ameliorate the insecurities prevalent in a society in transition.

[30] The patronage of the new cults is greatest in the larger centers with a higher degree of contact with European culture, rather than in the more remote sections. It must be noted that an economic factor is involved, since larger population and more money makes possible a larger number of religious practitioners, though these are also the areas where one would expect to find the highest degree of social tension. Increased communication has also been a factor in the spread of the cults.

15. Religious Acculturation
among the Anang Ibibio

Anang society affords a field laboratory situation for the study of acculturation, since the full impact of European culture was not felt until the First World War, when the region was brought under complete political control and the first mission and trading post established. Thus, it is possible through informants to reconstruct the indigenous culture as it existed during the first decade of this century—at the time the British arrived—and to note the changes wrought by acculturative pressures since then. This chapter will consider some of the major alterations in the religious beliefs and practices of these people resulting from the imposition of Christianity and other facets of European culture. Following a survey of traditional political and social forms and the main features of the religious system, the religious acculturation will be analyzed in terms of resistance to change, retention and loss of indigenous elements, acceptance of new ones, and reinterpretation. Finally, some attention will be paid to the effects of religious change upon other aspects of Anang culture.

Second largest of the six Ibibio-speaking groups of southeastern Nigeria, with an estimated population of three hundred and seventy-five thousand persons occupying an area of only eight hundred and fifty square miles, the Anang are located mainly in Ikot Ekpene and Abak Divisions of Calabar Province. They are bounded on the west by the Ngwa and Ndokki Ibo, on the north by the Isuorgu Ibo, and on the east and south by the Eastern Ibibio. They have no centralized government but are divided into twenty-eight subgroups (*iman*), each of which is a village group ruled by a hereditary chief (*okuku*) whose rights and duties are primarily of a religious character. Although the *iman* is the broadest political entity, the village community (*obio*) is the most important one; its hereditary leader (*ɔbɔŋ isɔŋ*) and a council of elders direct its political affairs and perform vital social and religious functions as well.

The patrilineage (*ɛkpuk*) is the largest social unit and is composed of a number of families (*idip*), both nuclear and extended, occupying a continuous tract of territory in the settlement. Leadership in the kin group usually is passed on from father to son, but in some patrilineages the oldest male assumes the position (*etɛ ɛkpuk*) if he possesses the requisite prestige symbols. Each family lives in a compound (*ikurɛ*) surrounded by forest, bush, and land belonging to its head (*idipetɛ*) and farmed by his wives and children. While polygyny is regarded as the ideal form of marriage, monogamy is practiced most commonly because only a very prosperous man can afford more than a single bride-wealth payment. Before the advent of the British, lineage endogamy prevailed, but with the cessation of intervillage conflict and the improvement of communications in the area, kin group and even village exogamy are becoming customary.

ANANG THEOLOGY AND WORLD VIEW

The central theme of Anang religion is the worship of an all-powerful deity (Abassi) who rules over the physical universe, other supernatural entities of lesser stature, and mankind. He is of gigantic proportions, invisible to human eyes, and he lives alone in a compound deep in the sky from which he occasionally emerges to roam about the earth. In the task of controlling the universe and regulating human conduct, he is aided by a multitude of spirits (*nnɛm*) who act as intermediaries between him and mankind and are considered as his helpers or messengers rather than as deities in their own right. They are not organized into pantheons, as in some African theologies, but operate independently, seldom being in contact with one another. All have normal, human, male and female figures and are visible only to religious specialists in a state of possession. They perform specific tasks for the deity and inhabit shrines (*idɛm*) where prayers and sacrifices are offered; these they deliver to Abassi, who sends power (*odudu*) to achieve the desired ends if the suppliants merit it. This power manipulated by the *nnɛm* is compared by elders to the wind which moves things yet cannot be seen, and by youth educated in the schools to electricity.

The tasks performed by the spirits can be classified as predominately economic, political, social, or religious. In the economic sphere, particular ones promote the safe clearing of the bush, the successful growth of various crops and palm trees, the ability of craftsmen to produce articles that will command good prices in the market, and the prosperity of traders. In the political realm, certain others protect the members of each of the *iman*, aid the villages' waging of war, and insure successful reigns for chiefs and community and patrilineage leaders. Some fulfil social functions by fostering reproduction, health, and longevity, by protecting the members of families and each of the secret societies, and by helping people to earn honorary titles. The greater number, however, are assigned religious tasks: to serve each of the types of religious practitioners by maintaining contact between them and the deity, to install souls and fates upon conception, and to observe the behavior of each human being and report it to Abassi for subsequent reward or punishment.

Of the more than thirty *nnɛm*, only three are female, and two of these —the earth (Ikpa Isɔŋ) and female fertility (Eka Abassi) spirits—are deemed the most important by the Anang. The former is responsible for the general health and protection of humanity and reports all conduct to the deity for evaluation. Although, as we have noted, he is omnipotent, it is she who is omnipresent and omniscient, and he always consults her before assigning the fate of a person or answering a prayer. Eka Abassi not only assures animal and human fertility but protects those who visit streams to bathe, wash clothes, and fish.

Shrines are usually individual trees or groves, but they also take the form of rocks, anthills, bushes, and pools. Many, also, are diminutive replicas of the Anang house made of branches and woven palm mats. They are established by and serve individuals, the members of families, patrilineages, villages, village groups, and secret societies; in the shrines serving a social or political unit, the leader of that unit acts as priest and alone may pray and sacrifice there in behalf of those in his group.

A person is thought to possess two souls; one inhabits the body (*ɛkpo*) and is immortal, while the other resides in a rock, tree, or animal in the bush and is called the "bush soul" (*ɛkpo ikɔt*). When an individual dies, his "bush soul" perishes, and his other soul either transmigrates to the village of souls (*obio ɛkpo*) beneath the earth to await reincarnation or becomes a ghost (*ɛkpo ɔnyɔŋ*), its destiny after death depending upon the fate of the person as ordained by the deity. The souls of ancestors living in the underworld are capable of giving aid to their relatives above and thus are worshiped at shrines to which they can return when requested to receive supplications and dispense benevolent power (*odudu*). They must, however, have the permission of the deity to furnish power, for, as an old man put it, "Abassi stands with the ancestors in aiding the lineage." Ghosts may not enter *obio ɛkpo* but are doomed to travel about the world alone and homeless forever, and they are feared by the Anang, since in their frustration they seek to harm human beings at every opportunity.

Once each year for a three-week period the souls of ancestors return to their patrilineages and are honored by a series of festivals in which everyone participates. During this time the members of the men's ancestral society (*ɛkpo*) perform day and night, singing esoteric songs, dancing, and wearing wooden masks to impersonate their dead relatives. Souls from the underworld are represented by masks carved and painted to portray beauty, while ghosts are depicted by masks which denote ugliness; when a member dons a mask, it is believed that his soul becomes possessed by an ancestor. The wearer of a beautiful mask moves gracefully, carrying colored cloths in his hands, and women and non-members of the society are permitted to observe him unmolested. On the other hand, if the possessing medium is a ghost, the masked member may run through the trails of the community, climb houses and trees, speak in an unintelligible jargon, and with a bow and arrows shoot women and non-members who fail to retreat at his approach; he is not held responsible, since his body is controlled by supernatural forces.

The Anang consider human conduct to be predicated upon fate (*emana*) as ordained by Abassi, but rather than remaining immutable following its assignment at conception, it can be modified by the individual through the exercise of free will within narrow limits. A divinely formulated moral code embracing every aspect of human behavior forms the basis for evaluating acts which transcend destiny, and should these acts conform to his code, Abassi will alter a person's fate so that future misfortunes are canceled; conversely, should freely perpetrated deeds result in transgressions against the code, he will compound predestined misfortunes for the individual either in this or in a future incarnation. Supernatural chastisement takes many forms, from the extreme of transforming the soul into a ghost at death to that of causing a woman to inflict a slight cut on her foot while hoeing; its severity depends upon the nature of the misdeed and the predilections of the deity.

The Anang stress acts that are punished rather than those that are rewarded when discussing free will and its consequences, indicating that negative sanctions influence their behavior far more than positive ones. They are also much more sensitive to external than to internal sanctions, there being little evidence of a highly structured conscience which evokes guilt feelings when a socially disapproved deed is committed. Belief in a divine moral code and the ability of Abassi to punish any deviations from its tenets is the most powerful mechanism of social control in the society.

These people have well-defined concepts of good and evil. Evil, or *idiok*, is recognized as the adversities that befall a person as the result of a fate which decrees them, the machinations of malevolent supernatural beings, or the attacks of a worker of evil magic; good, or *mfɔn*, is the absence of misfortunes induced by these agents. When punishing an individual, Abassi can destine that he be assaulted by a ghost, a "witch,"[1] or evil magic; however, attacks by these media often are not controlled by the deity, for they are thought to possess power to harm

---

[1] This term is used by Europeanized Anang to designate a supernatural entity whose attributes are discussed below.

mankind which he is unable to regulate, power that must be opposed through the use of good magic.

The course of a life can be altered not only by freely perpetrated acts and the uncontrolled assaults of malignant entities but also through prognostication. The person who desires knowledge of events to come, so that he may avoid harm and increase the benefits in store for him, consults a diviner (*abia idiɔŋ*). This specialist gains his insights from Abassi through the intercession of the spirit of divination; success at foretelling the future depends upon previous acts of the client as well as upon ritualistic perfection exercised by the diviner. The diviners of each village group are organized into a powerful society (*idiɔŋ*), membership in which is based upon being called into the profession by the deity through violent headaches, paying a large fee to the members, and undergoing a long and elaborate initiation ceremony. Among the numerous divining techniques, the most common one is to throw a handful of palm nuts on the ground and prognosticate by examining the pattern they form.

Workers of magic in each village group also form a society (*ibɔk*) whose membership requirements parallel those of the divining group, except that women are excluded. A practitioner offers one of three types of professional services—prescribing medicines (*abia ibɔk*), administering ordeals (*abia ukaŋ*), or controlling rain (*abia ɛdim*)—and he may divine as well, although few are members of both societies. Those (*abia ndomo*) who are not diviners but who do combine divination with another specialty usually use techniques of their own devising to foretell the future. Most practitioners deal in medicines, and within this rubric fall both charms and substances having actual curative qualities, which the Anang do not differentiate. Both are believed to contain power (*odudu*) to perform certain functions; the power emanates from the deity and is manipulated by the magic *nnɛm*.

Orthodox workers of magic, those who have been initiated into the society, ordinarily do not practice "black magic" but perform services beneficial to humanity. If a member of the society is discovered prescribing methods of evil magic, he is expelled and is subject to severe social censure; however, most workers of evil magic (*abia idiɔk ibɔk*) are former members who have renounced their orthodoxy, braving the disapproval of both Abassi and their fellow villagers, to practice their art for lucrative fees. The Anang greatly fear the power possessed by these specialists, and every individual of high status uses good magic to protect himself from jealous foes who might resort to evil magic.

Divining and to a lesser extent the use of magic provide means whereby fate and its modification through freely conceived acts can be transcended and the deity manipulated to a limited degree. This represents an area of inconsistency in the world view of these people, since everyone insists that Abassi is both absolutely omnipotent and absolutely just. As far as can be determined, there are no myths relating the origin of divining and magic which might present a complete rationale for their existence.

The oath givers (*mbiam*), who make up the third important category of religious practitioners, are neither organized into an association nor called into their profession by the deity; instead, the techniques of oath-swearing are passed on from father to son. It is a dangerous specialty to practice, for it requires complete mastery of numerous rituals, and the oath giver who is not efficient can be destroyed by the oath spirit. The primary duty of this *nnɛm* is to bring death to those who swear oaths falsely, although he can also protect property against theft and ward off ghosts, "witches," and evil magic. When an oath is sworn, the one being tested drinks a gourd of water treated by the *mbiam* so that the oath spirit enters the liquid; should he be lying, he will die within a period of time prescribed by the specialist. The presence of oath swearers in Anang tribunals assures the proficient functioning of the judiciary, for attached to every village group, village, and lineage court is an *mbiam* who can be directed to administer oaths to litigants making conflicting claims, and periodically the justices swear in his presence that they will not accept bribes or express favoritism.

As menacing a force as either ghosts or evil magic are "witches" (*ifɔt*), about whom information is difficult to obtain. The usual query as to their nature is countered by the proverb, "Only the trader knows the secrets of trading." The Anang believe that these beings form a society which an individual may join by seeking out a member and undergoing an esoteric initiation; on the other hand, a person can be made an *ifɔt* against his will by eating plantain dipped in oil in the presence of a member, by consuming food treated with "witch poison," or by having his soul stolen away at night by an *ifɔt*. Most of these beings are female, and children as well as adults can become members. During the day an *ifɔt* behaves as an ordinary human, but at night his soul ventures out to meet with his colleagues and perpetrate harmful deeds. Although the soul of a "witch" can maintain its invisible human form, it can also enter the body of an animal, usually that of a bat, firefly, or lizard. Medicines are procured to protect life and property from the machinations of *ifɔt*, and when a person suspected of being one is apprehended, his guilt or innocence can be ascertained by divination or an ordeal. Before the British arrived in the region, convicted "witches" were executed and sometimes eaten by the people.

When Anang culture as it exists today is compared with that of pre-conquest times, it can be seen that extensive changes have occurred in all its aspects. Change is most pronounced in the political, economic, and religious spheres, for it is these elements of European culture which were imposed most forcibly upon the Anang. The people have been most receptive to economic and religious innovations and have opposed the imposition of alien political forms, but they have been forced to yield to pressures exerted by the colonial government; their resistance, nevertheless, has been responsible in no little degree for several administrative reorganizations. Social and aesthetic changes are least evident and have been largely the by-products of other aspects of acculturation.

EUROPEAN CONTACT

The Ikot Ekpene region was penetrated by the British in 1901, when one column of the famous Aro expedition passed close to Ikot Ekpene village. Two years later the territory was explored by another military expedition, and in 1904 an administrative center was established at Ikot Ekpene. From that year until 1910 the interior peoples were brought under partial control by military means; complete political domination was not attained, however, until several more years passed, and as late as 1929 troops were stationed in the area to cope with local civil disturbances. Ikot Ekpene was a subdivision of the old Enyong District until 1914, at which time it became a district in its own right, subsuming what are now Ikot Ekpene, Abak, and Uyo Divisions and the Anang, Enyong, and Eastern Ibibio groups in their entirety. When the native authorities were set up in 1934, the present divisional organization emerged, and Ikot Ekpene Division came to include eight Anang, four Enyong, and three Eastern Ibibio village groups.

In 1951, at the time the research upon which this chapter is based was being conducted, local government was first instituted as a political experiment. The area was divided into four district councils—one urban and three rural—which were further subdivided into local councils, the latter corresponding rather closely to the village groups as far as the Anang were concerned. The judicial system, administered under a separate ordinance, has grown from a single court inaugurated at Ikot Ekpene village in 1904 to sixteen in the division at the present time; most of them serve a single village group, although the largest have two or more courts.

Economic exchange with European trading companies commenced on a large scale in 1919 with the building of the first trading post in the region at Ikot Ekpene village by the United Africa Company. The real development of external trade had to await pacification of the area, since in earlier days intervillage warfare was so frequent and intense that social and economic intercourse over a wide area was impossible. This state of affairs accounted for such conditions as patrilineage endogamy, markets serving only three or four contiguous communities, and hunters and fishermen seeking game no more than two miles from their homes. After 1910 a few men traveled to Itu and Utu Etim Ekpo, both within forty miles of Ikot Ekpene village, to purchase imported trade articles for resale in local markets and to sell palm oil and kernels to European firms or to Anang and Efik middlemen. As travel became safer during the years that followed, an increasing number of men became traders, the growth of this profession being stimulated by population pressures, the desire to gain wealth, and improved communications. With the cessation of armed conflict and the introduction of European medical techniques, there has been a phenomenal increase in Anang population. Landholdings are becoming smaller, while many young men inherit no land today; the result is that greater numbers of them are being forced into trading and other occupations and are emigrating to urban centers and other parts of Nigeria, the Cameroons, and Fernando Po.

The first Christian mission in the region was founded in 1919 at Ikot Ekpene village by the English Methodist church, so intensive economic and religious acculturation commenced simultaneously. Eight other Christian bodies, two of them African in origin, were installed between 1919 and 1948,[2] and today all maintain churches, some schools, and several hospitals. Missionary groups have provided the greater part of the formal education and medical care received by the Anang. All the denominations have had remarkable success in gaining converts during recent years, and more than half of the Anang now profess the Christian faith. The largest and most active bodies are the Roman Catholic, the Methodist, and the Christ Army.

In order to analyze religious acculturation most effectively, it has been decided to divide the Anang into three arbitrary age groups and to note the different manner in which each has reacted to religious proselytizing. The first includes the men and women who were past middle age when the first mission was established; the second, those who were young adults and middle-aged at that time; the third, those born after intensive acculturation had commenced.

THE ELDERS: SPIRITUALISM AND NATIVISM

The men in the oldest age category, for the most part, resisted the spread of Christianity during the first decade of missionary endeavor. It was they who made up the membership of the divining and magic societies and were oath swearers; as heads of families, patrilineages, and

[2] These are the Kwa Ibo (English interdenominational) established in 1920, the Roman Catholic (Irish order) in 1925, the American Lutheran (Missouri Synod) in 1936, the African Apostolic (African) in 1936, the Christ Army (African) in 1940, the American Assemblies of God in 1946, and the American Seventh Day Adventist in 1948.

villages, they were priests in charge of shrines serving the members of these social and political units. Their resistance was based upon the desire to maintain their positions of religious authority, and they held strong opinions as to the orthodoxy of Anang religion, believing that the acceptance of any elements of the alien religion would anger Abassi and provoke divine punishment. This attitude was contrary to that displayed by the elders of many West African societies who were willing to accept or reinterpret certain Christian beliefs and rituals. Among the Anang this type of reaction was limited to women of all ages and men in the two younger age groups.

The newly introduced denominations gained few converts during the 1920's, largely because of the resistance of Anang political leaders and religious specialists, but during 1930 a religious movement which swept southeastern Nigeria caused most of the people to accept certain elements of Christianity.[3] Originating in the south along the Guinea Coast, it spread northward from village to village and penetrated all the area occupied by the Ibibio-speaking and Eastern Ibo-speaking groups. Initially it was sponsored by dissatisfied adherents of the Kwa Ibo and Roman Catholic denominations; later it was embraced by members of all Christian churches, although missions strenuously opposed its expansion.

The principal belief of its Anang followers concerned the nature and capacities of the Christian Holy Spirit (Edisana Odudu), who was dissociated from the Trinity and conceived as the most powerful of the spirits, capable of curing all diseases and injuries, insuring longevity, bringing wealth, combating malicious supernatural forces, and rendering many other services. The Christian God (Ata Abassi) was syncretized with Abassi, and the Holy Spirit was thought to inhabit the church altar, which came to be regarded as a shrine (*idɛm*) where prayers and sacrifices could be made to Abassi. It was believed that the Holy Spirit could possess the souls of communicants; thus the denominations countenancing this kind of worship were called spiritualist churches, and the movement itself came to be known as the spiritualist movement. The African Christian, Kwa Ibo, Seventh Day Adventist, and Assembly of God bodies are still termed "spiritualist" because they stress possession and healing by the Holy Spirit.

The leaders of the movement attacked the indigenous religion, holding that its beliefs were inspired by Satan and that the grace of God could be gained only by renouncing them. Within a year Anang secret societies were abolished in most communities, while shrines were destroyed—

[3] Meek refers briefly to this movement as it affected the Ibo of Owerri Province (C. K. Meek, *Law and Authority in a Nigerian Tribe* [London: Oxford University Press, 1937], p. 86).

either burned or used to make pews in newly constructed churches. Many older men fought to stem the tide of conversion, especially priests and religious practitioners and those with political authority. Failing, some ceased their resistance and joined the spiritualists, becoming passive participators, while others continued to practice their religious professions and maintained their customary worship in secret.

The movement gained its major support from middle-aged men who had some political influence yet were not diviners, workers of magic, or priests; from women of all ages; and from young men. Especially active were women, who formed into large groups and marched about the villages burning shrines, singing hymns, and voicing ridicule of those who held to the indigenous ways. Open conflicts often resulted in which many persons were injured and killed.

Not only did membership in the European-sponsored denominations swell, but many nativist churches formed to carry on the new worship. Most of the latter were maintained for only brief periods, but while active they possessed large congregations. People crowded the churches and neglected other duties to participate in the daily services; many made their homes there, sleeping on pews and in the aisles, while others built temporary shelters on the church grounds so that they could dwell near the benevolent power of the Holy Spirit. African ministers (*akwa abassi*) presided over small congregations in rural areas which were isolated and not closely supervised by the missionaries and were thus able to practice the unorthodox rituals of the movement without reprimand. Many of them adopted Anang divining methods and sold their services to communicants, the Holy Spirit (Edisana Odudu) affording them power to prognosticate. Possession by this *nnɛm* was induced by ministers through the "laying on of hands," and it was thought that those in this condition, if true believers, would have their prayers answered by God (Ata Abassi). The state of possession resembled that of members of the ancestral society and was manifested in uncontrollable shaking of limbs, rolling on the ground, running through the village, and climbing trees and houses. Often one who had lost control of his senses spoke unintelligible words purported to be those of the deity injected into his mouth by the Holy Spirit. The spread of spiritualism from one community to another was accomplished largely by those who became most easily and violently possessed and who could speak the "language of God," thereby foretelling the miracles to be wrought for those who became converts. They were self-appointed evangelists (*mbio nkukut*) who had the ability to arouse the emotions of their followers to a high pitch.

The European missions fought the movement through church and school instruction and by excommunication, but they were unable to oppose it successfully because of insufficient numbers of missionaries and inadequately indoctrinated African ministers. Spiritualism flourished for eight years until eradicated almost completely by a revival of the traditional religion. The chief reason for this phenomenon was that the miracles promised by the leaders of the movement did not materialize; the Holy Spirit proved no more effective than Anang *nnɛm* in helping the people. In addition, during 1936 and 1937 locusts caused severe crop failures throughout much of Ikot Ekpene and Abak Divisions, and many important Anang leaders died; these events were interpreted as indications of the wrath of Abassi and contributed to the growing spirit of nativism. Partly responsible, however, were older men who had not participated actively in spiritualism, for they created political pressures for reform and propagandized against Christianity.

With nativism, secret societies were reinstated, shrines rebuilt, and worship at them resumed. There was a widespread withdrawal from Christian denominations, and now it was the turn of churches to be destroyed; but the eight years during which Anang religion was suppressed weakened it and paved the way for the supremacy of Christianity, once the nativistic revival had subsided. Renewed missionary effort, the introduction of four additional denominations, and economic and political changes of great magnitude also contributed to this process. During the 1940's the Christian groups, especially those which supported a modified form of spiritualism and sought to syncretize Christian and Anang dogmas, once again began to gain converts in large numbers.

At the present time,[4] men in the oldest age group are either antagonistic or indifferent toward the encroachment of Christianity and, almost without exception, are attempting to preserve the traditional religion. Incapable of arresting change, since they no longer possess social and political authority and since young people are turning to Christianity in ever greater numbers, the old men spend much of their time talking about the past and criticizing changes that are occurring. In particular they remonstrate against the immorality of the youth, asserting that all of the ills which have befallen the Anang are caused by the vindictiveness of Abassi, who is angry with young people for not obeying his religious mandates.

THE MIDDLE-AGED: SYNCRETISM

Men and women in the second age category—those who were young adults and middle-aged when missionary activity commenced—as well as women in the oldest age group have been much more susceptible to Christian proselytizing. Although declaring themselves Christians, few

---

[4] The following description of religious beliefs and practices, although rendered in the present tense, refers to conditions existing in 1951 and 1952, when research was carried on.

are what might be termed "true believers" according to mission stand-ards,[5] for they reinterpret Anang and Christian beliefs while still clinging to many indigenous forms of worship. The two African Christian de-nominations are supported almost entirely by those in this age category, for, as we have seen, old men are either anti-Christian or indifferent to the faith, while the youth choose to affiliate with "orthodox" churches—Roman Catholic, Methodist, or Lutheran.

Men in the second group are receptive to Christianity because they have not been subjected to a lifetime of religious enculturation that would have led to religious conservatism, and because few were religious specialists or priests of shrines when they were introduced to Christi-anity. Also, it is characteristic of West African societies to take over ele-ments of religion from each other.

In West Africa, tribal gods had been frequently borrowed, and there was no reason why the Christian concept of the universe and the powers that rule it . . . could not equally well be incorporated into their system of belief. West African gods are often described by the members of a tribe as having been taken over from another people, and one native explanation why this was done shows such insight into the psychology of the matter that it should be noted here. When one group conquered another, the superior power of the gods of the conquerors was self-evident, and it was thus to the advantage of the conquered to appease them.[6]

This African rationale was often voiced by Anang men of middle age. Many men choose to join a denomination because it costs far less than the traditional religion, which requires payments to oath swearers, work-ers of magic, and diviners for their professional services; materials for sacrifices conducted on numerous occasions; and the great expenses in-volved in joining a religious society. Being a Christian means making only a small monetary offering at the weekly church service. To many the Christian God (Ata Abassi) has superior power to cope with ghosts, evil magic, and "witchcraft," and this makes them receptive to the new faith. Finally, it must be realized that "rice Christians" are numerous among those in this age group, and they are interested only in obtaining schools, hospitals, and other material benefits from the missions.

Christianity always has had much greater support from Anang women of all ages than from men for several reasons. First, women believe that being Christian affords them more opportunity for religious expression, for in Anang religion manipulation of the supernatural rests largely in the hands of men. Women possess no shrines and are seldom allowed to take

[5] Lutheran statistics indicate that 50 per cent of the Anang and Eastern Ibibio profess Christianity, whereas an estimated 10 per cent are "true Christians." See H. Nau, *We Move into Africa* (St. Louis: Concordia Publishing House, 1945), p. 161.

[6] M. J. Herskovits, *Man and His Works* (New York: Alfred A. Knopf, 1948), p. 552.

part in rituals, although they may pray and sacrifice at the female fertility and farm *idɛm*. In the mission churches men and women worship together and are equally capable of receiving God's grace, while the nativist denominations favor women evangelists over men.

Another reason why women support Christianity is to gain protection from attacks by malevolent supernatural beings to whom they feel particularly vulnerable. This attitude is readily understandable when it is realized that infant mortality exceeds 40 per cent—miscarriages, stillbirths, and deaths during infancy usually are attributed to the machinations of the *ifɔt* and ghosts. Women believe that the power (*odudu*) possessed by the Christian deity will afford them protection, allowing them to perform successfully this most important female function.

Prior to the period of intensive acculturation, women did most of the farming and internal trading, but today men are encroaching upon both of these areas and control external trade almost completely. As a result women are coming to devote less time to trading and farming and more to religion, especially since churches sponsor many social activities in which they can use the time that in former years would have been spent in economic pursuits.

The degree of variation in religious expression among the middle-aged is considerable. Some have retained most of the elements of Anang religion and have remained aloof from formal Christian contacts; a few after joining mission churches have substituted new religious beliefs for old on a broad scale; most have had limited contact with mission groups or have joined African Christian denominations, and their worship reflects a blending of the two religions. The following generalizations apply, for the most part, to those in the last category.

There is a general tendency to syncretize Abassi with the Christian God. This entity is considered omniscient and omnipresent as well as omnipotent, thus not dependent upon the earth spirit for information concerning human conduct. The nature of the Trinity seldom is grasped by the Anang; the Holy Spirit is regarded as the most potent of the *nnɛm* aiding Ata Abassi—his chief task being to heal and foretell the future through soul possession—while Jesus is looked upon as the Son of God who was instructed to convert the peoples of the world to Christianity. Jesus plays an unimportant role in Anang worship, although many hold that belief in him as the offspring of God is a prerequisite for gaining entrance into heaven (*ɔnyɔŋ isɔŋ*) after death. Few Anang were able to explain the significance of Christ dying upon the cross to atone for the sins of mankind.

Anang spirits have been perpetuated, but those people most active in the European denominations are forbidden to erect shrines to house these beings. Nevertheless, many of them continue to sacrifice and pray before the spirits. Angels are regarded as *nnɛm* who carry messages for God; however, evidence of the syncretism of specific angels with specific spirits is lacking. Churches or prayer houses (*ufɔk abassi*) are held to be gigantic shrines visited directly by God and the *nnɛm*, and the deity is believed to dwell in the altar, whence he sends out power (*odudu*) through the cross. Prayers to him must be made in the church to be acted on most efficaciously, and animals are sacrificed to honor him only before the altars of the nativist churches.

Worship of ancestors has been little affected by religious acculturation. Missionaries have met their strongest resistance in trying to alter Anang beliefs in reincarnation, the power of the oath spirit, and the existence of "witches," ghosts, and evil magic. The village of souls and heaven are syncretized and are regarded as being located in the sky rather than beneath the earth and as ruled over by God and Jesus. Recognition of the existence of a "bush soul" and a soul within the body continues, the former perishing when the person dies and the latter being immortal. What happens to the soul after death is largely dependent upon the nature of the behavior of an individual while alive, for though fate is still regarded as a potent force in regulating human conduct, the emphasis has shifted to the exercise of free will and its consequences. If a person has led a righteous existence, his soul goes to heaven, but if he has failed to conduct himself according to God's dictates, his soul is assigned to hell (*idiɔk itiɛ*) where it becomes a ghost and serves the devil.

Traditionally, life in the underworld is looked upon as identical with life on earth, but under the impact of Christianity heaven is conceived as an abode of joy where everything a person might wish for is provided. Reincarnation eventually occurs, however, and those in heaven must rejoin their patrilineages below. Most Anang consider Satan to be an *nnɛm* who was once an angel but disobeyed the deity and was expelled from heaven. He lives in hell, a thick forest south of the Anang region, where he rules over lesser spirits, ghosts, and "witches." The harmful acts committed by these beings, as well as evil magic, are done at the direction of the devil with power emanating from him, for God (*Ata Abassi*) no longer is believed to punish humans by having them attacked by these entities; they are controlled by Satan alone and are as likely to harm sinners as those who are moral. This alteration in belief, according to many, accounts for the heightened fear of malevolent forces expressed by the Anang and has resulted in the increasing use of good magic and oaths.

Ancestral shrines are maintained by most men, worship before them taking place at customary times as well as upon Christian holidays, and the *ɛkpo* society still flourishes, but its functions are no longer primarily religious. Few of the younger members understand the significance of various customs associated with it, not realizing for instance that the two types of masks represent ghosts and souls. Possession of mask wearers seldom occurs, although those who don "ugly" masks still fire arrows at women and non-members, and police are often called upon to disband them when violence has been perpetrated. Members meet for social reasons and sing and dance together, and many youth who are away from their homes during the year return for these three weeks to visit their relatives and meet with old friends.

Similarities between the Christian moral code as expressed in the Bible (*nnwɛd abassi*) and the indigenous one often are commented on by the people, who emphasize that murder, theft, cheating, lying, bribery, and many other acts are regarded as sinful by both Christians and Anang. It is difficult for them, however, to accept the position of the missions in such matters as polygyny, warfare, sacrifices, killing twins at birth, and repaying bride-wealth upon divorce; in these cases they feel that Christian morality is in error. Confusion is created when they read in the Old Testament of polygyny and the sacrifice of animals to God, practices condemned by missionaries, or when they learn of the many wars Christians have fought in the name of their religion. Especially bewildered are the World War II veterans who fought for the British in foreign theaters, yet are prohibited from engaging in local armed conflict because the British consider warfare barbaric and uncivilized. The Anang tend to support their own moral convictions and to disregard those elements of Christian belief which contradict them; thus a staunch Christian is likely to practice polygyny, if prosperous enough, yet believe that his soul will go to heaven when he dies, and Christian mothers feel no guilt when they attempt to destroy twins born to them in mission hospitals.

Religious specialists are still numerous, but most of them are advanced in years and few new ones are being recruited. Men in the second age group are not likely to become practitioners, since they can earn more money through trading and other economic pursuits than through practicing divination or magic. Moreover, they feel that most of their religious needs are satisfied by adopting Christianity, especially by joining a nativist church whose evangelists are capable diviners and workers of magic (*abia ibɔk*). The behavior of these men is so economically oriented, and they are so Christian in their beliefs, that becoming specialists is out of the question for them; thus the various religious professions are on the verge of extinction.

Diviners have adopted new techniques as the result of European influences; they employ dice, playing cards, and dominoes in a variety of ways to prognosticate. Younger diviners call upon the Christian God to give them added power, and when Christians consult them, objects of that religion often are utilized. Some diviners throw the cross on the ground after a question is posed, and if the figure of Jesus faces up the answer is "yes," if down, "no." Another method involves opening the Bible at random and reading the advice contained on the page; even though most diviners cannot read, they profess the ability to ascertain the message from God there which reveals the answer to the client's problem.

European-trained doctors, medical dispensers, and midwives, as well as patent medicine salesmen, are giving workers of magic increasing competition. An African doctor practices in the government hospital at Ikot Ekpene, and each district council in the division is assigned a dispenser, who attends to the minor medical needs of people in his area, and a midwife, who advises expectant mothers and delivers infants in the patients' homes. In addition, several missions maintain small hospitals with doctors or dispensers in attendance. Medication and services in the hospitals and dispensaries can be procured at minimum expense. It took almost a decade to get the Anang to use these medical resources, but today hospitals are crowded and personnel overworked. Women were the first to note the advantages of delivery under a midwife's supervision or in a hospital, and after a time they came to depend less on the ministrations of workers of magic (*abia ibɔk*) and untrained midwives. The obvious superiority of European medicine and techniques proved to women that God is more powerful than Abassi and led many to renounce traditional religious beliefs. It took longer for men to shift their allegiances from Anang to European-trained specialists.

Many regard doctors and dispensers as workers of magic whose skills and medicines gain their efficacy through power dispensed by God and manipulated by the magic spirit, and persons who are ill or who have been injured often seek relief from both workers of magic and doctors. The fact that medicines and hospital treatment cost considerably less than services obtained from Anang practitioners has resulted in a rapidly growing number of people depending almost entirely upon government and mission facilities. It has also forced workers of magic to lower their prices and to provide new services, so that only those of high repute or with special skills can charge large enough fees to make their specialty pay; others less famous and those continuing traditional practices are forced to abandon the profession.

A new and important occupation—selling patent medicines—has developed recently. These medicines, imported from Europe and America and sold in most of the local markets by traders, have many exorbitant claims made for them. Some are purported to be aphrodisiacs and are popular among older men who are concerned with their waning potency; others are bought by students for their supposed ability to aid memorization; still others, advertised as blood purifiers, are purchased in large quantities because of the Anang belief that impure blood causes many bodily ills.[7]

Recognizing the growing fear of malevolent supernatural forces and spurred by competition from European-trained specialists, workers of magic are resorting to the sale of charms and medicines and abandoning their other pursuits. Indigenous charms are seldom prescribed, for new types are obtained from mail order houses in Europe and America dealing in magical and occult devices; these are thought to be effective, since manufactured and used by people living in Christian countries. "Black magic" continues to be practiced widely, although few specialists seem to be prescribing it. Certain patent medicines, including actual poisons, are thought to have harmful propensities and are used by persons resorting to evil magic.

Missionaries oppose swearing oaths more than any other traditional religious practice. As a result of their influence, the swearing of oaths was discontinued in native courts during 1947; swearing on the Bible was substituted, with grave consequences, since most Christians believe that God (Ata Abassi) will forgive any lies they may tell, and they are no longer compelled to take the dreaded oath *nnɛm* into their bodies. There is no longer any external compulsion to speak truthfully in court; this has slowed judicial procedure, placed undue emphasis on circumstantial evidence, and, according to Anang opinion, resulted in many unfair verdicts. Barring oath swearers from tribunals has brought about an increase in the practice of evil magic and oath-swearing. Persons who do not gain justice through the judiciary turn to magic and the oath spirit to punish their opponents who have escaped punishment by lying in court. After destroying the guilty party, the *nnɛm* attacks others in his patrilineage and community; thus many innocent people die.

Despite missionary resistance, oath givers are still numerous, and the oath spirit is still considered the primary avenging *nnɛm* of God, possessing vast power to punish those who tell falsehoods, preventing theft, and warding off attacks of malignant forces. New methods of giving oaths have been adopted, including holding the Bible and cross while swearing when the client is a Christian. After the oath spirit has been called into a compound or a plot of farm land to protect it from theft, the symbol of his presence erected as a warning is often a tall wooden cross rather than the traditional symbol.

"Witchcraft" is thought to be spreading at a rapid rate since the invasion of the region in recent years by members of an Efik "witch" society. Individuals who join this group are thought to be induced by Satan to do so, for it is believed that he constantly tries to enlarge his

[7] A number of these medicines were sent to the medical officer at Calabar for analysis, and they proved to be composed of sodium carbonate.

body of followers by tempting people to commit sins so that they will become ghosts following death, by commanding his *ifɔt* to force people to be witches by feeding them poison and stealing their souls at night, and by persuading them to join the Efik society. Charms to counteract the attacks of these beings are purchased from patent medicine salesmen and workers of magic, and doctors often are asked to prescribe medicines that will protect persons from *ifɔt*. Educated Anang know that Europeans and Americans believed in the existence of witches until early modern times, a fact that is emphasized when they defend their own convictions in the face of missionary ridicule.

YOUTH: THE NEW FAITH

Men and women in the third age category, those who were children when Christianity was introduced and those born since then, are the strongest supporters of the new faith. Many were reared as Christians and educated in mission schools, and most claim to be Christians whether or not they belong to a church. They have tended to join European denominations, mainly because only these can support well-equipped and adequately staffed schools and hospitals, and prestige is gained through membership in them. Formal education is prized by the youth, for it is an avenue to occupations which bring high income and prestige. Anything European, other than political and economic exploitation, is admired, and one who adopts European customs gains recognition as a result. African Christian denominations are denigrated, since they are severely criticized by missionaries for their pseudo-Christian dogmas, and they do not possess the financial resources to sponsor schools and hospitals; membership in them means "losing face" in the eyes of Europeanized Anang.

Young people are vague in their understanding of the indigenous religion. There are numerous reasons for this, one of the most important being that teachers in both government and mission schools inculcate Christian doctrines and denounce Anang beliefs. In government institutions this is done informally by instructors who for the most part have themselves been trained in mission schools. The youth who do not receive formal education are ridiculed by those who do if they manifest an interest in traditional ways, and the opinions of the educated ones strongly influence the uneducated. As elsewhere in Africa, "a distressingly large number of the younger people have cut themselves off from the past because of their feeling of shame, and are left today without any tradition of which they can be proud."[8]

The natural science curriculum in schools serves to undermine indige-

[8] W. R. Bascom, "African Culture and the Missionary," *Civilisations, Institut International des Civilisations Différentes* (Brussels), III, No. 4, 499.

nous views of the universe and mankind. Only those European scientific beliefs approved by the missions are disseminated—knowledge about organic and inorganic evolution is not taught generally, biblical interpretations being offered instead. Nevertheless, sufficient scientific knowledge is passed on to impress the students, and young scholars often can be observed explaining scientific information learned in school to persons their own age as well as to elders.

There are other reasons why young people are ignorant of Anang religion. Many of them leave home at an early age to follow occupations in urban communities and thus never receive sufficient religious indoctrination. Since women have been very receptive to Christianity, they militate against having their children taught what they consider false doctrines. Church services are attended by numerous children, since mothers are eager to give their offspring religious instruction as early as possible. Finally, with the decline of their social and political authority, older men are no longer in a position to command the obedience and respect of the youth and as a result are unable to impart religious knowledge with conviction.

In their desire to amass wealth and gain prestige, members of this age group have adopted ways of behaving—stealing, lying, bribing, cheating, and even murdering—regarded as immoral by missionaries, by representatives of the colonial government, and by older Africans themselves. This behavior actually has been fostered by the acceptance of the Christian concept of forgiveness. Both Roman Catholicism, by emphasizing remission of sins through confession and absolution, and Protestantism, by preaching an intellectual gospel of salvation through faith rather than good works, have implanted the belief that God will forgive all sins. Young people have tended to accept Christian morality, understanding that it is divinely sanctioned; yet the opinion prevails that these moral tenets may be disregarded without supernatural retribution if sins are confessed or if belief is maintained. Protestant sermons usually stress the sinfulness of man and the possibility of salvation through faith alone, while many Catholic priests, unable to speak Ibibio, pronounce absolution when unaware of the sins being confessed.

Whereas Abassi is unforgiving and punishes all misdemeanors, God is forgiving. We have seen that belief in a divine moral code and the ability of the deity to punish any deviation from its strictures is the most potent mechanism of social control in Anang society. The concept of a forgiving God has greatly reduced the effectiveness of negative supernatural sanctions as regulators of conduct, allowing young persons to engage in antisocial behavior without fear of punishment.

Political changes have stimulated the development of deviant behavior among the youth. Chiefs of village groups have been deposed and the powers of village heads and their councils of elders curtailed by the British, so young people can defy Anang custom and successfully resist the efforts of indigenous political bodies to exert their authority. The traditional judiciary has been abolished, and most cases now are tried in native courts. The members of the courts are often corrupt, for, with the exclusion of oath swearers from tribunals, judges are no longer compelled to swear that they will be honest and impartial. Furthermore, behavior once punished through court action now goes unpunished, since many acts formerly considered heinous by the Anang are not embodied in "native law and custom" as upheld by the British-introduced tribunals; and other acts that were severely punished in the past now draw minor fines. This reflects the strong influence of British concepts of justice as well as Christian morality. As Jeffreys says:

> Great Britain always has a clause in her colonial laws to the effect that Native Law and Custom are to be administered provided the application of them is . . . "not repugnant to natural justice, equity and good conscience." Natural justice has never been defined, but it appears to be a phrase deriving from the concept of nature which thus implies that natural justice must be interpreted in terms of Christian ethics.[9]

An Anang elder was overheard criticizing the law upheld in native and magistrates' courts for being contrary to "natural law" as set down by Abassi.

Ignorance of indigenous customs, reinforced by the concept of law entertained by the British, has helped to produce the disregard of certain strongly sanctioned traditional behavior by some district officers. When reviewing cases tried by native courts, these officials have been known to allow divorced women to return to the families without refunding the bride-wealth, being of the opinion that once a woman has served her husband for several years and borne him children, the debt is canceled. District officers also have disregarded pledging customs and have awarded pledged land to the individual who has farmed it for several years, holding that occupancy denotes possession. Unscrupulous youths have obtained land by asking a district officer known to hold this view to review cases involving land they have received on pledge and have worked for a period of time. This state of affairs has certainly intensified the conflict between older and younger generations and has created widespread demoralization.

The possibility of punishment through native and magistrates' courts is the major regulator of conduct among young persons today. The British judiciary, however, is held in contempt, and a person who has committed an offense often can bribe his way to freedom or gain a favor-

[9] M. D. W. Jeffreys, "Some Rules of Directed Culture Change under Roman Catholicism," *American Anthropologist*, LVIII, No. 4 (1956), 722.

able decision from a native court composed of kinsmen. Four types of punishment are meted out by the tribunals—whipping, imprisonment, execution, and fines—the last two being the only effective ones. Whipping is not feared, and often a convicted felon lives in greater prosperity and comfort in prison than at home. Having served a sentence may earn a young man the disfavor of elders, but in the eyes of his peers he gains prestige, for many of them regard a jail term as a mark of distinction.

Most young people, although accepting Christian dogma in most areas, maintain traditional beliefs concerning malevolent forces despite missionaries' efforts to discount their reality. No matter how Europeanized a person may be, he usually is able to recount his numerous experiences with *ifɔt* and ghosts[10] and can recite the Anang rationale for their existence. The only success elders have in exerting social control over youth is by resorting to the use of oaths, since the oath spirit is as greatly feared as "witches" or ghosts. Techniques of magic are widely employed by young persons to attain scholastic success, to win a girl's hand, to gain a desired position, to harm a rival, and for many other purposes. The tenacity of religious belief in this area is a constant source of irritation and frustration to missionaries and administrators alike.

Since social and aesthetic changes have been less sweeping, the effects of religious change upon these two aspects of Anang culture are not considered in this paper. Future research will present us with a better conception of how Africans all over the continent have reacted to religious acculturation and will also indicate whether certain patterns of change in Anang culture, as broadly outlined here, are discernible elsewhere.

[10] Several Anang and Eastern Ibibio pursuing education in the United States were questioned about these beings, and all claimed having had contact with them, both there and in Nigeria.

Contributors

AMES, DAVID W. Assistant Professor, Department of Sociology and Anthropology, University of Wisconsin. B.A. Wabash College, 1947; Ph.D. Northwestern University, 1953. Field research among the Wolof of the Gambia, 1950–51, as a fellow of the Social Science Research Council, with a supplementary grant from the Mackintosh Fund, Wabash College.

BASCOM, WILLIAM R. Director, Museum of Anthropology, and Professor, Department of Anthropology, University of California, Berkeley. B.A. University of Wisconsin, 1933; M.A. University of Wisconsin, 1936; Ph.D. Northwestern University, 1939. Field research among the Yoruba of Nigeria, 1937–38, as a fellow of the Social Science Research Council, and in 1950–51, as a Fulbright research scholar, with a supplemental grant from the Graduate School of Northwestern University. United States government service in Nigeria and Ghana, 1942–45.

CHRISTENSEN, JAMES B. Assistant Professor, Department of Sociology and Anthropology, Wayne State University. B.S. University of Utah, 1947; M.S. University of Utah, 1948; Ph.D. Northwestern University, 1952. Field research among the Fanti of Ghana, 1950–51, as a Fulbright fellow and as a fellow of the Social Science Research Council.

CORDWELL, JUSTINE M. Ph.B. Northwestern University College, 1947; Certificate, School of the Art Institute of Chicago, 1947; Ph.D. Northwestern University, 1952. Field research among the Yoruba and Bini of Nigeria and among the Dahomeans, 1949–50, as a fellow of the Rockefeller Foundation.

DORJAHN, VERNON ROBERT. Assistant Professor, Department of Anthropology, University of Oregon. B.S. Northwestern University, 1950; M.A. University of Wisconsin, 1951; Ph.D. Northwestern University, 1954. Field research among the Temne of Sierra Leone, 1954–55, as a post-doctoral research fellow of the National Science Foundation.

FULLER, CHARLES EDWARD. Professor, Department of Religious History and Theology, the Rural Seminary, University of Missouri. B.A. Juniata College, 1935; B.D. Garrett Biblical Institute, 1938; M.A. Northwestern University, 1938; Ph.D. Northwestern University, 1955. Missionary work in Portuguese East Africa, Southern Rhodesia, and the Union of South Africa, 1939–52. Field research in Portuguese East Africa, 1951, under a grant from the Wenner-Gren Foundation for Anthropological Research.

GREENBERG, JOSEPH H. Professor, Department of Anthropology, Columbia University. B.A. Columbia University, 1936; Ph.D. Northwestern University, 1940. Field research among the Maguzawa in Nigeria, 1938–39, as fellow of the Social Science Research Council, and linguistic survey of Jos Plateau, Nigeria, 1954–55, as fellow of the Guggenheim Foundation.

HAMMOND, PETER B. Assistant Professor of Anthropology, Administrative Science Center, University of Pittsburgh. A.B. Mexico City College, 1951. Field research among the Mossi in Upper Volta and French Sudan, 1954–56, as fellow of the Ford Foundation.

HERSKOVITS, MELVILLE J. Director, Program of African Studies, and Professor, Department of Anthropology, Northwestern University. Ph.B. University of Chicago, 1920; A.M. Columbia University, 1921; Ph.D. Columbia University, 1923. Field research in Dahomey, Nigeria, and the Gold Coast, 1931, in Africa south of the Sahara, 1953 and 1956–57.

LYSTAD, ROBERT A. Associate Professor, Department of Sociology and Anthropology, Tulane University. B.A. University of Wisconsin, 1941; B.D. Drew Theological Seminary, 1944; Ph.D. Northwestern University, 1951. Field research among the Ashanti of Ghana and the Agni of the Ivory Coast, 1949–50, as fellow of the Social Science Research Council.

MERRIAM, ALAN P. Associate Professor, Department of Anthropology, Northwestern University. B.A. Montana State University, 1947; M.M. Northwestern University, 1948; Ph.D. Northwestern University, 1951. Ethnomusicological studies in the Belgian Congo and Ruanda-Urundi, 1951–52, under post-doctoral grants from the Belgian-American Educational Foundation and the Wenner-Gren Foundation for Anthropological Research, and in co-operation with l'Institut pour la Recherche Scientifique en Afrique Centrale.

MESSENGER, JOHN C. Assistant Professor, Department of Social Science, Michigan State University. B.S. Lawrence College, 1947; Ph.D. Northwestern University, 1957. Field research among the Ibibio of Nigeria, 1951–52, as fellow of the Social Science Research Council.

OTTENBERG, PHOEBE V. B.S. University of Illinois, 1943; Ph.D. Northwestern University, 1958. Field research among the Ibo of Nigeria, 1951–53, as fellow of the Social Science Research Council.

OTTENBERG, SIMON. Assistant Professor, Department of Anthropology, University of Washington. B.A. University of Wisconsin, 1948; Ph.D. Northwestern University, 1957. Field research among the Ibo of Nigeria, 1951–53, as fellow of the Social Science Research Council.

SCHNEIDER, HAROLD K. Assistant Professor, Department of Anthropology, Lawrence College. B.A. Macalester College, 1946; Ph.D. Northwestern University, 1953. Field research among the Pakot of Kenya, 1951–52, as Fulbright fellow and as fellow of the Social Science Research Council.

WOLFE, ALVIN W. Assistant Professor, Department of Anthropology, Lafayette College. A.B. University of Nebraska, 1950; Ph.D. Northwestern University, 1957. Field research among the Ngombe of the Belgian Congo, 1952–53, as fellow of the Social Science Research Council.